Holocaust Angst

Holocaust Angst

THE FEDERAL REPUBLIC OF GERMANY AND AMERICAN HOLOCAUST MEMORY SINCE THE 1970s

JACOB S. EDER

OXFORD
UNIVERSITY PRESS

Oxford University Press is a department of the University of Oxford. It furthers
the University's objective of excellence in research, scholarship, and education
by publishing worldwide. Oxford is a registered trade mark of Oxford University
Press in the UK and certain other countries.

Published in the United States of America by Oxford University Press
198 Madison Avenue, New York, NY 10016, United States of America.

© Oxford University Press 2016

Library of Congress Cataloging-in-Publication Data
Names: Eder, Jacob S., author.
Title: Holocaust angst : the Federal Republic of Germany and American
Holocaust memory since the 1970s / Jacob S. Eder.
Description: New York, NY : Oxford University Press, [2016] | ?2016 |
Includes bibliographical references and index.
Identifiers: LCCN 2015050164| ISBN 9780190237820 (hardcover : alk. paper) |
ISBN 9780190237844 (epub)
Subjects: LCSH: Holocaust, Jewish (1939–1945)—Foreign public opinion, German. |
Memorialization—United States—Foreign public opinion, German. |
Public opinion—Germany (West) | Holocaust (Television program)—Influence. |
Holocaust, Jewish (1939–1945)—Historiography. | Antisemitism—Germany (West). |
Memorialization—United States. | Germany (West)—Ethnic relations.
Classification: LCC DS134.26.E34 2016 | DDC 940.53/1843—dc23
LC record available at http://lccn.loc.gov/2015050164

9 8 7 6 5 4 3 2 1
Printed by Sheridan Books, Inc., United States of America

This book is dedicated to the memory of
Katharina Buchhorn (1918–2011)
and
Michael Buchhorn (1949–2011)

Contents

Acknowledgments

A few years have passed since I completed my dissertation at the University of Pennsylvania, on which this book is based; even more years have passed since I finished my M.A. thesis at the University of Nebraska-Lincoln, where I spent a year on a Fulbright scholarship and began thinking about the topic of this book. It gives me great pleasure to thank the large number of people who have so generously provided encouraging feedback and productive criticism over the past years. I am above all indebted to Alan E. Steinweis, Susanna Schrafstetter, Philipp Gassert, and Norbert Frei (in the order we met). I am particularly grateful to Susanna Schrafstetter and Alan Steinweis, who have been a most significant source of advice since my stay in Lincoln, and the many conversations we have had there, in Munich, Burlington, and elsewhere have had a deep impact on my work. I wholeheartedly thank Philipp Gassert, the coadvisor of my dissertation, for many instructive discussions about German history, his indispensable advice and support, and for giving me numerous opportunities to present my project in Germany and abroad. I thank Norbert Frei for his very helpful advice at crucial stages of this project and for inviting me to join the Doktorandenschule of the Jena Center 20th Century History and later the Lehrstuhl für Neuere und Neueste Geschichte at the Friedrich-Schiller-Universität Jena. At Jena, I have very much benefitted from conversations and discussions with my wonderful (current and former) colleagues Tobias Freimüller, Marcel vom Lehn, Franka Maubach, Kristina Meyer, Dominik Rigoll, Tim Schanetzky, Dietmar Süß, Annette Weinke, and especially Daniel Stahl.

I also thank my dissertation committee at the University of Pennsylvania, particularly my advisor Thomas Childers, for helping me to navigate smoothly through graduate school. I cannot express my gratitude enough to Beth S. Wenger for expanding my knowledge of American Jewish history, but above all to Benjamin Nathans for his generous advice, his challenging questions, and especially for being a true mentor to me at Penn. I thank Kathy Peiss and Ronald J. Granieri for their advice in the early stages of this project, as well as

Frank Trommler for sharing his knowledge and expertise with me, both as a scholar and as a *Zeitzeuge*.

Over the past years, several colleagues have become true friends. I am incredibly grateful to Christine Friederich (née Hikel) and Chase Richards for their comments and feedback on the manuscript at its various stages of development. Chase deserves my undying gratitude not only for proofreading this book, but also for sharing all the burdens of being a doctoral student (and there were many). I wholeheartedly thank Philipp Stelzel, who has been a true friend for more than a decade and who has helped me with my work in more ways than I can mention here. I thank Hubert Leber, Christian Mentel, Katrin Schreiter, Fabian Schwanzar, and Mathew Turner, for their comments on various chapters, and I am particularly grateful to Deborah Barton for proofreading the final version of the manuscript in record time.

While working on this project, I had the privilege to receive suggestions and feedback from a number of colleagues and friends to whom I would like to express my gratitude. I thank Volker Berghahn, Elizabeth Borgwardt, Gregg Brazinsky, Suzanne Brown-Fleming, Martin Dean, Hasia R. Diner, Astrid M. Eckert, Lily Gardner Feldman, Tim Geiger, Hope Harrison, Jan-Holger Kirsch, Martin Klimke, Reinhild Kreis, Harold Marcuse, Gilad Margalit (1959–2014), Michael Meng, Claudia Moisel, Tina Morina, Bill Niven, Anke Ortlepp (and her Oberseminar in Munich), Jörg Osterloh, Nicole Phelps, Dieter Pohl, Thomas Raithel, Mark Roseman, Miriam Rürup, Bernd Schaefer, Hanna Schissler, Sybille Steinbacher, Corinna Unger, Richard Wetzell, Cornelia Wilhelm, and Meik Woyke. I am particularly grateful to Jürgen Matthäus for his advice during my two extended stays at the Center for Advanced Holocaust Studies, and to S. Jonathan Wiesen for his very helpful feedback during the revisions of the manuscript.

Moreover, I am grateful to the scholars, diplomats, and politicians who agreed to be interviewed for this project. A complete list of their names can be found in the bibliography, but I would like to express special thanks to Michael Mertes for granting me permission to access his files at the ACDP. As this project deals with a very recent history, getting access to classified documents posed a major challenge. Without the help of a number of archivists, I could have never navigated the pitfalls and challenges of this research. I thank above all Claudia Zenker-Oertel, Andrea Hänger, Beatrix Dietel (neé Kuchta), and Elisabeth Thalhofer of the Bundesarchiv, Jeffrey Carter of the United States Holocaust Memorial Museum Institutional Archives, and Charlotte Bonelli of the Archives of the American Jewish Committee.

The very generous financial support of a number of institutions made this transatlantic project possible. I am greatly indebted to the German-American Fulbright Commission; the History Department and the Norman and Bernice Harris Center for Judaic Studies of the University of Nebraska-Lincoln;

the University of Pennsylvania, especially the Department of History and the Jewish Studies Program; the Georg Eckert Institut für Internationale Schulbuchforschung (Braunschweig) and the German Historical Institute (Washington, DC) for doctoral fellowships; the Society for Historians of American Foreign Relations for a Samuel Flagg Bemis Research Grant and a Global Scholars Grant; the Jack, Joseph and Morton Mandel Center for Advanced Holocaust Studies of the United States Holocaust Memorial Museum (Washington, DC) for a Dorot Foundation Summer Research Assistant Fellowship and a Charles H. Revson Foundation Fellowship; and the Holocaust Educational Foundation (Evanston, IL) for a research grant. I am most grateful to the Gerda Henkel Foundation (Düsseldorf) for providing the funds for almost two years of uninterrupted research and writing. During my last year as a doctoral student, I was very lucky to receive a generous Mellon predoctoral fellowship in Cold War/ Post-1945 International History from The George Washington University's Elliott School of International Affairs.

The dissertation on which this book is based won the Fraenkel Prize in Contemporary History (Category B) of the Wiener Library, the Marko Feingold Dissertation Prize in Jewish Studies of University of Salzburg, and the Betty M. Unterberger Dissertation Prize of the Society for Historians of American Foreign Relations, which all greatly helped me while revising the manuscript. I also thank the Emerging Scholars Program of the Jack, Joseph and Morton Mandel Center for Advanced Holocaust Studies and the Jena Center 20th Century History for providing generous subsidies for the publication of this book. At Oxford University Press, I wholeheartedly thank my editor Susan Ferber for her incredibly helpful feedback on the manuscript as well as the two anonymous readers for their insightful comments and probing questions.

Last but certainly not least, I am deeply grateful to my family and friends— above all my mother Claudia, my brother Simon, his wife Valeska, and their son Leo—for their unconditional love and support. I sincerely thank Johanna Arnold, Jack Dwiggins, Julia Gunn, Matt Handelman, Sam Hirst, Jan Christoph Jähne, Nicole Kling, Konstanze and Alexander Kunst, Andrea and Holger Löwendorf, Christian Weilguny, Sven Ramones, and especially Josef Jaud and Daniel Eymer for their friendship and companionship.

Most importantly, I thank my wife, my best friend, my constant companion Amandine Barb for her love, her patience, and her support. Our journey has taken us from Heidelberg to New York, Paris, Munich, Washington, Philadelphia, Jena, and to our current home in Berlin. Only Amandine knows how strenuous and occasionally exasperating of a task it was to write this book, which I could have never finished without her loving and unwavering encouragement.

My grandmother Katharina Buchhorn and my uncle Michael Buchhorn did not live to see the completion of this book, which owes so much to their encouragement and intellectual inspiration. It is dedicated to their memory.

Abbreviations

AA	Auswärtiges Amt (German Foreign Office)
AAPD	Akten zur Auswärtigen Politik der Bundesrepublik Deutschland (Foreign Policy Records of the Federal Republic of Germany)
ACDP	Archiv für Christlich-Demokratische Politik (Archive for Christian Democratic Policy)
ADL	Anti-Defamation League
AICGS	American Institute for Contemporary German Studies
AJC	American Jewish Committee
AV	Auslandsvertretung (diplomatic representation)
BAarch	Bundesarchiv (German Federal Archives)
BArchG	Bundesarchivgesetz (Federal Archives Act)
Bd.	Band (volume)
BK	Bundeskanzler (German Chancellor)
BKAmt	Bundeskanzleramt (German Chancellery)
BMBF	Bundesministerium für Bildung und Forschung (Federal Ministry of Education and Research)
BM	Bundesminister (Federal Minister; Secretary)
BMBW	Bundesministerium für Bildung und Wissenschaft (Federal Ministry of Education and Science)
BMFT	Bundesministerium für Forschung und Technologie (Federal Ministry of Research and Technology)
BPA	Presse- und Informationsamt der Bundesregierung/ Bundespresseamt (Press and Information Office of the Federal Government)
CAHS	Center for Advanced Holocaust Studies of the USHMM (since 2014: Jack, Joseph and Morton Mandel Center for Advanced Holocaust Studies)
CDU	Christlich Demokratische Union Deutschlands (Christian Democratic Union of Germany)

CEO   Chief Executive Officer
ChBK   Chef des Bundeskanzleramts (Chief of the German Chancellery)
CSU   Christlich-Soziale Union in Bayern (Christian Social Union of
         Bavaria)
DAAD   Deutscher Akademischer Austauschdienst (German Academic
         Exchange Service)
DBT   Deutscher Bundestag
DHI   Deutsches Historisches Institut (German Historical Institute)
DM   Deutschmark
EU   European Union
FDP   Freie Demokratische Partei (Free Democratic Party)
FAZ   Frankfurter Allgemeine Zeitung
FES   Friedrich-Ebert-Stiftung (Friedrich Ebert Foundation)
FOIA   Freedom of Information Act
FRG   Federal Republic of Germany
GDR   German Democratic Republic
GEI   Georg Eckert Institut für international Schulbuchforschung (Georg
         Eckert Institute for International Textbook Research)
GHI   German Historical Institute
GI   Member of the United States Army
GIC   German Information Center, New York, NY
GK   Generalkonsulat (consulate general)
GK NY   Generalkonsulat (consulate general) in New York, NY
GMF   German Marshall Fund of the United States
HMC   Holocaust Memorial Center (Detroit)
IFG   Informationsfreiheitsgesetz (German Freedom of Information Act)
IfZ   Institut für Zeitgeschichte (Institute for Contemporary History)
IRC   International Relations Committee of the USHMC
KAS   Konrad-Adenauer-Stiftung e.V. (Konrad Adenauer Foundation)
MIT   Massachusetts Institute of Technology
NATO   North Atlantic Treaty Organization
NBC   National Broadcasting Company
n.d.   No date
NGO   Nongovernmental organization
NYPL   New York Public Library
OECD   Organisation for Economic Co-operation and Development
OSI   Office of Special Investigations of the US Department of Justice
PA AA   Politisches Archiv des Auswärtigen Amts (Political Archives of the
         [West] German Foreign Office)
PLO   Palestine Liberation Organization
POW   Prisoner of war
RTL   Radio Télévisioun Lëtzebuerg

SA	Sturmabteilung (Stormtroopers)
SDI	Strategic Defense Initiative
SPD	Sozialdemokratische Partei Deutschlands (Social Democratic Party of Germany)
SS	Schutzstaffel (lit. Defence Corps)
St	Staatssekretär (state secretary)
StM	Staatsminister (state minister)
SZ	Süddeutsche Zeitung
UC	University of California
UCLA	University of California, Los Angeles
US	United States
USHMC	United States Holocaust Memorial Council
USHMM	United States Holocaust Memorial Museum
USIA	United States Information Agency
UVM	University of Vermont
WJC	World Jewish Congress
WWF	World Wide Fund For Nature

Note on Terminology, Translations, and Sources

All translations from German sources into English in this book are mine unless otherwise noted. Wherever necessary, I have supplied short German quotations in parentheses. While I have translated the names of the vast majority of German government agencies, offices, institutions, and organizations in the text, the endnotes contain the original German name or an abbreviation, if use of the latter is common. For example, the Auswärtiges Amt is "Foreign Office" in the text, but "AA" in the endnotes. The names of organizations are not translated, such as Atlantik-Brücke (lit. "Atlantic Bridge"), unless they contain a generic term. For example, I refer to the "Konrad Adenauer Stiftung" as "Konrad Adenauer Foundation."

The vast majority of (West) German archival materials were made available to me in response to requests I filed in accordance with the Federal Archives Act (Bundesarchivgesetz) and the Freedom of Information Act (Informationsfreiheitsgesetz) before they had been properly processed, catalogued, and paginated by the Federal Archives (Bundesarchiv). Thus, page numbers are not available for these documents; in addition to the call numbers of the respective record groups and folders, I have included a precise description of each document in the endnotes. The same applies to records from the Institutional Archives of the United States Holocaust Memorial Museum, which were also accessed before they had been paginated.

I gained access to many files from the (West) German Foreign Office, the (West) German embassy in Washington, and various consulates general not through the Political Archives of the German Foreign Office (PA AA), but through the records of the Federal Chancellery in the Federal Archives (record group B 136). This not only demonstrates a way to circumvent the restrictive archival policies of the PA AA, but also—and more importantly—illustrates how closely the Federal Chancellery was involved in the foreign policy and diplomatic issues examined in this book.

Holocaust Angst

Introduction

"It is high time," German Chancellor Helmut Kohl wrote in 1990 to Rabbi Marvin Hier, dean of the Los Angeles-based Simon Wiesenthal Center (SWC), "for the positive things that have happened in Germany since 1945 to be discussed more intensively in the United States. I feel that, in this respect, there is an alarming lack of information."[1] At the time, Hier was heading up construction of the second-largest Holocaust museum in the United States, the Museum of Tolerance in Los Angeles. Government officials from the Federal Republic of Germany, or West Germany, had been monitoring American Jewish individuals and organizations involved in this and similar projects for more than a decade. Those monitored were held by the West German government to be the primary agents of the establishment of a specifically American Holocaust memorial culture that was—in their view—characterized by a lack of attention to the achievements of West German democracy after 1949.

Indeed, the Holocaust—the murder of almost six million European Jews by Nazi Germany and its allies—has become a central reference point in American political and popular culture. Within a period of roughly two decades, from the late 1970s to the mid-1990s, Holocaust memory became fully integrated into American life.[2] How Germans have perceived and reacted to Americans' public commemoration and remembrance of this horrific crime—one committed, above all, by German perpetrators—forms a key focus of this book. This question will be considered against the backdrop of the specific dynamics of West German–American postwar relations.[3] Since the end of the Second World War—and especially during the four decades of the "old" Federal Republic (1949–1990)—(West) Germany depended on, and benefited from, its alliance with the United States in a most significant way. The West German state sought and received economic support and military protection as well as ideological strength and political direction from its cooperation with America. Its fundamental transformation from the murderous Nazi dictatorship into a liberal democracy, firmly integrated into the Western alliance, would not have been possible without the United States. America played crucial roles in defeating

1

the Third Reich as an enemy and, even more so, in establishing the Federal Republic as an ally. After 1949 this close partnership and military alliance, especially at times of extreme tension during the Cold War, counted among the top priorities of West Germany's political leaders, from Konrad Adenauer (1949–1963) to Helmut Kohl (1982–1998). The former communist dictatorship in East Germany, the German Democratic Republic or GDR, does not receive significant attention in this book, as it had a divergent modus of engagement with the Nazi past, a virtually absent pluralistic and diverse public sphere, and fundamentally different premises of East German–American relations. In the context of the Cold War, these factors resulted in a dearth of significant ties between both countries.[4]

This book examines how West German political leaders, diplomats, civilians, and nongovernmental organizations reacted to the emergence of a highly visible Holocaust memorial culture in the United States between the late 1970s and the late 1990s. This development was marked by such crucial landmark events and turning points as the airing of the NBC miniseries *Holocaust* (1978/1979), the Bitburg controversy (1985), the establishment of the United States Holocaust Memorial Museum (USHMM, 1978–1993), the arrival of Steven Spielberg's *Schindler's List* (1993/1994) in movie theatres, and the publication of Daniel J. Goldhagen's *Hitler's Willing Executioners* (1996). Specifically, this book argues that a network of predominantly conservative West German politicians and government officials—some of whom were former Nazis or World War II veterans—and their associates in private organizations and foundations, centered around Chancellor Kohl, perceived themselves as "victims" of Holocaust remembrance and representation in America.

In most cases, they were members of or closely associated with the center-right party CDU (Christian Democratic Union). While Helmut Kohl, CDU chairman from 1973 to 1998, held centrist views on economic or social policies and fashioned himself as a "man of the middle," he pursued—opposing the political Left, the Social Democrats, the Greens, and left-leaning Liberals—a conservative rhetoric and policies toward German history and identity.[5] He was certainly not an apologist or revisionist, and he did not share the point of view of the national-conservative right wing of the CDU, represented for example by the long-term chairman of the CDU/CSU (Christian Social Union) group in the Bundestag, the nationalist and vehemently anticommunist Alfred Dregger.[6] Kohl's politics of history, however, corresponded to the views of many conservatives, who maintained that the Federal Republic needed to escape the "shadow of the Nazi past" and the "fixation on the Holocaust"; according to this position, history should serve as a source of "reassurance" for the nation-state, not as a burden.[7] In this context, Kohl acknowledged the "lessons" of the Nazi past for the Federal Republic but wanted to diminish its actual impact on the conduct of domestic and foreign policy; to his mind, the Federal Republic should be recognized as an equal by its Western partners.[8]

With regard to the United States, these politicians and officials were concerned that public manifestations of Holocaust memory—such as museums, monuments, movies, educational programs, and commemoration ceremonies—could severely damage the Federal Republic's reputation in the United States and even cause Americans to question the Federal Republic's status as a partner in the Western alliance.[9] This fear was not a ubiquitous phenomenon nor did it characterize all of Germany's political, diplomatic, or intellectual elites. In comparison to conservative positions toward history and identity, Social Democrats and left-leaning Liberals considered, broadly speaking, the German past a "warning and a burden for the nation state."[10] The government of Kohl's predecessor, the Social Democrat Helmut Schmidt (1974–1982), for instance, was made aware of the concerns held by German diplomats in the United States of the potential for American Holocaust memory to negatively influence West Germany's reputation abroad over an extended period. While Schmidt's government took notice of these developments and was certainly mindful of political and social tensions in German–American relations, it did not judge that the issue of American Holocaust memory required significant political action. Although Schmidt was the first chancellor to visit the Auschwitz concentration camp memorial, he did not make the German past a major priority of his government.[11]

In contrast, the German leadership around Kohl perceived the increasing interest of Americans in the history of the destruction of European Jewry and the growing public presence of Holocaust memory in the United States from the late 1970s on as a political threat to the Federal Republic.[12] From their perspective, American Holocaust memorial culture, as promoted and implemented by American Jewish organizations and individuals, constituted a stumbling block for West German–American relations. This book refers to their fears, catalyzed by these perceptions, as "Holocaust angst."[13] Representing the first comprehensive archival study of German efforts to cope with the Nazi past vis-à-vis its superpower ally, from the late 1970s to the 1990s, it focuses on various fields of interaction, including diplomatic, scholarly, and public spheres. In doing so, it unearths the complicated and often contradictory process of managing the legacies of genocide on an international stage.[14]

Yet why were the perceptions and reactions of the Kohl government during the 1980s distinctly different from those of its predecessors during earlier decades? Of course, the Nazi past had affected the image of the Federal Republic abroad as well its interactions with foreign countries since its existence.[15] In the 1950s, for example, both the West German and the US governments were keenly interested in showing the American public an image of Germans as "dedicated democrats" and reliable Cold War allies, not as Nazis.[16] Well into the 1960s, the Federal Republic's image in the United States was that of an economically successful country, yet one still characterized by the "residues of National Socialism."[17] For example, German diplomats feared that media and press coverage of the Eichmann Trial (1961) could reveal not only the extent of the Foreign Office's involvement in the Holocaust, but also damage the Federal Republic's reputation in the United States more generally.[18] Moreover, German politicians struggled to explain that major turning points in a confrontation with the Nazi past—such as the Auschwitz Trial of 1963–1965 and the legislative debates on the abolition of the statute of limitations for Nazi crimes since 1965—were not just reactions to political expectations or pressure from abroad.[19] In the course of the 1970s, however, a "relative indifference towards Nazism" characterized the political agenda of the Social Democratic governments, which faced more acute political challenges, such as the 1973 oil crisis and domestic terrorism.[20] In fact, political responses to German terrorists, especially the *Rote Armee Fraktion* (Red Army Faction), overshadowed the Federal Republic's image abroad: some European observers feared that counterterrorism could turn West Germany into a police state.[21] Vis-à-vis the United States, the Schmidt government initiated an overhaul of the Federal Republic's public diplomacy, which aimed at a more forceful, "imaginative" promotion of the achievements of German culture abroad.[22] It hoped to renew ties and to establish new political and societal connections between the two Cold War allies, but the Nazi past played only a minor role in this context.[23]

In the 1980s, however, the question of West Germany's broader image returned with pressing urgency. It was a central goal of the Kohl government to readjust the meaning of the Nazi past for West Germany's self-image at a time when the Federal Republic began to bid farewell to its status as a "provisional" entity and to redefine itself as a nation-state with its own tradition and history.[24] In this context Kohl pursued a specific politics of history, relying on history as a resource for domestic and foreign policy goals while simultaneously attempting to shape the general public's conception, consciousness, and understanding of German history.[25] Kohl maintained that the Nazi past rendered the conduct of foreign policy and the pursuit of national interests "extraordinarily difficult."[26] Yet compared to his predecessors, he wanted to orchestrate domestic and foreign policy mindful of this past, while recognizing the political potential of, and opportunities associated with, an active, state-directed politics of history.[27]

At this historical juncture, however, representatives of the American Jewish community, including several prominent Holocaust survivors, as well as other interest groups, were in the process of transplanting the perspective of Holocaust victims into the popular, academic, and political culture of the United States. American Jewish organizations, some of which had opposed the Federal Republic's rehabilitation in the 1950s, were by the 1980s spearheading a fundamental transformation of America's engagement with the history of the Holocaust.[28] This was a disturbing and distressing development for representatives of the West German state. Fear of an image abroad of the "ugly German" became deeply engrained in the minds of German politicians and diplomats.[29] Some American observers have even argued that this led to an "obsession with its international image" in the Federal Republic.[30] Kohl's biographer Hans-Peter Schwarz—granted, a leading conservative historian—expressed in hindsight his sympathy with the chancellor, who had opposed the "irresistible urge" of "the media, the lobbies of the victims, and leading politicians" in the West to "recycle the memory of German atrocities during the Second World War and to commemorate their own heroism at the same time" in the 1980s.[31]

More specifically, three developments overlapped since the late 1970s that forced West Germans to face a heightened level of international engagement with the crimes of Nazi Germany, and propelled them to take concrete political actions. The developments include the conservative discourses about German identity and the pursuit of a "usable past" against the backdrop of the Holocaust in the Federal Republic, the specific dynamics of German–American relations during the Cold War, and changes in American Holocaust memorial culture.[32] By insisting on the need for Germans in the Federal Republic to develop a sense of national identity, German conservative politicians as well as intellectuals aimed to "destigmatize the national past."[33] According to this view, as historian A. Dirk Moses has suggested, the Third Reich and the Holocaust constituted aberrations "in an otherwise healthy German past."[34] Such policies were partially a response to a growing critical engagement of West German society with the Nazi past and its aftermath. These resulted from generational change, the specific politics of history of the governments of the Social Democrats Willy Brandt and Helmut Schmidt, and a growing interest in the "history from below" and the "forgotten" victims of National Socialism.[35] The government of Helmut Kohl specifically devoted much energy to promoting, as historian Andreas Wirsching has remarked, a "balanced" interpretation of German history (*Geschichtsbalance*), which did not reject the "continuing relevance" of the Nazi past, but wanted to complement it with "positive aspects" of German history.[36] The 1980s thus saw numerous governmental initiatives to support a uniquely West German identity, intended to be based on the legacies of the Nazi past, the Federal Republic's "success story," and the long history of Germany's many positive achievements.[37] As a means of empowering West Germans to identify affirmatively with their history, there was to be a reduced public presence of the Nazi past—to be, in turn, contrasted with examples of German heroism, suffering, and sacrifice during the war, or integrated into a narrative according to which the democratic achievements after 1949 had redeemed Germans for the crimes of Nazi Germany.[38] As Kohl put it in a speech commemorating the fortieth anniversary of the liberation of the Bergen-Belsen Concentration Camp: "We have learned the lessons of history, especially the history of this century."[39] In the United States, the Kohl government attempted to disseminate an image of the Federal Republic based on the interpretation of West German history as a success story, heavily emphasizing the fundamental transformation it had experienced since the end of the war.[40] In this context, concern about the lack of knowledge of postwar German history in the United States was a crucial aspect of the West German government's Holocaust angst.[41]

The pursuit of equality and "normality" in international relations—while simultaneously contending with the stigma imposed by the Nazi past on the Federal Republic's reputation abroad—was a key characteristic of West German foreign policymaking.[42] Since its founding in 1949, the Federal Republic implemented a number of political, economic, and diplomatic measures to seek reconciliation with former enemies of its predecessor state, the Third Reich, and to compensate its victims for their suffering.[43] The legacies of the Nazi past, however, also burdened the sphere of public diplomacy, that is, that part of diplomacy that aims to create a positive image of one's own country abroad.[44] In this context, the Nazi past imposed limits on the scope of German policies. Given its history of imperialism, cultural chauvinism, and violent occupation, representatives of the post-Nazi state, West Germany, presented themselves and their country abroad with caution and self-restraint.[45] Debates in West Germany and among expatriates in the United States about how they *thought* they were seen abroad and how they *wanted* to be seen abroad are thus key to this analysis.[46]

While scholars have primarily been concerned with the various forms of West German self-representation abroad—such as trade fairs, exhibitions, sporting events, and the architecture of embassies—and German conversations about these representations, this book focuses instead on what West Germans *perceived* as representations of Germany in the United States. Elements of American Holocaust memorial culture became screens on to which Germans' Holocaust angst could be projected. By looking at these manifestations of Holocaust memory in America, and the German conversations about them, the interconnection between foreign and domestic policies becomes strikingly obvious.[47] For this reason, this book will rarely examine the daily business of West German public diplomacy in the United States, for example the work of the Goethe Institutes, a global network of centers promoting German culture and the study of the German language abroad, or the German Academic Exchange Service (DAAD), roughly the German equivalent of the Fulbright Commission.[48] Rather, it focuses on German government reactions to the development of an American Holocaust memorial culture and examines the ways these reactions reflected, as well as caused, changes in the discourses about the Nazi past in Germany.

The impact of Holocaust memory on German–American relations cannot be fully understood without taking the specific dynamics of the Cold War into consideration. The Federal Republic benefited from the alliance with the United States after World War II in a multitude of ways, and this relationship paved the way for the evolution of a civil and democratic society in a part of the former territory of the Third Reich.[49] Additionally, West Germany depended on the military protection offered by the Western alliance, and was—as the Iron Curtain divided East from West—permanently confronted unlike any other country, except perhaps Korea, with the realities of the Cold War. Since the late 1940s, the United States had heavily invested not only in the military alliance and West Germany's economic recovery, but also in building close societal ties between the two countries through the establishment of exchange programs, cultural centers, and various other initiatives in the field of public diplomacy.[50] In the 1970s and 1980s, however, observers on either side of the Atlantic noticed fundamental changes in both societies. The achievements of the founding generation of German–American friendship in the 1950s slowly eroded, and the so-called successor generation exhibited less commitment to the alliance.[51] From the German perspective, the declining interest of young Americans—illustrated, among other ways, by decreasing enrollments in exchange programs—in the language, culture, and history of Germany was particularly alarming. The dedication of future generations of Americans to the alliance—and hence to the Federal Republic—was the sine qua non of West German security, freedom, and prosperity. Moreover, many (young) Germans began to exhibit distinctly anti-American sentiments, particularly those associated with the Peace Movement against the modernization of American nuclear forces on German soil. This also became a source of concern for both countries.[52]

As a result, the 1980s saw a number of joint projects designed to strengthen German–American friendship and to build networks between future generations of leaders.[53] On the diplomatic level, both governments appointed "coordinators" for German–American cooperation. The celebration of the tricentennial of German immigration to the United States in 1983, the designation of October 6, 1987, as the first German-American Day by the US Congress, and the establishment of a German-American Friendship Garden between the Washington Monument and the White House in 1988 were intended to create powerful symbols of the close partnership between both countries. In order to generate the engagement and interest of young Americans in Germany, and vice versa, both countries established a number of educational programs, such as the joint student exchange program of the US Congress and the German parliament, the Bundestag. The German government further initiated a number of measures to spread a positive message about Germany and its history with respect to the United States. These initiatives aimed to reinforce ties between the two societies. For the Federal Republic, however, fear provided a decisive rationale. Should future generations of Americans remain uninformed about present-day Germany, their image of Germany would be dominated—and tainted—by those of the recent past: Hitler, World War II, and the Holocaust.

Despite the impact of Holocaust angst on German–American relations, as well as the formation of Holocaust memory in the Federal Republic, scholarly attention to this phenomenon remains cursory. While previous decades have seen a large and diverse body of scholarship on West Germany's success and failure in coping with the Nazi past and on American Holocaust memorial culture, studies taking a comparative or a transnational angle, based on archival sources, are rare.[54]

Indeed, the works of numerous historians, in Germany and abroad, have rendered the study of Germany's engagement with the Nazi past (*Vergangenheitsbewältigung*) a highly fruitful subfield of inquiry in the study of German contemporary history.[55] The events, debates, and developments investigated by scholars are multifarious. They range from the judicial, legal, and political consequences of the Third Reich (*Vergangenheitspolitik*), to the reparation efforts aimed at financially compensating the victims of National Socialism ("*Wiedergutmachung*"). A further area of examination is the private and public remembrance and commemoration of the Third Reich and the Holocaust in the Federal Republic. How the Nazi past impacted the political discourse surrounding memorial days, monuments, and museums forms a key question.[56] Historians have demonstrated in recent years that the history of West German engagement with the Nazi past, for example in the fields of *Vergangenheitspolitik* and "*Wiedergutmachung*," needs to be written using an international or transnational frame of reference.[57]

Historians of postwar American engagement with the Holocaust have also created a sizeable body of scholarship. Peter Novick—if one ignores the bestselling, controversial, though rather unscholarly diatribe on the *Holocaust Industry* by Norman Finkelstein—set the benchmark for the historiographical debate.[58] While many of Novick's findings were not new, nor have they remained uncontested, he established a master narrative that even his most serious critics have not been able to radically revise. Novick contends that while there was little public engagement with the Holocaust outside of Jewish communities in the postwar decades, discourse about the Holocaust has changed significantly in the United States since the 1970s.[59] It has become an "American memory," a moral point of reference in a variety of contexts, and provides alleged "universal lessons" for diverse groups, causes, and beliefs.[60] The American process of coming to terms with their withdrawal and failure to win the Vietnam War in the 1970s, and the end of the Cold War in the early 1990s, accelerated the "Americanization of the Holocaust."[61] These events overlapped with the impact of the NBC miniseries *Holocaust* in 1978, as well as the opening of the USHMM in 1993 and reactions to Steven Spielberg's acclaimed blockbuster *Schindler's List* the same year.

In fact, the heightened presence of discourse about the Holocaust in the early 1990s resulted in a whole body of scholarship dealing with various aspects of America's engagement with Holocaust memory.[62] The vast majority of these works examines developments in the United States and does not pay attention to the perception of Germans to this process. Edward Linenthal's book *Preserving Memory* on the founding of the USHMM, for example, argues that the museum enshrines the Holocaust as a Jewish "ethnic memory" from which all Americans could draw lessons. In his view, the museum "highlight[s] professed American values through stark presentation of their antithesis in Nazi Germany."[63] Linenthal, however, only devotes marginal attention to the perception of Germans to this process.[64] Even comparative histories do not concentrate on this field of interaction. Scholars such as Edward Young, Katrin Pieper, and Matthias Haß have compared the establishment of Holocaust memorials in the United States, Germany, Israel, and other countries, but pay little attention to the interactions between German and American actors on this subject.[65] The same holds true for Shlomo Shafir's *Ambiguous Relations: The American Jewish Community and Germany since 1945*, a comprehensive account of relations between American Jewish organizations and postwar Germany. While he provides a highly informed and detailed account of what he labels the American Jewish community's "ambiguous" attitudes toward the Federal Republic, Shafir offers little insight into the inverse: the attitudes of German officials toward American Jewish organizations and their assessment of American Holocaust memory.[66]

In recent years historians have begun to focus on international and transnational dimensions of Holocaust memory—a reaction to the emergence of such phenomena as well as to shifts in the historical discipline, which saw the arrival of a "new" international or diplomatic history and transnational history as a viable and promising subfield.[67] The past decade or so has seen a veritable boom in the study of transfers and exchanges, in public and cultural diplomacy, and in the significance of culture for the study of international affairs more generally.[68] With regard to Holocaust memory more specifically, scholars have explored its dimensions and implications that extend beyond the borders of a single nation-state, such as the "Europeanization," "internationalization," "universalization," or "globalization" of Holocaust memory.[69] They have fixed their gaze on the function of Holocaust memory in the development of the European Community after the end of the Cold War and on its role as a reference point for discourses about other instances of mass murder.[70] Scholars now also look at the emergence of Holocaust memory, museums, and study centers in Africa, South America, or Asia,[71] and they interrogate the impact of this development on the relationship between these regions and the "old" transatlantic West, where the Holocaust has become a major focal point of memorial culture.[72]

Considering that the Holocaust, a crime committed above all by Germans, has been "Americanized," and that American exports—such as the NBC miniseries *Holocaust*, Steven Spielberg's *Schindler's List*, and Daniel J. Goldhagen's *Hitler's Willing Executioners*—transformed debates about the Holocaust in the Federal Republic itself, German reactions to the discussion of the Holocaust in the United States warrant scholarly attention.[73] Indeed, historians such as Tony Judt have demanded that we examine "overlapping national cases" to "understand why the Holocaust has become what it is today."[74]

Beyond uncovering hitherto unknown dimensions of German–American relations and the commemoration and remembrance of the Holocaust, this book makes a number of contributions to the literature on postwar German history and Holocaust memory. First, it provides a comprehensive account of transnational memory management and the politics of history, focusing on attempts by German political actors to control, shape, and create historical narratives for political purposes.[75] The "nexus between memory and political power" must be taken into consideration here as the actions and decisions of politicians necessarily resulted, to a certain degree, from how they experienced and remembered the Nazi past.[76] This book, however, does not explore this kind of "political memory" in all its facets.[77] Rather, it focuses on the politics of history as well as political strategies employed by the generation of the descendants of Holocaust perpetrators, in competition with its victims, and those representing victims' interests, over how the history of the Nazi past and the Holocaust should be told, interpreted, and perceived by a broader audience in the United States.[78] This study illustrates how political elites—in democratic states, not just in dictatorships—have used institutional, financial, and intellectual resources to shape the writing and rewriting of history. This does not mean, however, that historians and other scholars occupy a marginal position in this story. Indeed, if history mattered, so did historians. German politicians relied on scholars as advisors and resources in their bid to wield their own influence over Holocaust remembrance and interpretation.[79] American academics, on the other hand, were also a primary target group of German initiatives in the United States.

Second, this book illustrates the impact of fears and prejudices on policymaking, specifically German perceptions of Jews.[80] Preconceived notions of collective character traits and the fear of Jewish influence and power in the United States constituted a core aspect of Holocaust angst. In this context, Kohl placed himself in the tradition of his political "grandfather," the first West German Chancellor Konrad Adenauer, who had claimed in the 1950s: "One should not, even today, especially in the United States, underestimate the power of the Jews."[81] American Jews held on average a negative attitude toward Germany and the Germans. Many Holocaust survivors settled in the United States after the war, where they opposed the rehabilitation of the Federal Republic as a partner in the Western alliance in the 1950s, and continued to exhibit, as Shafir has stated, a "grassroots dislike of Germany and the German people."[82] Many Holocaust survivors and other Jewish immigrants from Eastern Europe frequently held a particularly strong "aversion to Germans" after the war.[83] They had no positive associations with Germany before the Third Reich, unlike their German-Jewish counterparts, and, more importantly, had experienced the full force and brutality of Nazi Germany's war of annihilation in Eastern Europe. Given the traumatic experiences of forced ghettoization and imprisonment in concentration, labor, and extermination camps, it is hardly surprising that negative attitudes toward Germany were also passed on to the next generations.

While such attitudes certainly played an important role during encounters between American Jewish and German emissaries, in this book, the attitudes of the latter receive greater scrutiny that those of the former. A specific form of West German "secondary" anti-Semitism influenced the thoughts and deeds of several German figures in this book.[84] This form of anti-Jewish resentment arose from feelings of shame or guilt for the Holocaust and manifested itself above all as a defense mechanism against such feelings. It revealed itself in the assertions that (American) Jews could not "forgive" the Germans for the Holocaust and that they exploited the suffering of Jews during the Third Reich for profit—an alleged conspiracy that Norman Finkelstein later controversially termed the "Holocaust industry."[85] While the public actions and communication of German actors revealed no indicators of overt racial or religious anti-Semitism, several German protagonists exhibited—when no Jewish interlocutors were present—a certain degree of stereotypical thinking. Such latent prejudices found voice in references to the influence of a "Jewish lobby" or "Jewish money" in the United States, assumptions about certain collective characteristics of Jews (e.g., that they were "emotional"), and the use of derogatory terms (e.g., *Holocaust Eiferer*, that is, "Holocaust zealots") or coded language when speaking about Jews (e.g., the "East Coast" or the "readers of the *New York Times*").[86] German actors also concurrently expressed sincere moral concerns, remorse, regret, and shame, and they longed for reconciliation with the victims of Nazi persecution. The book therefore shows that earnest efforts toward reconciliation with Jewish victims and the perpetuation of anti-Semitic stereotypes were not mutually exclusive.

Third, this book uncovers a complex interaction of state and nonstate actors as well as nongovernmental organizations across and beyond national borders.[87] Numerous avenues of communication made these borders permeable and allowed for the transnational exchange of people, ideas, images, and, of course, interpretations of historical events. In contrast to traditional political or diplomatic history, this book looks not just at the state level, but also includes scholars, intellectuals, lobbyists, businessmen, private individuals, foundations, and scholarly institutions in this analysis. Politics in this study is not defined strictly as a top-down phenomenon—although it contains this element—but rather as "a system of relations that receives impulses from many directions."[88] Every political history has to address the question of power and how it manifested itself in the interaction between the state and other actors.[89] "Political power" in this context means the power of the West German government, and additionally that of the networks it built with private individuals and nongovernmental organizations.[90] It includes the power of American Jewish individuals and organizations in the formation of American Holocaust memorial culture. Furthermore, it encompasses the impact of those individuals and organizations that shape public opinion, such as the media and academic elites, who also contributed to the formation of German policies. It further includes individuals, such as Holocaust survivor and prominent author Elie Wiesel, who derive their influence primarily from moral authority. These actors occasionally both competed and collaborated in their attempts to define what the Holocaust meant for the United States, Germany, and the relationship between both countries. At times it is difficult to draw a line between state and nonstate actors, as some individuals moved from one position to another, held various offices at once, and acted or spoke on behalf of several institutions.

Fourth, while private individuals and nonstate actors receive significant attention, by no means are the key politician decision-makers absent. The book pays particular attention to Helmut Kohl's personalized style of governing, the "Kohl System," which was based on a wide network of confidants, with the Federal Chancellery (Bundeskanzleramt) at its center.[91] Unlike the Chancellery under his predecessor Helmut Schmidt, under Kohl the Chancellery was more than the administrative base of the chancellor, but rather the center of his political power over the cabinet, the CDU/CSU parliamentary group as well as the CDU party at large. Here, one's personal relationship to Kohl mattered more than ranks and hierarchies. It was a small circle of men—with one exception—who formed Kohl's "kitchen cabinet."[92] The chancellor chose his staff according to three principles: "loyalty, solidarity, and trustworthiness."[93] Consistent with such a personalized form of governing that privileged unofficial channels and informal committees over bureaucratic procedures, Kohl placed confidants in key positions from which they could effectively implement his policies.

Kohl relied on the advice of these confidants, which in turn gave them a significant amount of influence. Holocaust angst was, at least in part, possible because Kohl's advisors on the United States and international relations, such as the politicians Horst Teltschik and Walther Leisler Kiep and the political scientist Werner Weidenfeld, shared such fears. Dealing with the legacies of the Holocaust as part of the Federal Republic's foreign policy and diplomacy was *Chefsache*—that is, an issue with which the chancellor personally and through his closest advisors dealt. In fact, since the beginnings of the Federal Republic, chancellors have acted as "chief diplomat[s]" in this context and have allowed the foreign ministers little room for maneuver.[94] Accordingly, the foreign ministers, the Free Democrats (FDP) Hans-Dietrich Genscher (1974–1992, with a short interruption in 1982) and Klaus Kinkel (1992–1998), feature only marginally in this book.[95]

Writing contemporary history, especially that of the most recent past, presents a number of challenges.[96] While a truly overwhelming amount of published sources—many of them easily accessible online—are available to historians, archival sources are severely restricted. In most German and American archives, records are only declassified after a period of thirty years (with some exceptions). Writing this book brought with it not only the challenge of locating relevant archival collections before they had been propperly catalogued by archivists, but also of securing their declassification, a time-consuming and expensive enterprise.

The most important collections include the records of the Kohl government: the Federal Chancellery, several ministries, and the Federal Press Office in the Federal Archives in Koblenz (Bundesarchiv). Most of these documents have only been made accessible as a result of the requests filed as part of this research (according to Bundesarchivgesetz and Informationsfreiheitsgesetz, the German equivalent of the Freedom of Information Act), which represents the first instance of their consultation by a historian. As a result of these requests, documents from the Foreign Office also became accessible indirectly, even though the Archives of the Foreign Office refused to release them. While this archive upholds the thirty-year blocking period rather strictly and only allowed access up to the early 1980s, memoranda and correspondence between the German embassy in Washington, consulates general across the United States, and the Foreign Office in Bonn concerning German–American relations well into the 1990s were frequently forwarded or carbon-copied to the Chancellery and other ministries and can thus be accessed through the respective collections at the Bundesarchiv. In the United States, the core collections include the institutional records of the USHMM and the archives of the American Jewish Committee (AJC), which allowed unfettered access.

Practitioners of contemporary history face yet another challenge in treating the evidence offered by its many still-living protagonists, a number of whom contribute to the historiography about their lives and their times. This book thus engages to some extent with the autobiographies of its protagonists, albeit at a critical distance.[97] More than thirty interviews were conducted throughout the course of this research (a full list appears on p. 257), which proved crucial in shaping its focus and location of valuable written sources.[98]

Drawing on mostly undiscovered archival sources, this book explores the impact of Holocaust memory on German–American relations in five chapters. The first chapter offers a detailed assessment of how West Germans perceived and reacted to a significant shift in American Holocaust discourse at the end of the 1970s. A clear turning point was reached in the latter half of this decade for the public engagement of American society with this history. Accordingly, West German diplomats and officials at home began to consider American Holocaust memory a long-term political and diplomatic challenge to the Federal Republic. Yet Holocaust angst, to a certain extent a part of the day-to-day routine of German diplomats, reached new heights with the commencement of Helmut Kohl's tenure as chancellor in late 1982. The chancellor and his closest advisors personally dealt with these issues, and they viewed relations with American Jewish organizations as a particular challenge.

As such, the second chapter examines the relationship between the Kohl government and the organized American Jewish community during the 1980s. This chapter offers the first behind-the-scenes glimpse at some of the most contentious episodes in West German–Jewish relations during the 1980s, such as German plans to sell arms to Saudi Arabia and the Bitburg controversy. It also explores how German diplomats and politicians at home dealt with American memories of the Holocaust, as well as with Jewish organizations and Holocaust survivors in the United States. While in the late 1970s there were few official contacts, and a certain degree of antagonism as well as mutual stereotypes strained their relationship, within a decade the German government had managed to establish a stable and productive partnership with several American Jewish organizations.

In stark contrast to the development of this productive dialogue stood the opposition of the West German government and its associates to the establishment of the USHMM in Washington, the focus of the third chapter. Kohl and his advisors perceived this museum as a state-sanctioned reduction of German history to the Holocaust, and, as the German ambassador to the United States plainly stated it in the early 1980s, as an "anti-German museum."[99] For more than a decade, German intermediaries tried to persuade the museum planners to integrate postwar German history and the history of German anti-Nazi military resistance into the exhibition concept. Such attempts were designed to dispel any perception that all Germans had been Nazis and to stress that the Federal Republic was altogether different from Nazi Germany.

Yet these negotiations were not the only avenue the German government used to make a lasting impact on the image of Germany in the United States. Beyond the standard tools of cultural diplomacy, the German government specifically tried to shape the research agenda of American scholars of Germany as well as the teaching of German history in the United States. The fourth chapter explores these policies and pays close attention to the pivotal role of scholars in this context. Kohl, who considered it a central goal of his government to furnish Germans with a positive narrative about their country's history, closely collaborated with scholars who shared such views, and the chapter traces the origins of this cooperation in the early in 1970s. In order to achieve and promote its goals in the United States during the 1980s, the Kohl government attempted to establish effective bases within the American academic community, such as the German Historical Institute in Washington and Centers of Excellence for German Studies at American elite universities, namely Harvard University, the University of California, Berkeley, and Georgetown University.

The fifth chapter traces the evolution of Holocaust angst until the end of the Kohl era in 1998. Beginning in 1989, a series of new developments further stoked German fears. These included the skeptical stance of some American Jewish organizations to the prospect of a unified Germany as well as critical American press coverage of a series of attacks on foreigners and asylum seekers by right-wing extremists and neo-Nazi groups in the early 1990s. German unification also brought with it the revisiting of a previously decided issue, that of compensation payments for Eastern European victims of the Holocaust. Furthermore, the early 1990s saw German officials increasingly worried about what they called a "Holocaust industry" in the United States: namely, the growing instrumentalization of the Holocaust for commercial reasons. In the mid-1990s the Federal Republic also witnessed a new era of debate about the perpetrators of the Holocaust, propelled by American "products," such as the movie *Schindler's List* and Daniel Goldhagen's bestselling book *Hitler's Willing Executioners*. This unprecedented wave of Holocaust debate and publicity in a unified Germany catalyzed a learning process: the leadership around Kohl and its transatlantic network changed its policies toward Holocaust memory at home and vis-à-vis the United States. The book closes by reflecting on the challenges the aftermath of the Third Reich imposed upon a generation of German decision-makers too young to have been involved in Nazi crimes. In dealing with the legacies of the Holocaust on an international stage, they faced a predicament not of their own making, but one they could also not escape. In a sense, they were charged with the modern-day task of managing the ongoing aftermath of a genocide—a process which led to the acceptance and even self-identification of a state with a criminal past.

1

Holocaustomania

West German Diplomats and American Holocaust Memorial Culture in the Late 1970s

On July 9, 1977, the West German ambassador in Washington, Berndt von Staden, reported back to the Foreign Office in Bonn that "there are an increasing number of indicators that suggest attempts by the media, and in the public sphere, to re-awaken the memory of Jewish suffering during the Third Reich in the consciousness of Americans."[1] The ambassador worried that even though these developments were not anti-German in their intention, it would be "impossible to prevent such events from highlighting Germany in its darkest epoch." Indeed, there was an exponential growth in public manifestations of engagement with the Holocaust during the late 1970s in the United States. German diplomats monitored the establishment of Holocaust courses in high schools, seminars at universities, events held by American Jewish organizations, academic conferences and publications, plans for a television miniseries by the major television network NBC, and the creation of a President's Commission on the Holocaust. Staden's report, overall balanced and well-informed, concluded with a rather bleak assessment of the consequences of these developments in tainting the image of the Federal Republic in the United States. Despite a mostly indifferent American attitude toward the history of the Holocaust, its growing presence, especially its planned depiction on television, could have a "significantly negative impact" on the image of West Germany with the "general American public."[2]

It seems hardly surprising that West German diplomats, in charge of representing the Federal Republic's national interest abroad, were concerned about this development, which indicated a dramatic growth in the public presence of a crime carried out above all by German perpetrators. Of course, this was not the first time German diplomats had to face discussions abroad of the crimes committed by the Nazi regime. The horrors of the Third Reich and the Holocaust had affected the image of the Federal Republic since its founding in 1949, for example in the context of financial compensation for the victims of National Socialism, the reputation of West German corporations in the United States, or the well-documented opposition of the West German embassy in France to the screening of Alain Resnais's *Night and Fog* at the Cannes Film Festival in 1956.[3] More specifically, a number of events connected to the Nazi past had caused tensions between West Germany and American Jewish organizations, such as the defacing of the Cologne synagogue with swastikas in 1959 and the Eichmann Trial in 1961.[4] Toward the end of the 1970s, however, German diplomats became aware that the changes in American Holocaust memorial culture were not only tied to actual events, and thus had the potential to be more than just a momentary and passing phenomenon.

In the late 1970s, they began to observe and identify the individuals, institutions, fields of interactions, and the various meanings and functions of Holocaust memory for American society. This knowledge would serve as the basis both for a more concrete engagement with American Holocaust memorial culture and for the interventions staged under the chancellorship of Helmut Kohl. Under Kohl's predecessor, the Social Democrat Helmut Schmidt, German officials were reluctant to interfere with American debates about the Holocaust. They also lacked the tools and strategies to do so. Moreover, diplomatic personnel wanted to use caution and self-restraint in protecting German interests abroad, especially in the context of this sensitive issue.[5] During the last years of the 1970s and the beginning of the 1980s, German diplomats found themselves entangled in the complex, interconnected web of American Holocaust memory, West German domestic confrontation with the Nazi past, questions of personal responsibility, and the dynamics of international and German–American Cold War relations. These challenges become obvious by looking at three fields of interaction: the introduction of Holocaust courses in American high schools, which German diplomats monitored carefully; the broadcast of the NBC miniseries *Holocaust* in 1978/1979, which both marked a significant shift in Holocaust consciousness in the United States and served as the catalyst for discussion on the Federal Republic's coping with the Nazi past; and new contacts between German officials and representatives of American Jewish organizations, which would have a crucial, long-term impact on West German–American Jewish relations.

Holocaustomania in America

The debates among German diplomats over a growing Holocaust consciousness in the United States originated in the region where Germans first settled in North America. In early 1977, the Board of Education in Philadelphia published an official manual for a mandatory curriculum on the Holocaust in the city's high school system.[6] All ninth-graders were thereafter to study the history of the destruction of Europe's Jews as a part of their world history class. Considerations in Philadelphia had begun in 1975 with a conference on Teaching the Holocaust, organized by the local Jewish Community Relations Council.[7] While individual teachers had been teaching the history of the Holocaust since the early 1970s in American schools, and even earlier in a number of colleges, now a major American city—with both a large Jewish and a large German American population—decided that all high school students should learn about Nazi Germany's attempt to exterminate European Jewry. New York City saw a similar development, where the city's Board of Education also recommended a mandatory curriculum on the Holocaust in 1977.[8] The Anti-Defamation League of B'nai B'rith (ADL) was instrumental in this context. This organization, founded in 1913, was dedicated to defending the rights of Jews and fighting anti-Semitism, but also to protecting civil rights more broadly, which included supporting and funding educators and publications that facilitated teaching about the Holocaust.[9] In a *Teachers' Guide to the Holocaust*, published in 1977 to provide individual teachers with resources and materials, the ADL suggested that young Americans would tremendously benefit from studying this history. "In short," the booklet states, "a study unit on the Holocaust is a contribution to society and a compelling case study of human interaction. It can easily be adapted to classroom use for real educational growth."[10]

This statement encapsulates a paradigm shift in the United States' engagement with Holocaust memory. Naturally, the memory of the fate of the Jews under Nazi Germany had been a constant, if changing, presence in Jewish communities in the United States since the Second World War and had, at times, received significant public attention prior to the late 1970s.[11] For American Jews, the Six-Day War (1967) and the Yom Kippur War (1973) represented decisive turning points in their attitudes toward both the Holocaust and Israel. Although Israel was victorious in both wars, significant losses in the Yom Kippur War and an increasing international isolation shattered the notion of Israel's military invincibility. Contemporary threats to Israel and its vulnerable situation in the Middle East brought with them analogies to the suffering of Jews under Nazi Germany. As a result, the memory of the Holocaust became further integrated into American Jewish identity and consciousness, both a motivation and a discursive tool to gather support for Israel.[12]

Closely connected to a heightened public awareness of Jewish suffering under Nazism was an increased prominence of Holocaust survivors in America, marking the beginning of what Annette Wieviorka has called the "era of the witness."[13] As witnesses to this event, they enjoyed increasing public recognition during the 1970s, and some "have become sought-after authorities, even culture heroes."[14] Among them, the writer and scholar Elie Wiesel commanded unrivalled attention. Born in 1928 in Romania, Wiesel survived incarceration in the Auschwitz and Buchenwald concentration camps, moved to France after the war, and relocated to the United States in the 1950s. He published several dozen books on the Holocaust—most notably his memoir *Night*—and became arguably the central figure in shaping Holocaust consciousness in the United States, where he was considered the "archetypal survivor-witness."[15] During these years, survivors thus experienced a transformation to a position of "moral leadership" and engendered an "almost heroic" level of pride.[16] Several factors accounted for this transformation: an increase in self-confidence within the American Jewish community; the aforementioned wars in the Middle East; the growing temporal distance from the Holocaust; the impact of the Vietnam War on American society; and a certain fascination with "public and private disaster, destruction and victimization, surviving and survivalism."[17] Peter Novick has described the significance of a "culture of victimization" in the aftermath of the Vietnam War that compelled Holocaust survivors to share their stories.[18] Prior to these changes, they had—at least publicly—remained silent in a culture that was fixated on victory, progress, and war heroes.[19] The growth of Holocaust consciousness, however, also met considerable opposition from leading American Jewish intellectuals. For example, Jacob Neusner, a prolific scholar of Judaism, criticized what he termed the "Holocaustomania" of the 1970s.[20] He condemned the "obsession with 'the Holocaust' which want[ed] to make the tragedy into the principal subject of public discourse with Jews and about Judaism."[21] Others even argued that making the Holocaust the centerpiece of American Jewish identity would "grant a posthumous victory to Adolf Hitler."[22]

While the events of the 1960s and 1970s significantly changed how American Jews publicly spoke about the Holocaust, they also marked the beginning of the latter event's burgeoning public and discursive presence and a change in plot, as it were, that permeated American society. In parallel to the formation of a predominantly patriotic memory of World War II, the Eichmann Trial, the Six-Day War, the antiwar movement, and the civil rights movement—in which many Jews participated and opposed discrimination and anti-Semitism—all transformed mainstream America's engagement with the murder of European Jews.[23] For instance, the Holocaust came to be employed "as the standard by which to judge and oppose American actions in Vietnam."[24] Toward the end of the 1970s, the Holocaust thus went from being the "possession of American Jews" to a "national trust."[25] The introduction of Holocaust courses, the broadcast of the NBC miniseries *Holocaust*, and the establishment of a President's Commission on the Holocaust, which ultimately resulted in the establishment of the United States Holocaust Memorial Council and the construction of the USHMM, served to acquaint and confront Americans with this history.[26] Textbooks, museums, and even board games made the Holocaust a "moral compass" for millions of Americans.[27] The Holocaust was transformed into the ultimate benchmark for assessing human behavior, a unique "moral reference" point for all political strata of American society, and "the bearer of universal lessons" that rendered it, as Novick has argued, a "moral and ideological Rorschach test."[28] A central protagonist of American Holocaust memorial culture, the writer, rabbi, and museum expert Michael Berenbaum, who played a pivotal role in the establishment of the USHMM, summarized this intention by referring to the Holocaust as the "violation of every essential American value."[29] This "externalization of evil" thus equated a crime in which Germans had been the perpetrators with the negation of America's moral and ethical standards.[30]

This development raised red flags with German diplomats stationed in the United States. In May 1977, the Consul General in New York, Werner Ungerer, wrote a long and detailed assessment of the manual on the Holocaust to be used in history classes in Philadelphia.[31] In his analysis, he pointed out that the manual, which included course units on stereotypes perpetuated and prejudices held, as well as on the persecution and extermination policies against Jews during the Third Reich, appeared, on the whole, to be objective. It could not, Ungerer suggested, be considered an "anti-German concoction." Nevertheless, he was convinced that negative repercussions for the image of the Federal Republic were inevitable. For instance, the manual neglected to sufficiently explain, Ungerer pointed out, the Federal Republic's efforts to prosecute Nazi criminals or to compensate the victims of Nazism after 1949. Furthermore, it often used the terms "Nazi" and "German" interchangeably. Ungerer also criticized the manual's neglect of the "persecution of other racial and *völkisch* minorities" and its focus instead on the "specific sufferings of the Jews in the Holocaust."[32] Indeed, four out of six units specifically dealt with the persecution of Jews and were, Ungerer added, much more voluminous than the remaining two, more general chapters. Students, he concluded, would inevitably get the impression that "those who persecuted and killed Jews in such a manner belong to a barbaric nation."[33] This fear, that Americans would not be able to distinguish clearly between the postwar Federal Republic and Nazi Germany, found voice throughout the German observers' memoranda. It had its origins in the early postwar period when German—but also American—authorities actively tried to portray West Germans as democrats who were part of the Western alliance with the United States, rather than as Nazis.[34] In the 1970s, this fear received a new level of urgency in response to the changes in American Holocaust memory and constituted a core motive of German diplomats' confrontation with this memory.

Werner Ungerer was by no means an ardent nationalist, but he objected to a portrayal of the Federal Republic that focused solely on its inherited criminal history. Born in 1927, he studied economics and diplomacy and, from 1975 to 1979, headed the consulate general of West Germany based in New York.[35] Having joined the Foreign Service in 1952 as part of the third cohort ("crew") of

West German diplomats, he served as a diplomat for almost the entire period of the "old" Federal Republic (1949–1990). His field of expertise was European integration, to which he was deeply committed; he authored numerous scholarly articles, and he served as the Federal Republic's representative to the European Community in Brussels during the second half of the 1980s. Ungerer was old enough to have experienced ideological indoctrination during the Third Reich, and although the historical record is unclear, he may have fought in the Second World War. He later stated, however, that he had not been an active supporter of the Nazi regime, but had rather devoted his energies to building a "new Germany" from the ruins of the Third Reich.[36] Indeed, for many members of Ungerer's generation, the year 1945 marked the most crucial biographical turning point. This Flakhelfer-Generation—that is, youths who helped to operate anti-aircraft guns during the last years of the War, or "forty-fivers"—often fervently supported National Socialism in their youth, but as adults became thoroughly committed to the democratic regime of the Federal Republic. Prominent representatives dominated (West) German political and intellectual life from the 1970s until the late 1990s.[37]

Thus not only the Nazi period, but also the postwar years, had a distinctive formative impact on Ungerer, who took great pride in the democratic achievements of the Federal Republic and firmly believed that West Germans confronted the Holocaust, accepted it as part of their history, and had drawn important lessons from this event.[38] He had spent countless nights in air raid shelters and lost friends and family members during the war, but later recorded how, in his experience, all Germans had been treated as " 'collectively guilty' " after 1945. He also vividly recalled how, for many years, the Federal Republic had to face "hatred" from abroad, despite the "good will" many had demonstrated to build a "new Germany" and their dedication to reconciling with former enemies. Ungerer was committed to defending this "new Germany" against what he considered unjust and incorrect accusations from abroad, a commitment that both represented his assignment as the consul general and reflected his own deeply held, personal convictions. While he was tolerant of critical views of Germany—especially from those who had escaped Nazi persecution—he condemned the exploitation and misrepresentation of events in Germany for political or commercial reasons. For example, he lamented that American journalists exaggerated and distorted the prevalence of anti-Semitism in the Federal Republic, which did not correspond with the reality of a virtually impotent extreme right. Observers from abroad, he argued, also did not seem to understand that the prosecution of war criminals was a difficult process and sometimes led to disappointing results. Yet in comparison to other countries that had recovered from a dictatorship, Ungerer believed, the Federal Republic had been quite effective in punishing its own war criminals. Of course, he was aware that restitution payments could not "make good again" ("*wiedergutmachen*") on the damage the Nazi regime had caused, but he was disconcerted that the American public paid too little attention to German "good will" and compensation as a "gesture of reconciliation."

Ungerer's perspective allows insight into the broad reactions of German observers at the time. While they did not object in principle to the introduction of programs in American high schools to combat stereotypes and prejudices, they found it troubling that the example used was taken from German history. Learning about the Holocaust—without enlightening students on the positive developments in postwar West Germany—would inevitably result in anti-German sentiment among young Americans. German officials were convinced that the Federal Republic had sufficiently coped with the Nazi past by providing compensation to Nazi victims and putting war criminals on trial. In their view, Americans—American Jews in particular—devoted too much attention to the Holocaust without acknowledging the achievements of West German democracy.

Weighing Options

Even though West German diplomats had been generally pessimistic about the level of knowledge about the Federal Republic in the United States and assumed that Americans' knowledge about Germany was partially shaped by "wrong impressions," the transformation of American Holocaust memory in the late 1970s caught them by surprise.[39] To a greater extent perhaps than Ungerer, the tension between coming to terms with the Nazi past and promoting the "new" Germany was personified by the highest-ranking representative of German interests in the United States, Ambassador Berndt von Staden.[40] Staden was born in 1919 in Rostock as the son of a Baltic German aristocrat and grew up in Reval (Tallinn), Estonia. In 1938 he began to study law in Bonn, and, after a short return to Estonia, permanently resettled to Germany in late 1939 as a result of the Hitler-Stalin-Pact and the stationing of Soviet troops in his home country. Drafted into the Wehrmacht in 1940, he fought on the Eastern Front and in North Africa and was captured by British troops in May 1945. In his memoirs, he described his "mixed feelings" about the Third Reich, whose "atrociousness" he either did not fully grasp or wanted to disavow until the end of the war. His role within the Nazi apparatus, however, extended well beyond that of an average German soldier. Staden had enthusiastically welcomed the German "crusade," as he called it, against the Bolshevist Soviet Union, and also served in the Wehrmacht's intelligence unit, the Abwehr. He had intimate knowledge of the crimes against Jews through a personal connection: his cousin's son had—reluctantly, according to Staden—participated in the establishment of the Lodz Ghetto as a member of the Waffen-SS.[41] While Staden experienced the Third

Reich as a soldier, his wife, Wendelgard (b. 1926), a niece of the former Weimar Republic and Third Reich Foreign Minister Konstantin von Neurath, witnessed Nazi persecution policies first hand. In her memoirs, *Darkness over the Valley*, she recalls the establishment of a small concentration camp, Wiesengrund, in 1944 (officially satellite camp "Vaihingen"), close to the farm she grew up on, as well as her impressions of its malnourished Jewish prisoners and her attempts to help them.[42]

After a difficult period of readjustment to civilian life, Staden joined the West German Foreign Service in 1951. This marked the beginning of an extraordinary career in the West German civil service. In addition to his tenure as ambassador in Washington, Staden served in the Foreign Office in Bonn, for the European Economic Community, the Chancellery, and at the end of his career again in the Foreign Office as Undersecretary of State (*Staatssekretär*). From 1982 onward, he simultaneously served as the Coordinator for German–American relations. Staden was a close confidant of long-term Foreign Minister Hans-Dietrich Genscher, who placed Staden in strategically important positions.

As ambassador in Washington, Staden faced a number of national and international crises, including the Watergate scandal, the Vietnam and the Yom Kippur Wars, the ensuing Oil Crisis of 1973, debates about the modernization of nuclear forces in Europe, and a number of other political and economic issues that also significantly influenced German–American relations. The election of Jimmy Carter as US president in 1976 racheted up tensions in these relations at the highest government level. In the run-up to the elections, West German Chancellor Schmidt had favored the incumbent Gerald R. Ford. Schmidt was— as a sober, rational politician with significant experience in economic, financial, and defense policies—distinctly different from the rather emotional, moralizing, and deeply religious Carter. The resulting malaise between the two heads of state also affected key political issues, namely economic and armament policies, on which the positions of the United States and the Federal Republic often diverged. Staden exerted significant energy, minimizing the damage caused by a strained relationship between Carter and Schmidt to German–American relations.[43]

During those years he evolved as a "specialist for precise reporting and analysis," a great asset for the Federal Republic.[44] Increasing mutual trust and managing the flow of information between the two countries was therefore of particular importance in Staden's role as ambassador. Even though the changes in American Holocaust memory certainly complicated these goals, Staden did not mention them in his memoirs. In retrospect, the important political controversies and challenges may well have seemed more important to him. However, German diplomats and politicians were generally reluctant to broach the delicate question of how to deal with public memory of the Holocaust abroad.

By not making the Nazi past an official foreign policy matter, Staden may have been inspired to follow the example set by Chancellor Helmut Schmidt. To the chancellor, the commemoration of the Nazi past did not count among his political priorities. In contrast to his successor Kohl, Schmidt did not hold the Nazi past to be a major liability in promoting the image of the Federal Republic abroad. Even though he considered an "open engagement [*das saubere Umgehen*] with our recent past" an important factor for West German foreign policy, and expressed concern in late 1978 that "the memory of Auschwitz will—contrary to our hitherto existing expectations, experiences, and presumptions—play again a more significant role in the future,"[45] he opted for a pragmatic and "neutral" approach toward the Nazi past. In 1981, he famously remarked that the future foreign policy of the Federal Republic "must not be overshadowed by Auschwitz."[46] As such, Schmidt did not make the Holocaust "a major or even minor focus of his tenure as chancellor."[47]

Staden's internal memoranda and correspondence reveal, however, that he was indeed preoccupied with American Holocaust memory at that time. In contrast to earlier periods of heightened interest in the Nazi past, Staden and his staff realized in 1977 that they were witnessing a significant shift in American society's confrontation with the Holocaust. Specifically, they recorded a number of reasons for the growth of Holocaust memory that indicated a long-term change. These included the struggle against new and increasingly widespread forms of Holocaust denial in the United States, epitomized by the publication of *The Hoax of the Twentieth Century* by Arthur R. Butz in 1976. Most importantly, German diplomats observed that certain groups—what were referred to as "Jewish circles"—intended to mobilize and "emotionalize" American public opinion. By referring to the Holocaust, their goal was to gather support for Israel's national interests in light of Jimmy Carter's peace efforts in the Middle East. Finally, German diplomats identified efforts by "spiritual leaders" of American Judaism to reach an increasingly secular young generation of Jews in the country by referencing the fate of Jews during the Third Reich, aiming to create a "sustainable identity" for the Jewish community in the United States.[48]

Even though German diplomats assumed that this was above all a domestic debate that was not directed against Germany, they nevertheless feared a negative backlash for West Germany abroad.[49] As such, the embassy's staff weighed its options to confront this potential political threat, but they saw no obvious solutions. For example, Staden explored a suggestion from the German embassy in Tel Aviv and considered putting together a brochure documenting the twenty-fifth anniversary of the 1952 Luxemburg Agreement on reparations between West Germany and Israel.[50] In the 1950s, this agreement had, as historians have later concluded, "mollified the hostility of many American Jewish organizations" toward the Federal Republic.[51] The brochure, Staden suggested, should be "matter-of-fact" and "rather cool," and should feature not only a famous photo of an encounter between Konrad Adenauer and David Ben Gurion in the Waldorf Astoria Hotel in New York, but also "numerous photos of encounters between leading American Jews and German politicians."[52]

This PR idea had a Jewish audience primarily in mind. Around this time, however, the embassy became increasingly worried about how the majority of non-Jewish Americans would react when confronted with the history of the Holocaust. Such concerns were catalyzed by the plans of the television channel NBC to produce an eight-hour television program on the persecution and extermination of Jews by Nazi Germany. The embassy had learned of such plans in mid-1977 and assumed that NBC intended to replicate the emotional discussions that had followed its competitor ABC's blockbuster drama *Roots*, and that it hoped to achieve similar success with a miniseries on the Holocaust.[53] Staden feared that using such a "complex and sensitive topic" as the basis for a television series could have a "significantly negative impact" on public opinion toward Germany. He pointed out, however, that interfering with NBC and trying to change the script would not be a viable option.[54]

The United States desk at the Foreign Office in Bonn received Staden's suggestion to publish information about reparation payments with reservation and proposed in an internal memorandum not to engage in any form of direct public response for the time being. Officials assumed that the Federal Republic was not in a position to prevent discussions about the Third Reich or German anti-Semitism abroad.[55] Addressing such debates publicly only bore the risk of turning this "domestic issue" into a problem for German–American relations. Furthermore, taking a "demonstrative pro-Jewish and pro-Israeli stance in a third party country [i.e., the United States]" also had the potential to damage Germany's political position vis-à-vis Arab countries and in the Middle East. As a result, it would be in Germany's best interest to make clear to "leading personalities" that such "campaigns" could damage bilateral relations in the long run.

The Foreign Office repeated such reservations in its reply to Staden and clearly rejected the idea of using the twenty-fifth anniversary of the Luxembourg Agreement between the Federal Republic and Israel for public relations purposes. Not only was the agreement still controversial in Israel, but emphasizing the Federal Republic's payments for Holocaust victims and the Jewish state was also a rather delicate issue that could lead to undesirable political consequences. The Foreign Office advised diplomats in the United States to use restraint and caution when talking about compensation.[56] Emphasizing financial compensation for "atrocities committed against Jewry during the NS [National Socialist] period" could above all lead to the conclusion that the Federal Republic considered this a closed chapter in its history, an impression German officials wanted to avoid creating publicly.[57] Stressing the accomplishments of German compensation could also lead to new demands for such payments. In fact, since the early 1970s the Conference on Jewish Material Claims against Germany (Claims Conference) had been demanding financial support for Eastern European victims of Nazi persecution, especially those Jews who had left the Eastern Bloc after 1965.[58] German diplomats were not inclined to give the Claims Conference a renewed impetus for such demands. Not only had the Federal Republic hoped to permanently close the books on this issue in the 1960s, but the end of the postwar economic boom in 1973–1974 also made additional payments difficult financially for West Germany. Furthermore, raising this issue could potentially damage German–Arab relations. While the Foreign Office did not go into more detail on this issue, it is likely that payments to Jewish victims and to the state of Israel had triggered a negative reaction in the Arab world, as had the official establishment of diplomatic relations between West Germany and Israel in 1965. If nothing else, the oil crisis of 1973, an event with global repercussions, had demonstrated how much the West, including the Federal Republic, depended on economic cooperation with Arab states.

At the time, German foreign policy experts wanted to avoid such complications and agreed that no "offensive" reactions against the growing public presence of the Holocaust in the United States should occur.[59] The Foreign Office emphasized that the Federal Republic had to continue to "patiently" and "insistently" demonstrate to the United States that it was indeed "a different state than the 'Third Reich,'" was conscious of the crimes committed "in the name of Germany," and had learned its lessons from the past.[60] The thought that Americans, especially young people, the future generation of the Federal Republic's most important Cold War ally, could perceive present-day Germans as belonging to a "barbaric nation," as Ungerer had put it, was most unsettling to them.[61]

While West German diplomats in the United States and foreign policy experts in Bonn agreed not to openly confront or interfere with American Holocaust memorial culture, a further development complicated their position. The plans of the school boards in Philadelphia and New York to introduce Holocaust courses had caused "significant agitation," as Ungerer remarked, among Americans citizens of German ancestry.[62] German Americans also feared that such a course would not distinguish clearly enough between Germans and Nazis and would not pay sufficient attention to the persecution and murder of other minorities throughout history. In general, they were considerably displeased with the growing presence of the Holocaust in American life.[63] The president of the German-American Citizens League based in Cincinnati, Eugene von Riestenberg, for example, complained to NBC in mid-1977 that a TV program on the Holocaust would create "a whole new generation of German haters and is probably supposed to do exactly that."[64] German Americans' negative and defensive reactions to the public's heightened interest in the Holocaust were not limited to Ohio. In Philadelphia, the local German-American Committee was strongly "opposed to the teaching of the Holocaust."[65] The Committee's efforts to widen the focus of such a course to encompass the persecution of minorities and genocide throughout history more generally did, however, not succeed.[66] Ungerer noted that the prospects for such a change had not been unpromising until the "counterforces," by which he meant Jewish groups in Philadelphia, intervened via the school board and the media.[67] The city's mayor Frank Rizzo, characteristically and without so much as a whiff of political correctness, expressed his regrets to Ungerer about this development and suggested that for the future, "only cooperation" between "ethnic" Italians, Poles, Irish, and Germans could provide a "counterbalance" to the "overpowering influence of the Jews."[68] Such behind-the-scenes remarks certainly must have contributed to a growing antagonism against American Jewish organizations, but direct opposition was not an option for German diplomats.

Some German American organizations openly condemned American Jews, and some of these protests clearly had chauvinistic and anti-Semitic tendencies. For instance, the president of the Philadelphia chapter of the German American National Congress, Werner Barbye, called upon members of his organization to send protest letters to the *Philadelphia Inquirer* in opposition to the introduction of Holocaust courses.[69] He attributed the growing public presence of the Holocaust to the lack of "representatives of Germandom" on the school board, in television, and in the press, adding that "it has never been proven that six million Jews were killed." This was not an isolated incident. As the West German consulate general in New York City recorded, a number of other representatives of such organizations lamented "attacks" on German Americans by "international Jewry" and declared that it was time for German Americans to "wake up," expressions that obviously resonated with the diction of Nazi propaganda.[70]

West German diplomats could not completely ignore the actions of German Americans as they feared that such anti-Semitic statements would eventually come back to tarnish the image of the Federal Republic in the United States. After all, German American groups and associations "strongly identified" with their German heritage and their former home country.[71] Officially, German diplomats avoided dealing with such issues by insisting that German Americans were American citizens and that the Federal Republic could do nothing to influence them.[72] Behind the scenes, however, Ungerer was in discussions with their more moderate representatives. While he generally shared their opposition to a course that only focused on the Holocaust, he suggested that German Americans should not "dispute the right of the Jews to have their ethnic history taught in American schools."[73] Ungerer was happy to engage in fruitful discourse, but he had no tolerance for extreme views. His advice to the president of the German American Committee of Greater New York, Georg Pape, who had stated in the *New York Times* that "there was no real proof that the

Holocaust had actually happened," was to resign from his post.[74] After some hesitation, Pape withdrew his statement denying the Holocaust and eventually stepped down from his position, having lost the support of his own organization.[75]

Although German diplomats agreed not to interfere with American debates about Holocaust memory—unless this became absolutely necessary as in the case of German Americans—they tried to collect more information on the inner dynamics of this development. They were fully aware that organizations such as the ADL aimed to make this course on the Holocaust a permanent component of high school curricula not just in Philadelphia and New York, but across the country. In late 1977, German officials were presented with an opportunity to learn more about the goals of the ADL, which planned to hold a conference on Teaching about Genocide and the Nazi Holocaust in Secondary Schools, together with the National Council for the Social Studies in October in Glen Cove, Long Island, New York. In its invitation to Staden, the ADL made the goals of the conference abundantly clear, namely "the institutionalization of the teaching about the Holocaust; [and] the incorporation of the study of the Holocaust and its implications for society today into the school curriculum."[76] In the attached conference outline, the ADL added,

> The lessons of the Holocaust must be learned so that the early warning signs of genocide can be detected, so that all people, anywhere—whether religious, racial or political minorities, may be safeguarded.
> The lessons of the Holocaust must be learned so that we may truly value life, the life of an individual, a family, a group of people.[77]

This announcement, congruous with the development of an American Holocaust discourse at this time more generally, must have vindicated and accentuated German diplomats' concerns that such tendencies would perpetuate a negative image of the Federal Republic.

Around 150 participants gathered for the conference on Long Island, where a variety of questions relating to the teaching of the Holocaust in high schools were explored. Staden did not attend the conference, though the embassy managed to facilitate the participation of Siegfried Bachmann, a professor and director of the Georg Eckert Institute for International Textbook Research in Braunschweig (GEI).[78] Bachmann was a known expert on high school textbooks, and the ADL had also invited him to present a lecture on the treatment of the Holocaust in German textbooks. In his presentation, Bachmann aimed to underscore that West German secondary education did not ignore the Holocaust.[79] More importantly, at least from the perspective of the embassy, Bachmann monitored the proceedings and panels closely and submitted a detailed report about the conference to the embassy, in which he provided information on its content, as well as the mood and intentions of the participants.[80] His report confirmed what German diplomats had already noticed and would continue to emphasize in the future: that American Jewish engagement with the Holocaust was particularly impassioned and that their aim was to keep the Holocaust "in the consciousness of the American people" by appealing to their emotions.[81] For example, Bachmann pointed out the "emotional" language of the presentations by Elie Wiesel and the political scientist and historian Raul Hilberg, who had escaped Nazi persecution by leaving his birthplace, Vienna, in 1939.[82] According to Bachman, their presentations were based on personal experience and specifically addressed the "responsibility" of average Germans for the Holocaust. They resonated particularly well with Jewish conference participants of the "war time generation," whereas younger participants would have preferred a more "rational" approach to the history of the Holocaust.[83]

Bachmann maintained, however, that despite the ADL's goal to make the Holocaust relevant to all Americans, the conference proceedings showed that at the time the Holocaust was still predominantly a Jewish memory. He stated that virtually all attendees, most of them teachers or representatives of school boards, were "of the Jewish faith" and concluded that the ADL aimed above all at fostering "solidarity among Jewish groups" in the United States. "Winning sympathizers" was only a secondary goal. He closed his report by conveying a suggestion of the ADL's program director, Theodore A. Freedman, to possibly hold a German–American seminar on teaching the Holocaust in the future. Staden considered the idea of a joint seminar on textbooks worthy of further consideration, as it would give the "German side" a chance to "win the initiative" instead of being pushed "more and more into the role of apologists" by Jewish organizations in the United States.[84] While his reactions showed that German officials were beginning to ponder more pragmatic ways to confront American Holocaust memory, it would take years for German and American experts to actually meet and discuss high school textbooks.[85]

Toward the end of 1977, German diplomats drew some preliminary conclusions about the ADL's conference and the impact of Holocaust courses in America more generally, which they expected to be implemented in schools nationwide.[86] Staden remarked that Holocaust courses were not "anti-German propaganda" and did not aim at designing an "accentuated anti-German conception of history," but needed to be seen as part of a discourse about Jewish identity in America.[87] Nevertheless, he feared negative repercussions for the Federal Republic, and there was little room for maneuver: the embassy ruled out any effort to either "limit" the treatment of the Holocaust in high schools, nor to interfere with public discussion of the Holocaust.[88] While such initiatives' chances for success were slim from the outset, their engagement would also potentially allow Americans to perceive a link between the Federal Republic and the crimes of the Third Reich. This, of course, German representatives wanted to avoid at all cost.

Werner Ungerer, cognizant that the ADL had as its goal the introduction of Holocaust courses throughout the United States, even remarked that it was "idle" to ponder why exactly the ADL put so much energy into this initiative.[89] Instead, "the German side" should face the facts: the "existing anti-German bias of America's youth," he wrote, would certainly increase because of the "entanglement of the name of Germany with Nazi atrocities against European Jewry."[90] According to his assessment, American teenagers scarcely learned anything about present-day Germany in high school, but received most of their information from implicitly or even openly "anti-German" television programs. Exposure to a misrepresented version of German history in schools would thus confirm their clichéd notions and prejudices. While Ungerer, like Staden, hoped to find a way to make Holocaust courses more "balanced" in order to clearly distinguish the "democratic and liberal" Germany of the present from the Third Reich, he assumed that it was too late to make changes in Philadelphia and New York. Instead Ungerer warned that "without a doubt this topic is—even though more than one generation has passed—prone to stir highly emotional debates."[91] But at the end of 1977, no solution to this issue had been found.

The Watershed of 1978

In 1978 matters significantly worsened from the perspective of German diplomats. In addition to the airing of the most widely viewed television program on the mass murder of European Jews of all time, the NBC miniseries *Holocaust*, this year saw a number of other crucial events that accelerated America's confrontation with the memory of the Holocaust.[92] Indeed, the year 1978 marked a watershed for American Holocaust memorial culture. A group of American Nazis caused a national controversy over free speech when they threatened to hold a rally in Skokie, Illinois, a community with a large number of Jewish residents, including Holocaust survivors.[93] The Department of Justice's Office of Special Investigation (OSI) began to search for Nazi war criminals who had made their way to the United States, in order to put them on trial and deport them.[94] And, at the highest political level, Jimmy Carter's decision to establish a commission on the Holocaust, which eventually resulted in the construction of the USHMM, also gave official sanction to the institutionalization of Holocaust memory in the United States.[95]

The idea of creating a national Holocaust memorial was the result of domestic considerations in 1977.[96] Carter had alienated Jewish voters, who were traditionally close to the Democratic Party, by suggesting that the rights of

Palestinians be strengthened and by announcing plans for arms deals with Saudi Arabia and Egypt. Looking for ways to decrease the resulting tensions between the administration and Jewish voters, staff members suggested building a central Holocaust memorial to reinforce ties with American Jews, but also to send a clear affirmative signal of support to Israel. During the celebrations for Israel's thirtieth anniversary in the Rose Garden of the White House on May 1, 1978, attended by the Israeli Prime Minister Menachem Begin and more than one thousand rabbis, Carter announced the plans for a commission to find an appropriate form to commemorate the victims of the Holocaust. Since other plans for a national Holocaust monument existed at the time, the Carter administration had to move quickly to benefit politically from this decision. Thus on November 1, 1978, Carter established the President's Commission on the Holocaust, with its goal to develop a concept for the memorial and the organization of the Days of Remembrance of Victims of the Holocaust, which Congress had set for April 1979. During the Days of Remembrance, Carter later explained to the American people why the United States needed a national Holocaust memorial: American troops had liberated many concentration camps and many survivors had subsequently come to the United States.[97] However, the United States also bore a certain share of responsibility for the Holocaust, having failed to rescue Jews from Europe.[98] Finally, Americans should draw lessons from the Holocaust for the prevention of future genocides.

The President's Commission on the Holocaust was not the first initiative to build such a memorial in America.[99] In 1946, the National Organization of Polish Jews had tried to build a monument in New York City, a project that, as with a number of others proposed for the city, never materialized. A Holocaust museum in New York, the Museum of Jewish Heritage, only opened its doors to the public in 1997.[100] Before the establishment of the President's Commission, a number of smaller monuments existed or were in planning phases. These included the Babi Yar Park, established by the City Council of Denver in 1970, and the Los Angeles Holocaust Monument, conceived by Holocaust survivors in 1973 and completed in 1992. In the same city, the Los Angeles Museum of the Holocaust, designed by survivors and envisioned as a travelling exhibition in 1976, found a permanent location in 1978 in the building of the local Jewish Federation, making it the first "museum" for the victims of the Holocaust in America. Since 2010, it has occupied a building in Pan Pacific Park.[101] In 1977, also in Los Angeles, Marvin Hier founded the Simon Wiesenthal Center, which later established the Museum of Tolerance, in operation since 1993. Other major museums include the Detroit-based Holocaust Memorial Center, which was conceived in 1981 and completed in 1984.[102] The President's Commission on the Holocaust, however, was the first governmental as well as national initiative to permanently incorporate engagement with the Holocaust into American public, academic, and intellectual life, and it profoundly shaped Holocaust remembrance in the United States.[103]

While West German observers objected to the plans to build a national Holocaust museum in Washington throughout the 1980s, in 1978 their attention was focused on the NBC miniseries. Already before its broadcast, German diplomats expected that the miniseries would "deeply touch" Americans and feared that the history of the Holocaust would move from being an American-Jewish, and academic, point of interest, to a "phenomenon" that would reach a large segment of the American public.[104] Although Staden did not consider this development to be anti-German, he assumed that it would nevertheless have a negative effect on the reputation of the Federal Republic.[105] Yet to him, any attempt to change the script of the miniseries, which was already complete at this point, appeared futile. Such an intervention would only create the impression that the Federal Republic "identified" with Nazi Germany.[106] Even though it is hard to imagine how such an intervention could have even been accomplished, German attempts to directly interfere with the production of the miniseries would hardly have led to the desired outcome.

The broadcast of *Holocaust* was a turning point for discourse on the Nazi past in both the United States and Germany, where it was aired in April 1978 and January 1979, respectively. In the United States, it acted as a "catalyst" for the institutionalization of Holocaust memory, but its aftermath also accelerated German diplomats' fears about the image of the Federal Republic being tarnished in the United States.[107] Approximately 120 million viewers watched the four episodes in the United States, while about 20 million West Germans saw at least parts of the program.[108] In the aftermath of the recent wars in the Middle East, the Holocaust had in the United States become a "Jewish event" in public perception and was closely associated with the fate of Jews in Israel.[109] As a result of the wars, but also the liberation of Jewish hostages from a hijacked Air France plane in Uganda in 1976, Israel had been a constant feature in the news cycle throughout the 1970s. While this level of attention to Israel seemed to guarantee that a miniseries on the Holocaust would garner widespread interest, the script's writer Gerald Green nonetheless faced the challenge of making a history of the mass murder of European Jews appealing to a mass audience. Thus, he chose to tell the story through the eyes of the fictional middle-class German Jewish Weiss family, which allowed more viewers to empathize with the protagonists of *Holocaust*. In the miniseries, this family suffers from, or witnesses in some form or another, the escalation of Nazi anti-Jewish policies from 1935 to the end of the war. Only one family member survives the war. The antihero of the miniseries, the fictional SS-officer Erik Dorf, is a witness to the Nazi extermination and in some instances acts as the driving force behind its implementation. He is the "symbolic mastermind of the Final Solution," who escapes punishment by committing suicide while in US custody.[110] The miniseries depicts most of the important stages, events, and locations of the Holocaust, such as the Nuremberg Laws, Kristallnacht, the "euthanasia" program, forced labor, the Babi Yar massacre, the Wannsee Conference, the Warsaw Ghetto, and concentration and extermination camps, and is thus rightly considered a "mini-survey course" on the Holocaust.[111]

Despite some very critical reactions, including an attack by Elie Wiesel on the miniseries in the *New York Times*, it was a major success for NBC, boosted by a massive publicity campaign that preceded the broadcast.[112] NBC developed a viewers' guide, which it distributed across the United States with the help of several American Jewish organizations, including the ADL. These guides helped to make *Holocaust* a topic of discussion in synagogues and churches around the country before it was broadcast.[113] More than one million copies of a novel based on Green's script were distributed to American bookstores. The net effect of *Holocaust* was precisely what German diplomats had feared: it helped to establish the Holocaust as a "universal metaphor" that would serve as a "frame of reference for contemporary suffering."[114]

While this monumental influence of *Holocaust* could not be fully antici-pated, West German diplomats had used a variety of methods to follow and assess the impact of public debates and engagement with the Holocaust in the United States. They read publications about the Third Reich and the Holocaust, closely monitored the press, and used public opinion polls to gauge the mini-series' effect.[115] Prior to its airing, the embassy also wrote to the corporation responsible for the miniseries' distribution, in an attempt to collect informa-tion about its production and content.[116] German American organizations also corresponded with the embassy, forwarding copies of their own efforts to in-terfere or gather information, for example with NBC.[117]

It cannot be established whether Staden or Ungerer and their staff actu-ally watched the miniseries on NBC and, if they did, what their impressions were. Yet immediately after the telecast in April 1978, German emissaries in the United States were directly exposed to the opinions of Americans who had seen the program. The consulate general in New York City, for example, received a number of angry phone calls, with one representative being called a "German bastard" and accused of having participated in the Holocaust him-self, while another anonymous and particularly aggrieved caller even threat-ened to assassinate a German diplomat.[118] With no official instructions from the Foreign Office, the consulate general declined to issue a press release de-spite numerous requests for one.[119] Staden, however, was relieved that, in gen-eral, the "emotional reaction of the American public was much weaker than [he] had assumed."[120] Within a few weeks after its broadcast, the German embassy reported back to Bonn that *Holocaust* had caused less harm to the image of the Federal Republic than German diplomats had feared.[121] Accord-ing to his assessment, Americans had been "capable" of distinguishing clearly between the Third Reich and contemporary Germany, which made long-term negative damage to the Federal Republic's reputation in the United States unlikely. In retrospect, the decision not to issue a statement—and hence to officially recognize *Holocaust* as an image problem—had proven right, Staden argued.[122] The embassy further informed the Foreign Office that "Jewish circles" as well as Israeli Prime Minister Menachem Begin (Likud), who had recently visited the United States, "very consciously and determinedly pointed out the connections between the 'holocaust'-movie and the current threats to the Jewish state," albeit with mixed results. The "German side" should, however, not intervene in public, but illustrate through "low-key cooperation" its "wish for a fair and balanced representation," especially in the context of education.[123]

In the aftermath of *Holocaust*, the embassy assumed that its successful screening in the United States would lead to an increased demand in high school courses on the Holocaust and thereafter decided to take proactive measures in this regard. The embassy planned to distribute three feature films to high schools and colleges, which they considered would be more effective than "dull brochures" or "unemotional documentaries."[124] These films, *Die Brücke* ("The Bridge," 1959), *Des Teufels General* ("The Devil's General," 1955), and *Der 20. Juli* ("The Plot to Assassinate Hitler," 1955), were intended to show American students that "different"—that is non-Nazi—Germans had lived and suffered during World War II. Due to their content and production, the embassy considered these films "perfectly suited to convey a strikingly credible image of the situation Germans faced during those dark years."[125] It is remarkable that the films chosen were made in the 1950s, a time when the discussion of the Nazi past in West Germany mostly focused on the status of Germans as victims of National Socialism.[126] Indeed, these films portray the suffering of "ordinary" Germans, the diabolic nature of the Nazi regime, and the fate of the heroes of anti-Nazi resistance. They were "perfectly suited" to perpetuate the image of a state that was ruled by a small clique of criminals, but in which the vast majority of Germans had either been victims of Nazi rule themselves or had risked their lives to resist oppression.[127]

With the benefit of further hindsight, in January 1979 Staden pondered the reasons why the miniseries had not been the public relations catastrophe German diplomats had expected. According to his assessment, this had mostly been due to the "dulling" of American TV consumers with the interruption of the dramatic show by commercials, the weaknesses of the script, the excessive promotion of Israel, and the fair treatment of the issue of German collective guilt.[128] Staden did not provide more details on how he arrived at this conclusion, but he probably had in mind that one of the miniseries' moral heroes, Inga Helms-Weiss (played by Meryl Streep), was an average Christian German woman. To what extent American Jews would use *Holocaust* as a justification to raise public awareness of this "part of Jewish history" remained open to speculation, the ambassador added. However, even as discussion of the NBC miniseries abated, the German diplomatic establishment in the United States assumed that the public's preoccupation with the Holocaust itself would endure.[129] Not only had the broadcast significantly increased Holocaust consciousness in the United States, but it had also forcefully brought to German diplomats' attention two further areas of interaction: the Federal Republic's relations with American Jewish organizations and the impact of the Federal Republic's internal confrontation with the Nazi past on its reputation abroad. Having navigated the fallout from the miniseries in the United States, West Germans' reactions to the miniseries, scheduled to be broadcast in West Germany in January 1979, and the repercussions of their reception to the program would now come under scrutiny. The Foreign Office was well aware that foreign countries would closely watch how the citizens of the Federal Republic reacted to the screening of the miniseries.[130]

In the end, diplomats' concerns in this respect also turned out to be unfounded. In fact, the broadcast of *Holocaust* in the Federal Republic was a media event with an unprecedented impact on German historical consciousness, spreading knowledge and awareness of the crimes committed by the Nazi regime.[131] About 20 million West Germans saw at least parts of the program, which left them "in shock" and accelerated a process that repositioned the Holocaust from the periphery to the core of German memorial culture.[132] It also popularized the term "Holocaust" in Germany to describe the destruction of European Jews.[133] Even though there had been a number of programs addressing the Nazi past on West German television prior to *Holocaust*, the dramatic presentation of the story, as well as the debate that surrounded the broadcast, marked a sea change for West German discourse on the Nazi past.[134] The debate about the miniseries had begun prior to its German premiere in January 1979, and the German media and politicians had followed the broadcasting of the series in the United States closely.[135] In 1978, the popular left-leaning weekly, *Der Spiegel*, for example, opposed the screening of a miniseries about "gas chambers à la Hollywood" in Germany.[136] While prominent Social Democrats, such as Chancellor Helmut Schmidt and his predecessor Willy Brandt, supported the airing of the miniseries, conservatives, such as Bavarian Minister-President Franz Josef Strauß, vehemently opposed it.[137] Strauß directly attacked what he saw as the commercial motives behind the series by calling it a "fast-buck operation" (*Geschäftemacherei*), an assessment with clearly anti-American (and perhaps anti-Semitic) undertones.[138] In contrast, Germany's foreign policy elite at home recognized the opportunity to stress abroad the considerable impact of *Holocaust* on the West Germans. For example, the state minister (Staatsminister) in the Foreign Office, Hildegard Hamm-Brücher (FDP), concluded: "The shock with which German TV viewers reacted to *Holocaust* demonstrated abroad our willingness to learn from history far more convincingly than official measures and statements could have ever done."[139]

From the perspective of German diplomats in the United States, however, an impending legislative debate on the abolition of the statute of limitations for Nazi crimes had the potential to complicate this situation. As it had in 1965 and 1969, the year 1979 saw yet another debate in the Bundestag on the abolition of the statute.[140] At stake was the question of whether the Federal Republic would cease to prosecute Nazi criminals for murder, the statute of limitations for which ended after 1979. The Bundestag had extended the statute twice and would abolish it altogether in July 1979, but this was not clear at the beginning of that year.[141] To German diplomats in the United States, this controversial legal and moral question intensified fears that American observers, who followed the debate closely, would see the Federal Republic only in terms of its confrontation with the Nazi past. Already in early 1979, the embassy pointed out, "The whole Holocaust-discussion has so far not been directed against us. However, the danger exists that the discussion will move into that direction if it becomes connected to the discussion about the statute of limitations."[142] Ambassador von Staden also warned of the risk that this debate could prolong the discussion about *Holocaust* and lend it an anti-German note.[143] While the complex legal and moral implications of this debate meant that few average Americans would pay attention, with the power to influence the attitudes of American politicians in charge of foreign policy, the media could recognize an opportunity to sway public sentiment. German diplomats assumed that it was impossible to influence American citizens directly. That they would react negatively if the statute were not abolished could hardly be avoided, but any outrage was not expected to last for a long time.[144] This was entirely different from published opinion, which could very well cause an enduring change in American attitudes toward Germany. In this context, Staden specifically warned the Foreign Office of "those Jewish circles with particular influence in the realm of the media," who would ensure that any German decision to cease prosecuting Nazi war criminals would be met with a torrent of negative, daily newspaper headlines. He continued to explain that this posed a serious long-term threat to West Germany's reputation in the United States, as the media were likely to remind their audiences "at every possible opportunity" that the Federal Republic had stopped prosecuting Nazi criminals. The Federal Republic should consider very carefully whether it wanted to give such a "cue" for negative press coverage. He added, however, that by no means could the abolition of the statute result in positive press coverage for the Federal Republic.

The heightened public sensibilities about Nazi crimes after the airing of *Holocaust*, which had led to wide popular support of the abolition but also concerns about the Federal Republic's reputation abroad, shaped the Bundestag debate, and the parliament abolished the statute of limitations on July 3, 1979.[145] The debates over *Holocaust* and the statute, however, also accelerated a change in strategy among German diplomats in the United States. They concluded a recalibration of their relationship with American Jewish organizations was needed, as they had clearly identified them as opponents in the shaping of the Federal Republic's image in the United States.

Relations with American Jewish Organizations

The idea of reaching out specifically to American Jewish elites was not triggered by the impending broadcast of *Holocaust* in the United States, though it did lend impetus to a difficult conversation between Germans and Jews.[146] To New York Consul General Ungerer it was beyond doubt that the Federal Republic's image in the United States—and public opinion more generally—and the role of Jews in American society were inseparably intertwined. Already in November 1977, he had stated that "among the Jewish share of the American population and hence among many intellectuals and 'public opinion makers' [there] still exists a deep-rooted resentment against the Germans," which could, given the right occasion, turn directly against "us."[147] In fact, pointing to an alleged influence of American Jews on the media—without making an effort to greatly differentiate between various organizations or individuals—had been a fairly common practice for German diplomats. They considered them, as historian Shlomo Shafir later remarked, "a major stumbling block for a more assertive role of the Federal Republic in the world."[148] The German Foreign Office, for instance, had criticized in a similar context "the exceptionally large impact of the Jewish element in the formation of public opinion" in the United States.[149] Ungerer's assessment resulted from a meeting with eight Jewish community leaders who were concerned about "neo-Nazi tendencies" in the Federal Republic, to which Ungerer suggested that a visit to Germany might be useful to assess the situation there. The group included representatives of the American Jewish Committee (AJC), B'nai B'rith, and the Union of American Hebrew Congregations. Ungerer had proposed to invite them to Germany so that they could gain first-hand impressions of "democratic institutions and convictions" as well as of Germany's accomplishments with regard to compensating victims of National Socialism and successfully prosecuting Nazi war criminals.

At the time, the relationship between the Federal Republic and American Jewish organizations was fragile and complicated, and few official contacts existed.[150] More generally, West German–American Jewish relations suffered from preconceived notions and stereotypes. American Jews, if such a generalization is even possible, perceived the Federal Republic above all as the successor state of the Third Reich, while West German officials saw as a political problem for the Federal Republic the "obsession" of American Jews with the Holocaust, combined with an alleged refusal to acknowledge the significant democratic transformation Germany had experienced since 1945.[151] Not surprisingly, the legacies of the Holocaust had shaped the relationship between the German government and the American Jewish community since the founding of the Federal Republic.[152] For many American Jews, Germany continued to represent a "slaughterhouse" where millions of Jews had been murdered during the Third Reich, despite the integration of the Federal Republic into the Western alliance.[153]

Yet the changes in American Holocaust consciousness at the end of the decade propelled a fundamental and permanent transformation of West German–American Jewish relations. While the Foreign Office had initially rejected Ungerer's proposal to invite American Jewish leaders to the Federal Republic due to a lack of funds, the urgency of the "Holocaust discussion" led to a change of mind and the endorsement of Ungerer's suggestion.[154] German officials thus invited prominent representatives of American Jewish organizations to Germany and helped them to organize their trips if they came to the Federal Republic on their own initiative. Three delegations visited the Federal Republic subsequent to the broadcast of *Holocaust*: a group of five prominent representatives of the New York Jewish community, a delegation from the Simon Wiesenthal Center, and a delegation from the AJC.[155] While German diplomats in America and the Foreign Office in Bonn coordinated these trips, they sought to avoid giving the impression that they had been organized by German government authorities for public relations purposes.[156] In Germany these groups met with politicians, but also talked to students about Holocaust education in Germany and visited concentration camp memorial sites. All of these visits were considered very successful by German officials, as they served to demonstrate the existence of a progressive and democratic Germany to its visitors, showed that West Germany was openly confronting the Nazi past, and improved ties between the Federal Republic and these organizations.[157]

In early 1979, for the first time, several Holocaust survivors holding offices in American Jewish organizations met with Staden to campaign for the abolition of the statute of limitations.[158] The composition of this delegation, which included Soviet-born Abraham H. Foxman of the ADL, underscored the increasing prominence of Holocaust survivors within these organizations. Around the same time, the AJC also began to reengage its focus on the Federal Republic, a move catalyzed by German efforts to establish a dialogue, in reaction to the statute of limitations debate, and the impact of *Holocaust*. Founded in 1906 by German Jews in the United States for the purpose of protecting the rights of Jews at home and abroad, the AJC was one of the largest American Jewish organizations.[159] In an effort to improve relations, representatives of the AJC approached German officials directly to express their concerns about West Germany's reputation in the United States. The AJC reaffirmed its determination to "finally . . . normalize" relations between American Jews and the Federal Republic and wanted, as they told Staden, to act as the "pacemaker" (*Schrittmacher*) in this process.[160] To conduct these policies successfully, the AJC sought contacts at the highest West German political levels. It aimed to stabilize relations with the Federal Republic, which it came to recognize as a crucial NATO ally to the United States, an important partner of Israel, and as a central pillar of the European Community. In addition, the establishment of a network with future German elites could provide an opportunity to influence the country's means of coping with the Nazi past.[161]

In March and again in June 1979, Chancellor Schmidt, who had abstained from convening with the AJC in 1976, met with representatives of this organization.[162] At the first encounter, the debate over the statute of limitations topped the agenda, though Schmidt also discussed the Federal Republic's position toward the peace process in the Middle East, expressing his support for US policies in the region.[163] In relation to the statute, he assured the AJC that he supported the abolition, even though his public position was more reserved. He favored a calm debate on this issue in order to avoid a "polarization" of public opinion, which could hinder confrontation with the Nazi past more generally. Richard Mass, the AJC's president, applauded Schmidt for his standpoint and also informed him of a conversation he had had with Walther Leisler Kiep (CDU), then minister of finance in Lower Saxony, who would play an increasingly important role in West German–American Jewish relations under Kohl. According to Mass, Kiep had suggested reactivating an exchange program between the AJC and the Federal Republic, which the AJC had run in the early postwar years. The AJC signaled its interest in building ties and furthering reconciliation with the Federal Republic, and a participant of the trip to the Federal Republic earlier that month stated that he had been impressed with the "new Germany" and its efforts to confront the Nazi past. He did not fail to note, however, that representatives of the West German embassy and the consulates general in the United States seemed to be "deeply worried about the image of the Germans in America."[164]

As much as the ongoing debates about the legacies of the Holocaust influenced West German–American Jewish relations at the time, tensions between the Federal Republic and Israel, which had been the primary focus of West German reconciliation effort in the preceding decades, made improving ties with American Jewish organizations even more important from the German perspective. With the election of Begin as prime minister in 1977, relations between the two governments significantly deteriorated as a result of diverging views on the peace process and German plans to export arms to Saudi Arabia.[165] In fact, historians now consider the years Schmidt and Begin were in office the "most troubled period" of West German–Israeli relations.[166] Exemplified by Begin's assertions of German collective guilt for the Holocaust and his public criticism of Schmidt due to his past as a Wehrmacht officer, this crisis resulted in "a profound alienation between both countries, not only on the governmental, but even more on the societal level."[167] West German officials therefore also sought closer connections to American Jewish organizations as a way to balance tensions in the relationship with Israel.

It was, of course, no coincidence that Schmidt met to discuss these sensitive issues with representatives of the AJC and not another American Jewish organization. The AJC had already been in contact with various governmental agencies and private organizations in the Federal Republic in the 1950s, when it had launched several projects aimed at building ties with the fledgling West German state, such as an exchange program for teachers. However, these initiatives, designed to combat German anti-Semitism, failed due to a lack of governmental support on both sides of the Atlantic.[168] American Jewish organizations more generally had, at times, closely and critically watched the development of West German democracy and Germans' attitudes toward the Nazi past prior to the 1970s. Time and again they had called attention to what they perceived to be deficits in the Federal Republic's coping with the Nazi past. These included insufficient financial compensation for the victims of National Socialism, overly lenient custodial sentences for Nazi criminals, and the problem of anti-Semitism in the Federal Republic. Nonetheless, a period of nonengagement with the Federal Republic ensued as the generation in charge of these programs began to retire. American Jewish organizations also shifted their focus to Israel with the Six-Day War and the Yom Kippur War.[169]

Within the AJC, William (Bill) S. Trosten became the driving force in forging relations between this organization and the West German government. Born in Austerlitz, New York, in 1927, Trosten first encountered Germany as a young GI in 1945, where he met his German wife and developed an interest in the country. Eugene DuBow, a colleague at the AJC, later referred to him as a "textbook example of a Germanophile" who spoke the language fluently and had many influential friends in the Federal Republic.[170] Trosten joined the AJC in 1957 and served as its associate director from 1982 to 1990. In the late 1970s, he began to criticize American Holocaust memorial culture, which he feared would have negative consequences for the United States, American Jews, and German–American relations. A couple of years later, he became a key partner to the Kohl government in its engagement with American Holocaust memory. Trosten above all saw the Federal Republic as a crucial Cold War ally of the United States and Israel's most important partner in Europe. He contended that reinvigorated relations with the postwar West German state were in the interest not only of American Jews, but of the United States more generally as well as Israel. He assumed that there was a "dangerous ... lack of communication between the Amerian Jewish community and the current generation of Germans."[171] In 1980, Trosten stated, for example, in an autobiographical interview:

> The Germans have no understanding really of how American Jews view Israel. I mean, they know that—they read about the Jewish lobby obviously, but they really don't understand how we see ourselves. They don't understand the rationale, they don't understand the relationship. We don't understand theirs. I mean, we oversimplify, and they oversimplify. And I think that that's not a good situation, particularly when you have two such important areas, the United States and them.[172]

In a conversation with a diplomat at the German consulate general in New York, Wolf Calebow, Trosten suggested an intensification of West German–American Jewish dialogue, especially geared toward future generations.[173] As a matter of fact, Trosten shared some of the German observers' concerns about American Jews' preoccupation with the Holocaust and lamented that American Jews only traveled to Germany to visit Dachau or Bergen-Belsen.[174] In the very diverse spectrum of American Jewish organizations, then, the AJC represented something of an exception at the time, as it sought to establish permanent channels of communication with the Federal Republic, expressing concerns of negative attitudes toward the Federal Republic and the lack of dedication to the transatlantic alliance among many American Jews.[175] The Foreign Office considered such a dialogue highly desirable in 1979 and concluded:

> A conversation with representatives of this politically very important organization offers a great opportunity to have an impact on the opinions of a broad spectrum of American Jewry. Considering the status of Jewry in American society, this would probably also have a positive impact on German-American relations in general.[176]

To German diplomats, who may very well have been interested in furthering German–Jewish dialogue for the sake of reconciliation, the political benefits of such an exchange in the aftermath of *Holocaust* and in light of the debate on the statute of limitations was, of course, a top priority.[177] The fact that the AJC was reaching out to the Federal Republic respectively showed that "important groups of Jewish Americans" sought a stable relationship with the Federal Republic—"beyond all emotional preoccupations with these events."[178] This was by no means a token remark about the AJC, rather one in which it is clearly set apart from other American Jewish organizations and individuals who German diplomats judged to be potential liabilities. That the report specifically mentioned the "nonemotional" attitude of the AJC is remarkable, as the word "emotional" had been used to describe those voices and reactions to *Holo-caust* that the German diplomatic apparatus considered especially problematic.

In the late 1970s, the consulate general in New York and representatives of the AJC began to make plans for future cooperation. With Calebow of the consulate general, Trosten drafted a proposal for an exchange program between the Federal Republic and the American Jewish community.[179] The AJC officially handed the proposal to Helmut Schmidt during his second meeting with representatives of this organization in June 1979.[180] The proposal aimed to

> equip leading younger representatives of the American Jewish com-munity with objective knowledge about the Germany of today.... Simultaneously, Germans of the same younger age cohort ... are to be invited to the United States to familiarize themselves with the American Jewish community.[181]

The Chancellery welcomed this initiative, as German officials in charge of German–American relations at the time were acutely aware of a "genera-tion gap" developing between both societies.[182] However, the Chancellery was concerned about the funding for this program and doubted that it was le-gitimate for the federal government to establish an exchange program with a nongovernmental organization or association in a foreign country. In the government's view, this was a project more suited to a political foundation or a similar organization in Germany.[183] The Chancellery therefore passed the proposal on to the Foreign Office, which contacted the Federal Republic's four major political foundations, which were associated with (yet indepen-dent from) the major political parties: the Friedrich Ebert Foundation (SPD), the Konrad Adenauer Foundation (CDU), the Friedrich Naumann Foundation (FDP), and the Hanns Seidel Foundation (CSU). The Konrad Adenauer Foun-dation (Konrad Adenauer Stiftung, KAS) ultimately took up the offer. This foundation had opened an office in Washington in 1977 and considered the improvement of the Federal Republic's image in the United States to be one of its major tasks. "For the KAS," stated its former deputy general secretary Josef Thesing retrospectively, "the opportunity arose to win an important and influential partner in the American Jewish community."[184]

Based on this proposal, the AJC and the Konrad Adenauer Foundation devel-oped an exchange program for "future leaders of the Federal Republic and the American Jewish community," drawn from politics, universities, commerce, in-dustry, and the media.[185] Both sides had high expectations for the future role of this program in shaping West German–American Jewish relations. The spokes-man for the program's first German delegation, Wolfgang Pordzik of the KAS, was anything but modest about the anticipated impact of the initiative he had helped to create: "This program is a means to prevent it (the Holocaust) from happening again."[186]

Soon thereafter, Pordzik became director of the Konrad Adenauer Foundation's office in Washington and would be heavily involved in West German–American Jewish affairs well into the 1990s. He managed to establish a network with leaders of American Jewish organizations, above all the AJC, and worked toward intensifying West German–American Jewish relations, but also counted improving the image of the Federal Republic in the United States among his priorities. His legacy, however, is rather ambiguous. In the 1990s, some of his former partners, such as the AJC's executive director, David Harris, stated in retrospect that they were impressed with Pordzik's dedication to reconciliation, as well as his knowledge about American Jewish organizations. Others, however, maintained that Pordzik was only so heavily invested in West German–American Jewish relations for his own pride or solely for opportunistic reasons. Even William Trosten reportedly called him a "very difficult man." A senior official of a Jewish organization, who wanted to remain anonymous, stated vis-à-vis the *Washington Post* when asked about Pordzik in the 1990s, "people around Kohl believe American Jews have a lock on the American media and therefore on Germany's image in the United State." Pordzik himself conceded that such attitudes prevailed in the Federal Republic, but stated that he was working toward overcoming them.[187]

His reputation was permanently damaged when several former employees sued him in a Washington court in the mid-1990s for sexual harassment and anti-Semitic slurs. According to the suit, Pordzik had sexually harassed several female employees and also created a "hostile working environment" through his "repeated antisemitic remarks and actions," such as calling Jews "dirty" or insatiable and approving of Hitler's anti-Jewish policies. Pordzik vehemently rejected such accusations. "What is alleged is all lies," he retorted, "and we will prove that. From A to Z, from first word to last word, it is untrue and absurd. There is nothing that can hurt a German like an allegation of antisemitism, and that is why they have chosen to do this." A fierce controversy and legal battle ensued, during which representatives of several American Jewish organizations came forward in support of Pordzik. Even though Pordzik was acquitted of these charges, in 1996 he left the KAS to become a lobbyist for the German Postal Service.[188]

One and a half decades earlier, however, in the early 1980s, the cooperation between the KAS and the AJC marked the starting point of a top-level network that Chancellor Kohl and his staff later relied on to pursue policies connected to Holocaust memory in the United States. A few years later, another German nongovernmental organization, the elitist Atlantik-Brücke ("Atlantic Bridge"), joined this network.[189] Founded in the 1950s to cultivate German–American relations, the Atlantik-Brücke was officially a nonpartisan organization, but it had very close ties to the CDU. Its chairman from 1984 to 2000, Walther Leisler Kiep, held important positions in the CDU under Kohl, was the party's long-term treasurer, a foreign policy expert, and—last but not least—a key figure in several scandals stemming from illegal donations to the CDU and tax fraud from the 1970s to the early 2000s. He was Kohl's "guy for delicate missions," a Hanseatic man of the world with ample experience in senstitive negotiations and financial matters—and a notoriously bad memory.[190]

Although the exchange program resulted in the establishment of a transatlantic network of American Jews and West German conservatives, at its inception the deficits and problems in West German–American Jewish relations became strikingly obvious. Participants from both countries were generally—at least vis-à-vis the sponsors of the exchange—very pleased with the program.[191] Some prominent "multipliers," however, did not take away the intended lessons. The impressions of Deborah Lipstadt—who became a leading scholar of Jewish history in the United States—provide a case in point. After returning from Germany as part of an AJC-KAS exchange program delegation in 1982, she gave a public lecture at the University of California, Los Angeles, where she taught at the time. Lipstadt explained why she felt "pessimistic" about the question of whether the Federal Republic was "really different" from Nazi Germany and titled her presentation "Germany, 1982: Hiding from History?"[192] She denounced negative attitudes toward Turkish guest workers, public protests against Israel that equated Israeli policies with Nazi policies, and manifestations of anti-Semitism in Germany more generally. The main reason for her concern, however, was the Germans' supposed reluctance to openly confront the Nazi past: "When it comes to memory and history they live their lives in *einem Nebel*, a fog. . . . . The older generation has repressed its memory while the younger hides from history."[193]

This frank assessment points to the misconceptions that plagued West German–American Jewish relations during the 1980s. At a time when the conservative German philosopher Hermann Lübbe attested to a "cultural and political intrusiveness" of the memory of National Socialism in West Germany, which applied to memorial culture, the historical profession, and also the political left and a large number of civil society actors, speaking of a "fog" hardly seems justified.[194] Lipstadt's assessment met with clear disapproval within the AJC, and German participants also complained to the AJC about the "distorted image" "old and young Jewish Americans" had about the Federal Republic and Germany more generally.[195] Perhaps for that reason, Trosten contacted an American participant of the exchange program and encouraged him to write an article about his experiences in Germany, suggesting that it should conclude with an "upbeat statement on the importance of W. Germany to the U.S. and the unique place of Germany in the Jewish psyche."[196]

West German participants in the exchange faced other challenges in the United States. Many noted how difficult it was for them to speak about the Holocaust with American Jews, especially with Holocaust survivors and their children.[197] They expressed feelings of guilt and shame for the crimes of their parents' generation.[198] Yet they also brought their own prejudices and stereotypes to the United States. Trosten assumed that "the participants will have read a great deal about the so-called 'Jewish Lobby' and the inordinate political influence of the Jewish community in the United States," and the AJC therefore arranged seminars to specifically address this issue.[199] A Jewish member of a German delegation, historian Michael Wolffsohn, confirmed that such conversations would support the "de-demonization of the Jews and the United States."[200] He further suggested arranging encounters with American journalists in the future to "destroy the legend" of Jewish dominance over the American press (*"Verjudung" der US-Presse*).

The AJC-KAS exchange program illustrated that West German–American Jewish relations were heavily overshadowed by the memory of the Holocaust. Yet it provided a forum to address this issue. The long-term political consequence of the exchange program, however, should instead be seen in the network its organizers created, since many of them, as well as most of the German participants, were associated with the CDU or the Konrad Adenauer Foundation.[201] The ties between the AJC and the KAS—and later the Atlantik-Brücke—provided the crucial platform for discussions about the impact of American Holocaust memorial culture on German–American relations well into the 1990s. Once in power, Helmut Kohl and his staff relied on these contacts to conduct policies in this context.[202] Kohl and his staff also benefited from the advice and expertise of their American Jewish interlocutors, above all William Trosten. For representatives of the AJC, this network also proved beneficial: it granted them access to the highest German governmental authorities.[203] In the early 1980s, the foundations had been laid for a network that shaped, and to a considerable extent continues to shape, German–American Jewish relations.

Tensions in German–American Relations

In 1981, the new German ambassador to the United States, Peter Hermes, expressed his perplexity as to "why after 40 years the Jews in America have been playing up the memory of the Holocaust so dramatically for the past couple of years, what they are trying to achieve, because this doesn't make any sense to Germans in the United States."[204] While not all German diplomats in the United States exhibited such bewilderment, many of them—as well as German politicians at home—began to see the Federal Republic as the "victim" of the integration of Holocaust memory into American popular and political culture.[205] This marked the beginning of a transition from observing and analyzing American Holocaust memory to a more proactive agenda by German observers, fully implemented under Kohl.

German perceptions of the paradigm shift in American Holocaust memorial culture were therefore closely tied to the larger framework of German–American relations around the turn of the decade. After he took on his post as ambassador in Washington in late 1979, Hermes was confronted with a host of challenges for German–American relations. In the eyes of the Foreign Office's experts, a "fundamental wave of nationalism" had seized the United States under Ronald Reagan.[206] This led to a new phase of confrontation with the Soviet Union, which had recently invaded Afghanistan, but also created suspicion about any form of West German foreign policy that was not coordinated with the United States, especially efforts to decrease tensions between the blocs.[207] Of course, as the Cold War divided Germany in two, the Federal Republic was particularly interested in détente. The highly controversial NATO Double-Track Decision of 1979 had reminded Germans of the confrontation between the opposing blocs, particularly since the vast majority of new American nuclear weapons would be stationed in the Federal Republic.[208] A new level of Cold War tension thus coincided with the new stage in West German–American Jewish relations.

In contrast to his somewhat subtle and reserved predecessor, Staden, Peter Hermes was a rather outspoken critic of American Holocaust memorial culture. Born in 1922 in Berlin as the son of a high-ranking Weimar Republic politician, who was later imprisoned during the Third Reich as a result of his ties to the resistance against Hitler, Hermes had a reputation as a "staunch conservative" and a devout Catholic.[209] He fought in World War II and was a prisoner of war in the Soviet Union until 1950. Only a few weeks after his return to the Federal Republic, he joined the CDU and subsequently enjoyed a remarkable career as a diplomat and expert on economic issues. After completing law school in 1955, he joined the Foreign Service and was based, among other locations, in San Francisco (1956–1958), the Vatican (1958–1961, and again as ambassador 1984–1987), the OECD in Paris (1961–1965), and the Foreign Office in Bonn (1965–1979), being appointed state secretary (Staatssekretär) in 1975. Between the early 1950s and his retirement in 1987, he was deeply committed to the "rehabilitation of the good German name around the world."[210] In his memoirs, Hermes writes about his encounters with American Jewish organizations, including the "powerful Israel lobby" in passing, but emphasizes his dedication to reconciliation.[211] Nevertheless, he opposed the plans for the USHMM, which he saw as a threat to West Germany's reputation abroad, and criticized the museum for neglecting to consider German resistance against Hitler and

West German compensation efforts. He furthermore vehemently rejected the notion of German collective guilt, as well as the tendency to consider the "Holocaust as the quintessence of the German."[212]

The Foreign Office attributed the critical attitude of Americans toward the Federal Republic above all to political tensions between both countries.[213] These included the quarrel between Jimmy Carter and Helmut Schmidt; a skeptical attitude in the United States toward independent German economic policies; the broad public backing for the German peace movement that showed clearly anti-American tendencies; and concerns about German neutralism, which had existed since the days of *Ostpolitik*.[214] Yet beyond tension around isolated events, foreign policy experts in both countries attested to a more serious long-term challenge to German–American as well as Western European–American relations. According to this assessment, since the late 1970s it was above all the so-called successor generation—future leaders in Germany and the United States now in their twenties and thirties—who called the transatlantic alliance into question.[215] Not having experienced the high point in German–American friendship after World War II and how American support for the new West German republic enabled its growth, the successor generation in both countries showed a lack of commitment to the alliance. West German foreign policy experts identified a knowledge deficit as a key challenge. Young Americans knew too little about the Federal Republic, its culture, and its history. For their part, young Germans focused on racism and inequality in the United States, forgetting that the development of a free and democratic society in their own country had only been possible due to American support.[216] Remedies to address this deficit, analysts on both sides of the Atlantic agreed, had to be educational.[217]

In this context, questions of image, reputation, and prestige also played a crucial role, especially in the eyes of German observers. At the beginning of the 1980s, German officials assessed the developments of recent years as clearly negative. For instance, Konrad Seitz, director of the Foreign Office's policy planning division, attested in February 1982 that "broad segments of American society today have a *negative attitude towards the Federal Republic of Germany*," a new phenomenon for German–American relations since the end of World War II.[218] This was not an entirely correct assessment, but it nevertheless served as the basis for decision-making in the Foreign Office, which considered such a *"negative image* of the Germans," as well as anti-American tendencies in the Federal Republic, to be *"chains of our foreign policy"* (*Fesseln unserer Außenpolitik*).[219]

Chancellor Schmidt took these tensions seriously. Although he characterized relations with the Reagan administration as "excellent," he shared concerns about the danger that there could be a public opinion shift in Western Europe and the United States, one that was critical of the alliance.[220] Owing to its history and its geostrategic position, this development particularly affected the Federal Republic. This led to the creation of new positions in Germany and in the United States dedicated exclusively to improving relations between both countries. In the Federal Republic, Schmidt delegated this task to the state minister in the Foreign Office, Hildegard Hamm-Brücher, who had been working toward an invigoration of German–American relations, including nongovernmental actors, since the late 1970s.[221] As the first Coordinator for German-American Cooperation, she championed an expansion of exchange programs, political contacts, and encounters between future leaders of the successor generation, as well as a promotion of the Federal Republic in the American media, especially television.[222]

While such projects aimed at improving the relationship between future generations, the Foreign Office was also concerned about the role the German past played in this context. It clearly identified the American media as a particular cause for concern. Not only did the media reflect the negative image of the Federal Republic, but they were responsible for producing it in the first place.[223] The Foreign Office's policy planning division stated succinctly: "Our country and our people hardly stimulate American imagination, at least not in a positive way: the most interesting aspect about us is our Nazi past." [224] Some American observers shared such an assessment. The diplomat William R. Smyser, for example, saw the Nazi past as a great burden for the Federal Republic that rendered it "extremely vulnerable."[225] Even though young Germans vehemently denounced the crimes committed by the Nazi regime, many Americans were still "very conscious" of the Germans' Nazi past.[226] It was clear to German observers that a negative image of the Federal Republic in the United States would limit the country's room for political maneuver. Discussions about the successor generation connected the lack of dedication to the German–American alliance to a mutually deficient understanding of the societies and their histories. German diplomats and analysts could only conclude that the growing presence of the Nazi past in the United States would exacerbate the dearth of knowledge on the part of young Americans about the Federal Republic. If Americans would not learn more about the Germany of the present, one could ask, what would constitute the Federal Republic's future image in the United States, if not the German past?

By the early 1980s, West German officials had thus identified American Holocaust memorial culture as a distinct challenge for the Federal Republic. Holocaust-related educational and academic projects had directed their attention to the early stages of a process that reached a new level with the airing of *Holocaust*. The NBC miniseries forced German diplomats to weigh possible responses to a growing American interest in the history of the destruction of European Jews. The subsequent debate on the expiration of the statute of limitations served as an additional reminder that the Nazi past could provide a permanent challenge for the image of the Federal Republic in the United States. These instances put the issue of American Holocaust memorial culture on West Germany's diplomatic and political agenda and shaped the way West Germany would continue to deal with this phenomenon in the years to come. That German worries about the image of the Federal Republic in the United States overlapped with tensions in German–American relations more generally made their concerns all the more urgent. During these years, the foundations were laid in both countries that would define debates and discussions about the impact of Holocaust memory on these relations during the 1980s. But it took a chancellor who devoted great importance to the use of historical narratives for political purposes in order for Holocaust angst to result in tangible policies.

2

A Holocaust Syndrome?

Relations between the Federal Republic

and American Jewish Organizations in the 1980s

Under Chancellor Helmut Kohl, American Holocaust memory and West German–American Jewish relations became *Chefsache*, that is, "an issue for the boss." These interconnected issues emerged as significant factors for West German policies concerning the United States and—maybe even more importantly—for the Federal Republic's process of coping with the Nazi past on the government level.[1] At the beginning of the 1980s, two overlapping developments rendered American Holocaust memorial culture a pressing political problem in the eyes of German observers. First, an institutionalized infrastructure was created that granted the murder of European Jews at the hands of Nazi Germany a permanent presence in the American media, politics, educational system, and social discourse at large. Second, a crisis arose in German–American political relations, which contemporaries attributed to a declining lack of dedication of young Americans to the alliance with Germany and vice versa. The government of Helmut Kohl devoted significantly more attention to these issues and their concrete implications for the Federal Republic's reputation in the United States than the previous German government under Schmidt.[2]

In the Federal Republic, the Kohl government attempted to shape the discourse about the German past and to reposition West German society's attitudes toward its history.[3] Such policies aimed at putting an end to the exceptional position of the Federal Republic in an international context, the result of National Socialism and the Second World War.[4] At the end of the "long phase of *Vergangenheitsbewältigung*" (i.e., "coming to terms with the past") that had characterized the Federal Republic's discourse about the Nazi past during the 1960s and 1970s,[5] West Germany faced a fundamental challenge: a "longing for equality" as well as efforts to act as a self-confident, "normal" nation state in the international arena clashed with fears about the limits the growing international presence of Holocaust remembrance imposed on the country's reputation abroad.[6]

Concerns about the Federal Republic's image in the United States manifested themselves particularly in the West German government's relations with American Jewish organizations. The often difficult and ambivalent interactions between German officials and American Jews usually took place through diplomatic channels and were thus hidden from public view. However, occasional controversies caused a readjustment of previously held attitudes or changes in policies. Over the course of the 1980s, however, the relationship between the Federal Republic and some American Jewish organizations fundamentally changed. While in the late 1970s hardly any official contacts existed and a certain degree of antagonism as well as stereotypes strained the relationship, the Kohl government managed to establish a stable and productive partnership with several American Jewish organizations, above all the AJC. This dialogue offered to those organizations an opportunity to contribute to the shaping of West German policies as well as its domestic engagement with the Nazi past. The worries about the negative impact of American Holocaust memorial culture on German–American relations, the driving force on the German side, thus resulted in an intensification of West German–American Jewish dialogue.[7] For the Kohl government, this dialogue was also characterized by the quest for a new chapter in German–Jewish relations not to be overshadowed—as the historian Michael Wolffsohn put it—by a "Holocaust syndrome."[8]

Helmut Kohl, the Nazi Past, and American Jewish Organizations

The election of a conservative chancellor in October 1982 by a constructive vote of no confidence after more than a decade of Social Democratic rule marked a turning point not only for the history of postwar Germany, but also for West German–American Jewish relations. The new government of the long-term opposition leader in the Bundestag, Helmut Kohl, attributed great significance to the influence of Holocaust memorial culture on the image of the Federal Republic in the United States as well as an alleged influence of American Jews on the formation of public opinion in the United States more generally.[9] In their interactions with Jewish individuals and organizations, Kohl and his staff struggled with the impact of the Nazi past on this dialogue, especially in the conversation with survivors of the Holocaust in the United States and when the security of Israel was concerned.

In its critique of the growing presence of Holocaust remembrance in the United States, the Kohl government worked to increase mutual trust between Germany and the United States, as well as to "reinvent the memory of Nazism and lay to rest the burden of collective symbolic guilt," as historian Wulf Kansteiner has observed.[10] Both policy goals aimed at strengthening the German–American alliance and constituted crucial pillars of Kohl's foreign and domestic policy agenda. To Kohl, this partnership was of "existential" importance for West Germany's security and prosperity.[11] He generally had a very positive attitude toward the United States, though he lacked detailed knowledge about American society and did not speak English.[12] At a time when the Cold War confrontation between the blocks intensified, especially over the stationing of American nuclear missiles in the Federal Republic, the Kohl government not only wanted to confirm that the United States was firmly on the Federal Republic's side, but also to demonstrate its own commitment to NATO and the West.[13]

Kohl, who held a doctorate in history from the University of Heidelberg and frequently emphasized that he was the first chancellor who had not experienced the Third Reich as an adult, also prioritized the Federal Republic's engagement with its past.[14] He later maintained in his memoirs: "To recognize contemporary history [Zeitgeschichte] as a responsibility of the federal government and to take it seriously as such was of exceptional importance to me."[15] In fact, since the late 1970s the Federal Republic had experienced an almost proverbial "return of history."[16] This trend manifested itself in several sensationally successful historical exhibitions, for example on the history of Prussia in 1981, and rapidly growing interest in and research on the history of National Socialism. Asking "difficult questions" about the continuities of German history throughout the twentieth century became, as historian Ulrich Herbert has suggested, "the starting point for critical self-reflection on the part of West German society with respect to its prehistory."[17] This was in large part due to generational change as well as an increasing interest in the fate of "forgotten" victims of National Socialism and the everyday history of the Third Reich on the local level.[18] Taking advantage of this trend but opposing a fixation on the history of National Socialism, Kohl aimed to reinforce a particularly West German historical consciousness.[19] This placed the Federal Republic in the long-term continuities of German history, seeking to combine the legacies of the past with the positive aspects of German history and pride regarding the achievements of the Federal Republic, without losing sight of the ultimate—yet for the time being, unreachable—goal of German unification.

These politics cannot fully be understood without examining Kohl's Catholicism.[20] His Christian faith was a central component of his worldview, even though he supported a separation between the Christian churches and the routines of daily politics. Nevertheless, he was convinced that certain political convictions were diametrically opposed to the goals and aims of the Christian Democratic Union. Above all, "the skepticism of the Christian view of man erected in Kohl's mind a massive bulwark against totalitarian ambitions," as an official biography stated in 1992.[21] According to Kohl, a deep and sincere sympathy toward Judaism and the state of Israel was part and parcel of his Christian faith. He counted "*Wiedergutmachung,*" reconciliation, and a close partnership between the Federal Republic and Israel among his political priorities, and he saw himself in this context in the tradition of Konrad Adenauer "and all the democrats that gave this reconciliation a chance."[22] Time and again, Kohl condemned the crimes committed by the Nazi regime and pointed to the obligations resulting from the Nazi past, as well as to the lessons the citizens of the Federal Republic had learned from this past.

However, the chancellor's public engagement with the Nazi past was characterized by a dialectical tension between a moral vilification of the regime, especially its leader, and a lack of historical analysis of its functioning.[23] For instance, on the fiftieth anniversary of the Nazi seizure of power on January 30, 1983, Kohl wholeheartedly—albeit in the passive voice—condemned the regime's terror, violence, and crimes: "In the name of Germany, the face of humanity was defiled. As a result of this bitter experience, we Germans now hold a high responsibility for justice and peace, at home and in the world."[24] At the same time, he characterized Hitler as the "creature of a sick world," maintained that the "annihilation of millions" in Poland would not have been possible without "Stalin's complicity," and stated that the eight million German members of the Nazi party had "paid a high price for having been susceptible to seduction and enthusiasm, for conforming or participating." Kohl continued: "Yet it is also part of the truth that it was, if nothing else, this generation as a whole that looked to the future, that participated in building our free constitutional state and filled it with life." Not only did such an interpretation draw a clear parallel between the Third Reich and the communist Soviet Union, the "other totalitarian regime," from which "Germany and Europe" now needed to be protected, it also seemed to sympathize with the generation of Germans whose crimes he so forcefully condemned.[25] This ambiguity would surface time and again throughout the 1980s. In what bore a striking resemblance to the prevailing discourse about the nature of Nazi Germany in the 1950s, Kohl held that only a coterie of hardcore Nazis had been responsible for the criminal regime that had "blinded" the German people,[26] while the vast majority of Germans—civilians and soldiers alike—should be considered victims of war and tyranny.[27] In the early days of the Federal Republic, anticommunism in tandem with the close political alliance with the United States had popularized an interpretation of the Third Reich that equated National Socialism and communism as totalitarian regimes. The confrontation with the Eastern Bloc had given legitimacy and purpose to the young, provisional West German state, but had also offered to its elites a way to avoid a critical confrontation with the Nazi past.[28] As such, Kohl's politics of history in the 1980s seemed to return to leveling the distinctions between the perpetrators and the victims of the Third Reich and World War II.[29]

In addition to his interpreting National Socialism as a totalitarian regime of a small group of criminals, a number of other facets characterized Kohl's engagement with the Nazi past. When speaking of crimes committed by the Nazi regime, Kohl frequently used the expression "in the name of Germany" (*in deutschem Namen*), thus avoiding clearly identifying the perpetrators. While not denying the relevance of the Nazi past for the Federal Republic, Kohl maintained that its citizens had learned the lessons from this past.[30] As such, Kohl claimed to be able to govern "less biased" (*unbefangener*) by the Nazi past than his predecessors.[31] Indeed, unlike any chancellor before him, Kohl actively initiated and supported projects, such as monuments and museums, that would recalibrate West Germans' attitudes toward their country and their history. Already in his first government addresses, he announced his government's dedication to this end.[32] Such plans included a Central Memorial of the Federal Republic in Bonn (Zentrale Gedenkstätte) and two museums dealing with German history, the House of the History of the Federal Republic of Germany in Bonn (Haus der Geschichte der Bundesrepublik) and the German Historical Museum in Berlin (Deutsches Historisches Museum, DHM). Both museums only opened after unification. During the 1980s, however, the question of how to present the Nazi period in the broader context of German history in these institutions was highly controversial. Kohl's critics, especially on the political left, accused him of blurring the lines between victims and perpetrators of the Nazi regime and of pursuing apologetic policies in this context.[33] The museum in Bonn was supposed to cover the postwar period of German history, downgrading the Third Reich, as Kohl's critics argued, to "prehistory."[34] In contrast, the DHM would narrate German history from the year 900 to the present, rendering National Socialism just one period along a long continuum. Social Democrats in the Bundestag, such as Freimut Duve, suspected that Kohl's politics of history exhibited "a pathetic jealousy of the alleged normality of other nations."[35] The Greens, somewhat connected to the history workshop (*Geschichtswerkstätten*) movement that strove toward a critical reexamination of everyday life under National Socialism at the local level, were even more outspoken in their criticism. The left-wing politician and lawyer Hans-Christian Ströbele, for example, chastised in the Bundestag Kohl's museum projects as part of a "pattern" that aimed at an "abuse" as well as the "sanitization of our German history."[36]

Opponents of these projects doubted that the federal government had the right to "prescribe" an interpretation of history, which they considered one-sided and purely politically motivated.[37] Additionally, left-leaning liberals, such as Hildegard Hamm-Brücher, warned that Kohl's involvement with the museums could create a "state-sanitized image of history."[38] Critics of the plans for a Central Memorial, completed only in 1993 in unified Berlin, also widely opposed this project for its ambivalent message.[39] Dedicated to the "victims of war and tyranny," the plans for the memorial seemed to imply a "community of victimhood" of German dead and those killed by Germans during the war.[40] Some historians have even argued that here one can detect a core goal of the Kohl government's politics of history, namely a "systematic de-concretization" of the representation of the Nazi past in official memorials and museums.[41] While the memorial would not sufficiently differentiate between perpetrators and victims, the House of History would neglect to highlight to continuities between the Third Reich and the Federal Republic.

Such an ambiguity not only led to controversies in the Federal Republic, but also overshadowed West German foreign policy. Here the goals to readjust the Federal Republic's relationship to the Nazi past as well as end its exceptional position in the international community overlapped. This became obvious, for example, during Kohl's first state visit to Israel in 1984.[42] On the one hand, Kohl embraced, in a speech directed at Prime Minister Shamir, Germany's "responsibility" and expressed the pain he felt due to "the suffering brought upon the Jewish people by German doing [*von deutscher Hand*]."[43] On the other hand, Kohl claimed for himself the "grace of late birth" (*Gnade der späten Geburt*) in a speech in the Israeli parliament, the Knesset, but also included a former-Nazi-turned-right-wing-publisher, Kurt Ziesel, in his delegation.[44] In a similar vein as his aforementioned speech on January 30, 1983, an expression of moral remorse, solidarity with Israel, and empathy with the victims of National Socialism created ample room for misinterpretation and seemed to have apologetic tendencies. In the Federal Republic, the liberal and left-leaning media chastised Kohl's statement as an "attempt to absolve the postwar generation of its responsibility for the war and the murder of millions."[45] While leading Social Democrats, such as Horst Ehmke, deemed Kohl's insistence that he was unaffected by history (*Sich-geschichtlich-unbetroffen-Geben*) undignified and banal,[46] the Greens argued in the Bundestag that his government's way of coping with the Nazi past was "frivolous, macabre, and dangerous."[47] Jürgen Reents, a member of the Green Party's parliamentary group in the Bundestag, continued:

> This is the brief message that the chancellor has been trying to communicate time and again: the Federal Republic of today, with its chancellor barely 54 years of age, has nothing to do with the German past.[48]

Even though Kohl vehemently dismissed such a reading, it contributed to a growing opposition to his politics of history among his political opponents in the Federal Republic, negative press coverage, and a very critical reception in Israel.[49]

The majority of historians today agree that there was no master plan for the Kohl government's politics of history that aimed at drawing a line (*Schlußstrich*) under the Nazi past.[50] Kohl also did not embrace or support revisionist or obviously apologetic tendencies in his party, which, for example, saw a clear parallel between the Wehrmacht's "heroic struggle" against communism on the Eastern front and NATO's confrontation with the Soviet Union during the ongoing Cold War.[51] Nevertheless, the significance the chancellor devoted to history, his opposition to the "guilt complex" of the political left, and above all a number of ambivalent and contradictory statements do lead to the conclusion that Kohl aimed to change the discourse about the German past in the Federal Republic in a significant way, rendering a positive identification with this past possible.[52] Rather than follow a blueprint for a *geistig-moralische Wende* ("intellectual and moral change"), however, Kohl pursued such policies opportunistically, sometimes according to trial and error, but also with a great deal of stubbornness.[53] Expediency and responding to what he assumed the majority of Germans wanted also played a role. As *Der Spiegel* later remarked: "Kohl feels that the [German] people are longing for a *Schlußstrich*."[54] In fact, Kohl assumed that a majority of West Germans backed his politics of history.[55]

Proponents of an intensification of German–American relations as well as a "balanced" interpretation of German history were likely to take issue with the growing presence of the Holocaust in American life. After all, the United States was the most important partner of the Federal Republic in the Western alliance, and American initiatives commemorating the Holocaust clearly distinguished between (German) perpetrators and their (non-German) victims. Dealing with Jewish organizations in this context, however, necessitated a careful balancing act: while the Kohl government criticized the development of an American Holocaust memorial culture, it also considered American Jewish organizations and individuals key to the shaping of public opinion. As the political scientist Clay Clemens has remarked, Kohl saw them as part of influential "'anti-German' circles," which viewed "his country solely in terms of its Nazi past."[56] For example, Kohl considered Nancy Reagan's allegedly critical attitude toward the Federal Republic a result of her "private-personal contacts to important Jewish circles."[57] When Kohl visited Harvard University in mid-1990, he was very surprised by the enthusiastic support for German unification at the university, despite the fact that "roughly 30 percent of its graduates were of Jewish creed [*Überzeugung*] or origin."[58] Although Kohl maintained that he was "completely incapable of being anti-Semitic," such characterizations included at least latently anti-Semitic stereotypes about the influence and collective "creeds" of American Jews.[59]

Accordingly, the Kohl government had to engage with these circles in order to correct, as it were, their understanding of the Federal Republic. From the chancellor's perspective, the Nazi past was supposed to play only a marginal role in this dialogue with American Jewish organizations. Soon after his election, Kohl met with representatives of several major Jewish organizations, such as the ADL and the World Jewish Congress (WJC). On this occasion he proclaimed his government's attitude toward the Nazi past. Referring to himself as the political grandson of Konrad Adenauer, he readily accepted the legacy of Germany's first chancellor, which included friendship and partnership with Israel. Yet he also insisted that he was "the first German chancellor from the post-war generation and that he can speak and act free of any pre-war tradition."[60] Furthermore, he stressed that there had been no Nazis among his relatives and ancestors, a statement bound to be interpreted as a signal to close the books on the Nazi past.[61] According to Kohl, support for Israel was the most important lesson to be taken from the German past, yet making the Holocaust and the history of Nazi Germany a subject of prolonged discussion was not desirable as the Federal Republic had successfully completed the process of confronting this past. Kohl's Jewish interlocutors, such as Kenneth J. Bialkin and Abraham H. Foxman of the ADL, welcomed his firm commitment to Israel's security and were on the whole quite impressed by him. They expressed their hopes that Kohl would strengthen German-Israeli relations and visit the country as soon as possible.[62]

Yet relations between the Kohl government and American Jewish organizations were fragile. A conflict over possible German arms sales—including Leopard 2 tanks—to Saudi Arabia in 1984, for example, brought the Nazi past forcefully back on the agenda.[63] The question of whether the Federal Republic could conduct foreign policy irrespective of the implications of the Nazi past led to conflict with Holocaust survivors. Could the Federal Republic—as the United States, France, or the United Kingdom had for decades—provide an Arab state with weapons?[64] The government of Helmut Schmidt had already considered this arms deal, which had led to significant tensions with Israel.[65] In this context, Schmidt had also expressed his hopes that in a few decades German foreign policy should no longer be "overshadowed by Auschwitz."[66]

Kohl discussed the issue again during a state visit to the Middle East in 1983. However, he explicitly ruled out the sale of offensive weapons, especially Leopard 2 tanks, which Saudi Arabia hoped to purchase. In response to protests by the ADL against these plans, Kohl's foreign policy and security advisor Horst Teltschik wrote a long letter to Bialkin and Foxman. According to Teltschik, the federal government was motivated by economics, but also saw providing Saudi Arabia with defensive weapons as a way to increase stability in the region; with these weapons, Saudi Arabia could defend itself but could not pass them on to other states in the region for technological and logistical reasons or deploy them against Israel.[67]

Several American Jewish organizations vehemently objected to such considerations.[68] The American Gathering of Jewish Holocaust Survivors, for example, placed an advertisement in the *New York Times* on January 20, 1984, asking: "How many Jews will German weapons kill this time?"[69] This advertisement by the largest organization of Holocaust survivors in North America beseeched Kohl and the German minister of defense, Manfred Wörner, not to sell weapons to Saudi Arabia. The date of its publication—the forty-second anniversary of the notorious Wannsee Conference—was no coincidence. The American Gathering of Jewish Holocaust Survivors wanted to draw a clear parallel between West German arms deals with enemies of Israel and the Holocaust. Hence, the organization maintained in its advertisement, "Today, the new, democratic Germany is in danger of following the old Germany's footsteps." Adding to this viewpoint, the prominent author and Holocaust survivor Elie Wiesel referred to the Federal Republic as a "merchant of death" and the Germans as "people without memories."[70]

In the eyes of German officials, these were exactly the kind of appeals that would damage the Federal Republic's reputation in the United States, undermining trust in the motives and policies of the West German state. Despite the obvious distortions at play, the Chancellery could not ignore such accusations. They unambiguously called the transformation of the country from a murderous dictatorship into a respected Western democratic state into question. In light of Kohl's state visit to the United States scheduled for March 1984, German authorities felt compelled to act. In the United States (and also in Canada), organizations of Holocaust survivors threatened to stage "massive emotional demonstrations" against the chancellor to express their opposition to the arms deal.[71] Benjamin Meed, a Holocaust survivor and the president of the American Gathering of Jewish Holocaust Survivors, increased the pressure on the Kohl government by suggesting further media campaigns and demonstrations. He wrote to Kohl:

> dear mr. chancellor: we are under constant pressure from members of our organization—residing in every state in the union and in all the provinces of canada—who wish to actively protest the decision to sell arms to saudi arabia. the almost two hundred thousand survivors in the united states and canada are outraged and they have urged us to meet with you during your forthcoming visit to the united states. we believe that it is better that we speak directly with one another than at one another through the media or demonstrations. . . . in the past, survivors had painfully accepted the outstretched hand of friendship from the german people—itself reborn from the ashes of destruction. we ask the question: "is germany withdrawing its hand for friendship?"[72]

To be sure, public protests and newspaper advertisements were part of the political toolbox of any nongovernmental organization lacking formal political power. But Meed also pointed to what was at stake in the eyes of Holocaust survivors: the establishment of a working relationship between the Federal Republic and the North American Jewish communities after the Holocaust. To him, this was surely more than a power game. Rather, organizations like the American Gathering of Jewish Holocaust Survivors feared that the Kohl government was attempting to bring the Federal Republic into an era in which it would no longer see itself committed to the legacies of the Holocaust.[73]

During the run-up to the state visit, Germany's ambassador Peter Hermes, a critic of America's Holocaust memorial culture, took an ambivalent position toward survivors.[74] In an effort to ease the concerns of the survivor organizations' representatives, he strongly identified with what the first West German president, Theodor Heuss, had called "collective shame" for the crimes of the Nazi regime.[75] Hermes, born in 1922, also expressed his regret that a "normal" conversation between Holocaust survivors and Germans of his generation would never be possible due to the emotional barriers involved.[76] In a confidential memorandum to the Foreign Office and the Chancellery, however, he pleaded to take the protests seriously for different reasons. Urging the chancellor to meet with representatives of the Holocaust survivors, Hermes emphasized the potential damage that could result from entering into an open confrontation with this organization. According to the ambassador, the American Gathering of Jewish Holocaust Survivors

> possessed the greatest political potential to exert influence on American public opinion and to call for spontaneous actions, protests, and demonstrations.... I do not doubt at all that a failure to arrange a conversation with the chancellor will have disadvantageous consequences not only for German–Jewish, but also for German–American relations.[77]

From the German point of view, the fears of American Jews about the consequences of the arms deal with Saudi Arabia were irrational and illegitimate. German officials did not acknowledge that their opposition was, in the case of the Gathering of Jewish Holocaust Survivors, a concrete result of the persecution they had suffered from during the Third Reich. Yet they were taken seriously, as German diplomats feared their influence on the formation of public opinion and wanted to avert damage to German–American relations.

After Kohl had concluded talks with Reagan in Washington, he therefore met with representatives of the AJC, B'nai B'rith, the WJC, the Claims Conference, and representatives of Holocaust survivors.[78] The chancellor tried to ease their concerns about Israel's security in connection with the Saudi Arabian arms deal. Although his staff warned Kohl that "Jewish interlocutors may react purely emotionally and will not be receptive to rational reasoning,"

Figure 2.1 Helmut Kohl (b. 1930) and Ronald Reagan (1911–2004) at the White House, 1984. Ronald Reagan Library.

the chancellor's template for the meeting was based on solidly rational arguments.[79] Time and again, German officials pointed out that American Jews, especially Holocaust survivors, acted "emotionally" when it came to the Holocaust. They seemed to assume that the experience of victimhood had erased all sense of reason and logic, but they also probably concluded that such reactions would impose certain limitations on their interactions with Jewish interlocutors, as it would be difficult to confront emotions with the rational tools of diplomacy.

According to Kohl's template, the "Jewish claim"—an expression implying that these interlocutors spoke for all Jews—that the arms deal with Saudi Arabia bore the risk of a "Second Holocaust," as well as the survivors' opposition based on "moral" grounds, were illegitimate.[80] Saudi Arabia could neither employ the weapons for an attack on Israel, nor could they be passed on to other states for logistical reasons. In preparation for this meeting, however, Kohl's staff also pondered a different line of argumentation. Aware of the politically highly controversial implications, Kohl's staff had labeled it "Mit Vorsicht!," that is, "with caution!" The Chancellery considered warning American Jews against giving the West German population the impression that "the United States was being used as a cudgel [*Knüppel*] against us [the Federal Republic] by Israel" as this would endanger the "preferential treatment" West Germany granted Israel. In his state of the nation address about his controversial state visit to Israel on February 9, 1984, Kohl had already pleaded to keep third-party countries out of issues concerning German-Israeli relations.[81] Now, however, his staff contemplated telling American Jewish organizations that their support for Israel might end up hurting Israel. Such considerations underscore the conviction of German officials not only that American Jews were instrumentalizing the Holocaust for political gain, but also that they were receiving instructions from Israel and even had the power to shape US foreign policy toward the Federal Republic.[82] Kohl was probably aware that this was a highly problematic line of argument and did not make such a statement on the record in Washington. Representatives of American Jewish organizations had mixed feelings about their encounter with him. They considered it a success that Kohl had categorically excluded the possibility that Germany would sell Leopard 2 tanks to Saudi Arabia, but they regretted that he had not agreed to cancel the arms deal completely.[83]

Just a few weeks later, Ambassador Hermes sent another alarming message to Bonn. He emphasized that the Federal Republic had to prepare itself that in the context of the security of Israel, memorial days, and museums, the "Jewish efforts to keep the memory of the Holocaust as a warning alive" would not subside:

> All in all, the American public, not to mention the government and the Congress, have a sympathetic and positive attitude towards present day [West] Germany. One must not ignore, however, that the horrible Holocaust-issue [*schreckliche Holocaust-Thematik*] will—if only because of the Holocaust museums—be connected with the Germans for generations and will time and again nourish anti-German sentiment. People are quick to associate disagreeable behavior with the past.[84]

In light of this development, the federal government increasingly paid attention to the partnership the Konrad Adenauer Foundation had been building with the AJC. The AJC indeed did consider analogies between the Third Reich and the Federal Republic counterproductive and expressed its disapproval of the polemics of Elie Wiesel, a fierce critic of the arms deal with Saudi Arabia.[85]

Toward the end of the year, the new German ambassador in Washington, Günther van Well, suggested that it was crucial to intensify the dialogue with American Jewish organizations, in order to avert damage to German–American relations.[86] He warned the Foreign Office and the German Chancellery: "The intellectual confrontation in the United States with the Nazi persecution of the Jews will force us Germans—with a delay of 30 years—again into a new phase of coping with the past."[87] Mostly sharing the concerns of his predecessors, Well emphasized that American Holocaust memorial culture had developed above all two relevant ramifications for the Federal Republic. The question of financial compensation for the victims of National Socialism would continue to decrease in urgency as former concentration camp inmates passed away, while the centrality of Holocaust memory for Jewish identity in the United States would grow significantly in the future. The latter was underscored by the establishment of the Days of Remembrance, an annual commemoration ceremony for the victims of the Holocaust held in the US Capitol; large academic conferences; the construction of Holocaust museums, monuments, and study centers; and growing numbers of trips of American Jews to their former cites of incarceration in Germany, which often led to criticism of an alleged lack of historical consciousness in Germany.[88] Then again, the ambassador added, the number of American Jews and American Jewish organizations that were interested in a dialogue with the Federal Republic, one not exclusively focused on the Nazi past, had also grown. For the Kohl government, this was no reason for optimism, but it pointed to the possibilities an intensification of West German–American Jewish dialogue offered.

Burying the Nazi Past in Bitburg?

The public controversy over the visit of Ronald Reagan to a German military cemetery in 1985 was a watershed for West German–American Jewish relations.[89] At issue was the position of the Nazi past in German historical consciousness as well as of the Federal Republic in the Western alliance. The conflict, however, became a symbol of failure for Kohl's politics of history and marked a severe crisis for the Reagan presidency.[90] As historian Charles S. Maier has suggested, to "Kohl and his political advisers, the American president's visit was intended symbolically to wipe away the last moral residues of probation under which the Federal Republic still labored."[91] Kohl's party also faced important state elections in North Rhine-Westphalia only a week after Bitburg, which added significance to the encounter of the two political leaders.[92]

The visit was heavily contested in Germany, the United States, and elsewhere by opponents from a variety of religious, political, and social backgrounds.[93] Leading Social Democrats, such as Johannes Rau, not only opposed Kohl's political goals, but were also concerned that the chancellor's actions would damage the reputation of the Federal Republic abroad.[94] In the United States, German diplomats closely monitored the controversy and tried to assess its impact on German–American relations and the Federal Republic's status in the Western alliance, paying specific attention to the activities of American Jewish organizations. To many of these, the ceremony at Bitburg confirmed critical attitudes toward the Kohl government's politics of history. In the end, however, the Bitburg controversy had a paradoxical result. Despite the intensity of the debate, it led to an improvement in West German–American Jewish dialogue.[95] It also marked a significant stage in Kohl's "personal learning process," which shaped his politics of history into the 1990s.[96]

At the military cemetery Kolmeshöhe, west of the provincial German city of Bitburg, the Kohl government planned to commemorate the fallen soldiers of World War II, German as well as American. Scheduled for May 5, 1985, this ceremony took place only a few days before the fortieth anniversary of Nazi Germany's unconditional surrender on May 8, 1945. *Der Spiegel*, critical of Kohl's government, reported that already in late 1984, he had signalled to Reagan that he had been displeased about not having been invited to the fortieth anniversary of D-Day, when the Western World War II Allies had celebrated the victory over Hitler and the liberation of Europe from Nazism in France.[97] Kohl vehemently denied this report, yet stated with regard to the United States:

> But until to this day, a certain, I am sorry to say, Jewish party [*von jüdischer Seite*]—I do not usually go there, but it makes no sense to talk around it—is telling the American public that I had been very disconcerted about not having been invited to the celebrations on the occasion of the invasion. That is also an utter lie.[98]

In any event, Kohl's absence from the D-Day celebrations seemed to create an awkward and unjustified imbalance: while the Federal Republic made a most significant contribution to NATO's confrontation with Soviet Communism, the victory over National Socialism still appeared to yield stronger glue for the solidarity of the Federal Republic's Western partners than West Germany's accomplishments. Reagan had agreed to come to Bitburg at least in part out of gratitude for Kohl's unwavering support for the modernization of NATO's nuclear forces, including the unpopular deployment of Pershing II missiles in West Germany in 1983.[99] He also hoped for the German government's support for the controversial and costly Strategic Defense Initiative (SDI).[100]

In Bitburg, Kohl wanted to create a powerful symbol of German–American friendship and the close military alliance that had brought the two former enemies together.[101] His highly symbolic encounter with French President François Mitterrand over a mass grave at the World War I battlefield in Verdun in September 1984 was to serve as a model. Here, the two leaders, flanked by French and German soldiers, had held hands while a marching band played the Marseillaise.[102] It turned out, however, that a similar ceremony could not be held in Bitburg. During the planning process of the German–American ceremony, officials in charge had overlooked that not a single American GI, but a number of Waffen-SS men, were buried in the cemetery.[103] The ensuing controversy over the legitimacy and symbolism of the Bitburg visit showed that this cemetery was unsuitable to celebrate German–American friendship and reconciliation.[104]

In the United States, the Bitburg controversy began several months before Reagan's planned state visit to Germany. Contrary to initial plans and Kohl's original suggestion to include a visit to the Dachau concentration camp memorial, the president announced in January his intention not to visit a concentration camp memorial site while in Germany in order avoid confronting Germans with their past in an unnecessary way.[105] He stated in a press conference, "I don't think we ought to focus on the past. I want to focus on the future. I want to put that history behind me."[106] Reagan uttered a few more controversial statements in the months that followed, but the debate about Bitburg took a decisive turn only in April. On April 11, the official itinerary was announced, absent a stop at a concentration camp memorial site; in mid-April the press revealed that members of the Waffen-SS were buried in the cemetery. The president did nothing to defuse tensions, but provided even more reasons for his critics to oppose the visit. On April 18, for example, he referred to German soldiers buried at Bitburg as "victims, just as surely as the victims in the concentration camps."[107] In addition, Reagan referred to Nazi Germany as a "one man's totalitarian dictatorship," ascribing to an interpretation of the Third Reich in which only Hitler was to blame for Nazi crimes.[108] This statement resonated with the rhetoric of the early postwar period, when the United States had made a sustained effort to integrate the Federal Republic into the Western alliance in the struggle against the Soviet Union. In the 1950s as well as in the 1980s, "absolv[ing] most common Germans from responsibility for the Third Reich" therefore also aimed to strengthen the Cold War alliance with the Federal Republic.[109]

The Kohl government was probably glad to receive this kind of confirmation. Its spokesman Peter Boenisch, for example, clearly oblivious to the difference between a camp and a memorial, stated privately according to Der Spiegel: "It's quite outrageous that even 40 years after the end of the war, one has to walk through concentration camps."[110] Yet Reagan's historically false statements proved politically incendiary. Opponents of the visit called upon Reagan to cancel the trip, and the controversy in the United States culminated on April 19 when Elie Wiesel received the Congressional Gold Medal of Achievement. At this occasion, he appealed publicly to Reagan in the White House: "That place, Mr. President, is not your place. Your place is with the victims of the SS."[111] That Kohl and Reagan added a stop at the Bergen-Belsen concentration camp memorial site to the itinerary did not significantly ease opposition in the United States.

At Bergen-Belsen, Kohl had in fact given a sensitive speech on April 21, on the occasion of the fortieth anniversary of the liberation of the concentration camp. He forcefully condemned the barbarism of the regime, spoke with great empathy about the suffering of all groups who had been victims of National Socialism, not only Jews, and characterized May 8 as a "day of liberation for the Germans," an expression commonly attributed to Federal President von Weizsäcker's speech on May 8, 1985.[112] While Kohl's speech was less publicized than Weizsäcker's, some insiders have argued that Kohl only chose such language in order to ease the public criticism he faced over Bitburg from his domestic political opponents and the liberal and left-leaning press.[113] Even though Kohl indeed set a counterpoint to the impending ceremony at Bitburg, he also continued to characterize the Third Reich as a totalitarian regime and maintained that its crimes had been committed "in the name of Germany." His closing words allowed for an ambiguous interpretation. While he firmly embraced the importance of preserving the memory of Nazi crimes, he concluded, quoting a Jewish mystic, "The secret of redemption lies in remembrance."[114] This statement at least implied that the Federal Republic had or was in the process of redeeming itself with its efforts to commemorate, as Kohl said, the "darkest, most painful chapter in German history."

Only a day after the ceremony at Bergen-Belsen, Kohl expressed his anger about the public controversy over Bitburg in the United States to the CDU's federal committee (Bundesvorstand).[115] To him, holding the ceremony at Bitburg made sense not only because of the military cemetery, but also because of the "total symbiosis" between Germans and Americans in this city, which had resulted in well over five thousand marriages. He further maintained that it was impossible to find a German military cemetery where no Waffen-SS men were buried. As far as he knew at that point in time, those buried in Bitburg had been very young men. If they "had not had the misfortune to lose their lives during the war," they would have returned home and would probably have been granted amnesty immediately after the war. Kohl thus considered the reactions of most American Jewish organizations—especially in the context of the question of whether to also hold a ceremony at a concentration camp memorial with Reagan—"irrational," but he stressed his empathy for those opponents of the visit who had survived Nazi concentration camps. Nevertheless, he was particularly displeased about the public statements by "Mister Wiesel, who came from Auschwitz and who is operating in this matter with a particular severity against us, to a degree that I cannot completely understand, as I wish politely to put it." Kohl continued that the Federal Republic, however, suffered not only from the actions of "certain organizations," but also deserved a share of the blame because of its

> abysmal politics of representing the new Germany in America, the complete lack for 30 years of a representation of what the Federal Republic is really like. . . . I am steadfastly determined—I want to tell you clearly—to change that.

The encounter at Bitburg was designed as a large-scale media event, under-scoring the partnership between the two Cold War allies. The ceremony was moreover an attempt to reduce the burden of the Nazi past on the Federal Republic's reputation abroad and to delegitimize criticism of German policies in this context.[116] The White House agreed that "bygones should be bygones."[117] Reagan's staff assumed that Kohl wanted this ceremony at a symbolic place on a symbolic date to "show that he is a sovereign leader meeting with the Americans as an equal," but also that "he needed to be seen in the Rhineland (where the Bitburg cemetery is located) burying the past."[118] The president's public relations advisors, however, were deeply concerned about the impact of the Bitburg controversy on Reagan's reputation, and the *New York Times* later refered to Bitburg as "probably the biggest fiasco" of his presidency.[119] Even though Kohl and Reagan had agreed in a phone conversation on April 23—in which Kohl allegedly stated that his government would fall if Reagan can-celled the visit—to go ahead with the ceremony despite massive opposition, the president's advisors hoped that the chancellor would withdraw the invita-tion.[120] They knew that the reactions to the Bitburg plans had "created a situa-tion where the *purpose* of the visit"—"reconciliation and good will between two great countries"—"cannot be accomplished."[121] However, they were also aware that the fierceness of the Bitburg controversy resulted from the fact that the visit was supposed to legitimize an interpretation of the history of the Third Reich that many Americans, and Germans on the left, considered unaccept-able. Marshall Breger, Special Assistant to the President for Public Liaison, ex-plained to Reagan's Chief of Staff, Donald Regan:

> The CDU, and in particular, Chancellor Kohl, view the German people as having been controlled by a group of madmen during World War II. Thus, in their calendar, May 8 is a day of liberation for Germany as well as for the allies—it is the day in [sic] which the bulk of the German people were liberated from Nazism. Following this view, it is under-standable why the German "dough boys" (excepting certified war crim-inals) are to be viewed as akin to GI Joes. It is this version of history which the President will legitimate by the Bitberg [sic] wreath-laying.[122]

Hence Reagan would support an interpretation of Nazism according to which only a small group of criminals had been responsible for Nazi crimes, with the vast majority of Germans as innocent victims of the dictatorship.[123] Such a read-ing matched the position held by leading right-wing German conservatives, for example the majority leader in the Bundestag, Alfred Dregger (CDU). An open letter he sent to the United States Senate sparked further debate. Dregger made clear that he would consider a cancellation of the visit an "insult" to the fallen German soldiers, most of whom had been "decent" men.[124] Behind closed doors,

Kohl expressed his explicit approval of Dregger's protest and noted the ignorance of many Germans, especially on the left, about German losses during the war:

> To us it is important not to deny the burden of history with its horrible chapters, but that we also recognize the other side of these soldiers, who lost their lives. . . . Now you will understand why I am pursing this monument for the war dead in Bonn [Central Memorial] with such an intensity.[125]

A series of articles in *Newsweek* showed that Germany's struggle to come to terms with its history did not escape the attention of Americans. One commentator attested to the need of the German people to "forget" the Holocaust and quoted a Reagan staffer who suggested that Kohl wanted "to put all this guilt the Germans have been carrying around behind them."[126] Another article spoke about the need and the yearning of a younger German generation to free themselves of the burden of their history.[127] Holocaust survivors in the United States, however, considered Bitburg an indicator that the Kohl government wanted to close the books on the Nazi past and that it had been able to win the US president's support for this endeavor. Members of the United States Holocaust Memorial Council, over which Wiesel and other Holocaust survivors

Figure 2.2 Helmut Kohl, General (Ret.) Johannes Steinhoff (1913–1994), Ronald Reagan, and General (Ret.) Matthew B. Ridgway (1895–1993) visit the Bitburg Military Cemetery, 1985. Bundesregierung/Ulrich Wienke.

presided and which was in charge of building the USHMM, were puzzled by Reagan's alleged willingness to support the rehabilitation of West Germany. From their perspective, Bitburg clashed with the Holocaust Council's mission, which Reagan had so far supported: commemorating and increasing awareness of the Holocaust. Reagan's plans, and particularly his comments about the Holocaust and its victims, almost led to the resignation of the entire Council and the termination of the project to build an American Holocaust memorial in Washington.[128]

Although no Council member resigned over Bitburg, Holocaust survivors felt betrayed by Reagan and offended by Kohl. Sigmund Strochlitz, a survivor of Auschwitz and member of the Council, was outraged that Reagan had refused to visit the Dachau concentration camp, but was going "to honor those who perpetrated the Jewish people and killed American prisoners."[129] The former Polish partisan Miles Lerman, who became the Council's chairman in 1993, suggested that "a true reconciliation" with the German people—something he did not necessarily desire—demanded first of all that the Germans recognize that "there was a Holocaust."[130] Many survivors saw Bitburg as evidence that West Germany was still in denial about the Holocaust, that the country lacked adequate Holocaust education, and that this necessarily created an "opportunity for the revival of Neo-Nazism."[131] Despite such inaccurate assumptions about the Federal Republic, most Council members were not opposed to reconciliation with West Germany in general. Yet they deeply rejected any attempt to relativize the Holocaust.[132] As Wiesel stated in a live television interview with Tom Brokaw on the day of the Bitburg visit:

> I feel sadness, very profound sadness. I never thought I would live to see this day. The road from Bergen-Belsen to Bitburg is a very long one, and I thought it would take centuries for humankind to cross it. And the president of the United States has just crossed it in less than one hour.[133]

In the long run, Bitburg permanently damaged Kohl's reputation with the Council and Holocaust survivors in the United States.[134]

The AJC also vehemently opposed the Bitburg visit and positioned itself in this debate with clear reference to its dialogue with the Federal Republic. Due to its intimate knowledge of the country, for example through the exchange program with the Konrad Adenauer Foundation, the AJC saw itself in "a unique position to explain ... why the Bitburg visit was not an acceptable sign of reconciliation."[135] The organization called upon representatives of the White House as well as the state minister in the Foreign Office, Alois Mertes, also the representative of the Bitburg electoral district, to cancel the visit. In fact, the AJC's President Howard Friedman and its Associate Director William Trosten persuaded Mertes to plead with Kohl to visit the tomb of Konrad Adenauer with Reagan instead of the cemeterey.[136] Even though Kohl refused to cancel the visit to the cemetery, he added Adenauer's tomb to the itinerary and cut the ceremony at the cemetery to a few minutes.[137]

The diplomat Wolf Calebow, who played an increasingly important role in West German–American Jewish affairs in the second half of the 1980s, suggests in his memoirs an alternative reading of the AJC's role in the run-up to the Bitburg visit. Calebow had—in private capacity—asked Trosten, whom he had known since the 1970s, to intervene on behalf of the Kohl government in Washington.[138] In fact, Trosten and Friedman had held a series of meetings with White House officials in Washington and the West German Foreign Office in Bonn, including Mertes, trying to prevent the ceremony at Bitburg.[139] It was during these meetings that they suggested changing the location of the reconciliation ceremony to the grave of West Germany's first chancellor, Konrad Adenauer.

In his conversation with Trosten, however, Calebow had argued that a cancellation of Bitburg would politically only benefit anti-American voices in the Federal Republic and would damage German–American relations. As a result, Calebow maintains, a delegation of the AJC, including Friedman and Trosten, had signaled to Reagan during a meeting at the White House on April 29 that they would support the visit to Bitburg if the itinerary were amended.[140] According to Calebow's account, Reagan only then decided to proceed with the visit. It cannot be said with certainty if this version, which traces Reagan's decision not to cancel Bitburg back to Calebow's initiative, is correct. Other evidence suggests that it is more likely that the AJC did not change its stance on Bitburg, but nevertheless strongly endorsed a shift of priorities in Germany vis-à-vis Reagan: a shortening of the visit to the cemetery without a speech; a long, emotional speech by Reagan in Bergen-Belsen; and a wreath laying at Adenauer's grave.[141]

Bitburg became a turning point for West German–American Jewish relations due to the opposition of American Jewish organizations to the visit, as well as the weight German observers put on these protests and their initiators. In fact, not only Jewish groups, but the vast majority of the American media, as well as a broad coalition of religious groups, civil rights activists, and veteran organizations, opposed the Bitburg visit.[142] The public protests diminished Reagan's approval ratings and his popularity.[143] The White House noted that Reagan had become a "target for Jewish groups and vets alike," and the majority of Americans even considered the veterans' opposition, which included the conservative American Legion, "more persuasive" than Jewish protests.[144] Important political leaders, including leading Republicans Bob Dole and Newt Gingrich, as well as majorities in both houses of Congress, expressed their disapproval of the Bitburg visit.[145] Above all, they rejected the symbolic visit on moral grounds as the ceremony could be misinterpreted as paying respect to the Waffen-SS, in their eyes a symbol for Nazi tyranny and the Holocaust.[146]

Yet leading conservative German politicians, diplomats, and journalists thought that a "Jewish-American media machine" was pulling the strings behind the scenes, as the sociologist Werner Bergmann has observed.[147] The German embassy in Washington and the Chancellery in Bonn closely monitored and analyzed the coverage of the Bitburg controversy in the mass media as well as the protests of American Jewish organizations.[148] While most of the protests in the United States were directed against Reagan, German observers were naturally more concerned about a negative impact on the image of the Federal Republic.[149] West Germany appeared as a country that had only insufficiently confronted the Nazi past, and the chancellor received a lion's share of the blame.[150] To German diplomats, the coverage in the *Washington Post* provided a case in point. On April 22, for example, the *Post* reported on the massive protests of Holocaust survivors against Bitburg and quoted Benjamin Meed: "How many Germans sleep today on mattresses which are still filled with Jewish hair? How many Germans adorn their houses with art confiscated from Jewish homes?"[151] In the Chancellery, such attempts to scandalize the Federal Republic and its policies inevitably fueled fears about the negative impact of American Jewish organizations on German–American relations.

There was also room for moderate conversation, at least when German diplomats directly interacted with leaders of the American Jewish community. Already before the debate about Bitburg had reached its apex, Ambassador van Well had tried to ease the tensions with some American Jewish organizations. In March, he met with representatives of the ADL to rebut their concerns about a lack of willingness among the German youth to confront the history of the Holocaust as well as worries about the Federal Republic's commitment to Israel's security.[152] Both sides agreed about there being a shortage of opportunities for Germans and American Jews of the postwar generation to engage with one another, which resulted in a number of stereotypes and misconceptions.

As the public controversy over Bitburg heated up, German diplomats sent highly detailed summaries of the media debates and the activities of American Jewish organizations and individuals to the Foreign Office and the Chancellery. On April 13, for example, Theodor Wallau, a diplomat at the embassy who later served as ambassador to Israel from 1996 to 2000, described the press coverage on Bitburg:

> The discussions about the plans for the wreath-laying of the US president at the Bitburg military cemetery continue to be intense. . . . The main consensus is that the cancellation of the visit to Dachau—which the press had considered a set part of the program—should make an honoring of the fallen German soldiers in Bitburg impossible.

The claim that the visit to Bitburg was Kohl's idea is new. Some of the press demands a cancellation of the visit to the cemetery, some call for an expansion of the program to commemorate the victims of the Nazis. The White House seems to be open to this idea. Representatives of organized Jewry and veterans receive ample space in these discussions, politicians take advantage of this issue to point to the president's and his advisors' tactlessness.[153]

About a week later, Wallau described the recent coverage of the Bitburg controversy as "excessively fierce and even hysterical."[154] On April 23 alone Ambassador van Well sent four messages to Bonn, analyzing the controversy in the United States. He paid particular attention to the perception of West Germany, Kohl, and reports about the activities of Jewish groups in the media. According to Well, Kohl appeared as a "decent German," but also as a "provincial" politician, one who was "not very bright."[155] Public opinion, Well reported, seemed to be shifting "more and more against Jewish circles, which according to the view of many Americans want to exert an exaggerated influence on the president."[156] With regard to Jewish opposition to Bitburg, Well stated that

> contacts with rabbis, the Jewish upper upper-middle class [*jüdischen großbürgern*], and intellectuals (with the exception of the "Holocaust zealots" [*holocaust-eiferer*]) are unaffected by the Bitburg discussion, [they] continue to work pleasantly.[157]

In general, the ambassador mostly held American Jews responsible for the political and public opposition to Bitburg. Implying that this protest was merely zealotry, he reduced their opposition to a mere instrumentalization of the Holocaust for political reasons.[158] Well seemed to block out the personal suffering many of these opponents had endured under the Nazi regime, instead seeing their opposition as a political campaign, one with West Germany as its ultimate victim. Furthermore, he saw the resolution of Congress against the Bitburg visit as a response to the "growing pressure of Jewish circles." In his view this also applied to the electoral strategies of individual senators, who he assumed were worried that their opponents might receive "Jewish money," which would endanger their prospects of reelection.[159] On April 25, Well warned the Foreign Office and the Chancellery:

> 14 days of "manufactured" opinion in the media have made an impact with officials, journalists, and among the general public, which gives reason to fear that the campaign will eventually affect our political relations directly. This danger would then exist all the more if cheap and manipulative [*stimmungsmachende*] television

coverage from Germany were to augment the strong rhetoric [*verbale kraftakte*] that already exists.[160]

Well considered Menachem Rosensaft, chairman of the International Network of Children of Jewish Holocaust Survivors, "one of the most active spokespersons and initiators of the campaign against the wreath-laying" and warned that he was organizing public protests to take place in Bitburg, which could produce negative coverage.[161] Wallau, summarizing the press coverage on April 29, also paid close attention to commentaries by Jewish journalists, some of whom, such as Meg Greenfield of the *Washington Post* or Dorothy Rabinowitz of the *Washington Times*, allegedly maintained "that there is German collective guilt."[162] Even though such analyses by the ambassador and his staff cannot be considered openly anti-Semitic, they reinforced the stereotypical notion that American Jews held significant influence over the media and political decision-making processes and also that they exploited the memory of the Holocaust politically.[163] As a result, German officials based their strategic considerations on such assumptions.

Some journalists in the Federal Republic shared such views. Fritz Ullrich Fack, an editor of the highly-respected, conservative *Frankfurter Allgemeine Zeitung (FAZ)*, blamed—without an explicit reference to the American Jewish community—a "powerful media machine" for perpetuating the image of the "ugly German" in the United States.[164] Another *FAZ* commentator stated that "reasonable people" should warn "certain Jewish circles" that their exaggerated opposition to Bitburg could damage the "moral unity" of the West and thus endanger the "fate of Israel."[165] The lowbrow magazine *Quick* directly attacked the "legendary Jewish lobby" in the United States.[166] Yet such clichés also preoccupied German political decision-makers. According to the memoirs of Secretary of State Shultz, Kohl's foreign policy advisor Horst Teltschik made clear to the designated US ambassador to the Federal Republic, Richard Burt, that protests by Americans against Bitburg would lead to an increase in anti-Semitism in the Federal Republic: "'Young Germans,' he said 'are saying that watching the power of the American Jews to pressure the president, they now understand the problem Germany faced prior to World War II.'"[167] This statement confused action and reaction. Without question, nearly every major American Jewish organization opposed the Bitburg visit. However, the German side did not make an effort to analyze in depth the reasons for this position, which could have led to a reconsideration of the entire ceremony and its highly problematic symbolic implications.

Only two days prior to the visit, the embassy acknowledged that efforts to justify the Bitburg ceremony would be in vain.[168] As a consequence, diplomats turned their thoughts to the future of West German–American Jewish relations.[169] Considering the fatal impression the Bitburg affair had created about the status of the Federal Republic's coping with the Nazi past, this would be a challenging task. The embassy warned the Foreign Office and the Chancellery on May 3, only two days before Bitburg:

> The Bitburg visit will probably leave its mark on Jewish circles in the long run. Some call something into question that they had considered self-evident: the unconditional damnation of the crimes of the Third Reich, symbolized by the SS, and the agreement that these crimes will never be forgotten.... We will have to engage in extensive conversations with Jewish circles to make clear that we also do not want to forget the crimes of the Third Reich, but consider them a calling to prevent similar events in the future.[170]

The embassy further concluded that West German efforts to explain "our position toward the past of the Third Reich" had been insufficient and that German emissaries had to be found who could make clear "the place of the topic in its historical context." According to this view, the Third Reich was neither an "'accident,' nor the logical consequence of German history."[171]

Despite the intensity of the Bitburg controversy, it ebbed away soon after Reagan had visited the cemetery. Only a few days after the ceremony, Well was almost able to give the all-clear to Kohl: the "campaign of the media" and the protests of the "Jewish lobby" had not significantly damaged German–American relations; a majority of Americans had not shared their opposition after all; and American Jewish organizations were now intent on easing tensions with the Reagan administration.[172] Nevertheless, he made clear that Bitburg had to be considered a failure as an attempt to convey the Kohl government's approach to the Nazi past in the United States. To the contrary, "the controversy about the visit to the cemetery has revitalized the Nazi past, more than it suits us, and it has especially burdened the memory with new emotions."[173] For the future, this posed a considerable challenge for the reputation of the Federal Republic. Above all Holocaust survivors and organizations representing their interests considered Bitburg a confirmation that the Federal Republic was not capable of dealing responsibly, as it were, with its past. However, they also welcomed this opportunity to inform Americans—even "the entire world"—about the history of the Holocaust.[174]

Several top-level German officials tried to reverse the damage caused by the controversy.[175] Alois Mertes met with representatives of the AJC, the Anti-Defamation League of B'nai B'rith, and the Conference of Presidents of Major American Jewish Organizations, an umbrella organization. A sensitive mediator who showed sympathy for the "emotional reactions" of Jewish victims of Nazi persecution and their relatives, Mertes tried to explain that the Bitburg visit was an "expression of grief for all victims of war and tyranny," not an act of "hero worship." This was meant as a sincere expression of remorse, but the leveling of the distinctions between perpetrators and victims of Nazi Germany, which Mertes's explanation at least implied, was an interpretation that closely corresponded with the dominant interpretation of the Nazi past among German conservatives.[176] His interlocutors could not share such an interpretation because of the "symbolism of the SS," which made a clear distinction between perpetrators and victims absolutely necessary.[177] Both sides agreed, however, that the conflict offered an opportunity to increase West German–American Jewish dialogue.

Berndt von Staden came to a similar conclusion. The former ambassador to the United States and current Coordinator for German-American Cooperation in the Foreign Office visited Washington in mid-May and stated that the debate about Bitburg had underscored the necessity of expanding the reciprocal exchange of information between both countries.[178] Finally, Ambassador van Well hoped to strengthen the exchange with American Jewish organizations and gave a public talk about "Germans and Jews—After Bitburg" in front of a Jewish audience in May.[179] In a generally cooperative atmosphere, the audience criticized what they considered the shortcomings of West Germany's engagement with the Nazi past. But for the Federal Republic, there was reason for hope: Well's audience expressed its admiration for Weizsäcker's address to the Bundestag on May 8, 1985. The German president's speech soon evolved as a countertype to Kohl's Bitburg ceremony, as Weizsäcker placed the murder of European Jews at the center of his elaborations.[180] Well further stated that the Federal Republic now considered American Jews the "main torch bearers of the Ashkenazi heritage."[181] On behalf of the German government, he invited the president and the vice president of B'nai B'rith to Germany. They made clear that they had realized during the Bitburg controversy that "the coping with the Nazi past in German-Israeli relations was much more advanced and comprehensive than in West German-American Jewish relations."[182] In the years following Bitburg, the ADL and B'nai B'rith began a youth exchange program with the Federal Republic.[183]

Finally, the chancellor himself sent a signal to the United States in late 1985. That December, he gave the opening speech to the first conference of the Leo Baeck Institute in Germany, which historian Lucy S. Dawidowicz considered "Germany's Answer to Bitburg."[184] However, in addressing the Atlantik-Brücke in June 1985, an audience that was certainly supportive of Kohl, the chancellor presented a different set of conclusions from Bitburg.[185] He saw Reagan's visit to Germany as a powerful sign of reconciliation between the former enemy nations. While the visit had shown that the "wounds of the past" had remained "sensitive," he insisted that the Federal Republic had openly confronted the Nazi past and learned its lessons from this history. Yet:

> At the same time, we have to cope with all the problems resulting from coping with the Nazi past [*Vergangenheitsbewältigung*], also

in our relationship with foreign countries [*zum Ausland*], exactly because we, as Germans, embrace our entire history and do not attempt to rewrite this history.

The great resolve with which President Reagan, in accordance with his unshakeable moral conviction, held to the program of the visit, has met with widespread sympathy and respect here. There was also no room for misunderstanding over the meaning of said gesture, which lay in the joint visit to a German military cemetery. The reaction is, because of its intensity, cause for reflection. We need to show sympathy, especially where individual persecution during the Third Reich does not allow one to forgive, much less to forget. If today one or two critics in the United States have already arrived at a reconciliatory interpretation, we can already detect here the results of a clarification process [*Klärungsprozess*] from which the relationship of both peoples will benefit in the end.[186]

Even though Kohl expressed empathy with the victims of National Socialism, he refused to acknowledge that the visit to the Bitburg cemetery had created ample room for misunderstanding. He attributed the fierce opposition against Bitburg abroad not to the ceremony's ambiguous message, but to the "problems" resulting from a preoccupation with the Nazi past abroad. Here Kohl echoed a common view among German conservatives, who argued, in short, that the Federal Republic had successfully "coped" with Hitler, but not with the "coping with Hitler."[187]

Although the controversy over Bitburg indeed triggered a "clarification process," which eventually led to improved relations between the Federal Republic and some American Jewish organizations and also contributed to long-term change in the Kohl government's politics of history, this had hardly been Kohl's original calculation. Despite Kohl's refusal to take responsibility for Bitburg's failure, his government abandoned for the time being plans for a Central Memorial of the Federal Republic in Bonn, which had been intended to convey a similar controversial message.[188] Bitburg also forced many American Jewish organizations, for the first time since the 1950s, to broadly engage with the Federal Republic and its relationship to the Nazi past.[189] Many felt justified in their critical attitude toward the Federal Republic.

A Pragmatic Partnership? West German–American Jewish Relations after Bitburg

Bitburg, however, set in motion a process that led to an unprecedented expansion of interaction between the Federal Republic and American Jewish organizations, above all the AJC. The Kohl government realized in the aftermath of Bitburg the full extent of the Holocaust's impact on American political culture. For the future, German officials knew that if only for pragmatic reasons, public controversies of this kind had to be avoided and relationships with American Jewish organizations had to be redefined. Thus in subsequent months and years, the German government and its partners made a concerted effort to reach out to American Jewish organizations.

By October 1985, the Foreign Office already considered this new stage in the relationship a "very positive result" of the discussion about Bitburg: the visit to the military cemetery had contributed to an "intensification of our conversation with the Jewish organizations in the United States."[190] A stronger German–Jewish dialogue was—as stated earlier—hardly the intended motivation for Bitburg, but both German officials and representatives of some American Jewish organizations realized after this low point that continuing an antagonistic stance toward each other would hurt the political interests of both sides in the long run. The West German government continued to be concerned about the impact of the Nazi past on the Federal Republic's image during the second half of the 1980s and took the relationship with American Jewish organizations very seriously.[191] This new phase of West German–American Jewish dialogue was not without new conflicts and setbacks. Nevertheless, between 1985 and 1990 a series of initiatives aimed at reducing the tensions the Bitburg controversy had so forcefully brought to the surface. Both sides agreed that misperceptions and a lack of knowledge about each other constituted a crucial challenge.

This change was only possible because most American Jewish organizations decided very soon after Bitburg to put this issue aside. The AJC, for example, publicly declared that Reagan's visit to the military cemetery had been the "mistake of a friend—not the sin of an enemy," and willingly expanded exchange and educational programs with the Federal Republic.[192] The Anti-Defamation League and B'nai B'rith International hoped to follow the example of the AJC and sent delegations to Germany, trying to build closer relations with the German government.[193] These did not result in a similarly stable long-term cooperation, however. The AJC launched an educational program with the Friedrich Ebert Foundation, which was closely associated with the SPD, to distribute teaching materials about the history of the American Jewish community to German high schools.[194] In general, American Jewish organizations took stock of their attitudes toward the Federal Republic, and some acknowledged that German realities did not fit their critical image. During a visit to West Germany in October 1985, a top-level delegation of the AJC concluded that the country now was "truly a democracy."[195] Such a recognition of the political realities in the Federal Republic, by all standards a model democracy in the 1980s, was a crucial condition for closer relations. The AJC was so heavily

invested in building this partnership because it recognized the Federal Republic as a critical ally of Israel and a central power in the European Community.
Furthermore, the AJC was interested in protecting American Jewish interests
in Germany.[196]

This new level of openness toward the Federal Republic was, however, not
representative of the entire spectrum of American Jewish organizations. Those
organizations representing the interests of Holocaust survivors or concerned
with the institutionalization of Holocaust memory in the United States, such
as the Gathering of Jewish Holocaust Survivors and the United States Holocaust Memorial Council, maintained a distinctly critical attitude toward the
Federal Republic. In Kohl they saw a revisionist politician who wanted to sup-
press the memory of the Holocaust.[197] They considered the German government's attempts to deepen ties with American Jewish organizations, such as
the AJC, as a mere ruse for political rehabilitation. Representatives of these
organizations thought that the Federal Republic did not deserve to be rehabil-
itated because of its alleged refusal to cope with the Nazi past, as epitomized
by Bitburg.[198]

The Kohl government and its associates also realized that it had not made a
sufficient effort to understand the political goals of American Jewish organizations, as well as the significance of Holocaust memory for Jews and American political culture more generally. In addition to the established channels
of the Konrad Adenauer Foundation with the AJC, the Atlantik-Brücke under
the leadership of Walther Leisler Kiep and Beate Lindemann became heavily
involved in West German–American Jewish relations and would play an increasingly important role toward the end of the decade. Kohl attributed great
significance to this network, while AJC representatives tried to correspond directly with the chancellor's office.[199]

The installation, on the suggestion of Berndt von Staden, of a liaison for
West German–American Jewish relations in the German embassy in 1986 further illustrates efforts for establishing ties with—but also gaining a better understanding of—the functioning of the American Jewish community.[200] This
liaison, the aforementioned diplomat Wolf Calebow, played a key role in the
further development of West German–American Jewish dialogue. Calebow
had been in conversation with American Jewish organizations since 1977, in
part on his own initiative. In 1979, for instance, he had jointly drafted the proposal with William Trosten that resulted in the exchange program between
the AJC and the Konrad Adenauer Foundation. From 1986, he was officially in
charge of improving the relationship with American Jewish organizations at
the German embassy in Washington.[201]

However, he played an ambivalent role; while claiming to work toward a
better understanding between the Federal Republic and American Jewish organizations, he also nurtured a number of misconceptions about their motives.

Calebow held a number of positions in the West Germany Foreign Service, but clearly devoted most of his energies to what he referred to as "normalizing" the relationship between the Federal Republic and American Jews. As he explained in his working memoirs *Auf dem Weg zur Normalisierung* (*Towards Normalization*), and later in a number of letters to the editor of the conservative daily *Frankfurter Allgemeine Zeitung*, Calebow was convinced that a number of influential American Jewish organizations vehemently opposed any kind of normalization between Germany and Jews after the Holocaust.[202] To underscore his position, he came up with a peculiar analogy, which he often repeated: Was it compatible with "the tradition and content of Jewish thought" if now that the "Jews had finally been released from two thousand years of discrimination for the alleged murder of Jesus Christ, the Germans should—because of their responsibility for the Holocaust—be put into a maybe comparable special relationship at least vis-à-vis the Jews for now and forever"?[203]

Calebow seemed convinced that—with few exceptions—American Jewish organizations had a vital political interest in keeping a negative image of Germany alive.[204] The "continuous demonization of Germany, not Nazi Germany, but of the democratic Federal Republic," Calebow argued in 2006, served the political needs of the leaders of Jewish organizations and communities, especially in the United States.[205] Painting Germany and anti-Semitism more generally as a threat not only furthered the inner cohesion of these groups, but also assisted the goals of the American "Pro-Israel-Lobby," which bore a large share of responsibility for the "Israeli policies of expansion and repression of the Palestinians."[206] Calebow's critical stance toward Jews was thus not limited to America, but extended to the state of Israel as well. Although he made most of these statements after he retired from active service, they illustrate his basic convictions as he explicitly referred to his experiences as a diplomat in the United States. In retrospect it appears that Calebow was hardly suited to improve the dialogue between the Federal Republic and American Jews.

During the 1980s, however, he acted as an important hinge between the United States and Germany as not only the Foreign Office, but also the Chancellery, took his assessments into consideration. In 1988 he produced a detailed analysis of West German–American Jewish relations, reflecting on the past and making suggestions for the future.[207] According to his evaluation, the efforts of a diverse range of American Jewish organizations to establish museums, monuments, and educational programs that all aimed at keeping the memory of the Holocaust alive should not be interpreted as conscious attacks on the Federal Republic. Germany was, however, the "victim" of such initiatives.[208] As such, a confrontation with American Holocaust memorial culture was inevitable. This report confirmed, but also added more substance, to the experiences of German diplomats since the late 1970s. Calebow suggested that two questions clearly divided the American Jewish community: first, positions toward Israel, and second, attitudes toward the memory of the Holocaust. The German government, he concluded, had to concentrate its energies on those American Jewish organizations that did not consider the "instrumentalization of the Holocaust" an "adequate means for practical politics today."[209] To Calebow, it was beyond doubt that improving the relationship with the American Jewish community was a vital foreign policy interest of the Federal Republic.[210] He therefore forcefully recommended closer cooperation with the AJC, which he considered the only organization whose projects were "oriented towards the future."[211]

In this manner, cooperation with the AJC might serve as a template for dialogue with other American Jewish organizations. For the time being, however, Calebow considered the position of the Chancellery and the embassy to also speak with representatives of B'nai B'rith or the World Jewish Congress problematic. Allegedly, such equal treatment would be counterproductive, as these organizations were not interested in improving mutual understanding and could lead to neglecting relations with the AJC.[212] Of course, the German government should engage in conversations with representatives of Holocaust museums and Holocaust education, but had to be aware that they did not count among advocates of West German–American Jewish dialogue. At present, Calebow made clear, only members of the AJC, above all its associate director, William Trosten, were willing to accommodate the interests of the Federal Republic in the United States.

Even before Calebow's extensive assessment circulated between the desks of West German officials, the Atlantik-Brücke, especially its chairman Kiep, had begun to develop closer ties with the AJC. Trosten saw in the cooperation with the Atlantik-Brücke a way to achieve certain political goals in the Federal Republic. For instance, he hoped not only to contribute to a stabilization of German–American as well as German–Israeli relations, but also to affect the Federal Republic's engagement with the Nazi past. Both sides agreed to hold annual conferences on West German–American Jewish relations and to cooperate on questions concerning Holocaust museums and Holocaust education in the United States. In particular, they concurred that the American engagement with the Holocaust required a "positive epilogue" (*positive Schlußnote*),[213] by which they meant an explicit reference to the success story of the Federal Republic.[214] For this purpose, the AJC developed materials for teaching the history of West Germany at American high schools. This program, tellingly titled "Phoenix from the Ashes," enjoyed the backing and the financial support of the Foreign Office.[215] In addition, the AJC initiated—in collaboration with the Atlantik-Brücke—a program for American Holocaust educators. Once a year a delegation of high school teachers would visit the Federal Republic, where they could experience, as it were, German democracy in action. These efforts, which Kohl personally deemed very important, continued well into the 1990s.[216]

The first AJC-Atlantik-Brücke conference, however, held in Bonn in November 1987, made the challenges for West German–American Jewish relations rather obvious.[217] Both organizations agreed that insufficient knowledge about each other was responsible for the lack of understanding. According to their assessment, American Jews knew too little about the history of the Federal Republic and its partnership with Israel, while Germans did not know enough about Jewish life in the United States and the significance of Holocaust memory in this context in particular. The AJC noted that Bitburg had pointed to an "emotional and intellectual chasm between American Jews and Germans, a cleavage that prompts each side to apply the worst interpretation on the actions of the other."[218]

Accordingly, many American Jews continued to be under the impression "that Germans wish to forget the past," which led, in tandem with the growing presence of Holocaust memory in the United States, to a negative attitude toward the Federal Republic.[219] The American participants in the conference, however, also considered domestic German debates over the legacies of the Holocaust as epitomized by Bitburg and the so-called Historians' Controversy a great threat to future German–Jewish relations:[220] "Should the attempt to relativize the past succeed, such a move would take out from underneath us virtually the only ground on which Germans and Jews can presently meet."[221] In the eyes of the representatives of the AJC, Germans were not making a sufficient effort to understand the motives of American Jews and their critical attitude toward the Federal Republic. The German participants in the conference stressed that the Federal Republic was a stable democracy, but also acknowledged certain deficits in the Federal Republic's coping with the Nazi past.[222] However, they opposed the omnipresence of the Nazi past in the United States, as it "burdens Germany's international image."[223] Plans for the national Holocaust museum in Washington exemplified this development, as they did not allow for an integration of the history of postwar West Germany into the exhibition. To the German delegation, this would necessarily result in an unbalanced representation of Germany: "The past, some implied, should no more be allowed to overwhelm the present than be forgotten."[224] Both sides concurred that the media in both countries deserved a significant share of the responsibility for tensions in West German–American Jewish relations: the American media focused above all on negative developments in the Federal Republic without providing proper context, while the German media resorted to the cliché of the "'Jewish lobby,' thereby reinforcing a stereotype and missing the deeper causes of American concern."[225] These problems could only be solved, representatives of both sides conceded, by a concerted effort from American Jewish organizations and German foundations as well as the German government.

Despite this rather pessimistic assessment, optimism prevailed in Germany. The Foreign Office hoped that the cooperation with the AJC would leave a positive mark on West German–American Jewish relations, and officials considered the AJC a pioneer in this context.[226] They saw the organization as a key to improve the Federal Republic's standing in the American Jewish community and in the United States more generally. In December 1988, Kiep and Trosten met with Kohl, who had had several conversations with AJC members in the past, to discuss the current state of affairs. Joint projects of the AJC and the Atlantik-Brücke now included efforts to integrate a chapter on the history of the Federal Republic into American Holocaust courses, an issue that had been on the agenda of German observers since the late 1970s.[227] The chancellor deemed these efforts "eminently important" and later expressed his hopes that this project would improve the Federal Republic's image significantly, which he considered "constrained" to the period from 1933 to 1945.[228]

In the aftermath of Bitburg and through his conversations with the Konrad Adenauer Foundation and the Atlantik-Brücke, William Trosten evolved as the Kohl government's most important partner in the American Jewish community. Not only had he been a major driving force in the establishment of several projects that connected the Federal Republic with the AJC, but he also acted as an informal advisor to German diplomats and officials in the Chancellery. That he was granted access to Kohl underscores the weight the chancellor attributed to the impact of American Holocaust memorial culture on Germany's image in the United States, West German–American Jewish dialogue, and Trosten's advice in this context. When Trosten was due to retire from his position at the AJC in 1989, the Chancellery even considered hiring him directly as a lobbyist in the United States.[229]

Trosten, however, chose a different path. After his retirement in 1989, he cofounded the so-called Armonk Institute with former AJC president Theodore Ellenoff, an organization focused exclusively on improving West German–American Jewish relations, a goal that Trosten and Ellenoff deemed difficult to reach under the new AJC leadership.[230] Even though the Armonk Institute still exists according to public records, it probably ceased its activities after Trosten passed away in 2001.[231] According to its mission statement, the

The Armonk Institute seeks to improve American German relations by focussing on contemporary Germany (post 1945) in order to:

- Promote better understanding between Americans and Germans;
- Overcome historic stereotypes;
- Convey to the American public an objective view of the democratic evolution of the Federal Republic of Germany after World War II;
- Provide Germans with information about Jewish life in America.[232]

The central component of the Armonk Institute's program focused on American high school teachers. During the 1990s, it sent about six hundred teachers on "intensive study trips to Germany where they have the opportunity to meet with their teacher colleagues, political and economic leaders as well as civil servants in the foreign office and other federal state agencies."[233]

Despite its name it was not an institute, but rather an instrument with which Trosten could continue his activities between American Jewry and the Federal Republic, and as such it did not have a real membership. It operated out of an office at Squadron, Ellenoff, Plesent & Sheinfeld, a New York City-based law firm whose founders had included Ellenoff and Howard Squadron, who had served as the AJC's president from 1978 to 1984. The precise sources of the Armonk Institute's funding are not clear. It raised funds, however, through the high-profile Vernon A. Walters Award ceremony, a high-priced event it jointly held with the Atlantik-Brücke almost every year during the 1990s. With one exception, the winners of this award "for outstanding achievements in the strengthening of the relationship between Germany and the United States" were captains of German industry, such as the CEOs of BMW, Merdeces-Benz, Deutsche Bank, and Bertelsmann.[234] Especially to companies that had operated during the Third Reich and now pursued business interests in the United States, this award by a Jewish institution was highly desirable. For example, in 1998 Thomas Middelhoff, the designated CEO of the Bertelsmann publishing house, happily accepted the Walters Award. Bertelsmann had just acquired Random House, a merger that Vanity Fair had criticized as being part of a German "blitzkrieg" against American publishing houses.[235] Praised by his eulogist Walther Leisler Kiep as a "global leader," Middelhoff tried to ease such criticism by insisting that Bertelsmann had actually been a "Christian resistance publishing house" during the Third Reich. After the speech, however, journalists widely reported that the opposite had in fact been true, which forced the publishing house to install an independent commission of historians to examine Bertelsmann's role during the Third Reich.[236] Despite this certainly unintended outcome of the ceremony, the decision to bestow the Walters Award upon Middelhoff illustrates that the efforts of Trosten's Armonk Institute to further German–American partnership also included serving German business interests in the United States.

In taking a more direct stance against American Holocaust memory during the 1980s, the Kohl government valued Trosten highly. After Trosten's death in 2001, the German conservative elite publicly expressed its appreciation for his efforts. For instance, historian Michael Stürmer, who participated in the Kohl government's efforts to shape Americans' understanding of German history during the 1980s, wrote an obituary for Trosten in the conservative daily Die Welt. Stürmer stated that "the Germans did not remain stigmatized by World War II and Nazi atrocities forever after 1945 not only because of the geostrategic location and the economic potential of the country, but also because of people like Bill Trosten."[237]

In 1989, Trosten hoped with the Armonk Institute to take over the programs the AJC had conducted with the Atlantik-Brücke, such as excursions of American educators to the Federal Republic. Trosten stressed the challenges for the Federal Republic that resulted from the emphasis American Jewish organizations put on Holocaust memory in the United States. He demanded that Germany designed a "responsible, offensive public relations strategy" to react to the consequences.[238] He was driven by his dedication to the German–American alliance, but also by his commitment to Israel's security, stating, "American Jewish 'Activists' have little or no knowledge either of the importance of the Federal Republic to the long range geo-political interests of the United States or the extent of German economic and political aid to the State of Israel."[239] At this point in time, Trosten had therefore become not only a partner, but also a de facto advisor to the German government, and his analyses contributed to policymaking in the Chancellery. In the years following Bitburg, then, the federal government had established a stable network with some representatives of American Jewish organizations. These contacts with individuals, above all Trosten, were not only necessary to implement certain policy goals in the United States, but also to understand the inner workings and political agendas of these organizations. For Trosten and his American associates, this cooperation resulted in contacts with the highest German authorities, including the chancellor, which gave their small and new organization, the Armonk Institute, a significant amount of influence and power.

During the 1980s, West German authorities thus won important allies in their efforts to improve the country's image in the United States. At the same time, however, they had been engaged in a struggle with a much less predictable outcome. While constructing a network with some representatives of American Jewish organizations, the Kohl government also devoted significant energies to another development, closely connected to the debates about the impact of American Holocaust memory on the image of the Federal Republic in the United States: the planning and establishment of the USHMM in Washington. In a sense West German Holocaust angst culminated in the opposition to this institution, which preoccupied German observers and emissaries throughout the 1980s and even into the 1990s.

3

Confronting the Anti-German Museum

(West) Germany and the United States
Holocaust Memorial Museum, 1979–1993

In the eyes of the Kohl government—and of the chancellor himself—building a Holocaust museum in Washington, on the symbolically charged ground of the National Mall, was an outrageous idea. Helmut Kohl exhibited a highly skeptical attitude toward the establishment of an institution that would permanently anchor the Holocaust in American life.[1] His government's concerns about American Holocaust memorial culture culminated in opposition to the USHMM, which it considered a reduction of German history to the history of the Holocaust, sanctioned by the US government.[2] West German officials assumed that the USHMM would propagate a narrative that portrayed Jews as victims, Americans as liberators, and Germans as perpetrators. Such a narrative not only collided with the Kohl government's domestic politics of history, but it also seemed to pose a threat to the Federal Republic's reputation in the United States. Hence, representatives of the Kohl government and unofficial intermediaries set out to influence the design of the museum's content, especially its permanent exhibition.

Attempts by one government to interfere with the design of a national memorial of another government posed tremendous challenges. Through a series of behind-the-scenes interventions, a network of official and unofficial representatives of the Federal Republic tried to change the concept of the USHMM. German actors, government officials, nongovernmental organizations, and individuals were driven by fear as well as a claim for a right of codetermination with regard to how the history of the Holocaust should be told.[3] West Germany's Holocaust angst was not limited to questions of image and prestige, but extended into the sphere of foreign policymaking.[4] The Kohl government feared that visiting a Holocaust museum in Washington would cause Americans to question the Federal Republic's status as a partner in the Western alliance—the pillar of West German security and prosperity during the Cold War. In accordance with the debates about the successor generation on both sides of the Atlantic, this applied specifically to younger generations of Americans.[5] A key advisor on US policy and public relations to Helmut Kohl, Hubertus von Morr, summarized this attitude in the Federal Chancellery: "We cannot understand why America wants its young people to go to that museum and come out saying, 'My God, how can we be allies with that den of devils?'"[6]

A National Holocaust Museum for the United States

On November 1, 1978, Jimmy Carter established the President's Commission on the Holocaust. Its task was to develop a concept for a national memorial and museum and to organize the Days of Remembrance of Victims of the Holocaust in 1979.[7] In 1980, the US Senate created the Presidential Commission's successor organization, the United States Holocaust Memorial Council, to implement the Commission's suggestions for an American Holocaust memorial. To this day, the Council functions as the governing body of the USHMM. Carter nominated Elie Wiesel as both chairman of the Commission and later of the Council. Wiesel handed over the Commission's final report to Carter on September 27, 1979. In a letter accompanying the report, Wiesel presented the key findings of the Commission and outlined some of the guidelines for the museum.[8] Even though the construction of the USHMM did not begin until 1988 (and its doors only opened five years later), he already set some of the parameters as to how the Holocaust would be defined in the museum. This interpretation—like the make-up of the Council—was heavily contested at the time. Carter supported a broad and inclusive definition of who counted as victims of the Holocaust—following a number suggested by Simon Wiesnthal, he spoke of 11 million victims—and demanded that an accordingly diverse number of non-Jewish representatives should be on the Council.[9] Wiesel, on the other hand, emphasized that only Jews were targeted for total destruction by the Nazi regime. "There exists," he wrote, "a moral imperative for special emphasis on the six million Jews. While not all victims were Jews, *all* Jews were victims, destined for annihilation solely because they were born Jewish."[10] Nevertheless, *all* Americans could draw lessons from this unique crime, irrespective of religion or ethnicity: "The universality of the Holocaust lies in its uniqueness: the Event [*sic*] is essentially Jewish, yet its interpretation is universal."[11]

This position also contributed to the dominant position of Holocaust survivors on the boards of the Council, who subsequently managed to implement a "careful hierarchy of victimization" in the museum, where non-Jewish victims of Nazi persecution are "situated in relation to the Jewish center."[12] In particular Wiesel's interpretation of the Holocaust as a "sacred mystery" increased the

Figure 3.1 President Jimmy Carter (b. 1924) shakes the hand of Vladka Meed (1921–2012), a member of Jewish resistance in Poland and wife of Benjamin Meed (1918–2006), during a ceremony in the White House rose garden occasioned by the formal presentation to the president of the report of the US Holocaust Commission (pictured from left to right: Vladka Meed, Benjamin Meed, and Jimmy Carter). Jimmy Carter Library.

survivor's position as a somehow "holy" interpreter of the event.[13] At the core of these discussions was the question as to how the suffering of non-Jewish victims of National Socialism would fit into the Holocaust narrative. These debates, however, were not accessible to West German observers.[14] Nevertheless, it would later become clear to them that this concept would not leave much space for a nuanced analysis of German patterns of behavior during and after the Third Reich.

The Commission also outlined plans for the creation of a "living memorial," which would house a research institute as well as a "Committee on Conscience" for genocide prevention.[15] Though it offered no concrete ideas for the eventual design of the USHMM and its exhibition, the Commission set certain limits for the future institution. It demanded that the museum would become a federal institution built in the nation's capital. Federal land was provided for the USHMM, but its construction would have to be financed by private donations.[16] In Washington it would serve as a counterweight to the museums of the Smithsonian

Institution, which represented the positive and progressive aspects of human life.[17] Particular emphasis was to be devoted to American involvement with the Holocaust, which included the liberation of Nazi concentration camps and the immigration to the United States of many Holocaust survivors, but also the failure of providing refugees a safe haven and not putting genocide prevention on the military agenda.[18] Nevertheless, an idealized history of Americans as liberators would become a dominant motif of the USHMM.

In its final form, the USHMM did not provide a forum for self-promotion to the German government. Architect James Ingo Freed attempted to capture architectural features associated with the Holocaust, thereby almost creating "a self-sufficient memorial monument to the victims of the Holocaust."[19] The building's most prominent features include a large entrance hall, the Hall of Witness, and a hexagonal Hall of Remembrance, which can be reached on the second floor. It functions as the USHMM's "formal memorial space," houses an eternal flame, and features the names of the most notorious Nazi concentration and extermination camps on the walls.[20] Steel, glass, and red brick dominate the Hall of Witness, which resembles a cathedral as well as a waiting hall in a train station. The hall's specific features evoke powerful associations with the Holocaust. Windows and doors remind the visitors of crematoria and the elevators, which take the visitors to the entrance of the permanent exhibition,

Figure 3.2 15th Street Eisenhower Plaza entrance to the United States Holocaust Memorial Museum (USHMM) with the Hall of Remembrance on the right.

of gas chambers. From the outside, the building takes the shape of a row of concentration camp watchtowers.[21]

For the concept of the permanent exhibition, the planning team decided to combine chronological, geographical, and thematic elements.[22] The exhibition is divided into three exhibition floors, each of which addresses a period of Holocaust history. Museum visitors enter the permanent exhibition on the mostly text-based fourth floor, which chronologically narrates the history of

Figure 3.3 USHMM, interior view of the Hall of Witness.

Figure 3.4 USHMM Permanent Exhibition Opening Floor: "Nazi Assault 1933–1939." USHMM/Edward Owen.

the "Nazi Assault" from Hitler's rise to power in 1933 until the beginning of the Second World War in 1939. They then descend to the third floor, which covers the period of the "Final Solution," based on the display of artifacts from ghettos and death camps. This section of the permanent exhibition is arranged into thematic sections, describing life and death in the ghettos, deportation trains, and camps. The exhibition's final floor then explores the "Last Chapter" of the Holocaust, including death marches, liberation, and war crimes trials, in a more or less chronological order. In addition, this floor contains segments on the rescue of Jews by "righteous gentiles" and resistance against Nazi perpetrators.

First Impressions

The dominant role of Holocaust survivors on the boards of the USHMM significantly influenced the relationship between the museum and West German officials. Their experiences led to a skeptical stance toward Gemany and to "a high degree of anti-German sentiment," as the USHMM's founding director

Figure 3.5 USHMM Permanent Exhibition Middle Floor: "The 'Final Solution' 1940–1945." USHMM/Edward Owen.

Jeshajahu ("Shaike") Weinberg later recorded.[23] Both the chairman and vice chairman of the Council, Wiesel and William J. Lowenberg, were survivors of the Auschwitz extermination camp. Hadassah Rosensaft, a member of the museum's content committee, had been incarcerated at Auschwitz and Bergen-Belsen. Museum representatives who were able to escape the Nazi extermination machinery also remained affected by their experiences during the Third Reich. For example, a key historical advisor during the planning phase of the museum, Raul Hilberg, managed to leave his birthplace, Vienna, in 1939.[24] Miles Lerman, the head of the Council's International Relations Committee, had fought against German occupation forces as a partisan in Poland.[25]

Holocaust survivors and immigrants from Eastern Europe, including Wiesel, in particular were highly skeptical toward West German intermediaries.[26] In contrast to many German-born survivors, they did not have any positive prewar connection to German culture and language. More significantly, however, they had experienced the Nazi war of annihilation in Eastern Europe, which aimed at the total and irrevocable destruction of Jewish life and culture as well as the degradation of large parts of Eastern Europe to colonies of a German empire. Negative attitudes toward Germany among some survivors were, at times, not limited to Germans of the Nazi generation. During the postwar

Figure 3.6 USHMM Permanent Exhibition Final Floor: "Last Chapter." USHMM/ Edward Owen.

years, such an aversion resulted, for example, in a boycott of German products and public efforts to stigmatize the Cold War ally West Germany for the crimes of the Nazi regime.[27] A prime example is the case of Benjamin Meed, a forced laborer in the Warsaw Ghetto and a member of the Jewish underground, who helped to prepare the Warsaw Ghetto uprising.[28] Having established himself as a successful businessman in the United States, Meed cofounded the American Gathering of Jewish Holocaust Survivors in 1981 and held several important offices in the Presidential Commission and the United States Holocaust Memorial Council. For instance, he chaired the museum's content committee, in charge of the design of the permanent exhibition. As the president of the Gathering, he often drew explicit parallels between Nazi Germany and the Federal Republic.[29]

Such attitudes, while certainly an understandable result of traumatizing experiences, posed a significant problem for the Kohl government in its negotiations with the Council. The museum planners in Washington saw in Kohl a politician who wanted to bring "Germany truly into the post-Holocaust era," as the museum's former project director and first director of its research institute, Michael Berenbaum, remarked in retrospect.[30] Political scandals of the 1980s, such as the Bitburg controversy and the persistence of German emissaries vis-à-vis the USHMM, created the impression that German officials were not interested in a serious dialogue about the legacies of the Holocaust, but in implementing a political agenda. This sense of antagonism, partially based on personal experiences, was already apparent during the first encounters between the Council and representatives of the Federal Republic.

The plans for the USHMM had been of some concern to German diplomats in Washington before Kohl became chancellor. Already in 1979, their considerations included the question of whether the Federal Republic would or could contribute to the museum, even though German diplomats had at first very limited knowledge about the project and were not even sure if it would be built at all.[31] Early on, the Foreign Office suggested that German diplomats should try to "influence" the concept of the memorial so that the Federal Republic would not be identified with the "enterprise of the Holocaust" (Holocaustvorhaben).[32] The representative of the White House in charge of the President's Commission on the Holocaust had given the German embassy the impression that the Federal Republic might be asked for a donation of artifacts.[33] According to the assessment of Ambassador von Staden, such a donation could serve as a "gesture of reconciliation" to "militant Jewish organizations," implying that such a necessity existed—and that donating artifacts might be a venue to influence West Germany's image in the United States.[34] Museum planners also debated at the time what kind of contribution they could expect from the Federal Republic. The Council ruled out a financial contribution, but hoped for the support in securing access to archival materials, including inviting archivists to Germany.[35] Due to the expected size and significance of the USHMM, Staden's successor, Peter Hermes, assumed in 1981 that the Federal Republic could not abstain from assisting the Council altogether, and should communicate "our willingness to cooperate."[36]

Voicing Objections

In the summer of 1982, while he was still opposition leader in Bonn, Kohl already expressed his concerns about the USHMM to a group of CDU parliamentarians, but was skeptical the Federal Republic could prevent the museum from being built or even influence its content.[37] Peter Petersen, a CDU member of the Bundestag, recorded what Kohl had said about the museum, which "the Jews," as Petersen put it, were building in Washington.[38] In the early 1980s, Petersen repeated Kohl's words to journalist Judith Miller, who was working on a book about Holocaust memory at the time:

> What would a young German visiting the United States think when he passed the Holocaust Museum on the Mall? ... What would he feel when he saw his country's entire history reduced to these twelve

terrible years? Was this the way in which the United States was going to treat its most valued European ally?[39]

Attributing the USHMM to "the Jews"—and not to the officially secular President's Commission or Council—shows that Petersen did not perceive the museum primarily as a government institution. Furthermore, this choice of language clearly conveys a sense of antagonism, which would affect Petersen's further interactions with the Council. Yet Kohl's concerns, as summarized by Petersen, went beyond the question of German image in the United States. Worried about *German* visitors and their feelings when exposed to a Holocaust museum in the United States, Kohl also aimed at protecting Germans from being confronted with the history of the Holocaust abroad. It may be no coincidence that such fears existed at a time when the alliance between Germany and the United States was especially tense. In particular, young Germans, associated with the peace movement, called this alliance into question and expressed their criticism often in anti-American terms.[40] Maybe Kohl feared that he could no longer convincingly demonstrate that Germans and Americans were true allies if Americans were building a monument to Germany's most horrendous crime in Washington.

Within a year after Kohl took office in Bonn in late 1982, several German emissaries had already contacted the representatives of the Council in Washington. Among the first to get in touch with the museum in order to explore the possibility of negotiations was ambassador Peter Hermes.[41] He was at first highly skeptical about the USHMM, probably because he believed that American Jewish organizations would use the museum to exert political pressure on

Figure 3.7 Peter Petersen (1926–2005). DBT/Foto- und Bildstelle.

the Federal Republic.[42] A member of the Council and the Washington representative of the AJC, Hyman Bookbinder, had given Hermes the impression that the USHMM would indeed include a chapter on postwar West Germany—and that there could be a connection between the Federal Republic's foreign policy and its portrayal in the museum. He had written to Hermes in January 1981:

> I am actively engaged in developing plans for the American memorial museum. How Germany will be treated in that museum might well be affected by the decision you make pertaining to the sale of arms to Saudi Arabia.[43]

Maybe because of such encounters, Hermes became a fierce critic of the plans for a USHMM. When two Jewish members of Congress, most likely Eliot Levitas and James Scheuer, contacted him to discuss Germany's concerns about the USHMM, Hermes refused to meet with them.[44] As Petersen later wrote in a letter to Kohl, Hermes had told the congressmen that the "Germans did not want to have anything to do with this anti-German museum."[45]

Nevertheless, Hermes changed his mind due to the expected significance of the USHMM for German and foreign policy interests. In March 1983, he wrote to the Foreign Office that the Holocaust memorial in Washington "concerns us directly and indirectly to a considerable extent."[46] From an article in the *Washington Post*, the ambassador had received detailed information about the plans for the museum, which he thought would be completed in 1987, and suggested a German contribution beyond the requested help for building up the archives.[47] As he assumed, based on the article, the Council planned to build a memorial for all victims of National Socialism, not only Jews. German officials should encourage such plans and work toward the integration of German victims as well as German resistance against the Nazi regime. Hermes was very clear about the threat the future museum posed to the Federal Republic's reputation. He wrote in early 1983:

> 15 million tourists visit Washington annually. We can assume that the majority of them will include a visit to the memorial into their plans, despite the fact that it will be located at the periphery of the famous "Museum island" of the capital. The information provided by the memorial about the course of German history and the Germans' behavior during the years from 1933 to 1945 will be the only point of contact with Germany for many American visitors, especially adolescents; it will again abet the danger—which has not disappeared since the end of the War—of an identification of the entire German people with Hitler's totalitarian regime for an indefinite period of time.[48]

Therefore, he invited Elie Wiesel to the German embassy for an exploratory talk and offered him funding for a trip of two archivists to the Federal Republic where they could discuss a possible cooperation with German authorities.[49] Wiesel was generally receptive to such an invitation, yet he postponed the archivists' trip, most likely because the offer had been made too early in the museum's planning process.[50]

About a month later, Helmut Kohl, for the first time, spoke in detail to the CDU's federal committee about the plans for the USHMM. At the time, he expected the museum to open in 1984. After providing some background information about the expected size, location, and number of visitors, he went on to comment on the institution, for whose construction, as he stated, "the American Jews have collected 120 million dollars."[51] In an unusually direct appeal for help, Kohl outlined his concerns:[52]

The intention of leading American Jews is, of course, not primarily an anti-German one—some of them do not even understand this intention, if one insinuates that they hold it—but they want for all intents and purposes to apply a moral lever to continuously tell the American public, you have to support Israel for better or for worse. Thus, the intention is to tell Americans that [the] Holocaust was possible and must never become possible again; a repetition would strike Israel. This is why support for Israel is a top priority of American politics, from a moral perspective as well. What drops down to us from this byproduct is that the image of Auschwitz, Mauthausen, SS-men, the whole suffering of the Jewish people in their experience with Germans becomes apparent. Of course, these were Nazis. But now [try to] make this distinction in a country that knows as much about Germany as the average German does about Americans. That means we are faced with a problem that I consider to be of enormous dimensions. I still do not have a solution. However, we need to come up with something, not in the sense that we fight it—that would be deadly—but in the sense that we counter it with something like the history of German-American commonality in history. . . . This is the only chance I see to thwart this. I would be very grateful if you could think about what could be done here. This is not just any issue. Please do not misunderstand me. At the moment, we are having trouble in agricultural policy with the United States and its protectionism. This is, however, secondary compared to what is developing here psychologically. Maybe we will find a solution, maybe even soon, so that German cheese can be introduced there. Then this problem will be gone. But if an entire generation of school students grows up to perceive German as a synonym for Holocaust, then this is a terrible thing. Things are much worse today than during the Adenauer years. This is an important point, and I really ask you for your assistance with respect to what specifically we can do.[53]

Even though he was not present at said meeting, Peter Petersen emerged as the Kohl government's key link to the Council during the 1980s. Since he first heard in summer 1982 from the chancellor about the plans for a Holocaust museum in Washington, he was determined to "win over the decisive Jews as friends, so that they begin the design of this museum with a different attitude towards Germany."[54] Petersen made a determined effort so "that we get the chance to design a hall in this museum to put the history of the new Germany on display."[55] In a letter to Mark Talisman, vice chairman of the Council, he elaborated this objective in late 1984:

> Therefore my firends and I—and that includes Chancellor Kohl personally—like the idea that in the Holocaust-Museum would be a hall or a big room in which the story of a different Germany is told. Not so much the story of the resistance against Hitler by Germans (many of whom, as you know, were murdered—and as impressive and important those people are), but more how we as a people have learnt after the war which will prevent a recurrence of such colossal moral failure on a national scale which made Hitler possible in the first place.
>
> Also the contents in this room could open the door into a future which otherwise might be barred by the shock and hurt and bitterness which will come alive again in every decent human being that goes in that museum.[56]

A backbencher in the Bundestag who never reached high office, Petersen probably never desired an official mandate, as he considered his style of conducting foreign policy through personal connections and friendships more effective than the official policies of the embassy.[57] He lamented the lack of commitment of Germany's diplomats to fostering interpersonal ties with American politicians and to using such connections to influence decision-making processes. This kind of unofficial or "second-track diplomacy" was consistent with Kohl's way of governing, relying on personal connections instead of or in addition to the official diplomatic channels.[58]

At first glance, Petersen was not really suited to become the Federal Republic's messenger to the United States Holocaust Memorial Council. As he stated in the mid-1980s, he had been a staunch supporter of the Hitler regime as a teenager and never doubted until the end of the Third Reich that "the Jews [were] our misfortune."[59] Born in 1926, he was a student at a Napola, an elite Nazi boarding school, served in the Wehrmacht division Großdeutschland, and wanted to join the SS.[60] As journalist Judith Miller, who had interviewed Petersen for her book on Holocaust memory, remarked: "For him, Hitler was God, National Socialism was his religion."[61] However, the end of the war marked a fundamental turning point for Petersen. When his father arranged for him to meet a survivor from Bergen-Belsen—the first Jewish person Petersen ever talked to—this experience "converted" Petersen into a Christian, an enthusiastic supporter of the West German democracy, and an opponent of Nazism. Subsequently, he never tried to hide his Nazi past. In his conversations in the United States as well as at home, Petersen repeatedly told the story of a remarkable transformation and fashioned himself as the embodiment of the "repentant sinner."[62]

When first elected to the Bundestag in 1965, Petersen was one of its youngest parliamentarians.[63] While he negotiated with the Council, he was a member of the Bundestag's defense committee, an issue that was also of personal importance to him. In 1984, he wrote a book, titled *Sind wir noch zu retten? (Can we still be saved?)*, addressed to his nineteen-year-old son and his generation, the generation of the peace movement, trying to explain why the West needed to remain strong in its confrontation with the Soviet Union.[64] Petersen later also stressed that his opposition to the USHMM in part resulted from his son's experiences abroad, where the latter had been "blamed for the mess" Petersen's generation had caused.[65] However, Petersen did not want to be reduced to the role of strengthening the Western alliance at home, but wanted to play an active role in the Federal Republic's foreign policy matters.[66]

Two encounters, in 1980 and 1981 respectively, shaped his attitudes toward American Jews and American Holocaust memorial culture. During his frequent visits to the United States, Petersen had noticed that a Jewish congressman, the Democrat James Scheuer, consistently avoided talking to him. Thus Petersen approached him directly in 1980.[67] In the course of this conversation, it became clear that Scheuer had not wanted to speak with a German of Petersen's generation, the generation old enough to have been involved in Nazi crimes. Petersen took the initiative and told Scheuer about his experiences during the Third Reich and his subsequent conversion to Christianity. His openness paid off, as he told his constituents at home in a newsletter: "Since that day, the Federal Republic and I personally do not have a better friend in the American Congress."[68] The other key moment followed a meeting between Chancellor Schmidt and Howard Squadron, the chairman of the Conference of Presidents of Major American Jewish Organizations, on May 21, 1981.[69] This meeting resulted in a fierce discussion about the Federal Republic's policy toward Israel, which caused Squadron to publish a negative article about Schmidt in the

New York Post.[70] According to Petersen's assessment—as well as the assessment of the Chancellery—this meeting was a "fiasco" and the image of Schmidt in the American mass media had deteriorated "abruptly and dramatically."[71]

Such events were crucial in shaping Petersen's attitude toward the role of Jews in American society and the "Holocaust problem" in German–American relations.[72] They furthermore point to the significance of personal connections for foreign policy making and also allow some broader conclusions about the relationship between Germans and Jews. Petersen concluded that Germans could not escape the "special relationship" with Jews, but if they were open, sincere, and considerate, they could "gain the best friends."[73] To him, the importance of the Holocaust for America's Jews was a result of Israel's threatened status in the Middle East as well as attempts to make sense of the millions of deaths by working toward making the world "more sensitive" to human rights catastrophes. Helmut Schmidt had accordingly neither understood that the subject of Israel required special sensitivity nor that he, as a World War II veteran, would be treated with a certain degree of suspicion. Despite such insightful considerations as well as Petersen's honesty about his Nazi past, he was also open about his rather pragmatic concerns, which, in the end, closely resembled old anti-Semitic stereotypes: "It is impossible," he wrote in 1981 in a report on Jewish life in America, "to overestimate the Jewish influence on the mass media."[74] That Petersen would act on such assumptions about an alleged influence of Jews over the mass media became obvious after the Bitburg controversy. In reference to Schmidt's encounter with Squadron and concerned about Kohl's image in the United States, he tried to prevent Kohl from making the same "mistakes."[75]

Petersen also laid the most important foundation for the Kohl government's interaction with the Holocaust Council: establishing a personal relationship with Elie Wiesel. Petersen and Wiesel met for the first time in late 1984.[76] At this occasion, Petersen informed Wiesel of Kohl's worries about the potential negative impact of the USHMM on German–American relations and West Germany's image in the United States. To avoid such damage, the close relationship between both countries as well as between the Federal Republic and Israel should, according to Petersen, be represented in the museum's exhibition.[77] Even though this first encounter did not produce concrete results, Petersen managed to establish a "friendship" with Wiesel. He would usually put this word in quotation marks when talking about Wiesel, illustrating a certain degree of ambiguity about their relationship. They continued to meet and even set up a committee—the United States-German Committee on Learning and Remembrance—to discuss issues related to the USHMM in 1985, which existed until Wiesel's resignation as Council chairman in December 1986.

It is possible that Petersen's biography appealed to Wiesel.[78] However, Wiesel's commitment to reconciliation and preserving the memory of the

Holocaust notwithstanding, his willingness to meet with Petersen and even to support his plans to set up a committee to discuss the concept of the USHMM were probably not entirely altruistic. Even though Wiesel later maintained that he had "had no contact with Kohl's government," he benefitted directly from cooperating with Petersen.[79] For several years, he had been a contender for a Nobel Prize, both in literature and for the Peace Prize.[80] Efforts on behalf of the Council to support his candidacy also included lobbying with the German government for support.[81] In the Federal Republic, it was Petersen who orchestrated a campaign of the Bundestag to support Wiesel's bid for the Nobel Peace Price both in 1985 and 1986, the year it was successful.[82] At the USHMM, Petersen came to be known as "the person who had the campaign in the Bundestag to get signatures for the Nobel for Elie."[83] He was also the only German officially invited to the award ceremony for Wiesel in Oslo, and it was clear to him that his efforts to negotiate with Wiesel received a "significant boost" through the Nobel Prize.[84]

Even though Petersen would later only speak with respect about Wiesel, during the early years of their acquaintance, his motives oscillated between self-interest and genuine admiration. While considering various ways to facilitate a conversation about the design of the museum, supporting

Figure 3.8 Elie Wiesel (b. 1928) at a press conference in the mid-1980s. Evangelischer Pressedienst, Frankfurt/M.

Wiesel's Nobel Prize campaign evolved as the most promising strategy. In order to convince the museum planners to accommodate the Kohl government's suggestions, Petersen wrote, "we would have to get the leading American Jews on our side, and for this purpose it would be ideal to support the efforts of the most prominent Jew, Prof. Elie Wiesel, to get the Nobel Prize."[85] In his correspondence with other members of the Bundestag, Petersen was quite explicit that it was necessary to appease "the Jews" because they—and especially his "'friend' Wiesel"—were politically extremely powerful.[86] According to Petersen, this had become clear when fifty-three US senators signed a protest letter against Reagan's visit to Bitburg in early 1985. In an almost cynical assessment with clearly anti-Semitic undertones, Petersen warned that the protest, allegedly orchestrated by American Jews, had the potential to "effectively poison" the Western alliance, "unless we manage to satisfy or at least neutralize the influential Jews in America."[87] In order to protect the alliance, Petersen considered a certain policy necessary:

> I will continue to do everything to win over the Jews of America, not because they are particularly nice people (some of them really aren't), but because I want to avert damage from the alliance; because what's the use of insisting on our principles and end up facing a ruined alliance. . . . Especially in this context, we cannot choose our partners, and there is simply no way around Wiesel and his Holocaust-Council, even if it would be easy to imagine more pleasant partners.[88]

It may not have been a coincidence that Petersen chose such confrontational language in a letter to Alfred Dregger, a most outspoken critic of American protest against the Bitburg visit, who also saw the alliance threatened by "forces which would like to abuse the commemoration of May 8, 1945."[89] Petersen probably assumed that criticism of these "forces" would resonate well with Dregger, who had been a member of the Nazi Party, but—in contrast to Petersen—never talked about his Nazi past publicly.[90]

Incidentally, the German extreme right vehemently disapproved of Petersen's efforts vis-à-vis the Council. The *Deutsche National-Zeitung* (*German National Newspaper*), for instance, not only severely criticized the plans for an American Holocaust museum, but also personally attacked Petersen. As the United States showed no "shame" for the "extermination of the Indians" as well as a "multitude of the most terrible crimes against humanity," plans to build a museum about "German acts of moral turpitude" were particularly inappropriate. Former Nazis like Petersen, the paper argued, acted as accomplices to such an endeavor, which made it impossible for the Federal Republic to escape the Nazi past. Instead of cooperating with a Holocaust museum abroad, they should rather come to terms with "their own past."[91]

In any event, the letters Petersen and about eighty additional members of the Bundestag sent to Oslo in support of Wiesel's bid for the Nobel Peace Prize did have the desired effect—certainly in Washington. When he met with Wiesel in early 1985, Petersen showed him the impressive list of signatures under the support letter he had drafted and made the suggestion to create the Committee on Learning and Remembrance to which Wiesel agreed.[92] Not surprisingly, the wording of the official German recommendation differed from what Petersen had told his colleagues in the Bundestag. Its members recommended awarding Wiesel the Nobel Peace Prize not because he was the United States' "most prominent Jew," but because

> with great persuasion he has encouraged people around the world to reach a higher grade of moral sensitivity.... It would be a great encouragement for all, among them the German people, who dedicate themselves to reconciliation.[93]

Later, Petersen would take all the credit for "having secured" the Nobel Peace Prize for Wiesel, which had "opened a lot of doors" in the "Jewish world of the USA" for him.[94] Yet Petersen further claimed that Wiesel's first visit to Germany since 1945, which he had arranged, had completely changed the latter's "attitude toward Germany."[95] Despite the fact that Wiesel later denied some form of quid pro quo with Petersen, Council members also assumed that the two had struck a deal. In 2000 the former vice chairman of the Council, William Lowenberg, went on the record stating that Wiesel had been, unlike himself, much more willing to accommodate German requests to negotiate the design of the museum: "Elie helped them, didn't he? Elie tried. Why do you think he got the Nobel? [The] Nobel was awarded ... you know that story."[96]

The Nobel Prize episode points to Petersen's ambivalence toward the Council in general and his Jewish interlocutors in particular. On the one hand, Petersen's writings to his Bundestag colleagues were full of stereotypes about the alleged character of Jews and their power over American public opinion. On the other hand, his respect and empathy for Wiesel were deep and sincere. This ambiguity becomes quite obvious in a letter Petersen sent to the foreign and security policy expert and vice chairman of the CDU/CSU parliamentary group, Volker Rühe:

> If a man, who saw his sister being burned alive and whose father died in his arms when he was only 15 years old, agrees to talk to us, I am grateful and will not make any demands. If the same man is given an award, which has only been conferred 40 times throughout history, by the president in the White House following a resolution of

Congress, if he and his friends then manage within two days to collect 80 signatures in the Senate and 400 in the House of Representatives against the arrangement of his president's visit to Germany,
this then reveals, how much influence these people hold.[97]

His characterization of American Jews, whom he either referred to as "the
Jews," "these people," or Elie Wiesel's "friends," suggests that it was not unusual
in internal correspondence to speak of Jews pejoratively, but also to assume
that American Jews formed a single, coordinated community with a significant
influence over the political establishment in Washington—the stereotype of
the "Jewish lobby," which neglected the diversity of opinion and policies in the
American Jewish community. Petersen's ambivalence represented more than
just the tactics and inner conflicts of a human being with clear political interests. It was indicative of a more general postwar German unease about dealing
with the survivors of the Holocaust. Expressions of guilt, compassion, and empathy were in conflict with still existing anti-Semitic notions of Jewish power
and influence.

The United States Holocaust Memorial Council
and the Federal Republic

Despite such tensions on a political level, Council representatives in general
established good relations with German archivists and representatives of
concentration camp memorials in the mid-1980s. Nevertheless, some representatives had distinctively negative experiences in the Federal Republic,
which corroborated their critical position. For example, when a small delegation visited a number of European concentration camp memorial sites and
archives to inspect documents and artifacts in fall 1984, they realized that
several German institutions feared competition from the Council's plan to
establish a major Holocaust-related archive as part of the museum.[98] In November 1985, the Council's senior historian, Sybil Milton, went on an exploratory trip to Germany to meet with German archivists and representatives of
concentration camp memorial sites. At a seminar organized by Action Recon-
ciliation/Service for Peace (Aktion Sühnezeichen/Friedensdienste) and the
Friedrich Ebert Foundation, she attempted to calm the concerns of German
representatives of memorial sites that the Council would try to influence
German–American relations.[99] Since the Council had launched a campaign
against Ronald Reagan's visit to Bitburg just six months earlier, however,
Milton's statement was hardly credible. Milton was furthermore confronted
with the assumption that the United States government wanted to divert

attention from its own past crimes against Native Americans or slavery by building a monument to the Holocaust and thereby "externalizing evil," a view that could be found in Germany until well into the 2000s.[100] Milton countered such accusations by pointing to the fact that the Council's mandate was limited to the Holocaust and did not include dealing with the legacies of United States policies toward Native Americans and slavery.

Back in the United States, she took a rather critical stance toward the Federal Republic's process of coping with the Nazi past. She particularly lamented the absence of a monument for the victims of the Holocaust in Berlin.[101] Furthermore, she found fault with the Gedenkstätte Deutscher Widerstand (the memorial for German anti-Nazi resistance) in Berlin. She considered the exaggerated importance of the German military resistance for the democratic tradition of West Germany a "blatant falsification of history" for "dubious ends."[102] Helmut Kohl's devotion to this memorial—he stressed the resistance's relevance for West German dignity and considered it an act of "self-liberation"— was, according to Milton, "inadequate" and "imbalanced."[103] In general, Milton concluded that West Berlin's memorial work was insufficient as far as the memorialization of the Holocaust was concerned.[104] In addition, exhibition "plans for the 1987 750th centenary of the city of Berlin" did not "include either the Jews or the Nazi period in Berlin." "Official support" for such projects was not likely.[105] Milton summarized:

> The nature of memorial work in West Berlin and its inadequacy is of central importance to the USHMC [United States Holocaust Memorial Council], since it reflects the voiced and unvoiced objections of many German CDU politicians to the USHMC in Washington and enables us to understand the position of Helmut Kohl, that the USH Memorial Museum is by definition anti-German.[106]

Not only did such an assessment confirm assumptions about the insufficiency of the Federal Republic's coping with the Nazi past as well as corroborate a skeptical stance toward German officials more generally, but it also substantiated a global claim for leadership with regard to Holocaust memory. In a world where Germans seemed incapable of coming to terms with their own history, it was up to the United States to take over the power of interpretation and to "preserve" the memory of the Holocaust.[107]

In early 1985, the Council had come to a similar conclusion in the context of Reagan's controversial visit to Bitburg. In a series of emergency meetings, Council members discussed ways to prevent Reagan from visiting the cemetery and even considered resigning in protest.[108] The Council saw Bitburg above all as a domestic crisis as the actions of the president seemed to threaten its project to integrate the memory of the Holocaust into American historical con-sciousness.[109] Yet Bitburg also weakened Bonn's position vis-à-vis the USHMM as the event confirmed the impression in Washington that the Federal Repub-lic could not deal responsibly with the Nazi past.[110] One Council member was candid in his criticism of Kohl and questioned whether the chancellor was "sin-cere about reconciliation."[111]

Such a highly critical assessment hardly corresponded with the truth. Kohl had been criticized for his insistence on the Bitburg visit as well as its ambigu-ous implications, but he was a credible opponent of any kind of neo-Nazi revival and certainly no revisionist.[112] A nuanced evaluation that took the German position into consideration did not occur in the Council. What mattered for the negotiations with German emissaries were negative impressions of a defi-cient memorial culture in Berlin and scandals related to the Nazi past. The first encounters between representatives of the USHMM and the Federal Republic thus illustrate a certain degree of antagonism, but also a lack of knowledge about each other's cultural frames of reference. They further reveal how in-strumental personal experiences during the period of the Third Reich—and thereafter—were for German–American-Jewish dialogue as well as German–American relations in general.[113] Holocaust survivors involved in the creation of the USHMM had a generally negative attitude toward West Germany, shaped by their individual suffering, but also by a certain cultural imprint. Then again, German emissaries had multiple, conflicting items on their agenda: reaching certain political objectives against what they perceived as Jewish power and in-fluence in the United States, but also creating the impression that they sought to make a sincere gesture of reconciliation. All of these strands came together in Petersen, who in a way embodied the transformation from Nazism to democ-racy that (West) Germany as a whole had experienced. This learning process—from perpetrator to partner in the Western alliance—created a demand for respect on behalf of the Federal Republic as well as Petersen. Survivors of the Holocaust were, however, very reluctant to show such respect.

Learning and Remembering

Despite such a difficult constellation, a series of formal meetings between museum representatives and intermediaries of the West German government took place beginning in mid-1985 under the umbrella of the United States-German Committee on Learning and Remembrance, which Elie Wiesel and Peter Petersen created in 1985.[114] A few weeks after this encounter, Wiesel met with Ambassador van Well and left him with the impression that German in-volvement in the design of the exhibition of the museum would be a central task of this committee.[115] Petersen also reported to Kohl that he had suggested to Wiesel the idea of creating a small study group of "two Germans" and "two Jews" to jointly design a hall in the museum in which "our concept" could be put on display.[116] Wiesel was, according to Petersen, excited about this idea and decided to expand the group to include five representatives from each country who should discuss "what we have learned jointly" from history.[117] For Petersen and Kohl, who officially nominated the members of the German delegation, it was clear that the design of the exhibition was subject to discussion, and that lessons that both sides had learned from the Holocaust would be part of this process of negotiations.

Even though the committee existed only for a short period of time, it was the sole instance in which Council representatives officially discussed issues concerning the museum with German emissaries. These talks gave both sides an opportunity to debate their diverging views on the establishment of the Holocaust museum and were supposed to provide a basis for future mutual understanding.[118] To Wiesel, who had asked political scientist and historian Raul Hilberg to join the committee, educational cooperation—especially improvement of Holocaust education in West Germany—was the main goal of this endeavor. The German delegation had a different agenda: the discussion of the content of the museum's permanent exhibition.[119] Kohl took this project very seriously and nominated in addition to Petersen two well-established public relations experts—a member of his "kitchen cabinet" and an official in the Press and Information Office of the Federal Government (Bundespresseamt), Wolfgang Bergsdorf, and the former Social Democratic Lord Mayor of Berlin, ambassador to Israel, and now head of Germany's international broadcaster *Deutsche Welle*, Klaus Schütz.[120] While no information on the precise reasons for these appointments is available, it is likely that Kohl chose Schütz because of his close connections to the Berlin Jewish community, to give the delegation a bipartisan appearance, and because of Schütz' expertise in the field of public diplomacy.[121] Kohl also appointed historian Klaus Hildebrand, who was one of the most influential conservative historians in the Federal Republic and would soon thereafter find himself on the defense along with Ernst Nolte, Andreas Hillgruber, and Michael Stürmer during the Historians' Controversy.[122]

In Germany, Petersen explained to his colleagues, for example to Volker Rühe, the rationale behind the committee. According to Petersen it aimed at expanding the museum's concept beyond "German-Jewish history"—a euphemism for the Holocaust—to speak about the "crimes that man was capable to do to other men in this century so that we could appeal to humanity's conscience."[123] Two diverging views of a "universalized" Holocaust narrative thus collided during these negotiations: while representatives of the USHMM aimed at making the Holocaust the benchmark for assessing human evil, German officials wanted to see the Holocaust as one event in an extremely violent century, during which other countries had committed mass murder and genocide as well. Petersen thus planned to convince "the Jews in Washington," as he stated, not only to talk about "the crimes Germans committed against Jews," but also "human rights violations more generally."[124] This expansion of the focus of the museum's exhibition aimed at taking a comparative approach toward the representation of genocide and rejected the notion of the Holocaust as a "singular" or "unique" event. Such an effort to adjust the museum's focus would eventually also destigmatize the Federal Republic as not only Germans would be portrayed as perpetrators. While the flight from German specificities and to generalize beyond the Holocaust to other episodes of genocide were not unique to conservatives and existed across the political spectrum, this line of argument indeed served to underscore Petersen's case in Washington.[125] Kohl, in any event, was highly supportive of Petersen's endeavors, as the latter reported to the leading CDU politician and president of the Bundestag, Philipp Jenninger.[126]

The committee convened for the first time on June 24, 1985, in New York City.[127] Wiesel held high hopes for its future role and stated that it would open "'a new avenue' in German–American relations without forgetting the Holocaust."[128] Even though the committee was not created in reaction to the Bitburg visit, it could have prevented this controversy had it been founded earlier, Wiesel explained.[129] Ambassador van Well—not officially a member of the committee—spoke on behalf of the German government and appealed to the museum representatives to integrate the success story of the Federal Republic in the exhibition concept. He emphasized the merits of the new Germany and offered to help the USHMM "to give as whole and complete an account of the truth as possible."[130] In addition to restitution payments to Israel, Germany's Western integration, and the joint struggle with the United States against Communism, this "truth" included:

> The all-pervasive forces of totalitarianism, the lures and terror of systematic perversion of the human mind, the German resistance, the tortures and the blood sacrifices connected to the 20th of July, 1944, the untold heroism of German families standing by their Jewish friends in the face of terror and intimidation, and their scroll of Honor remembered in Israel.[131]

Well neither addressed the extent of the involvement of German society in the crimes of National Socialism, nor did he clearly identify the perpetrators of the Holocaust. Ultimately, so it seems, the Holocaust was supposed to be told in the museum as a story where the role of perpetrators fell to only a small criminal clique, while the vast majority of Germans had been seduced or terrorized by a totalitarian regime, and had become its victims or even heroes of anti-Nazi resistance. Even though the historical profession would make the Holocaust only a major focus of research in the 1990s, it was certainly known during the 1980s that neither resistance nor heroism had been the predominant forms of experience of the average German during the Third Reich.[132]

Schütz and Petersen also suggested cooperation between the USHMM and the German Historical Museum in Berlin. Still in the planning stages, the German Historical Museum was to be a centerpiece of Helmut Kohl's domestic politics of history:[133] If the Council allowed the German delegation to "have input into" the design of the USHMM's permanent exhibition, "we could have your input as to how we can tell the story of the Jews."[134] Petersen stressed that the delegation was in close consultation with the chancellor on this issue.[135] In fact, Kohl later even explained in his memoirs that he conceived the idea for a German Historical Museum when he learned about the plans for the USHMM.[136] However, the American delegation did not want to discuss the design of the permanent exhibition at this point in time.

The committee also explored other fields of possible cooperation, such as education and scholarship.[137] At the center of their attention was the question of how to educate the youth about the Holocaust. With regards to young Germans, the committee acknowledged that this was a particularly difficult task, as they needed to accept the legacy of the Holocaust without feeling guilty for it. Further ideas, such as a student exchange program or a joint publishing program, were also postponed. Raul Hilberg suggested improvements that could be made for scholars.[138] He was particularly concerned about the restrictive protection of Holocaust perpetrators' personal data by German privacy laws and severely criticized working conditions for young Holocaust historians in Germany. Even though Germany had excellent scholars, choosing the Holocaust as a field of study meant that they "will not have a career,"[139] which Hilberg considered an indicator for a boycott of Holocaust studies by German universities.[140] The committee could therefore provide a forum for German historians to present their research to larger audiences. Hildebrand rejected this idea, stating that it was a "general fate" of historians not to find employment, which had nothing to do with the fact that they studied the Holocaust.

The first meeting thus ended without concrete results, but the positions of both sides had become clear. For the German delegation, German heroism and victimization as well as the history of the "new Germany" were part and parcel of the "truth" about the Holocaust and thus should be represented in the museum. It needs to be stressed that at least Petersen and Schütz did not aim at suppressing the public remembrance of the Holocaust in general. To them, however, it should also include the history of the "new Germany." Petersen's statements revealed that he was genuinely interested in intellectual exchange. For instance, he cautioned the committee against incorporating the West German claim, as supported by Hildebrand, that the Holocaust provided a primary motivation for the July 20, 1944, group's attempt to assassinate

Hitler. Nevertheless, the American delegation felt confirmed in their skepticism toward the Kohl government.[141]

Despite disagreement on key issues, Ambassador van Well sent a positive assessment of this first formal meeting back to the Foreign Office, which passed it on to the Chancellery. Accordingly, the German delegation had suggested a focus beyond "topics such as Auschwitz" during the first meeting. More importantly, Well stressed that Wiesel had guaranteed Petersen, in a private conversation, that the museum "would under no circumstance have an anti-German character."[142] Well even assumed that Wiesel and the Council were at the time overwhelmed with the task of building a museum and had not made final decisions about its concept. In the event that the joint committee would prove to be a success, the opportunity might arise to design the museum together. The German embassy's "obvious concern" that the "German side" would have to make a financial contribution in such a scenario had "thus far not been confirmed. Money had not been mentioned at the meeting."[143] Considering the rather unproductive discussion of the meeting and the lukewarm attitude of several American members toward their German counterparts, this optimism was rather surprising—and indeed, it would not last long.

The second—and at the same time last—official meetings of the committee took place in Bonn and Berlin in January 1986.[144] This was also Wiesel's first visit to Germany since his liberation from the Buchenwald concentration camp. The committee members met with high-ranking German politicians and functionaries, such as the Lord Mayor of Berlin, Eberhard Diepgen; a vice president of the Bundestag, Heinz Westphal (SPD); and Werner Nachmann, the chairman of the Central Council of Jews in Germany. The committee visited the center of the Berlin Jewish community and the House of the Wannsee Conference, at the time a school youth hostel of the Neukölln district,[145] and it is possible that the visit to the Wannsee Villa gave the impetus for the creation of a memorial museum in this location.[146] In addition to several ceremonies, the committee discussed Holocaust education in the United States, Germany, and Israel.[147] Contrary to initial plans, Helmut Kohl did not meet with the group in Bonn, and also the discussion of the museum's exhibition proved rather unproductive.[148] Petersen again stressed that Kohl was concerned that the "manner of representation of the Holocaust" in the United States would damage German–American relations, and that the museum in Washington might become "a demonstration against Germany."[149] Yet beyond reiterating their established positions, the committee members did not reach any concrete decisions. To some members of the American delegation the purpose of the committee seemed questionable, maybe even pointless, and the group as a whole was unable to come up with a precise statement to pass on to the press. Hilberg even wondered: "What is the task of this group?"[150] And Wiesel concluded rather ambiguously: "We have made progress, but it is not tangible."[151]

Nevertheless, "The Week in Germany," the New York-based German Information Center's weekly newsletter, announced on January 24 that "one of the first results of the meeting was the decision . . . that the West German side will contribute to the development of the Holocaust Memorial Museum to be built in Washington."[152] In contrast to the American delegation, the German delegation saw a major breakthrough for their project of shaping the future content of the museum. Given the attitudes of Americans, the Germans' optimism is puzzling. Maybe Wiesel created false hopes—perhaps even in return for the Nobel Peace Prize nomination—or his German interlocutors simply misread him. In any event, Wiesel must have known that other Council members vehemently rejected his negotiations with German delegates. Petersen would soon find out about their position toward the Kohl government and its efforts vis-à-vis the museum.

On December 4, 1986, Petersen and Schütz were scheduled to speak to the entire Council in Washington.[153] The night before, Petersen was supposed to meet with Wiesel to plan a strategy for his presentation to the Council as well as public presentations, meetings, and photo opportunities with Reagan and Vice President Bush for 1987.[154] This would have meant official approval for their project from the highest authorities in the United States. However, Petersen's hopes were to be disappointed as his and Schütz's visit to the Council overlapped with unforeseen circumstances. The very day of the scheduled presentation, Wiesel submitted his letter of resignation to Reagan, a fact known neither to the Council nor to the German emissaries.[155] As the museum project was entering a critical stage and demanded a chairman with "expertise in management, administration, finance, and construction," Wiesel decided to resign.[156] As a matter of fact, controversies between the "spiritual" leader Wiesel and more experienced fundraisers, such as Albert Abramson and Harvey M. Meyerhoff, had created serious tensions within the Council. Furthermore, Wiesel's mystical understanding of the Holocaust had made the implementation of such an interpretation in the museum rather complicated.[157]

Despite Wiesel's absence, Petersen and Schütz spoke at the Council meeting, yet they did not address their concerns regarding the exhibit content. As they were pressed for time, they only spoke about Holocaust education in Germany and made an offer to cooperate in the design of the future memorial in the Wannsee Villa.[158] The majority of the Council was not aware that Wiesel had invited Petersen and Schütz to attend the meeting on December 4 and was "appalled" when they learned about it.[159] The future vice chairman of the Council, William Lowenberg, expressed his refusal to meet for further talks or even negotiations: "I don't make deals with Germans."[160] This negative attitude toward the successor state of the Third Reich notwithstanding, Lowenberg would later become one of the key contacts of unofficial German messengers at the Council. It is almost ironic that one of them, Walther Leisler Kiep, remarked a few years later about Lowenberg: "Despite [his] cruel fate, he is neither bitter nor inaccessible for our objective."[161] While museum representatives openly communicated a critical stance about the Germans when they were among themselves, the German delegation was not exposed to such attitudes directly. After Wiesel's resignation, the Council unofficially agreed not to meet with German officials to discuss the museum project.[162] No further meetings of the Committee on Learning and Remembrance took place as Wiesel's successor as Council Chairman, Harvey Meyerhoff, dissolved it in December 1986.[163]

The brief history of this committee illustrates how seriously the West German government took the issue of the USHMM. The series of meetings on both sides of the Atlantic included some of Kohl's close advisors and experts for questions of public relations and history. The goals of the German delegation were clear from the outset: to adjust the future concept of the USHMM in a way to compare the Holocaust with other genocides, as well as to include references to German history that would send a positive message about the Federal Republic. The American delegation was, at the very least, reluctant to discuss such proposals, much less willing to provide a forum for self-promotion to West Germany. This confrontation, in combination with previously established antagonistic attitudes on both sides, resulted in a fundamental misunderstanding about the purpose of the committee and, ultimately, its dissolution. In his conversations with Petersen, Wiesel had created hopes that were impossible to fulfill. Yet the explicit opposition of other Council members to accommodating West German political goals could not have been a secret to him. Wiesel's role in this episode remains ambiguous.

Challenges and Dilemmas for the Council

The dissolution of the Committee on Learning and Remembrance did not—as some Council members intended—end the dialogue between the Council and Petersen.[164] Petersen continued to correspond with the Council's International Relations Committee (IRC), chaired by Miles Lerman, who refused to set up a new formal committee with German representatives.[165] The IRC was, among other things, in charge of securing artifacts and archival materials abroad for the USHMM. The discussions at this stage illustrate a slight change in position of Council representatives, which resulted in a series of dilemmas: while they refused to engage in official dialogue with German emissaries, they were aware that the museum could not be built entirely without cooperation with German authorities. Museum representatives also acknowledged that the Federal Republic was not Nazi Germany, and that some of their worries were irrational. The German side, which had lost an important advocate with the departure of Wiesel, continued to stress concerns about the USHMM. But German intermediaries went even further. On several occasions, they claimed for themselves a right of codetermination in regard to the shaping of Holocaust memory abroad on the basis of their nationality. They maintained that the museum should not only tell the story of the Holocaust until 1945, but needed to include the development of a postwar democratic Germany.

A first conversation during this phase of the negotiations took place in late June 1987.[166] On this occasion, Petersen offered an official donation of artifacts to the USHMM by the German government and also suggested that he would help museum archivists get access to German archives. In return, he hoped to arrange a meeting of the dissolved Committee on Learning and Remembrance, the IRC, and the USHMM's Content Committee, which was in charge of designing the permanent exhibition.[167] The position of the museum's representatives, however, remained unchanged: they welcomed a donation in the form of artifacts or archival materials, but wanted to avoid any gesture that could be interpreted as an invitation to discuss the museum design.[168] Project director Berenbaum did not want to negotiate with the Kohl government regarding the gift at all, but rather wanted to compile a "shopping list" of archival materials it could provide to the USHMM. He furthermore emphasized that the Council's main task was to "preserve Holocaust materials," not to "develop German-Jewish dialogue" or to conduct "foreign policy."[169] This marked a significant departure from Wiesel's position a few years earlier.

In 1988, conversations between Petersen and the IRC continued. In a meeting in February with Lerman and Benjamin Meed, a prominent spokesperson for Holocaust survivors and the chairman of the USHMM's content committee, Petersen again probed the chances for an integration of the history of the new Germany into the museum's exhibition.[170] Lerman and Meed replied that the museum intended to speak about German Nazi victims and opponents, such as Martin Niemöller, yet vehemently stressed that Petersen's initiatives would not alter the narrative of the museum: "Efforts to sanitize the past will not even be considered."[171] Lerman and Meed "made it clear to Mr. Petersen that the Council was not interested in any money for the construction of the U.S. museum," but stated that they were willing to consider an invitation of the museum's archivists and historians to the Federal Republic.[172] Furthermore, they were skeptical about Petersen's suggestion to arrange a meeting with historians "who have the confidence of Chancellor Helmut Kohl," as they were well aware of their position toward the museum.[173] Such a meeting and the donation of artifacts could only occur, Lerman and Meed argued, if the Federal Republic did not expect any concession with regard to the exhibition design in return. This put Petersen in a difficult situation. He wanted to demonstrate willingness to support the museum, but also stressed that the federal government could not make a donation "without knowing what the full museum treatment of Germany would be."[174] Despite the fact that the IRC signaled certain room for negotiation, Petersen could not agree to their terms. Giving up the claim for codetermination of the exhibition design would have defeated the whole purpose of his endeavors.

In May 1988, the IRC decided to contact Petersen and asked for a "specific proposal."[175] In his reply, Petersen spoke about Kohl's concerns, his relationship with Wiesel and the campaign for the Nobel Prize, and again asked for an opportunity to meet with the content committee to discuss the USHMM's exhibition design. He restated the concerns and expectations of the West German government and fortified the claim that the Federal Republic should be consulted in the telling of the history of the Holocaust:

> [The] Holocaust is part of your history. It is also part of our history, the darkest part any people can carry. If we Germans face the truth—and only the truth can make us free—then obviously that truth will have to have formed the basis of the Federal Republic. We would like to have a chance to show how this has been translated into our constitution, our laws, our relationship to Israel, the attempts of restitution. . . . In another way Israel, of course, is also a result of the Holocaust, and here we could imagine that the story of the Federal Republic and the story of Israel should have a part in a Holocaust Museum, not in an attempt to cover up anything, but as an encouragement for people and nations to learn from the past and become free for the future.[176]

The IRC's reaction to this letter is unknown, and there are no indicators for further interaction between Petersen and the Council.[177] In July 1989, Lerman remarked that Petersen had not contacted him again.[178] A meeting with Petersen had been scheduled for September, which Lerman cancelled because of time constraints; this caused great irritation with Petersen, who complained to Philipp Jenninger that "the Jews have cancelled once again and postponed the talks."[179] While it is not entirely clear why the contact between Petersen and the museum collapsed, Petersen's withdrawal and his replacement by other emissaries were probably connected to tensions with his colleagues at home. In particular, Volker Rühe, the CDU/CSU parliamentary vice chairman in charge of approving the funding for Petersen's trips to the United States, had not been supportive of Petersen's efforts. Although Rühe shared the skeptical attitude of other major CDU politicians toward the plans for the USHMM, he demanded a rather forceful intervention, expected Petersen "not to give in to the Jews," and thought that his attempts to negotiate with museum representatives were pointless.[180] Also known among his colleagues as "Volker Rüpel"[181]—"Volker the Boor"—he was quite frank in his disapproval of Petersen's negotiations with the representatives of the museum, to which Petersen replied in a letter:

Even if you think this is all nonsense ("Your shitty museum"), I will continue. Even if I will not benefit from this politicially at all, I hold the naïve opinion that we all serve a purpose that is bigger than each and every one of us.[182]

Petersen kept on stressing the benefits of personal diplomacy, despite his frustration with the lack of support from his parliamentary group.[183]

In May 1989 Petersen explained to Kohl that the current representatives of the Council were not willing to continue the negotiations with German emissaries.[184] This could change, however, once the newly elected president, George H. W. Bush, appointed new members to the Council. For the time being, Petersen suggested to Kohl a change in strategy: to turn inward and change the way the story of the Holocaust and its aftermath were told in German concentration camp memorials. Instead of only representing "the horror," these sites could show what "Germans and Jews" have "learned and achieved together over the past 40 years." The Federal Republic needed to provide "the American Jews" with an example of how the history of Holocaust could be told, thus preventing the USHMM from becoming a "symbol of hate and hopelessness."[185] Given the difficult process and the fierce controversies over finding acceptable forms of memorialization at these former sites of Nazi terror (as well as the question of local authority), it is highly unlikely that the kind of positive addition that Petersen imagined could have been installed at such a site.

Even with Petersen out of the picture, German opposition to the USHMM continued. In September 1988, another unofficial messenger of Kohl, a close confidant and head of his office as the CDU's chairman in Bonn, Michael Roik, met with Sybil Milton and Michael Berenbaum in Washington.[186] That Kohl sent Roik, who had no official political or diplomatic mandate, was in keeping with his way of governing.[187] Kohl often delegated delicate issues to close confidants who would take care of them outside of the context of their formally assigned positions. In the United States, Roik went on a tour exploring several sites of Holocaust memorialization in the United States. During his stop in Washington, Milton and Berenbaum showed him slides of the museum layout and explained the concept of the exhibition and the building. Roik, the first German intermediary to get a tangible impression of the USHMM's concept, was not pleased by what he saw. He objected to the plans for the USHMM, also explicitly in the name of Kohl. As Milton recorded in a memorandum, Roik expressed his disapproval with reference to the slides: "'Wouldn't this upset young German visitors to the Museum?' . . . 'Wouldn't this be virtually meaningless to young Americans, prejudicing their reaction to West German democracy today?'"[188] Stressing the impact on young Germans and Americans, Roik clearly alluded to the debates about the successor generation and the future of German–American relations. His concerns point to a twofold objective: to defend the reputation of the Federal Republic abroad as well as to protect Germans from being exposed to a Holocaust museum in the United States. Maybe he even feared that German voters would blame such a lack of protection of West Germany's image abroad on Kohl and his government. In any event, Roik manifested the opposition of the Kohl government to the USHMM. Repeated efforts by Milton to convince Roik that his fears were unfounded and that Americans would not judge the Federal Republic based on what would be shown in the USHMM were in vain. Milton concluded:

> There seems to be no way we can convince the CDU that it is not our intention to malign nor praise the FRG, but that we intend to tell the full historical truth as it happened, without concern about West German prestige or image.[189]

Still, the IRC continued to deal with German reservations. In July 1989, the IRC agreed that no "formal" or "institutionalized" dialogue with the Federal Republic that went beyond the acquisition of artifacts, documents, or books was desired from the museum's perspective.[190] At this meeting, Lerman also posed the question of how the IRC should proceed in case a monetary gift were made by "a German individual or government."[191] For the time being the IRC agreed with the suggestion of Raul Hilberg not to reject such money, but to use it for the acquisition of archival documents and books in Germany. This may have been the case because securing the necessary funds to build a large museum with an extensive archive and library had proven to be more difficult than the planners of the museum had imagined.

Again in April 1990, the IRC put relations with the Federal Republic on its agenda as the German government and German corporations—their names were not mentioned in the minutes—had apparently offered money to the USHMM. Lerman explained, without going into detail:

> Monetary gifts. I'm talking about monetary gifts. We made it clear that at one juncture, it was put out to us by the German Government [sic], by the West German Government [sic], whether we would entertain an idea for accepting a very large gift from them, and we gave them a resounding "no."[192]

Even though it had come at a time when the USHMM faced fundraising problems, Lerman suggested treating offers from German companies in the same way. Among the IRC members were several Holocaust survivors and former forced laborers who had vehemently rejected accepting such donations.[193] Thus, the IRC unanimously adopted a resolution, acknowledging the democratic character of the Federal Republic and rejecting the notion of collective guilt for the

German people. However, the members of the IRC found "accepting moneys from German governments or corporations or industries for the United States Holocaust Memorial Museum both troublesome and unacceptable."[194] Yet this resolution put the IRC in another dilemma. Since making it public would have threatened the IRC's access to the archives of German corporations, it was resolved that the statement would not be publicized but communicated to the relevant corporation through unofficial channels.[195]

Despite the need for delicate balancing acts—for example, needing money but not wanting to accept it from German sources; or securing archival materials in order to document crimes committed by their providers—it was clear to the members of the IRC that the Federal Republic was not Nazi Germany. The incongruity of some of their reservations against dealing with representatives of West German institutions became obvious by comparison to the IRC's attitudes toward East Germany.[196] In August 1989, Council Chairman Meyerhoff and Lerman had negotiated an agreement with representatives of the GDR about the donation of East German artifacts to the USHMM.[197] The GDR had for decades rejected responsibility for Nazi crimes and refused compensation payments, for instance to the Claims Conference. When the GDR leadership wanted to improve economic relations with the United States in the 1980s,

Figure 3.9 Standing before the grand staircase in the unfinished Hall of Witness are, from left, Miles Lerman (1920–2008), Leslie Wexner (b. 1937), Bella Wexner (1908–2001), Harvey M. Meyerhoff (b. 1927), Albert Ratner (b. 1927), and Albert Abramson (1917–2012). USHMM/Paula Darte.

they hoped to do so by appeasing what they considered "Jewish" demands. According to their understanding, American Jews were in control of the United States government, which rendered closer contacts to American Jewish organizations essential for their economic and political goals.[198] In this context, the GDR also began to cooperate with the Council.

Taking the difficult relationship to West Germany and its government into consideration, the official agreement with the East German government created a dilemma for the Council, as West German archives and museums had been willing to work together with the Council since the early 1980s. Lerman suggested:

> If we are dealing with East Germany, a country that for 45 years has stonewalled us and didn't want to cooperate with us, how can we stonewall West Germany? We need to start some kind of dialogue with them, not a political dialogue. We need a dialogue with an historian and an archivist that unofficially are working with us all along.[199]

The limits were, however, very clear to Lerman: top priority was the acquisition of materials for the museum without making compromises with regard to the content of the exhibition. Ideally, negotiations with the GDR could serve as an example: "We were in East Germany, and you know that we didn't give them anything. All we did is we have gotten stuff."[200]

The discussions between the IRC and West German emissaries continued to be problematic. The already difficult relationship was exacerbated by the fact that prominent Council members failed to communicate their disapproval of cooperating with Germans to German intermediaries. Despite their negative attitude, they created hopes that could not be fulfilled. William Lowenberg reported to the IRC that the leadership of the West German Atlantik-Brücke, Walther Leisler Kiep and Beate Lindemann, a known critic of "American preoccupation with crimes of the Third Reich," had approached him several times.[201] They wanted, as Lowenberg later remarked, "a piece of the action, in plain English," and kept "begging and pleading and pleading."[202] Kiep and Lindemann had asked Lowenberg to add a positive portrayal of West Germany to the USHMM's permanent exhibition on several occasions.[203] Furthermore, Kiep had urged Lowenberg in 1989 that the museum "must portray to the American people that the young Germans are a new breed," a statement that was, all things considered, hard to argue with. Lowenberg informed the IRC that he had clearly rejected any form of cooperation at these meetings.

The German side, however, had taken away a different impression from these encounters, which William Trosten had arranged, who was also present on both occasions. In this instance, the former AJC associate director acted on behalf of his Armonk Institute, which enjoyed close contacts to the Atlantik-Brücke as well as the Chancellery. In a summary for Kohl, Trosten stated that Lowenberg had encouraged his interlocutors "to make a specific proposal."[204] Furthermore, Trosten told Kohl that "after much discussion Mr. Lowenberg stated that he agreed in principle to the inclusion of exhibition material pertaining to the Federal Republic of Germany in the Holocaust Museum."[205]

The internal discussions of these encounters by the IRC, however, revealed a much more critical attitude toward German intermediaries. In addition to Lowenberg's negotiations, Lerman also reported that the Konrad Adenauer Foundation had approached him in early 1990.[206] He emphasized that this foundation embraced the policies of President von Weizsäcker, whom the IRC regarded to be morally impeccable.[207] Thus, contacts with "people of this caliber" were "desirable." Museum director Jeshajahu Weinberg, however, objected. Born in Warsaw, Weinberg grew up in Berlin and emigrated to Palestine in 1933. He had served as the founding director of the Museum of the Jewish Diaspora in Tel Aviv in 1970 before he took over the position in Washington in 1989.[208] In the conversation with Lerman in 1990, he verbalized a concern that many museum representatives shared when he suggested that Kohl's CDU wanted "political rehabilitation, very much in the eyes of the Jews, where I don't think we want to give them political rehabilitation, and I really don't think they deserve it."[209] The IRC also disapproved of the involvement of other American Jewish organizations, such as the AJC, and agreed that future talks would only be acceptable if German emissaries approached the IRC directly and did not use "brokers."[210] In addition, the IRC was only willing to talk to "decent" Germans "with a clean record," even though they were allegedly a "rare breed." Weinberg further remarked that the CDU was "totally present with ex-Nazis, and Kohl belongs to the group that does not want a change."[211] Nevertheless, museum representatives were not willing to burn the bridges with representatives of the West German government completely, thus leaving them with the impression that the museum's content was still up for negotiation.

Concerted Efforts

The years between 1990 and 1992 saw a number of concrete initiatives from various German individuals that went beyond the negotiations and suggestions of the previous years. The opening of the USHMM was approaching, which added urgency to German efforts. On the political level, the fall of the Berlin Wall in late 1989 and preparations for unification also had an impact on policies toward the Council. At a moment when the recreation of the German nation-state seemed within reach, the Chancellery considered any comparisons between the Federal Republic and the Third Reich from abroad particularly harmful.[212]

In 1990, the Chancellery, the Atlantik-Brücke, and the Armonk Institute thus made a concerted effort to produce a convincing proposal for the representation of the Federal Republic in the USHMM. Lowenberg had created the impression that the Council would review such a proposal.[213] In February 1990, Kohl met personally with representatives of the Armonk Institute, including Trosten and Ellenoff, in Bonn.[214] Present at this meeting was also Michael Mertes, the son of the late state minister in the Foreign Office Alois Mertes, a speechwriter and advisor to Kohl, who dealt with contacts to American Jewish organizations in the Chancellery. At this meeting, they decided that the Chancellery would cooperate with the Armonk Institute in the design and transmission of a concept to the Council.[215] The preparation was delegated to Hermann Schäfer, the founding director of the House of History of the Federal Republic in Bonn—a key element of Kohl's politics of history. The Atlantik-Brücke then passed it on to Trosten, who was supposed to place it with the USHMM. Kohl wrote to Schäfer:

> With great pleasure I heard from Mr. Kiep that you are willing to produce a concept for the representation of postwar Germany in the context of the National Holocaust Memorial [sic] that is being planned in the USA.
>
> I consider this project of extraordinary importance and would like to encourage you explicitly to put forth your expertise and the possibilities of the House of History of the Federal Republic.[216]

For questions about details, Kohl concluded, Schäfer should be in touch with Kiep and Lindemann, who acted as unofficial emissaries on his behalf. Schäfer's concept, titled "Coping with the National Socialist Past and German Identity Today," aimed at demonstrating to an American audience the manifold ways in which the Federal Republic had successfully confronted the Nazi Past.[217] A large number of examples and artifacts were also supposed to show that the Federal Republic was distinctly different from the Third Reich. Furthermore, the concept fortified the claim that the Federal Republic's history was an essential component of the history of the Holocaust's aftermath. In light of German unification and the fact that major Holocaust museums were being built not only in Washington, but also in Los Angeles and New York, the concept was to serve as the basis for a travelling exhibition. Even though Lowenberg met with Kiep, Lindemann, and Trosten again in December 1990, it is not clear if Schäfer's concept ever reached Lowenberg or anyone else at the Council.[218] It certainly had no impact on the design of the USHMM's permanent exhibition.

Around the same time, the German embassy became involved in the negotiations. Diplomat Wolf Calebow, who was stationed in the United States from
1977 to 1980 and again from 1986 to 1992, played the key role,[219] including
serving as the embassy's liaison to American Jewish organizations.[220] Already
in the mid-1980s, Calebow had tried in cooperation with Petersen to negotiate
between the Council and the West German government. A few years later, he
again talked to the Council to explore the chances for an exhibit on the history of the Federal Republic, its relationship with Israel, and German anti-Nazi
resistance.[221] In 1990, for example, Calebow corresponded with the Council's
executive director, Sara Bloomfield—who became director of the USHMM in
1999—to arrange an opportunity to discuss the museum's content. In June
1990 Calebow also met with Abraham Foxman, a member of the Council and
the museum's content committee, as well as the director of the ADL. Foxman,
who refused to transmit Calebow's concerns about the USHMM to the Council,
recommended a different solution. The Federal Republic could offer to donate
artifacts connected to German resistance movements of such value that the
museum could not easily reject them. These plans failed, however, because
the German side did not manage to provide Foxman with adequate artifacts.
Furthermore, Calebow was in close contact with Kiep and Lindemann of the
Atlantik-Brücke during their negotiations with Lowenberg and with officials
in the German Chancellery, including Michael Mertes. At this point, a network
of German politicians, diplomats, high-ranking civil servants, and others cooperated closely to implement the federal government's project to change the
design of the USHMM's exhibition.

In February 1991, the Kohl government's most important ally at this stage
of the negotiations, William Trosten, in close collaboration with Calebow
and the Atlantik-Brücke, again tested the waters for the implementation of
German goals in the USHMM.[222] Trosten wrote to Kohl that negotiations had
to be conducted through him as the question about a German contribution was
"politically so charged" that direct talks with Germans were "not possible."[223]
As a result of Trosten's efforts, the museum agreed to consider featuring a segment on West German restitution payments to Israel in the permanent exhibition. In addition, museum director Weinberg agreed to integrate a chapter
on German resistance into the exhibition narrative. However, he categorically
refused even to consider the July 20, 1944, group, which he deemed "anti-
Semitic," yet told Trosten that a segment on the Munich student resistance
group the White Rose might be possible.

In December 1991, German ambassador Jürgen Ruhfus and Calebow met
with Weinberg and Berenbaum to view a model of the museum.[224] At this occasion as well, the German delegation addressed the issue of military resistance.
Calebow hoped to illustrate the causal connection between the Holocaust and
the motivation for the July 20, 1944, assassination attempt on Hitler. For this

purpose, Calebow tried to establish a conversation between Berenbaum and Peter Hoffmann, an expert on German military resistance at McGill University.[225] This line of argumentation was of central importance to his mission as he saw the resisters as the prototypes of "good Germans." It was also necessary to document this—indeed nonexistent connection—between the Holocaust and the resistors' motivation to justify an integration of a segment on military resistance into the USHMM's exhibition.[226] The museum planners were aware that these had the status of "martyrs of German anti-Nazi resistance" in the Federal Republic,[227] but they did not agree with this interpretation due to the ideological congruency of the national conservative group of conspirators with the Nazi regime almost until the end of the war. Raul Hilberg later remarked, for instance, that it was simply unthinkable to feature the "reasonable anti-Semitism" of a Claus Schenk Graf von Stauffenberg in a memorial museum dedicated to the victims of the Holocaust.[228]

As a consequence, the hopes of German negotiators began to wane. Ambassador Ruhfus, for example, suggested that the realization of German goals in the USHMM were unlikely. Instead, the Foreign Office should begin to prepare measures, perhaps in cooperation with the German Historical Institute in Washington, to balance the media coverage of the opening of the museum in 1993. However, Ruhfus also recorded that the USHMM would "omit all attacks which appear to be specifically directed against us."[229] Even though he already anticipated the eventual failure of German efforts, this assessment may also have served to ease some of the concerns of those who had indeed feared such "attacks."

Yet the negotiations were far from over. On February 5, 1992, Lowenberg signaled to Trosten that the USHMM would review photo materials dealing with West German-Israeli relations and Germany's coping with the Nazi past, if the Federal Republic provided such materials.[230] Around the same time, more detailed information about the design of the future USHMM reached Bonn. An internal memorandum of the Chancellery summarized:

> According to the project director Michael Barnbaum [sic], the most important goal of the exhibition will be to enable the visitor to *identify with the victims*. The memorial is supposed to show a "terrible, despicable historical event" and to personalize the history of the victims.[231]

This served as an additional reminder that the USHMM planners envisioned a transformative impact of the museum on its visitors. Through the Foreign Office in Bonn, Calebow compiled a collection of photographs, which Trosten handed to Lowenberg in March. These included pictures of German politicians visiting Israel or meeting with Israelis, German teenagers working in Israeli kibbutzim and at the Dachau concentration camp memorial. The centerpiece of this exhibit was a famous photo of the first encounter between Konrad Ade- nauer and David Ben Gurion at the Waldorf Astoria Hotel in New York in 1960, illustrating the development of positive relations between the Federal Republic and Israel. Kohl was informed about this project and was highly supportive of it, while the Foreign Office had done everything within its power to organize appropriate images as quickly as possible.[232]

The photo collection also included the iconic picture of German Chancel- lor Willy Brandt's kneeling at the Warsaw Ghetto Memorial. Ironically, some museum planners also suggested integrating this image into the permanent exhibition. Weinberg and Berenbaum saw it as an opportunity to counteract Holocaust denial through Brandt's admittance of German guilt.[233] While the German side saw Brandt's gesture as a sincere symbol of reconciliation, the American side wanted to use the image for different purposes. Holocaust sur- vivors on the content committee, however, rejected featuring this image in the permanent exhibition,[234] as they did not want to imply that the museum was entitled to express forgiveness.[235]

A generally skeptical attitude toward the Federal Republic, combined with the restriction of the museum's charter to tell the story of the Holocaust from 1933 to 1945, led to the rejection of the entire German photo collection. De- spite the concerted effort of the Chancellery, the Foreign Office, and the Press and Information Office of the Federal Government, the Council's response was negative.[236] On July 23, 1992, Lowenberg informed Trosten of this decision.[237] Calebow expressed his disappointment very clearly in his memoirs: "That was it. No concessions, not even the slightest indication of a concession."[238] Frustrated that the museum planners were not willing to make the smallest compromise after several years of negotiations, Calebow returned to Germany in 1992. After this failure, the chancellor and his aides decided to no longer pursue their plan to shape the USHMM's exhibition. They had not changed their critical attitude toward American Holocaust memorial culture, but realized that "our goal," and the "goals of the Memorial Council" were simply incompatible.[239] As Hubertus von Morr, a key advisor on US policy and public relations to Kohl in the Chancellery, further summarized:

> Our longstanding *efforts* to achieve in the Holocaust Memorial Museum, built in Washington on federal land close to the Mall, a consideration of German postwar history (member of the Bundestag Petersen, W. Leisler-Kiep [sic], Armonk Institute) have remained *without result*.[240]

Morr suggested that the Chancellery should, explicitly also for *"reasons of self- respect,"* stop all efforts to influence the design of the museum's exhibition, a suggestion Kohl approved in the marginalia. However, Kohl agreed that the German government should continue to supplement the "*narrow representation of German history by making an offer for broad engagement with German postwar history.*"[241]

The same year another attempt to shape the American Holocaust discourse had already failed, albeit for more profane reasons. German officials were also in discussion with another American Holocaust museum, the Detroit-based Holocaust Memorial Center (HMC). To journalist Günther Gillessen of the conservative *Frankfurter Allgemeine Zeitung*, the HMC was another indicator that some "do not want to let the wound of the mass murder heal" and are thus responsible that "current and future generations in Germany will be identified with the crime of the fathers forever."[242]

When the HMC had asked the German embassy for financial support in 1985, the embassy had declined this request.[243] In 1990, however, German officials rediscovered the HMC as an opportunity to work toward a "rational," less "emotional" portrayal of the history of the Holocaust. A close confidant of Kohl, the political scientist Werner Weidenfeld, negotiated with the HMC in Detroit. In his capacity as Coordinator for German-American Cooperation in the Foreign Office, he lobbied for a significant financial contribution—eight to ten million US dollars—to the HMC.[244] This money was supposed to be used for the construction of an Institute of the Righteous, which had the potential, as an internal memorandum of the Foreign Office argued, to change the "up to this point in time very one-sided discussion of the Holocaust in the USA."[245] Charles Rosenzveig, a rabbi and the founder of the HMC in 1984, had been trying to raise funds with the German government for several years and was now willing to conceptualize the new institute in cooperation with the Federal Republic.[246] The German consulate general in Detroit immediately recognized an opportunity to contrast "the Germany of yesterday" with the "Germany of today and of tomorrow":[247]

> An Institute of the Righteous and a permanent exhibition with the intention described above would become the first institution of this kind in the world, and would certainly be unique in the United States. . . . It would probably for many years have a substantial positive impact on Germany's image with Jewish and other circles in the United States.[248]

Weidenfeld, instrumental in shaping Kohl's policies to create a positive identity for the Federal Republic, saw a unique opportunity. Beyond the Detroit consulate general's rather broad assessment of the situation, Weidenfeld was more nuanced and explicit in his evaluation of the project vis-à-vis Kohl.[249] The

HMC aimed, according to Weidenfeld, to promote tolerance and fight xenophobia, not to "hit the visitor over the head with a staged emotional poignancy." Rosenzveig had therefore also left the United States Holocaust Memorial Council, because he rejected the expected "inappropriate emotional razzle-dazzle" (*emotionale Effekthascherei*) of the USHMM, as Weidenfeld wrote to Kohl. To him, Rosenzveig was the perfect ally to promote a "rational" interpretation of the history of the Holocaust and its aftermath. He deserved German financial support, Weidenfeld stressed, because his project "corresponded exactly with German interests." More importantly, he would not be able to complete this project against the "opposition of Jewish hardliners" without German support.[250]

Yet the West German Ministry of Finance blocked Weidenfeld's plans because of a lack of money, despite the support of the Foreign Office.[251] Limited available funds for such purposes were going to be spent to support the memorial at the Auschwitz concentration camp. Even though the Foreign Office mentioned that it would be possible to apply for funding with the Federal Ministry of Finance again in 1994, the chances for success were uncertain due to a general recession in Europe and the cost of German unification. During the early postunification years, more urgent matters needed to be addressed. In the end, albeit for different reasons, all German efforts to change the concepts of American Holocaust museums failed. The German claim that the Holocaust belonged—at least in part—also to the Germans could not be established in the United States. The agendas on the two sides were too contradictory, the resentments too strong to find common ground.

A Scandalous End?

A few weeks before the opening of the USHMM, journalist Marc Fisher landed a scoop in the *Washington Post*:

> The German government, worried that the Holocaust Memorial Museum opening in Washington next month will damage Germany's democratic image, offered museum organizers "millions of dollars" to include an exhibit on postwar Germany, according to museum officials and aides to Helmut Kohl. This offer was immediately rejected, said Miles Lerman, chairman of international relations for the U.S. Holocaust Memorial Council.[252]

This revelation could not have come at a worse time for the Kohl government. Already afraid of the effect of the USHMM on the image of the Federal Republic, such scandalous news could only exacerbate the situation. The chancellery and the Konrad Adenauer Foundation perceived the article as an assault by the press on the Federal Republic, as a "negative campaign" with the intention of damaging the reputation of the Kohl government.[253] It caused great dismay among governmental officials and their associates. Wolfgang Pordzik, the director of the Washington office of the KAS, tried to convince the editors of the *Washington Post* that Fisher's article was "factually wrong" and that no offer of a gift to the Council had been made.[254] The *Post* responded right away, insisting that the "reporting was correct on the main thrust of the story," but offered to publish a letter to the editor.[255] Pordzik took advantage of this option—as did the government spokesman Dieter Vogel on Kohl's orders.[256] Denying that the federal government ever offered money to the USHMM, Vogel's reply in the *Post* stated that

> the Federal Government would have welcomed it if the museum had included information on German resistance to National Socialism as well as on the successful construction of a state based on the rule of law and of a liberal democracy in postwar Germany, and if account had been taken of the fact that Germany is not only a close ally of the United States but also a friend and partner of Israel.[257]

The Kohl government thus made no secret of its disapproval of the design of the USHHM. Details on the financial offer, however, remain inconclusive.[258] On-the-record statements by museum representatives as well as Marc Fisher's investigation indicate that representatives acting on behalf of the German federal government indeed made such an offer. It is possible that it was made with the support of a member of the KAS and a representative of the German embassy.[259] The diplomat Wolf Calebow raised another possibility, namely the likelihood of an attempt by Walter Wallmann (CDU) in 1989, then prime minister of the state of Hesse, to donate a large sum of money to the Council.[260] The Hessian government indeed discussed a contribution with a representative of the AJC, who let them know that the Council would not accept it.[261] This conversation took place in June or July 1989, and it is possible, but not certain that this was the offer that Lerman mentioned to Fisher. But precise information about the amount of the donation is lacking. Former museum representatives Berenbaum, Lerman, and Lowenberg spoke of a sum between ten and fifty million dollars.[262] They all agreed that this donation was supposed to convince the museum planners to accommodate West German reservations about the exhibition design.

In 1991, however, German diplomats had recorded that the Federal Republic did not, "as a matter of principle," support American Holocaust museums with federal money.[263] In 1993, there was therefore some confusion among German diplomats in the United States about this question. The embassy tried to get some clarity about Fisher's allegations and contacted Lerman directly, who now stated that Petersen had made the offer in 1989 or 1990.[264] Accordingly, Petersen had insinuated to Lerman that "the german [sic] government could be of very, very substantial support" if changes were made to the exhibition design.[265] Having checked the available documentation, the embassy reported to the Foreign Office and the Chancellery that "the Federal Government was neither asked by the Holocaust Memorial Council for financial support nor did it offer such support."[266]

Officials in the Chancellery also had no knowledge of such an offer. They wrote in a summary of the events to Kohl: "As part of the numerous attempts by the federal government vis-à-vis the Holocaust Memorial Council to work towards a consideration of the development of Germany after the war as well, *money has never been an issue.*"[267] In the context of possible financial support for the HMC in Detroit, the Foreign Office explicitly mentioned to the Chancellery that this was a "unique" case and would not create a precedent for payments to other American memorials or museums.[268] Thus the accessible records of the German Chancellery do not allow the conclusion that, if such an offer was ever made, federal money would have been used. Petersen (or someone else) may have vaguely suggested the possibility of a donation without having thought about how to secure the money—or he knew of a way to find the necessary funds through other channels.

It was only revealed much later, in 1999, that the CDU possessed a large amount of funds, hidden in foreign bank accounts. With the hindsight knowledge of these secret accounts, it appears possible that enough money was available to finance projects close to the chancellor's heart. The discovery of the CDU's illegal party donations scheme in 1999 seriously damaged the reputation of Kohl and a number of other high-ranking CDU politicians, including Kiep, Wallmann, and several other CDU leaders. Indeed, it marked the nadir in the former chancellor's political career. These funds, used among other things for financing election campaigns, were transferred from foreign bank accounts to the Federal Republic and were officially declared as "Jewish bequests" (*jüdische Vermächtnisse*). That the CDU implied that their illegal donations were actually pecuniary legacies by Jewish émigrés caused a tremendous scandal in the Federal Republic.[269] Whether this money could have been used for an offer to the Council, however, remains a purely speculative question. In 1993, German officials seemed to oppose such a financial contribution. A German diplomat, for example, concluded from the rumors about a German attempt to "bribe" the USHMM that it was "absurd to offer money for additional presentations about 'postwar Germany, German-Israeli relations.'"[270]

Exaggerated Fears

The opening ceremony of the USHMM on April 22, 1993, took place without the German chancellor, even though he had been invited alongside a number of other international political leaders. In his invitation to Kohl, Council Chairman Meyerhoff called upon him to speak as the "voice of modern Germany," to make a strong statement about Germany's historical responsibility, and to commit to a central goal of the USHMM, namely "a brighter future based upon an international respect for democracy and human rights, freedom and liberty."[271] Both Kohl and Weizsäcker turned down an invitation to attend the opening ceremony, but in March Kohl had toured the USHMM with Weidenfeld prior to its opening and issued an official statement on April 24, 1993.[272] It is hardly surprising that Kohl did not attend the event. It would have been nearly impossible for him to give a speech that would have been considered appropriate by all interest groups involved.[273] He probably also wanted to avoid a potentially embarrassing scenario. Despite the official invitation, museum representatives, including Lerman and Weinberg, had signaled to the German ambassador, Immo Stabreit, that the "basis" had not "forgotten" the Bitburg visit and could put the chancellor on the spot.[274]

Figure 3.10 Helmut Kohl receiving a tour of the USHMM prior to its opening (pictured left of Kohl is Albert Abramson; pictured first from the right is Sara Bloomfield; pictured third from the rights is Werner Weidenfeld; tour guide is historian David M. Luebke). USHMM.

Eventually Foreign Minister Kinkel represented the federal government, but did not speak at the ceremony.

During his visit to the United States in March, Kohl had also met with newly elected President Clinton. In May, he reported on this encounter and expressed optimism concerning the future of German–American relations to the CDU's federal committee. With regard to Clinton, he stated:

> With relation to the Germans, it is very important that this is a different generation. The opening of the Holocaust museum has just taken place, which was very critical for us. In contrast to Bush and also to Reagan, President Clinton is a man who did not personally experience the war and the Nazi period.... For Clinton, the Germans are now the Germans of today.[275]

Even though Kohl did not take advantage of the opportunity to praise the achievements of the new Germany at the opening ceremony of the USHMM, German officials acknowledged that their fears had been vastly exaggerated. Though some of the German press reacted critically to the opening of the museum, and the Foreign Office took its usual precautions, preparing information about compensation payments for the victims of National Socialism and (West) German efforts to cope with the Nazi Past more generally, the museum soon lost its ominous character.[276] Already on the day of its opening, the embassy reported to the Foreign Office that "the fears about the emergence of 'anti-German' coverage in the media in the context of the opening of the hmm [Holocaust Memorial Museum] have so far not proven true."[277] An examination of the coverage of the opening ceremony in the US press by German diplomats confirmed this assessment.[278] An evaluation by the CDU also sent a reassuring message to the Chancellery. A few days before the opening, a delegation of CDU/CSU members of the Bundestag, other party officials, and members of state governments toured the USHMM as guests of the AJC. Summarizing the report for Kohl, an official in the Chancellery wrote:

> According to the report, the vast majority of the participants view the content of the exhibition as balanced. There is no reason to fear that the Museum would discredit the image of contemporary Germany. The behavior of the USA with regard to knowledge about the annihilation of the Jews in Germany is examined critically.[279]

The report itself provided further reason for relief: "The exhibition makes unmistakably clear that the Holocaust was an act of the Nazis and not of all Germans."[280]

Had all the efforts of the past decade thus been in vain? There is no easy answer to this question. The federal government had perceived the plans for the USHMM as a major threat to (West) Germany's reputation abroad as well as for German–American relations in general. As such, Holocaust angst was a political reality. Government officials and their partners thus had to take measures they considered appropriate to protect Germany's foreign policy interests.[281] This does not mean, however, that the absence of anti-German reactions to the opening of the USHMM fundamentally altered their position. Helmut Kohl and his transatlantic network of confidants and allies would continue to insist

Figure 3.11 President Bill Clinton (b. 1946; center), Elie Wiesel (right) and Harvey M. Meyerhoff (left) light the eternal flame outside on the Eisenhower Plaza during the dedication ceremony of the USHMM. USHMM.

that the dominant American Holocaust narrative was incomplete without references to German anti-Nazi resistance as well as the Federal Republic's success story of coming to terms with the Nazi past and friendship with Israel.[282]

The large number of German individuals and organizations involved in the negotiations and the persistence with which they tried to achieve their goals in the United States is striking. The Chancellery, the CDU party headquarters, the embassy, members of the German parliament, and representatives of the KAS and the Atlantik-Brücke tried for more than a decade to influence the design of the USHMM's exhibition. When their efforts became the subject of press coverage after the opening of the USHMM, some representatives of American Jewish organizations were even sympathetic toward their concerns. Daniel Mariaschin of B'nai B'rith, for example, stated that it was understandable that the German government had feared that Americans were presented with a one-sided interpretation of German history in the USHMM. However, he continued, "this museum was organized and created largely by survivors who have a deep need to tell their story of those years, and not the story of Konrad Adenauer or Ludwig Erhard."[283] The Kohl government and its intermediaries in Washington did not seem willing or able to make this distinction and to accept the existence and workings of a specifically American Holocaust memorial culture.[284]

4

Politicians and Professors

The Politics of German History in the American
Academy from the 1970s to 1990

Efforts to influence the concept of the USHMM's permanent exhibition were not the only avenue the Kohl government took to make a long-term impact on the Federal Republic's image in the United States. During the second half of the 1980s, the Chancellery, in collaboration with other government agencies and a number of prominent conservative scholars, decided to target American universities, scholars working on German history, and their students. The German leadership around Kohl sought to provide incentives to American academics and institutions to engage with the "success story" of the Federal Republic. Changing the scholarly discourse about German history in the United States, however, imposed significant challenges on them.

In order to make an impact on American scholarship about Germany, the Federal Republic needed to establish academically legitimate and effective institutions in the United States and to create new networks with current and future academic elites. Such efforts become most apparent in the establishment of the German Historical Institute (GHI) in Washington, and the founding of three Centers of Excellence for German studies. These centers made up the central component of the so-called Initiative of the Federal Chancellor for the Intensification of German-American Academic Relations (Bundeskanzler-Initiative zur Intensivierung der deutsch-amerikanischen Wissenschaftsbeziehungen) of 1988. To German officials, the growing presence of Holocaust remembrance in the United States during the 1980s illustrated the necessity to raise awareness of "positive" aspects of German history. In this way, both endeavors were supposed to differ in their conceptualization from other educational and exchange programs that were—due to their size, history, or the specific institutions involved—rather impervious to direct and immediate interference from outside, such as the programs administered by the DAAD.[1]

The emergence of an American Holocaust memorial culture was not the only incentive to increase scholarly cooperation between the Federal Republic and the United States. The aforementioned debate about the successor generation revealed, in the eyes of contemporaries, a decrease in expertise, interest, and dedication to Germany in the United States and vice versa.[2] However, the motivation to create new bilateral avenues of cooperation cannot be reduced to the growing gulf between the societies. The retirement and passing of the generation that had built German–American friendship after World War II does not fully explain West German concerns about the future of German–American relations: who—or perhaps what—would shape the image of Germany in the United States if those who knew the "good" Germany were gone? According to the Kohl government, the answer was obvious: ignorance and stereotypes. The result would be a blanket image of Germans as villains and Nazis.

In the design and implementation of the two initiatives, the founding of the GHI and the Centers of Excellence, German scholars played a crucial role. Beyond concrete advice and expertise, they gave academic legitimacy to the policies pursued by the Kohl government.[3] In general, professorial and other academic appointments have been often much more overtly politicized in Germany than in the United States. Kohl was the not the only one who collaborated with German academics.[4] The leadership of the Social Democrats, for instance, founded a Historical Commission in the 1980s in order to "revitalize" the SPD's "political self-confidence."[5] This commission was composed of left-leaning historians, who often opposed the Kohl government's politics of history.[6] However, Kohl, a historian by training, granted a small group of academics an unprecedented amount of influence.[7] For a chancellor who attributed great significance to history and historical consciousness, it only seemed logical to rely on the advice of scholars he trusted. Indeed, the Kohl government could not have engaged in the politics of history without the knowledge and advice provided by scholars.[8]

Politicians and Professors: Origins of Helmut Kohl's Alliance with German Scholars

The origins of the alliance between conservative politicians and scholars, which came to fruition during the 1980s, lay in the early to mid-1970s. Since that time, German conservatives had engaged in debates about (West) German identity and history against the backdrop of a more general experience of crisis during the 1970s.[9] After the end of the period of Social Democratic reforms, a series of economic crises as well as a wave of terrorism in the Federal Republic exacerbated what contemporaries perceived as a challenge for German democracy. This shift was caused by the oil shock of 1973, the new phenomenon of mass unemployment, and what was construed as a fundamental change in society's values, especially since 1968, which seemed to be ever-accelerating in the eyes of contemporaries. This perception was closely connected to the search for a new German identity in the "provisional" Federal Republic. Conservatives wanted to balance the Federal Republic's transition into the postindustrial age by creating bases for identification and orientation. The buzzword *Tendenzwende* ("turnaround") served as a slogan for this constellation.[10] A general description of a time of economic changes marking the end of the postwar boom, *Tendenzwende* also became a catch phrase for conservatives to call for a fundamental change of social values and a key slogan in the struggle to regain political power from the left. The CDU in particular employed a shortened version, *Wende* ("change" or "reversal"), to oppose the government of Helmut Schmidt and to call for rolling back post-1968 cultural liberalization and a loss of power to the Social Democrats in 1969.[11]

Helmut Kohl emerged as the future leader of German conservatism during the 1970s, when the Social Democrats Willy Brandt and Helmut Schmidt governed West Germany. In 1973, Kohl took over the chairmanship of the CDU and installed confidants in key positions. At this time, questions about the values of German society and German identity also gained importance in the CDU.[12] It was above all conservatives who had suggested since the middle of the decade that the Federal Republic "lacked" identity.[13] Behind closed doors—and in stark contrast to its official rhetoric, which maintained that unification was the ultimate end of the Federal Republic—the CDU started to ponder a specifically *West* German identity, based on the assumption that the Federal Republic was a "definite" entity.[14] As a member of a commission organized by Horst Teltschik, later Kohl's foreign policy advisor in the Chancellery, Werner Weidenfeld provided the intellectual basis for the discussion, arguing that it would have to be a central task of West Germany's future political leadership to clearly define the Federal Republic's self-image.[15]

In the 1970s, as during preceding decades, questions about how to deal with the legacies of National Socialism divided West German political culture.[16] Conservative politicians and intellectuals aimed to foster German patriotism as well as a West German identity, while the left opposed such tendencies. The latter proposed a country "divorced from corrupted national traditions," while the former favored an "imperative for positive, national continuities."[17] Conservatives considered it a crucial function of the historical profession to provide the basis for an affirmative interpretation of the German past, one that would strengthen Germans' identification with the Federal Republic. Historians examining the ruptures and continuities in German history as well as the Federal Republic's search for "normality" prepared advice, intellectual frameworks, concepts, key terms, and forums for discussion.[18] In the rhetoric of conservatives, demanding more "historical consciousness" and pointing to a lack of "identity" were calls for a new West German patriotism.[19] They also targeted what they perceived as a dominance of the left over German political culture and the prevailing impact of the Nazi past in setting the terms of the debate. For them, the state needed to occupy a more assertive role in this discussion.[20]

Conservative politicians and intellectuals were not the only ones contributing to a discourse about identity and German history. To a sociopolitical milieu mainly associated with the Social Democratic Party and the emerging "Green" movement, the Holocaust evolved at this time as a benchmark for a critical assessment of German identity.[21] They favored a critical examination of German history and identity; according to this view, the Holocaust had rendered impossible the kind of affirmative approach to this history suggested by conservatives. For example, the main political proponents of the airing of the NBC miniseries *Holocaust* on German television were Social Democrats, while prominent members of the Union parties opposed the broadcast and attempted to discredit the miniseries.[22] Furthermore, the emerging "memorial movement" (*Gedenkstättenbewegung*), which significantly advanced the establishment of memorials at former sites of Nazi terror, was above all a movement of left-leaning milieux.[23] Finally, scholars like Hans Mommsen, a Social Democrat, made major contributions to the historiography of the Holocaust in the 1980s.[24] As a cofounder of the SPD's historical commission, he also opposed the right's politics of history because he assumed that it not only aimed to reduce perceived German responsibility for World War II and obscure the broad social backing of National Socialism, but also threatened the pluralist political consensus of the Federal Republic.[25]

In fact, this divison between the left and the right would shape political debates about the German past well into the 1980s. Critics of Kohl's politics of history accused the chancellor of blurring the lines between Nazi perpetrators and victims of National Socialism.[26] This confrontation reached its apex in the Historians' Controversy of the mid-1980s.[27] Not simply a debate about the uniqueness of the Holocaust, this dispute was more importantly a struggle over politico-cultural hegemony in the Federal Republic, the Kohl government's politics of history, and the significance of the Holocaust for West German identity.[28] At the height of this debate, the conservative historian Michael Stürmer, a professor of history at the University of Erlangen-Nuremberg, wrote:

> A loss of orientation and a search for identity are closely related. But anyone who believes that this trend will have no effect on politics and the future is ignoring the fact that in a land without history, the future is controlled by those who determine the content of memory, who coin concepts and interpret the past.[29]

Stürmer believed that the dissemination of a certain interpretation of German history had the potential to shape German national identity and thus could have a crucial effect on the country's future. As a young historian, Stürmer had counted among the up-and-coming liberal and left-leaning historians, but moved to the right as a consequence of his struggles with leftist student radicals in the aftermath of 1968.[30] During the Historians' Controversy of the mid-1980s, he was one of the most vocal and eloquent combatants, supporting the claim that the Federal Republic needed to find a usable past as a precondition for a "normal" national identity.[31]

A few years earlier, Werner Weidenfeld, a professor of political science at the University of Mainz and an expert on the history of German foreign policy and the Adenauer era, also pondered the identity of the Germans in a number of book publications and articles.[32] Weidenfeld, who considered himself a political scientist and a historian, argued that in light of the "loss of orientation" and "crisis of identity" which the individual experienced in modern times, society needed to create a collective identity.[33] Even though the state could not do so by decree, it had to respond to the Germans' "longing for an undamaged identity."[34] However, according to Weidenfeld, "deficits of history, the catastrophe of National Socialism, and the withholding of German unification" stood in its way.[35] Yet for Weidenfeld, shaping a specific West German identity also served to prevent the revival of a dangerous kind of German nationalism, one that had been prevalent during the first half of the twentieth century. He considered the German–American postwar alliance, and European integration, to form the backbone of the Federal Republic's national security, though additionally wished that these alliances would become integral in how the republic defined itself as a nation. Strong ties to the West, especially the United States, were thus a necessity of Cold War foreign policy, as well as a means to fundamentally and permanently transform German political culture. As such, his academic and political agenda must be seen as part of a larger "struggle for the acceptance of the model of Western democracy and rationality" in the Federal Republic, as *Die Zeit* noted in an article on the "prompters [*Souffleure*] of the chancellors" in 1983.[36]

Both Weidenfeld and Stürmer—and a number of other scholars and intellectuals—contributed to the discourse about identity and the Germans' relationship to the past that had characterized much of the conservative political spectrum in West Germany since the mid-1970s.[37] While they differed in their analyses and approaches, they nevertheless suggested that the state should play a key role in the shaping of Germans' attitude toward their past, creating an affirmative narrative that rendered a positive identification with German history possible. Both scholars also shared a proximity to political power. Indeed, they provided advice, ideas, templates for speeches, and suggestions for history-related projects to Helmut Kohl.[38]

In 1971 had Kohl made the acquaintance of Weidenfeld in Mainz, the capital of Rhineland-Palatinate, where the former was minister-president and the latter a young and ambitious scholar, venturing into the field of political consulting.[39] Since the early 1970s Weidenfeld had contributed to Kohl's speeches, but officially retained his independence as a scholar. Only in 1987 did he receive an official assignment as Coordinator for German-American Relations in the Foreign Office. At this point in time, Weidenfeld had proven himself as a close advisor, speechwriter, and confidant of Kohl. His appointment in the Foreign Office at the suggestion of the chancellor marked a perfect example of Kohl's personalized style of governing, the "Kohl system," placing trusted individuals in key positions from which they could implement his policies.[40] This is remarkable because Weidenfeld remains the only nonpolitician or nondiplomat to have held this office. He also had closer connections to the chancellor than to the foreign ministers, the Free Democrats Hans-Dietrich Genscher and later Klaus Kinkel, to whom he officially reported.

In the early 1980s, Kohl and Stürmer met at a birthday party of the chancellor's dissertation advisor, historian Walther Peter Fuchs, who Stürmer had succeeded as a professor of modern history at the University Erlangen-Nuremberg. Stürmer allegedly insinuated to Kohl that the German public "widely underestimated" the chancellor's actual political importance.[41] Stürmer's flattering comment apparently struck a chord with Kohl. In the following years, Stürmer, an expert on imperial Germany and Bismarck, served as an advisor and speech writer to Kohl on historical topics and projects, such as the German Historical Museum, and significantly shaped the latter's politics of history.[42] Fashioning himself as an "advisor to the chancellor" (*Kanzlerberater*), Stürmer publicly reinforced the impression that his views shaped governmental policies.[43] Allegedly, Kohl and his inner circle in the chancellery disapproved of Stürmer's boastful and self-important behavior, and Kohl would later distance himself from Stürmer publicly.[44]

Stürmer also participated directly in public debates, for example by writing op-eds for the leading German conservative daily newspaper *Frankfurter Allgemeine Zeitung*. He argued that German history should not be reduced to the Nazi past, but that Germans had to be able to identify with their history positively to battle a loss of orientation and to foster West German patriotism.[45] His major contribution to German historiography was in his geographical approach, arguing that Germany's *Mittellage* (location at the center of Europe) explained much of its—at times violent—political history.[46] This was a "traditional conservative" interpretation, going back to the Weimar Republic, that aimed at reducing Germany's individual responsibility, for example, for the outbreak of the First World War.[47]

Kohl, and the CDU more generally, relied on the advice of scholars such as Weidenfeld and Stürmer, who shaped the intellectual concepts and the language for the debates. Weidenfeld in particular defined and propagated key terms in this context, such as the Germans' supposed crises of identity and orientation.[48] In the early 1980s, he published and edited a number of books further clarifying his claims, suggesting that Germans experienced a fundamental lack of orientation.[49] To conservative politicians and intellectuals, strengthening the historical consciousness of Germans promised an adequate response to confront what they saw as a loss of orientation and values in contemporary West German society.

Already in his first state of the nation address of 1982, coauthored by Weidenfeld, Kohl made clear how important he considered a "reflection on German history" (Besinnung auf die deutsche Geschichte).[50] It was a central component of the necessary "renewal" his government would bring about after the Social Democrats had governed for over a decade. History was supposed to provide, other conservatives demanded as well, the power to overcome the Federal Republic's identity crisis. Addressing West Germany's historians directly on the occasion of the thirty-fourth Annual Conference of the German Historical Association, federal president and former CDU majority leader Karl Carstens, for example, called for a way to enable Germans to "identify positively" with their history.[51] This marked a striking contrast to one of Carstens's predecessors, the Social Democrat Gustav Heinemann, who had called for a critical engagement with German history.[52] Around this time, Michael Stürmer embarked on a "search for a lost national master narrative for German history" and stated that national history could no longer give all the answers for the question of German identity, especially in a European framework.[53] However, history provided indispensable "sign posts to identity, anchorages in the cataracts of progress."[54]

Despite the fact that this productive alliance of politicians and professors was concerned with the identity and historical consciousness of the citizens of the Federal Republic, its effects were not limited to West Germany. What use would a new German patriotism and an affirmative interpretation of German history emphasizing positive traditions and achievements be, if others, above all Germany's most important international partners, did not take notice of it? In the eyes of Helmut Kohl and his academic advisors, Germans had every right to be "proud" of the Federal Republic.[55] Yet in order for the Federal Republic to be able to present itself in the international arena as a "normal," self-confident nation state, its allies had to share this reading of West Germany's patriotism and understanding of its own history. In correspondence with long-term projects in the Federal Republic proper as well as its policies vis-à-vis the USHMM, the Kohl government hoped to inscribe such a reading of German history in the work of current and future American experts on Germany. If they could shape not only America's image of the Federal Republic, but also channel its research and scholarship on German matters, they could make a significant impact on the image of the Federal Republic in the United States in the long run.

A Visible Presence for German Understanding of History in Washington

While the idea for the German Historical Institute in Washington, DC originated in the mid-1970s in connection with the debate about a drifting apart of German and American societies, it was only realized in the 1980s. The GHI was founded, according to the intentions of a small group of officials in the Chancellery and other government offices, as an instrument to promote a positive interpretation of German history in the United States. While they aimed to establish a scholarly institution that appeared independent to outside observers, they pursued a political agenda behind the scenes. According to a memorandum prepared for Kohl's cabinet in late 1985, the Minister for Research and Technology Heinz Riesenhuber (CDU) wanted the institute to become a "visible presence for German understanding of history" (*eine erkennbare Präsenz deutschen Geschichtsverständnisses*) in Washington.[56]

The GHI was established to promulgate an interpretation of German history that did not focus exclusively on the Nazi past. For government officials and diplomats, Holocaust angst provided a core motive for its establishment. The debates spurred by the NBC miniseries *Holocaust* in the late 1970s as well as the presumed negative impact of the USHMM in Washington made German officials conclude that the Federal Republic needed to make a direct impact on the writing of German history in the United States. The GHI's founding history illustrates not only the significance of the relationship between politicians and professors, but also the tension between the two in the implementation of political goals. Scholars involved in its establishment opposed government efforts to interfere with its research agenda, which caused a dilemma for the Kohl government. In order for the GHI to be accepted as a legitimate institution in the United States, all indicators of government interference had to be concealed. After all, the existence of a historical profession that can work independently from government interference constitutes a core component of every democratic society, and without the reputation of academic freedom, the GHI would have failed as a scholarly institution. Nevertheless, government officials tried to influence its agenda prior to its opening and also attempted to shape the concept of one of the GHI's first major projects, namely a conference celebrating the success story of the Federal Republic on the occasion of its fortieth anniversary in 1989.

The GHI in Washington was not the first historical institute the Federal Republic had founded abroad. Precursors of such institutions existed in Paris and Rome prior to World War II, and West Germany established a GHI in London in 1976.[57] As the founding of the GHI Paris in 1958 illustrates, the creation of a historical institute abroad cannot be separated from more general foreign policy goals. In the 1950s, the reorientation of the West German historical profession after the Third Reich "converged" with key political aims of the Adenauer government, namely reconciliation and rapprochement with the Federal Republic's western neighbors, especially France.[58] A German Historical Institute in Paris thus provided a forum for dialogue between German and French historians, while building trust for the Federal Republic abroad and contributing to the young country's "political emancipation."[59] In the eyes of the German government at the time, scholarly cooperation had the potential to help dissipate the "hereditary enmity" between Germany and France.[60] The most recent additions to the GHI network were institutes in Warsaw (1993) and Moscow (2005) after the end of the Cold War, which can also be seen as instruments of reconciliation with former enemy nations. Naturally, it is difficult to separate the establishment of such institutions from political and diplomatic agendas. The establishment of the GHI in Washington, however, illustrates the tension between national interest and historical truth against the backdrop of the growing presence of Holocaust memory in the United States.

In 1976, the consulate general in Boston first suggested establishing a historical institute at one of the large universities on the East Coast.[61] Modeled after the institutes in Paris and London, a dependency in the United States might foster academic exchange between both countries at a time when members of the generation of émigré scholars were reaching the ends of their careers. While (mostly Jewish) scholars and academics, having fled or emigrated from Nazi Germany during the 1930s and 1940s, had helped to maintain ties with the Federal Republic, their successor generation was, according to the consulate general's assessment, less interested in Germany.[62] Furthermore, key academic motives to create a GHI in the United States included the positive experiences with the GHIs in Europe, expanding international connections and ties of the German historical profession, the growing significance of the role of historians in postwar American society, and access to a number of key archives and libraries—the National Archives and the Library of Congress—as well as universities.[63]

For the next several years, the Foreign Office discussed these plans with other government agencies—above all the Ministry of Research and Technology (Bundesministerium für Forschung und Technologie; BMFT), which assumed formal responsibility for the project in 1978, but also the German Fulbright Commission and the Alexander von Humboldt Foundation—in regard to the location, target audience, and organization of such an institute.

The latter organizations were rather skeptical about the necessity and precise purpose of an American GHI, but attested that the "influence of German emigrants on the political and intellectual life in the United States" needed to be perpetuated and German cultural diplomacy in the United States intensified.[64] Both foundations engaged with a proposal that Michael Stürmer had written in 1977, criticizing the Humboldt Foundation for only funding junior faculty under the age of forty and the German Fulbright Commission for spreading money according to the "principle of the watering can."[65] Instead, money available for such ventures was supposed to be concentrated at America's leading universities, for instance at Harvard, where, according to the Foreign Office, the chair for German history had been vacant for ten years.[66]

As a result of these discussions, the BMFT suggested in 1978 a conference series involving German and American historians; these events could probe ideas and eventually prepare the establishment of a historical institute.[67] Even though the Foreign Office supported the establishment of a GHI in the United States,[68] German diplomats feared that the ministry's plans to give historians the central role were "too academic," insular, and would miss the institute's "political purpose."[69] Emphasizing the "political motivation behind its suggestion to establish a German historical institute," the Boston consulate general wrote a slightly derogatory letter to the Foreign Office, criticizing the BMFT's intentions:

> Of course, it is nice [*erfreulich*] if interested historians from both countries get together for seminars and aim for more intensive contacts in the future. The consulate general, however, intended to provide long-term institutional security for such rather random contacts. The establishment of a German Historical Institute at a university on the East Coast should serve the political purpose of stimulating and channeling American historical research on Germany and Europe in the long run.[70]

The consulate general hoped that the Foreign Office would insist on this strategy vis-à-vis the BMFT. The embassy in Washington supported this version of the project and was even more specific about the political dimension toward the end of 1978: "The establishment of a German Historical Institute ... has become an even more urgent matter due to the considerations about the 'Holocaust' issue and 'improvement of knowledge about German history in the United States' respectively."[71] Due to such concerns of German cultural diplomacy—a clear reference to the NBC miniseries—the embassy strongly suggested the establishment of a permanent institute that would specifically target scholars, even though the precise format and tasks of this institution were still up for debate.

In early 1980, the embassy again weighed in on the establishment of a GHI in the United States. While the teaching of German history and the German language were well established in the United States, historical research dealt to a disproportionately large extent with the history of the Third Reich. In this context, a GHI, according to the embassy, should encourage encounters between German and American historians to confront "the lack of knowledge about and understanding of the Federal Republic of Germany as a progressive and liberal, modern and industrialized nation that can be considered a model in certain areas."[72] To convey such knowledge about postwar German history and the Federal Republic "here and now," the institute would have to offer courses or classes and should be located in Washington. Even though the establishment of the GHI fell into the realm of the BMFT, German diplomats were not willing to watch the fulfillment of these plans from the sidelines. Instead, the Foreign Office would have liked to take control over the institute and integrate it into other projects that aimed at "an intensification of our cultural engagement" in the United States targeting academic elites.[73]

Some American academics shared German worries about a lack of knowledge of the Federal Republic among Americans. For this reason, the foreign policy expert Robert Gerald Livingston, a United States citizen, pitched to the Chancellery under Helmut Schmidt the idea to found an Institute for Contemporary German Studies in the United States, intended to address the problem of the successor generation.[74] Livingston wrote, "The United States—and Germany too for that matter—will soon lack those capable of 'interpreting' the two countries to each other, as a generation of leaders was able to do during the late 1940s, and the 1950s and 1960s."[75] The Chancellery welcomed the idea of such an institute.[76] Yet both sides agreed that this institute—founded as the American Institute for Contemporary German Studies (AICGS) in connection with Johns Hopkins University in Washington, DC, in 1983—would be an American project and funded with American money.[77]

The German side therefore focused on the establishment of a German Historical Institute. The discussions about such an institution continued for quite some time, but they illustrate the importance West German officials attributed to academic elites for German–American relations. Already in the late 1970s it was clear to German diplomats that they needed to reach out to current and future historians if they wanted to make a lasting impact on the writing of German history in the United States. Providing incentives to American historians to study and research non-Holocaust-related aspects of German history thus came to be seen as a crucial component of the larger project of promoting the success story of the Federal Republic.

When Kohl became chancellor in late 1982, the country gained a leader who attributed great weight to history in general, but also to shaping historical consciousness in a specific way. Under Kohl, the plans to establish a GHI in the

United States gained significant momentum and were eventually completed in 1987.[78] The chancellery not only took the credit for establishing the institute, but later even considered the GHI the chancellor's idea.[79] Early on, the Kohl government paid close attention to the political implications of such an institute. Horst Teltschik, who was in the process of compiling a list of German historians to be nominated for the German delegation to the USHMM's Committee on Learning and Remembrance, informed Kohl about the plans for the GHI in 1984:

> At this occasion, I would like to inform you that Minister Riesenhuber is in charge of the establishment of an Institute for German history in Washington. It would be important that the establishment of this institute could, under certain circumstances, also happen as a counterweight to the Holocaust-museum.[80]

To observers in Washington, the connection between the plans for the GHI and the USHMM were anything but secret. For example, a trustee of the AICGS, Thomas L. Farmer, who was concerned that the GHI could compete with the AIGCS for funding, wrote:

> The Bundeskanzleramt [Federal Chancellery] is particularly interested in an outreach program for the Institute, since it appears to be interested in *establishing in the United States some counterbalance to the Holocaust Museum* and its study facilities.[81]

Despite the objections of the AICGS, an institution also designed to foster German–American academic relations, the federal government continued to pursue the project. Upon the BMFT's initiative, the Council of Science and Humanities (Wissenschaftsrat), West Germany's most important academic advisory board to state and federal governments, developed a proposal for a GHI in 1984.[82] Referring to concerns that had dominated the debates about the GHI during the preceding years, such as the passing of the generation of emigrants, the Council of Science and Humanities fully supported the establishment of the institute.[83] Its proposal was based on strictly academic motivations: to stimulate German research about the United States and vice-versa, to intensify and institutionalize the dialogue between German and American scholars, and to secure access to sources on German and European history located in the United States.[84]

Government agencies welcomed this proposal but underscored the political dimension of the project. In an internal memorandum, the BMFT agreed that such an institute could build a bridge to American historians and demonstrate the Federal Republic's interest in academic exchange, while serving the political goals of the Kohl government, as it "could contribute in the United States to a more complete image of Germany, in contrast to its being represented by way of Romanticism on the one hand, the Nazi era and the Holocaust on the other."[85] However, the necessary funds for such an endeavor had not yet been secured. The ministry thus contacted Walther Leisler Kiep, who was in the process of negotiating a West German follow-up contribution to the German Marshall Fund of the United States (GMF), which the Federal Republic had set up in 1972 as an "expression of special gratitude" for American postwar aid.[86] Hans-Hilger Haunschild, state secretary in the BMFT, asked Kiep to look into whether part of the GMF's funds could be used for the establishment of the GHI and whether it could even be established under the GMF's umbrella. Emphasizing the significance Kohl attributed to this project, Haunschild wrote: "In this context, the chancellor pointed to the need to update the representation of German history in the United States [*Nachholbedarf bei der Darstellung deutscher Geschichte*] as well as the great political significance of this task."[87] Kiep, however, dismissed this request. He was certain that the GMF's board of trustees would reject any attempt at direct government interference, which would cause a "scandal" and could even endanger the GMF's future altogether.[88] While Kiep successfully negotiated an extension of West German funding for the GMF of DM 100 million in late 1985, the funds for the GHI would have to come from the federal budget.[89]

In the further course of the considerations, the BMFT decided in conversation with Michael Stürmer that the GHI would be established in Washington, as it could reach the most important audiences in this way but also facilitate access to archives and libraries.[90] Other government departments also showed great interest in the GHI. The Foreign Office, for example, attached "great importance" to being represented on its board of trustees (Stiftungsrat) in order to guarantee "coordination" with its own projects concerning Germany and German history in the United States.[91] Despite such ambitious plans, key protagonists tried to remain realistic about a GHI. The Minister for Research and Technology, Heinz Riesenhuber, tried to dampen the expectations. In October 1985, he wrote to Wolfgang Schäuble, the chief of the Chancellery:

> The plans to establish an institute as analyzed and recommended by the Council of Science and Humanities corresponds to the chancellor's wish to institutionalize a visible presence for German understanding of history in Washington, even though it will not even be remotely comparable to the Holocaust Museum pursued [*betrieben*] by American Jews.[92]

By identifying the USHMM as a project "betrieben"—a verb with a negative connotation in this context—by "American Jews," the Ministry of Research and Technology ascribed to the antagonistic position of the Chancellery toward the USHMM. Yet the official statement of the ministry about the founding of the GHI did not contain the slightest reference to such political considerations, which would have endangered the legitimacy of the project from the start.[93] After overcoming budgetary concerns from the Ministry of Finance, the German government decided on November 6, 1985, to establish the GHI, which opened in 1987.[94]

Choosing the right person as founding director would be indispensable for the implementation of their political goals, government officials knew. In accordance with what Hans-Ulrich Wehler, a leading left-leaning historian, at the time called a core principle of "neoconservative academic politics," officials tried to install a person willing to carry out these goals.[95] In early 1986, the BMFT began the search for a historian who would be responsible for the GHI's agenda, in coordination with the future institute's academic staff and its academic advisory board (Wissenschaftlicher Beirat).[96] The BMFT officially always insisted that it would not interfere with the GHI's internal affairs. Behind the scenes, however, both the BMFT and the Chancellery tried to find a suitable candidate for the position of director. The Chancellery favored two highly esteemed scholars, Karl Dietrich Bracher and Thomas Nipperdey, for this position.[97] Bracher, a political scientist and historian born in 1922, is one of the leading scholars of twentieth-century German history. He published widely on the history of democracy and totalitarianism and taught for almost forty years at the University of Bonn, where he supervised over one hundred dissertations.[98] In 1984, he had advised the Chancellery during the negotiations with the United States Holocaust Memorial Council. In 1986, however, he was already sixty-four years old and declined the offer to become the GHI's founding director.[99]

Hence, two historians who cooperated closely with Kohl on historical questions and who would serve on the GHI's academic advisory board, Michael Stürmer and Klaus Hildebrand, tried to persuade the alternative candidate, Thomas Nipperdey.[100] Nipperdey, who taught in Munich at the time, was the author of a colossal three-volume history of Germany from 1800 to 1918. His argument to consider the history of the German Empire in its own right—and not as the prehistory of the Third Reich—is perhaps his best-known contribution to historiography.[101] Yet Nipperdey, who died of cancer in 1992, was also not interested in the position, likely for family reasons.[102]

Making matters even more difficult for the Chancellery was the fact that of the twenty-six applicants who had responded to the job announcement for the position as director, only two were full professors ("C 4," according to the German classification), namely Hartmut Lehmann and Jürgen Kocka.[103] Neither was a specialist of the history of postwar Germany, meant to be a major focus of the institute. Lehmann was a specialist on early modern history. In the late 1950s, he had written a dissertation on the First World War and, about ten years later, produced a second book on the history of pietism in the German state of Wurttemberg since the seventeenth century.[104] In 1980, he published a study on the age of Absolutism.[105] Born in 1936, Lehmann had studied history, English, and political science in Germany, Austria, and England and held research fellowships at a number of American institutions, including UCLA, the University of Chicago, and the Institute for Advanced Studies in Princeton.[106] Since 1969, he had taught as a professor at the University of Kiel. While the Chancellery considered Lehmann academically suitable, he was, according to the staff's assessment, a largely "unknown" historian. Then again, Kocka appeared even less ideal a candidate because his field of expertise was labor and social history and he was, even worse, a "well-known Social Democrat," as Claus A. Lutz, an advisor and speech writer for Kohl in the Chancellery, pointed out to the chancellor.[107] The challenge to find a fairly prominent, well-established candidate, willing and able to implement political goals endangered the expectations of the Chancellery for the GHI. Lutz thus recommended to Kohl that he discuss these issues in detail with Stürmer or Hildebrand because of the "political significance" of the institute:

> Also in the United States, interest in historical questions is growing. We should take advantage of the opportunity to help with words and deeds with the representation of German and European history in the United States.
>
> A first task of the institute could hence be, for example, to promote the exhibition concepts of the House of History of the Federal Republic (including the history of the German resistance, which is largely unknown in the United States) and of the German Historical Museum.[108]

In addition to promoting the success story of West Germany, the GHI was thus also supposed to acquaint Americans with the history of German anti-Nazi resistance. These objectives directly corresponded with the efforts of German negotiators vis-à-vis the United States Holocaust Memorial Council.

At this crucial stage, Michael Stürmer intervened in the Chancellery.[109] In a confidential letter to Lutz, he elaborated his opposition to Kocka and Lehmann. He considered both candidates not suitable for the position of director and suggested that the BMFT should continue its efforts to convince Bracher or Nipperdey—whom he favored—to take over the position. The ministry should make use of its prerogative to make the final decision about the position and should not leave it up to the academic advisory board. According to Stürmer, Lehmann was a "very well respected" historian but did not have the necessary experience in the United States and lacked expertise in twentieth-century history. Furthermore, he was not sufficiently "outgoing"—Stümer actually used the English word—to "make an impact in America." Kocka, on the other hand, whom Stürmer considered the "most interesting and talented candidate," did not have the right academic profile for the position as founding director. While he had published important works on labor history and the nineteenth century, he had not worked on contemporary history and international relations, "the actual and necessary focal points" of the institute. Furthermore—and maybe more importantly—the majority of centrist and right-of-center historians had, as Stürmer stressed, strong reservations about Kocka. Kocka had been a "determined 68er" and had in the late 1970s positioned himself, along with Heinrich August Winkler, Hans Mommsen, Hans-Ulrich Wehler, and others, as an opponent of an affirmative interpretation of German history, which aimed at fostering German identity. Instead, he stressed the emancipatory role of a critical historical profession.[110] With such a devastating assessment and no other candidates available, Lehmann became the GHI's founding director. He did not take up his position right away, and from April 1 to August 1, historian Hermann-Josef Rupieper served as acting director.[111]

The Chancellery had considerable reservations about Lehmann's appointment. Lutz wrote to Wolfgang Bergsdorf: "Prof. Lehmann will become director after all (for 5! years)."[112] He was also not happy with the choice of Rupieper as acting and deputy director because the latter allegedly was a "pinko" (*links angehaucht*).[113] Some of Germany's leading historians shared the Chancellery's reservations. Arnulf Baring, for example, noted that Lehmann's five-month delay in starting his job and his lack of "organizing ability" put the future of the institute in jeopardy. Baring did not doubt at all, however, that the GHI would not become a research institute, but a "cultural stage for the government" (*Kulturtribüne der Regierung*).[114] Ambassador Ruhfus, however, sent a positive assessment of the GHI's opening ceremony on November 18, 1987, to the Foreign Office and was also pleased with Lehmann's "friendly and competent" inaugural address.[115] He pointed out that the ceremony had served to dispel the reservations of American scholars in general and of "Jewish academic circles in particular" against the institute. The audience had, according to the ambassador, specifically appreciated the intention to make the Nazi past an "important topic" for the GHI. He concluded optimistically that the institute would play a "significant role" in the intensification of German–American relations in the cultural sphere.

Despite—or maybe because of—the reservations against Lehmann among some government officials, he managed to establish himself as a politically independent founding director. Lehmann must have known that the GHI could build the reputation of a legitimate scholarly institution in the United States only if he could succeed in safeguarding it from political attempts to instrumentalize the brand-new institute. This was, however, not an easy task. Lehmann may not have been aware that key political players perceived the USHMM and

American Holocaust memorial culture more generally as a problem for the Federal Republic's reputation and that they had accelerated the establishment of the GHI for this reason. To him, as he stated in an interview in 2008, the "connection between the official opening of the Holocaust Memorial Museum and the German Historical Institute" was merely a "rumor."[116] It was only in 2012 that the GHI officially acknowledged the connection between its establishment and the plans for the USHMM during the 1980s. On the occasion of the GHI's twenty-fifth anniversary, Hartmut Berghoff, the GHI's director from 2008 to 2015, and Richard F. Wetzell wrote in a short history of the institute:

> Regarding the larger political context, there can be little doubt that the U.S. government's decision (1980) to establish a Holocaust Museum in the nation's capital made the proposal for a German Historical Institute especially timely in the eyes of some officials and politicians in Bonn.[117]

When Lehmann expressed his intention, however, to enter into a scholarly dialogue with the evolving USHMM in 1988, the German embassy requested that such endeavors be coordinated with German diplomats.[118] In fact, the first official joint event of the two institutions—the presentation of an *Encyclopedia of Camps and Ghettos*, published by the USHMM—only took place in 2010, almost twenty-five years after the founding of the GHI.[119] Since then, the GHI and the USHMM's Center for Advanced Holocaust Studies have regularly cooperated on seminars and book presentations.[120]

Although neither the Chancellery nor the BMFT, who had jurisdiction in this matter, could install a candidate of choice as director, government officials tried to implement their goals in the aftermath of the institute's opening. In this context, Kohl's expert on German–American relations, Werner Weidenfeld, and the director of the GHI's board of trustees and an official in the BMFT, Josef Rembser, played the central role. The first substantial conflict between politicians and professors over the GHI's activities was closely connected to the question of what the GHI could and should actually do—or not do—to promote the success story of the Federal Republic in the United States.

In early 1988, the embassy sent a reminder to the Foreign Office expressing its expectation that the GHI should soon take a "significant role in the field of historical scholarship with a strong effect [*starker Ausstrahlung*] on German-American cultural relations more generally."[121] The Foreign Office forwarded this reminder to the BMFT, where Rembser had been pondering this question as well. In March 1988, he met with Weidenfeld to discuss potential fields of collaboration.[122] Weidenfeld explained to Rembser that he—by order of Kohl—aimed to intensify the Federal Republic's presence in the United States and to generate more and new interest in Germany among average Americans, but also specifically among American Jewish organizations. He suggested that the GHI should actively engage in "public relations work" (*Public-Relations-Arbeit*) to improve German–American relations.[123] The fortieth anniversary of the Federal Republic, to be celebrated in May 1989, would provide an ideal opportunity for such an initiative. In the context of the debates about the Federal Republic's identity and Weidenfeld's role in these debates, it was clear that the latter had the promotion of the success story of the Federal Republic in mind. While Rembser welcomed Weidenfeld's suggestion, he also pointed to the fact that scholars working at the GHI wanted to focus on their research projects, not engage in public relations activities.

In the aftermath of this meeting, the BMFT contacted Lehmann and forwarded Weidenfeld's suggestion to hold a "representative event" for the fortieth anniversary of the Federal Republic.[124] In fact, this date—only about half a year prior to the fall of the Berlin Wall—became the ultimate self-recognition of West Germany as a nation-state in its own right, and outside observers even compared the celebrations in the Federal Republic with the bicentennial celebrations of American independence in 1976.[125] Lehmann agreed to organize such a conference as long as it would be "strictly academic," and no interference with regard to the program or the participants on behalf of the ministry would arise.[126] Coincidentally, Charles S. Maier of Harvard University's Minda de Gunzberg Center for European Studies had approached Lehmann to hold a conference on the Federal Republic's history in fall 1989, and the two historians decided to collaborate. The conference eventually took place at Harvard University from October 27–29, 1989, under the title "1949–1989: The Federal Republic as History."[127] Maier, one of the most influential historians of European history in the United States, had just completed a book on political and economic stability after the two World Wars. In 1988, the year he corresponded with Lehman, he also published *The Unmasterable Past*, an account of the Historians' Controversy. This book also included a very critical assessment of the Kohl government's politics of history, dubbed "Bitburg History" by Maier, which he defined as a blurring of the lines between Nazi perpetrators and their victims, denial of German collective responsibility for the legacies of the Holocaust, and rejection of the singularity of the Holocaust.[128] At first, however, neither Weidenfeld, the embassy, the BMFT, nor the chair of the GHI's academic advisory board, Erich Angermann, had any objections to these arrangements. The ministry decided to sponsor the project with DM 90,000 (ca. $53,000 at the time).

The run-up to the conference, however, strikingly exposed the goals but also the limits of government interference with institutions such as the GHI. The BMFT was thoroughly displeased with the conference proposal prepared by Maier and Lehmann. Their concept portrayed the history of the Federal Republic as a "series of learning experiences," to be explored in seven panels with titles such as "Learning to Live with Opposition," "Learning to Live with Plural-ism," "Learning to be an Ally," or "Learning to be Western." Based on the prem-ise that the Federal Republic was no longer a "tentative regime," the conference aimed to illustrate "West German achievements as struggles to overcome the legacy of earlier intolerance and authoritarianism."[129] Such a critical introspec-tion into West German history clearly ran counter to the kind of affirmative narrative government officials had envisioned.

Despite earlier support, Lehmann received a phone call from the BMFT in September 1988 and was told that the conference proposal was not "bal-anced" enough and that the BMFT would not fund the conference unless he changed the program.[130] Furthermore, the BMFT requested to be informed about the further development of the program and the list of speakers, an in-tervention that was, according to Lehmann, unheard of in the history of all German Historical Institutes. He underscored, in correspondence with mem-bers of the academic advisory board, that the GHI was operating on "thin ice" in the United States. Deepening the dialogue with American historians would only be possible if the GHI addressed topics that were of interest to them as well. More importantly, however, Lehmann stressed that "political steering" (politische Steuerung) of the GHI's activities severely damaged the institute's academic reputation. If the conference could not be organized without taking the BMFT's objections into consideration, Lehmann suggested, it should not take place at all.[131] Considering the fact that his partner in convening the con-ference, Maier, had established himself as a critic of the Kohl government's politics of history, Lehmann's concerns were certainly justified. It is nothing short of unthinkable that Maier, highly skeptical of Kohl's "insensitive" ap-proach to history, would have supported a public relations conference of the West German government.[132]

The chairman of the GHI's academic advisory board, Erich Angermann, also objected to the proposal Lehmann and Maier had developed.[133] Above all, he criticized the program for scholarly reasons, as he thought it only covered topics of "marginal relevance," and did not pay enough attention to crucial turning points in the country's development, such as the "economic miracle" or Adenauer's policies of reconciliation. However, he also considered its message politically problematic and thought the proposal was "obtrusively condescend-ing," as it painted the image of a country that was nothing more than the "more or less docile apprentice of the Western powers." He accused Lehmann of not being able to understand and execute the task he was given, namely to organize a "representative" event. Yet in addition to these objections, Angermann was also concerned about protecting the academic independence of the GHI. He feared that the BMFT could take the GHI's failure to meet political expecta-tions as a reason to use the board of trustees to interfere with the institute's academic agenda. He suggested, almost in a form of anticipatory obedience, that the GHI had to maintain certain academic standards as well as guarantee the "political 'tolerability'" (*politische "Verträglichkeit"*) of the event for the Federal Republic's fortieth anniversary.[134]

When all parties convened to discuss this complicated situation in late November, Lehmann and Maier had already revised the conference proposal. The latest draft had taken some of the previous criticism and suggestions into consideration.[135] Gone was what Angermann had considered "condescending" language, and they had expanded the thematic focus as well. The proposal now put more emphasis on the Federal Republic's "forty-year achievement . . . as a successful effort to overcome the legacy of earlier intolerance, authoritarianism, and social cleavages." The members of the GHI's academic advisory board welcomed these changes. While Lehmann would be responsible for the conference, the advisory board claimed responsibility for making sure that the BMFT could raise no "legitimate political objections." In this meeting, however, the BMFT corroborated its position, namely that it had the *right* to interfere with the GHI's agenda if this was politically necessary. All scholars present at the meeting, even the critics of the conference, rejected this position. They insisted that the GHI's academic agenda had to remain completely beyond the ministry's sphere of influence. This insistence aimed not only at protecting what scholars considered their domain, but also served to protect the institute as a whole. For its academic reputation, it was of "the *greatest* significance" to avoid even the remotest "*semblance* of governmental interference" (Anschein *gouvernementaler Einflußnahme*).[136]

In the end, Angermann was content with the revised conference program, which the BMFT now also deemed acceptable.[137] Nevertheless, Josef Rembser, who had been irritated with Lehmann's efforts to plan the conference without consulting the BMFT, requested that Angermann keep him informed about the proceedings.[138] Ominously, he concluded that the GHI, the academic advisory board, the board of trustees, and the BMFT would learn how to cooperate in the future. Lehmann had, in the end, managed to protect the institute from the interference of government officials, who had expected the GHI to grant academic legitimacy to an affirmative interpretation of the Federal Republic's success story.

The discussions about the GHI's agenda and key personnel provide a striking example of how the Kohl government tried to set the agenda of the institute behind the scenes.[139] Yet during this process officials realized that for the sake of the GHI's scholarly reputation, signs of such efforts had to be concealed at all cost. While scholars like Angermann sought to preemptively meet the expectations of the German government to avoid conflict with the BMFT, Lehmann insisted on his autonomy as the director of an institution whose purpose he considered above all academic and only to a much lesser extent political. From the perspective of government officials, the real problem lay in the choice of

Lehmann as the GHI's director.[140] Officials in the Chancellery critically monitored his activities and, especially after Stürmer and Hildebrand left the academic advisory board, worried that the institute invited too many "left-wing" historians as speakers.[141] This even compelled the chancellor to personally call upon the head of the Konrad Adenauer Foundation, Bruno Heck, to sponsor lectures at the GHI, whose establishment Kohl, after all, had "emphatically" supported.[142] German diplomats also continued to call for the GHI to take a more active role in German public relations in the United States, above all to prepare "measures" to balance the media coverage that would accompany the opening of the USHMM in 1993.[143] However, if political actors did not want to jeopardize the institute's academic reputation, the boundaries for efforts to influence its agenda were necessarily very narrow. The establishment of the GHI was, however, not the only example of cooperation between politicians and professors during the 1980s to change the image of Germany in the United States. Only a year after the founding of this institute, Werner Weidenfeld launched an even larger academic initiative in the United States.

Thinking Big: Werner Weidenfeld and the Chancellor's Initiative

In his state of the nation address in March 1987, Kohl announced to the German parliament his decision to improve "our image in the United States" as well as German perceptions of America in the near future.[144] Friendship and partnership with the United States were, after all, of "existential importance" for the Federal Republic.[145] In the same address, Kohl once again pointed to the centrality of German history as a "source of reassurance" for the German people and added that the "image of the Federal Republic abroad" should correspond to its "economic, social, and cultural realities" and include "German history in its entirety with all the high points and low points."[146] In Kohl's rhetoric, demanding such a complete or balanced approach toward German history was clearly a critique of a lack of attention to German history's "high points."[147]

While it was the consensus in the Chancellery in early 1987 that the Federal Republic's image in the United States was on the whole positive, officials considered the Nazi past a central source of potential irritations in German–American relations.[148] A number of other issues strained this relationship, including questions about security, arms reduction, détente, and economic tensions. Yet irrespective of such political and economic concerns, officials saw the "*Nazi past* and the Holocaust" as a latent threat for the image of the Federal Republic in the United States, which could manifest "at any given time."[149] These considerations also increased awareness of the long-term structural challenges the Federal Republic faced in shaping Americans' perceptions of Germany. These included a generally low degree of awareness among Americans of Germany, the geographic size of the United States, the relatively minimal coverage of foreign affairs in most American newspapers, and the inaccessibility of American television networks for public relations efforts. Due to the lack of opportunities to address Americans en masse, German public relations efforts had to focus on America's elites: select print journalists, politicians, members of political organizations, and universities and colleges. In fact, German officials had considered establishing a German TV channel in the United States for years, but had postponed this project again and again due to the "chaotic character" of the market in the United States.[150]

In 1987, Kohl delegated the task to improve the Federal Republic's image in the United States to Werner Weidenfeld. On October 1, Foreign Minister Genscher officially appointed Weidenfeld the new Coordinator for German-American Cooperation. This was an office created in 1981 as a means to strengthen the ties between both countries. While the first Coordinator, Hildegard Hamm-Brücher, had put forward a number of initiatives to strengthen German–American relations, her successor, former Ambassador von Staden, was less productive. Weidenfeld would quickly change that. While officially in the employ of the Foreign Office, he coordinated his initiatives directly with Kohl and the Chancellery.[151] At times, it appeared as if the foreign minister and the Foreign Office's staff were watching from the sidelines while Weidenfeld in correspondence with the Chancellery created public diplomacy initiatives.[152] Kohl trusted Weidenfeld, and the latter took advantage of an extraordinary amount of power in the design and conceptualization of new projects concerning German–American relations.

Prior to his tenure in the Foreign Office, Weidenfeld had already been advising the CDU and Kohl on questions concerning German identity, history, and foreign policy as a "prominent," "well respected," yet "independent" professor.[153] In the 1980s, Weidenfeld published a series of books and chapters addressing issues related to German history, identity, patriotism, and historical consciousness in the 1980s.[154] For example in 1987, he edited a volume on the historical consciousness of the Germans. Here, he also put forward his own considerations on the relationship between history and politics.[155] The two were in his estimation inextricably linked and converged in the Germans' quest for identity.[156] According to Weidenfeld, this quest was the driving force behind German history, from the Middle Ages to the present, responsible for the "extreme energy" released by Germans, their greatest achievements and deepest low points, including the "perversion of political thought under the National Socialist tyranny [*Herrschaftswahn*]."[157] Yet according to this line of argument, the heightened interest in history, which the Federal Republic had experienced since the late 1970s, was also a result of the Federal Republic's lack of identity.

Weidenfeld considered the challenges of the postmodern, postindustrial age a crucial factor for the "loss of orientation" at the time; it was the duty of the state to respond to these problems. Furthermore, he argued that the Federal Republic's problems were—just as much as those of German–American relations in general—also generational: the foundation of the Federal Republic's success story, built in the Adenauer era of the 1950s, had withered over the decades.[158] It is striking that many new German initiatives, such as exchange programs and the establishment of new institutes, echoed the tools of American cultural diplomacy in the 1950s.[159]

As Coordinator for German-American Cooperation, Weidenfeld could combine, as he stated in his inaugural address, the "theoretical-analytical work" of the "political scientist and historian" with the opportunity to implement policies.[160] He saw his new tasks as closely connected to his earlier scholarly reflections on identity. American support for the reconstruction of the Federal Republic and Europe was as much a part of German identity as the contribution of Germans and Europeans to the history of the United States. He explained in the same address:

> If in this way the question about the identity of the Federal Republic of Germany and the question about the American self-image constitute the key issue of German-American relations, then the coordinator's central tasks are obvious: He will above all attend to those individuals and institutions whose impact on identity formation [identitätsprägende Wirkung] is particularly noticeable.[161]

Weidenfeld thus not only produced scholarly manifestos on the issue of "identity," but actually wanted to have an impact on "identity formation." He listed the American mass media, "opinion leaders" of the "younger generation," and politicians as key target groups, but put another field on top of the list: academia. Here he wanted to make it a central task to create and sustain "images corresponding to reality" of the transatlantic partners on both sides of the Atlantic.[162]

Weidenfeld expended much energy to create programs that would build new connections between Germany and the United States as well as improve the reputation of the Federal Republic abroad. Already during his first year as Coordinator, several high-publicity events took place, for example the establishment of a Council for German-American Youth Exchange; a Joint Resolution of the United States Congress designating October 6, 1988, "German-American Day"; and the dedication of a "German-American Friendship Garden" on the National Mall in Washington.[163] These were reciprocal projects, at least in theory. In practice, however, the Federal Republic often was the driving force behind initiatives deepening German–American relations and also provided significant funding for these measures.[164]

Kohl expanded Weidenfeld's competencies in 1988 to include German public relations work in the United States more generally. At the beginning of his term as Coordinator, however, he focused above all on academic initiatives. They aimed to change and channel discourse about the Federal Republic in the United States in the long run by targeting students, scholars, and professors, as well as future "opinion leaders." All of them were supposed to learn more about the success story of the Federal Republic and also be encouraged to become experts on issues related to Germany and its history. For this purpose, Weidenfeld designed a grand strategy with a programmatic title in 1988: the Initiative of the Federal Chancellor for the Intensification of German-American Academic Relations.[165]

The establishment of so-called Centers of Excellence for German studies at three highly prestigious American universities formed the core of the Chancellor's Initiative. These centers aimed to maintain as well as broaden knowledge about Germany and Europe, especially within the humanities and social sciences.[166] In these fields, the Kohl government saw a specific deficit in the United States as well as the potential to make a lasting impact on the Federal Republic's image. In total the German government invested about DM 50 million in this project over a period of ten years. It hoped not only to generate new interest in the Federal Republic and broaden Americans' understanding of the country and its history among students and their academic teachers, but also to have an impact on American society at large, even though expectations in this regard remained rather vague. The centers were thus supposed to provide a long-term opportunity to channel and shape curricula and research agendas in the United States. The selection of ten young members of the "American academic elite" per year for a Chancellor's Fellowship, modeled after the highly prestigious Rhodes Scholarships, accompanied the establishment of the centers.[167]

Concerned about the status quo and the future orientation of American universities vis-à-vis Europe and Germany, Weidenfeld outlined this project and defined its purpose and limits in 1987.[168] In this context, he emphasized the necessity for the Federal Republic to support German studies departments at American universities. The German government viewed these departments as crucial nodes and multipliers in a network from which much larger audiences could be reached. The key challenge lay in initiating a conversation with elite American universities. German officials knew that it would be difficult to enter into a dialogue with these institutions, especially if such a conversation concerned decisions related to their academic agendas.[169] As the centers were supposed to benefit from their prestige and already existing infrastructures, it was clear to Weidenfeld that the federal government had to be willing to compromise as well as to provide incentives. In order to make such a proposal more attractive for American universities, the centers' focus may have had to be expanded to all of Europe, not just Germany. At this stage of the process, Kohl got involved. The chancellor invited the presidents of about ten leading American universities, the American Association of Universities, and the Council of Learned Societies to Germany.[170] This was the first time a German chancellor directly reached out to American academic functionaries in such a manner. The personal invitation by the chancellor underscored the importance that he attributed to this enterprise, but also served as an incentive for his American guests to take the trip. Representatives of a very select group of universities—including Harvard University, MIT, Johns Hopkins University, Georgetown University, the University of California Berkeley, the University of Chicago, and Washington University in St. Louis—accepted Kohl's invitation.

The visit was scheduled for early July 1988, and Weidenfeld and his staff and partners knew that this would be a decisive moment for the future of their efforts to spread knowledge about the Federal Republic in the United States.[171] At the time, the Federal Republic entertained several programs promoting German studies in the United States, such as chairs at a few universities, DAAD lectureships, and a cooperation with the German Studies Association (GSA). But these efforts were not, in the estimation of the Foreign Office, sufficient. The Foreign Office also emphasized that the Federal Republic's most recent project, the German Historical Institute, was at the time not able to stimulate research about Germany, as its academic advisory board had declared the GHI staff's own research projects its top priority for the time being. The establishment of new centers thus seemed an ideal solution to this problem. However, it would have to be made clear to the American university representatives that their visit to Germany was not only a fundraising event: while the federal government was willing to pay for the centers, they expected to reach the goal of stimulating German studies in the United States in return. German officials planned to establish three centers, which would be staffed with "high-ranking" German professors (full professors, "C 3" or "C 4" according to the German classification), their *Assistenten* (German equivalent of an assistant professor yet directly subordinate to a full professor), and research assistants. In addition, they would offer five to six yearlong fellowships for young German scholars.[172] In short, the centers were supposed to implant the structure of the German university into elite American universities, establishing mini-institutes staffed with German scholars.

In light of such grandiose plans, other government experts on academic policies were considerably less enthusiastic. Weidenfeld had at several occasions in the past proposed new, large-scale projects, which experts with more practical experience considered premature.[173] They also complained that Weidenfeld made decisions that affected the domains of other ministries without making a sufficient attempt to coordinate his efforts.[174] But they knew that he had the full backing of Kohl, who would make sure that additional and necessary funding would be available, even if it meant adjusting the federal budget.[175] And it was the chancellor's explicit wish to establish bases at American universities where the discourse about Germany and German history could be shaped.

On July 6, 1988, Kohl announced his plans to his American guests.[176] However, the reaction of the university presidents to the Chancellor's Initiative was at first rather lukewarm. Even though American universities showed the "greatest willingness" to develop programs on European and German studies with the federal government, they put heavy emphasis on the European context of such programs. German studies could only constitute a "small part" of these endeavors. In addition, the university presidents were very reluctant to commit to institutional agreements with the German government about centers at their own universities. Clearly, they wanted to safeguard their institutions from external influence, especially that of a foreign government. Nevertheless, all universities present at this meeting submitted a proposal for the funding competition that Kohl publicly announced that same day.[177] In addition to the Centers of Excellence and the Chancellor's Fellowship, Kohl also announced his plans to establish a German-American Academy of Humanities and Social Sciences in the not too distant future. Because of administrative and budget related problems, this project was only implemented as the German-American Academic Council in 1993, with an expanded focus on the sciences, engineering, and technology.[178]

The invitation of presidents of elite universities served the purpose of establishing contacts with these institutions, but Weidenfeld also hoped that it would function as a signal to major American private foundations and encourage investments in future projects.[179] As such it was only logical for Kohl to invite the presidents of such foundations, including the Rockefeller, Pew, and MacArthur Foundations, to Bonn the following year. All told, three such Chancellor's Roundtables with high-ranking guests convened between 1988 and 1990, including several intellectuals and opinion leaders for the third roundtable.[180] The meeting with the foundation's presidents in late September 1989 was, of course, overshadowed by the political changes taking place in Eastern Europe. Yet these political shifts that eventually led to the end of the Cold War served to underscore Kohl's emphasis on strengthening cooperation with American elites.[181]

While the meeting in 1989 did not lead to any concrete results, the foundations' presidents emphasized their commitment to a partnership with Europe and signaled interest in intensifying their engagement on the other side of the Atlantic.[182] The majority of foundation representatives were willing to support collaborative research projects, but were also skeptical toward the establishment of new institutions, especially if they only focused on German–American cooperation. Joint projects should, they argued, be conceived much rather in a European–American than a German–American framework. In this context, Kohl was specifically interested in his guests' assessment of the image of the Federal Republic and of Europe in the United States.[183] They attested to a generally positive attitude on the part of Americans toward Germany and the Germans, but suggested that improvements could be made in terms of knowledge about the country's culture and language. According to the Chancellery's assessment, the guests also appreciated "our aversion to having to see the Germans often portrayed in the American media as [a] 'villain,' as a Nazi with a thick accent."[184] Kohl stated that he knew that the injustice "committed in the name of Germany" could never literally be "made good" again, but he wondered if Americans knew enough about what the Federal Republic had actually accomplished in terms of financial compensation for the victims of National Socialism. Despite such rather delicate issues, the German side considered the invitation of the prominent—and financially potent—guests as a success: not only had they been very pleased by the reception in Germany, which had included meetings with other high-ranking German government officials and President von Weizsäcker, but they had also expressed their willingness to continue the conversation about future projects with Weidenfeld.[185]

Questions about the Federal Republic's image were not at the top of the agenda of the chancellor's meeting with the presidents of major American private foundations, although the impact of the Nazi past on the reputation of Germany abroad was key to German officials during the planning phase of these academic projects. In November 1988, for example, Kohl traveled to the United States to bid farewell to Reagan and meet President-elect Bush. He was scheduled to give a speech in honor of Simon Wiesenthal's eightieth birthday in New York and to receive an honorary PhD from Georgetown University.[186] Prior to his departure, the Foreign Office warned the Chancellery that due to the temporal proximity to the fortieth anniversary of the Kristallnacht pogrom, the image of Germany would be "*burdened*" during the visit of the chancellor.[187] According to this warning, large-scale newspaper ads as well as radio spots advertised events, symposia, exhibitions, and films commemorating the pogrom.[188] In New York alone, at least thirty events were to take place, including the groundbreaking ceremony for the city's Holocaust memorial museum.[189] In addition, the controversy surrounding Philipp Jenninger's address to the Bundestag on November 9, 1988, shadowed the chancellor's state visit. Jenninger, president of the Bundestag, had delivered a speech in commemoration of Kristallnacht that clearly condemned Nazi crimes, but had employed Nazi terminology—not to endorse it, but to reconstruct the thinking of the millions of Germans who followed it. Nevertheless, his speech lent itself to misinterpretation, leading to a wave of protest and ultimately Jenninger's resignation.[190] Marvin Hier of the SWC, in charge of organizing Wiesenthal's birthday event, and the "Nazi hunter" himself protested with German diplomats in Washington and New York. Wiesenthal conceded that Kohl's speech commemorating Kristallnacht in Frankfurt "could not have been better and phrased more masterfully,"[191] but agreed with Hier, who demanded "clarification" from Kohl with regard to Jenninger.[192] Reflecting on the state of German–American relations in connection with this visit, Kohl recorded in his memoirs his discontent with the image of the Federal Republic in the American media.[193]

Maybe as a result of these experiences, in late 1988 Kohl significantly expanded Weidenfeld's responsibilities to improve Germany's image in the United States more broadly. Weidenfeld was charged with developing strategies to reach out to audiences beyond academic elites.[194] For the next few years, he gathered information on this issue and began preparing a "master plan" for German public relations efforts in the United States. However, he postponed the completion of his proposal several times, and the entire project was temporarily shelved in 1990, when German unification had improved the Federal Republic's image to an extent that the Chancellery could never have achieved on its own, even "with the best concept."[195] He only completed his proposal in 1992, when global power structures had shifted fundamentally.[196] Weidenfeld's suggestions of 1992, however, were inextricably linked to his activities in academia before unification.

In 1989, before the fall of the Berlin Wall, a series of meetings, conferences, and roundtables took place, and drafts and proposals circulated between Bonn, Washington, and New York suggesting new ways and means the Federal Republic could use to present itself in the United States.[197] In New York, a committee composed of German diplomats from the embassy and various consulate generals came to the conclusion that significant changes had to be made to the representation of the Federal Republic in the United States, among other things to "underscore a *humane image of the Germans* in light, for example, of SS clichés in American movies and television shows."[198] Weidenfeld's office announced in this context his decision to integrate the American Jewish community as a new target group into the Coordinator's future projects.[199] For Weidenfeld, Holocaust angst was only one of a number reasons to change the discourse about the Federal Republic, albeit an important one. In the early 1990s, for instance, he tried to negotiate a positive portrayal of the Federal Republic in the Holocaust Memorial Center in Detroit.[200] When he finally completed his master plan for German public relations in April 1992, his assessment strongly resonated with the convictions of other German officials during the 1980s:

> The crimes of National Socialism, the Holocaust, totalitarianism have become deeply engrained in American collective perception. Since an especially important American elite, Jewish citizens, are affected in a traumatic way, this image maintains its pressing presence [*bedrängende Gegenwart*].[201]

In the early 1990s, his efforts to confront this challenge would build on the achievements of the Chancellor's Initiative of 1988.

The founding of three Centers of Excellence marked the core of this initiative. In 1989, after several months of deliberation, Kohl decided to establish these centers at Georgetown, Harvard, and the University of California Berkeley. While the Foreign Office and some officials in the Chancellery had—in accordance with the original plan to establish a center in the Midwest—favored the University of Chicago, Kohl and Weidenfeld chose Harvard instead.[202] Behind the scenes in Bonn, there had been a series of controversies over the appropriate form and source of funding for the centers.[203] Yet the chancellor's decision to establish three highly prestigious centers with a direct impact beyond academia was implemented despite such resistance.[204] To the Chancellery, four criteria were decisive: a center would have to make a substantial and new contribution to the field of German and European studies; it would have to influence other universities and the public at large; the German contribution to the establishment would have to be clearly visible; and the universities themselves would have to guarantee funding after a period of ten years.[205] Until then—that is, until 2000—the German government planned to provide each center with ca. DM 1.5 million annually. Weidenfeld negotiated the contracts with the three universities, which representatives of the DAAD and the universities signed on November 1, 1990, in Washington, DC. The DAAD was from then on in charge of dispensing the funds to the centers and received annual reports. All universities agreed to rapidly establish the centers, hire new professors, design new curricula, and award fellowships.[206]

The centers, especially the one at Georgetown (now called the BMW Center for German and European Studies), are an indicator of how important the transatlantic partnership with academics was to the Kohl government. However, the original goal to channel scholarship on Germany and maybe even install German professors with their staff at universities like Harvard or Georgetown failed. The actual agreements between the DAAD and the respective universities were clearly tailored to the agendas and needs of those universities rather than to the original political goals of the German government. During the planning phase, it must have become obvious to German officials that exporting or establishing a German institute staffed with German scholars at an American university, from which they could shape future research on Germany, could not be realized. According to the agreement with Berkeley, for example, German expectations as to the quality of scholarship, the center's visibility, and its impact on other universities and beyond academia were very high.[207] Yet in terms of the center's research and teaching agendas, the demands were very moderate: the centers focused not on German–American, but clearly on European–American relations; courses and degree programs were developed as additions to already existing curricula at Berkeley; and a European, not necessarily a German, visiting professor taught at the center. The DAAD only had a moderate request, hoping that German professors would be invited to participate in the evaluation of the center's activities. Considering that the German government invested a large amount of money in the center's activities—courses, fellowships, conferences, and so forth—its influence on its agenda was indeed very limited.

The centers could not have been established without making these concessions. After all, Berkeley also agreed to a significant investment (less than $1 million per year) for public relations, adult education, conferences, and new faculty positions. Perhaps German officials realized that funding an independent academic center—without expecting to have a say in its scholarly agenda—would put the Federal Republic in an even better light than all the efforts to convey the image of a Germany that had fundamentally changed since 1945. After all, wasn't academic freedom a crucial aspect of this reversal? When in 1996 a commission of six German and American professors was tasked with evaluating the centers, their assessment was thoroughly positive.[208] The centers had, according to the evaluation, perfectly served the purpose of strengthening German and European studies in the United States. While the attempt to directly channel American scholarship on Germany had failed, the establishment of such institutions in the end perfectly served the purpose of promoting a truly democratic and progressive image of Germany. Who in the United States could, all things considered, complain about millions of Deutschmark for the noble cause of scholarship? That Holocaust angst and the promotion of a certain interpretation of German history had been at the origins of these projects was probably not common knowledge at American universities.

The goal to inscribe the success story of the Federal Republic into the historical consciousness of Americans and reduce the presence of the Nazi past and the Holocaust could only be achieved indirectly—if at all. The cooperation of German political actors with German scholars thus cannot be reduced to a one-way relationship of professors advising decision-makers. Instead, it should be seen as a conversation, one that created its own internal dynamics and in which scholars were able to pursue their own (academic) goals. As a matter of fact, a multitude of political players and academics vied to influence the purposes, design, and function of joint projects. While the Chancellery played the dominant role in the political sphere, other German government agencies, particularly the Foreign Office and the Federal Ministry of Research and Technology, in charge of some of Germany's academic projects abroad, pursued their own agendas. Some scholars indeed acted as academic advisors to the federal government, some sought to defend academic freedom against political interference, and some fell somewhere in the middle. For these reasons, both projects, the GHI and the Centers of Excellence, in their final version significantly differed from the original intentions of the political leadership around Kohl. These institutions are thus to a certain degree an unintended outcome of the Kohl government's politics of German history.

5

After Unification

The Transformation of Holocaust Memory, 1990–1998

In September 1998, only ten days before the Bundestag elections that would end his sixteen-year tenure as chancellor, the *Frankfurter Allgemeine Zeitung* featured a long interview with Helmut Kohl. Campaigning for reelection, but also already shaping his legacy, Kohl justified the plans for the highly controversial Monument to the Murdered Jews of Europe in Berlin.[1] He proclaimed:

> Here, the core of our self-concept as a nation is at stake. The parliament, the government, and the public agree to a large degree that Germany bears a special responsibility to keep the memory of the Holocaust alive.[2]

Addressing those who opposed the plans for the monument, Kohl continued:

> Many people still have not understood how closely not only the [German] Jewish community but also the world is following our debate. We are not talking about just any issue. We are talking about the Holocaust and how it should be commemorated in Germany in an appropriate way.

Kohl's support for the construction of a massive Holocaust monument in Berlin suggests a significant transformation in his government's politics of history over the course of roughly one and a half decades. While Kohl had, for example, in Bergen-Belsen in 1985 expressed his dedication to preserving the memory of the Holocaust,[3] he now made explicit a conclusion that had manifested itself throughout the preceding years: that Holocaust memory *in* Germany and the country's reputation *abroad* were deeply intertwined. Yet while the German government could do little to shape memorial cultures abroad, it could indeed exert such influence at home. After sixteen years in office, Kohl seemed no longer to perceive Holocaust memory only as a burden; he had possibly discovered its potential to become a "positive resource," as historian Jan-Holger Kirsch has remarked, for domestic and above all foreign policy goals.[4]

This transformation of the Kohl government's politics of Holocaust memory in the Federal Republic cannot be explained without taking its engagement with American Holocaust memorial culture into consideration. During and after German unification, Holocaust angst of German officials—within Kohl's Chancellery and at crucial places of the networks established in the 1980s—continued to manifest themselves in two critical ways: first, a fixation about an assumed influence of American Jews on public opinion, who portrayed Germany only as a "Holocaustland," and, second, a growing concern about tendencies to instrumentalize Holocaust memory for fundraising and other commercial purposes.[5] At the same time, German officials became increasingly aware that all of their direct efforts to manage American Holocaust memory had or would fail. It is possible to continue exploring the further development of Holocaust angst beyond 1990 as there was a significant degree of continuity of personnel between West and unified Germany. De jure, the GDR joined the Federal Republic and the West's governmental structures were expanded to the East.[6] Kohl soon appointed some East Germans to government positions, among them a rather inconspicuous "girl" by the name of Angela Merkel, who became Federal Minister for Family and Youth in 1991.[7] Yet the key positions in the "system Kohl" remained firmly in the hands of the old West German elites.

Holocaust Memory in Unified Germany

The end of the Cold War changed the global political power structure fundamentally, including German–American relations: while Germany depended less and less on the military support of the United States, German officials became increasingly concerned about the declining dedication of the United States to its former Cold War ally. This change in the geopolitical landscape after 1989/90 also did not put an end to German discussions about the Nazi past. To the contrary, the emergence of a larger German nation-state, the most populous and economically strongest country at the center of a rapidly changing European continent, raised new questions as to how to engage with the Nazi past and the Holocaust. These political transformations quickly put an end to the Kohl government's efforts to shape a specifically West German identity. Yet how the impact of the Nazi past and the Holocaust would play out on the new Germany's identity in the long run was all but clear at the beginning of the decade.

Debates over the Nazi past, the Holocaust, its perpetrators, and its victims boomed in the 1990s.[8] Unification erased the interpretative frameworks the Cold War had imposed on the engagement with the Nazi past in both German states. The East German reading, perceiving National Socialism as fascism and thus as a result of capitalism, reducing it to an assault on communism, was no longer tenable.[9] In the "old" Federal Republic, of course, no such state doctrine existed. Nevertheless, the paradigm of totalitarianism, popular particularly with conservatives, for instance during the Bitburg controversy, was modified. It had considered both Nazism and Soviet Communism as totalitarianism and suggested that the Federal Republic's contribution to the struggle against Communism should outweigh the legacies of the Nazi past.[10] After unification, a different kind of debate about totalitarianism emerged, focusing on the political impact of the post-GDR left as well as on questions of how coming to terms with the Communist past would compare to coping with the Nazi past.[11] Beyond the end or the revision of such paradigms, unified Germany faced a multitude of new debates and controversies about the Nazi past and its impact on German identity.

Already the question of the legitimacy of German unification itself led to fierce political debates, resulting from diverging lessons drawn from the Nazi past. In contrast to the political right, the left and the generation of 1968, generally speaking, as well as the Federal Republic's leading liberal intellectuals, such as Jürgen Habermas, were critical of unification.[12] They based such criticism explicitly on fears that a new German nation-state could abandon the "republican consciousness" and the self-imposed limits of West Germany, for example in the realm of foreign policy.[13] Yet very soon it became obvious that unification resulted in an entirely new dynamic of engagement with the Nazi past. At the end of the 1990s, the Holocaust had indeed become the "central paradigm of the political culture of the Federal Republic."[14] A large number of important anniversaries, but also debates and controversies about the Nazi past propelled unified Germany to reassess questions of guilt and responsibility, perpetration and victimhood.[15] For example, the fiftieth anniversary of the end of World War II in 1995 illustrated a broad consensus among Germany's political elites about the significance of the Nazi past for the nation's historical consciousness. In a striking contrast to Bitburg ten years earlier, the Kohl government made no attempt to contrast the crimes committed by the Nazi regime with the suffering of German soldiers or civilians; May 8, 1945 had irrevocably become a day of liberation. The former Allies' reactions on this occasion also indicated that the Federal Republic "could now pay less attention to memory politics and focus more exclusively on the 'real' political challenge of becoming a first-rate European and global power broker."[16]

To take another example from the domestic context, an exhibition about "Crimes of the Wehrmacht," designed by the Hamburg Institute for Social

Research, broke a major societal taboo by shattering the myth of the "clean Wehrmacht."[17] This and other discussions about the involvement of "ordinary" Germans in the Holocaust stood in stark contrast to the former West German emphasis on German suffering and victimhood.[18] To some, this extended what they considered necessary and bearable. In 1998, for example, the German novelist Martin Walser spoke out against what he perceived as an "incessant presentation of our shame," which made him want to "look away."[19]

American Jewish Organizations and German Unification

The fall of the Berlin Wall on November 9, 1989, also interrupted the phase of rapprochement between the West German government and American Jewish organizations that had intensified in the aftermath of Bitburg. Questions about the future of Germany also put the German past back on the agenda.[20] In 1990 an open conflict between several American Jewish organizations and the Kohl government erupted about the legitimacy and the implications of German unification. In this context, the Kohl government benefited from its partnership with the AJC and the Armonk Institute, who not only welcomed the political changes, but also directly opposed criticism by other American Jewish organizations.

The majority of Americans supported the idea of a unified Germany.[21] Some American Jewish organizations, such as the World Jewish Congress, however, showed little enthusiasm for a larger, stronger German state at the heart of Europe and took a reserved and skeptical stance.[22] They knew that their position would not change the course of events and alter American political support for German unification.[23] Nevertheless, they warned of the danger of a new German nationalism and militarism and expressed their worries that a unified Germany could neglect "Jewish concerns," such as financial compensation for the victims of National Socialism, Israel's security, prevention of anti-Semitism, and the support for Holocaust memory.[24] These objections specifically concerned the population of the GDR, which lacked the experience of living in a democratic state and had been exposed to anti-Zionist propaganda for decades.[25] Furthermore, the prospect of unification brought the question of East German compensation payments and restitution back on the agenda, which the GDR government had refused to address almost until the end of the regime.[26] Several American Jewish organizations and publicists heavily criticized the Kohl government's efforts to reach German unification as quickly as possible.[27] The WJC, prominent Holocaust survivors such as Elie Wiesel and Benjamin Meed, as well as organizations that explicitly focused on the legacies of the Nazi past, such as the Simon Wiesenthal Center, warned that a unified Germany might forget the "lessons of history."[28] According to Wiesel, Germany was not yet "ready" for unification.[29] And the SWC's dean, Marvin Hier, wrote to Kohl on February 9, 1990:

> I must tell you, I am not among those in the cheering section applauding the rush towards German unification. However, if that is the inevitable course, let us at least place on record our concerns. . . . The fears are real because those who bear the scars of the last "unified Germany" do not see their concerns being addressed in the current reunification discussions between world leaders. They open the papers each day and read about proposals concerning the demilitarization of armed forces; about monetary union and the rate of exchange of the Deutsche Mark. All very legitimate, but not a single word is said publicly about the great internal questions of how to educate millions of people who have been cut off from the real world for more than forty years and how to prevent their ignorance of the past from negatively affecting the course of the future. To the victims of Nazism, Mr. Chancellor, it is not the potential weakness of the Deutsche Mark that is critical, but the consequences that may lead to a weak "Deutsche memory."[30]

This letter struck a chord in the Chancellery, especially since Hier had also made it public via the *New York Times*.[31] His catalogue of requests revealed his lack of knowledge about the Federal Republic, but his intervention was bound to upset a chancellor so concerned with Germany's reputation abroad. In addition to reasonable requests concerning the redesign of concentration camp memorials and revitalizing Jewish life in East Germany, Hier incorrectly depicted the Federal Republic as a country without Holocaust education in high schools, which tolerated "hate crimes" and anti-Israeli "terrorist organizations" that "have enjoyed respectability in East Germany."[32] While the last claim was indeed true,[33] Hier's characterization of the Federal Republic did not correspond with reality: neither did West German schools refuse to teach the history of the Holocaust, nor was there a need to ban German terrorist organizations, such as the Red Army Faction or the Revolutionary Cells, outlawed and prosecuted since their inception in the 1970s.[34] Kohl was outraged about this letter and with a thick black pen underlined the words "cheering section" twice, adding to the top of the document "So sind Sie" (best translated as: "That is typical of you").[35] His response to Hier, however, was more measured. In a long and detailed letter, he expressed his surprise and disappointment about Hier's assessment as well as the fact that the latter had made his letter public.[36] As Hier spoke on behalf of an institution that bore the name of the famous "Nazi hunter"

Simon Wiesenthal, whom Kohl greatly admired, the chancellor also contacted Wiesenthal directly.[37] Even though Wiesenthal had only lent the Center his name and was not involved in its activities, Kohl made clear to him that he was "deeply disappointed" about Hier's letter.[38] In the further course of the dispute, Hier clarified that his objections only concerned the population of the GDR.[39]

Yet this did not mean that the SWC approved of German unification and the Kohl government's policies in this context. For example, when he addressed the National Leadership Conference of the SWC in Washington in March 1990, German ambassador Jürgen Ruhfus recorded a "fundamentally negative attitude towards us."[40] Ruhfus, however, noted that other American Jewish organizations would eventually abandon their critical stance toward German unification. He believed that while Hier could not be persuaded, "a patient approach towards American Jewish organizations" would have a positive effect in the end. An encounter a few days later confirmed Ruhfus in his judgment. A member of the National Security Council staff at the White House sympathized with the ambassador: the White House knew how "difficult the dialog with Jewish organizations could be at times."[41] However, the "German cause" would in the end benefit if German representatives would continue to seek a dialogue with "patience and persistence."[42]

While these discussions with one spectrum of American Jewish organizations caused dismay within the Kohl government, it intensified its cooperation with its partners, the AJC and the Armonk Institute, significantly. In correspondence with Michael Mertes, in charge of relations with American Jewish organizations in the Chancellery, William Trosten had criticized the "propaganda and agitation (e.g., Elie Wiesel interview in *Der Spiegel*) especially from American Jews" against German unification.[43] In a memorandum for Kohl, Mertes deemed the readiness of Trosten's Armonk Institute to reduce "Jewish fears about a reunification of Germany" to be "immensely valuable" for the Federal Republic.[44] The Armonk Institute planned symposia, interventions with the American mass media, and the continuation of projects concerning Holocaust education in the United States.[45] These initiatives were particularly useful for the Kohl government as they emerged from within the American Jewish community and so could not be interpreted as outside interventions into Jewish (and American) affairs by the Federal Republic.

The AJC expressed a number of concerns and expectations in regard to the prospect of a unified Germany, yet was generally optimistic about the future development of the Federal Republic.[46] Considering the stability of German democracy and its past efforts to confront the Nazi past, the AJC hoped for a similarly positive development on the territory of the GDR, where it perceived significant deficits in terms of Holocaust education, the content of former sites of Nazi terror (which indeed all but ignored Jewish victims in favor of Communist interpretations of National Socialism), and open claims for financial compensation.[47] Yet also for West Germany, the AJC lamented deficits with regard to the engagement with the Nazi past and hoped that a further institutionalization of Holocaust memory would take place in a unified Germany. In so doing the AJC made clear that American opinion about the "new" Germany—especially among American Jews—would in the long run depend upon the Federal Republic's domestic engagement with the Nazi past.[48]

The Return of the Ugly German

In the years following German unification, a series of events propelled new anxieties about a negative image of the Federal Republic in the United States.[49] In this context, German officials maintained their critical stance toward Holocaust memory in the United States and American Jewish organizations. For example, the refusal of the German government to send troops to participate in the Gulf War of 1991 caused tensions between the Federal Republic and some American Jewish organizations, who perceived this as a lack of support for Israel, especially in light of accusations that German companies had contributed to Iraq's chemical weapons program. Even the Armonk Institute cancelled a trip to Germany for this reason.[50] However, it was above all American reports about the rise of right-wing extremist, neo-Nazi, and anti-Semitic violence against foreigners and asylum seekers in unified Germany that alarmed German diplomats.[51] In November 1992, the new German ambassador Immo Stabreit (1992–1995) sent an alarming message to the Foreign Office:

> The news about the murder of the three Turkish women in Mölln and of one German in Wuppertal (according to the press here, the attack was caused by the latter's pronouncement that he was Jewish) have come as a real bombshell [*wie eine Bombe eingeschlagen*]. From a conversation that I had this morning with a local, exceptionally influential journalist, I record that we now have to prepare ourselves for exceptionally bad press. . . . Jewish circles in particular were deeply worried and agitated.[52]

Against the backdrop of a reform of German immigration laws, a wave of right-wing extremist violence hit the Federal Republic in the early 1990s. Between 1991 and 1993, extremists committed in total 4,500 acts of violence against refugees, immigrants, and Jews, resulting in twenty-six murders and 1,800 injuries.[53] Attacks on foreigners in cities such as Hoyerswerda, Rostock-Lichtenhagen, Mölln, and Solingen, where five Turkish women died in 1993, as well as attacks on synagogues, marked an unprecedented outbreak of racist and anti-Semitic violence. Hordes of neo-Nazis giving the Hitler salute, scanting "Germany to the Germans, foreigners out!" and "Sieg Heil!," created images reminiscent of SA violence during the Weimar Republic and of Nazi pogroms that were sent around the globe. To this day, the video recordings of the Rostock-Lichtenhagen pogrom as well as the reactions and comments by the bystanders remain deeply disturbing.

In the eyes of critical observers, the state governments often appeared helpless or refused to acknowledge the true extent of the problem.[54] For example, when in Hoyerswerda the police could no longer protect a shelter for asylum seekers during a riot, they were escorted and relocated by police officers (and soon thereafter, expelled from Germany). With the help of the state, it appeared, right-wing extremists indirectly achieved an explicit goal: to "liberate" certain areas of foreigners.[55] These violent incidents were in no way indicative of the overwhelming majority of Germans, even though right-wing parties gained support and numerous bystanders in local communities sympathized with the extremists.[56] However, hundreds of thousands of German citizens protested the wave of violence by arranging mass demonstrations and candle-light vigils all over Germany.[57] But the executive—above all the state governments in charge of the police—were unable to swiftly stop the wave of violence and to protect German and foreign citizens and refugees alike.

The foreign as well as the German press reported in great detail about these events. Coverage abroad—and in the Federal Republic—put major blame on the Kohl government for failing to find appropriate and effective responses.[58] The chancellor took criticism in American newspapers personally and felt "wrongly attacked," as Stabreit recorded in a letter.[59] In general, German diplomats stationed in the United States paid specifically close attention to articles written by American Jewish journalists, some of whom indeed held critical views of Germany.[60] The *New York Times* columnist Abraham Michael ("A. M.") Rosenthal, for example, wrote an acerbic analysis of the Kohl government's failure to adequately protect minorities, explicitly referring to the "victims of the previous one-Germany." Rosenthal continued:

> In history, Germany was not the only criminal nation, just the most vile. The problem is not that inescapable, realistic fears remain but that Germany has a way of perpetuating them.
>
> Yes, other countries use their economic power careless of what it does to others. Other countries have riots against foreigners and sometimes deport them.
>
> But when Germany swings the economic steel ball, when so many Germans approve of the anti-foreign violence of their youngish Nazis, when Germany decides the answer to refugees is to tighten asylum, when Germany prepares to deport gypsies, among the first

victims of older Nazis, Europeans are seized by desire to rethink union with the new Germany until they are sure it is entirely new.[61]

Fritz Ziefer, director of the embassy's New York-based public diplomacy department German Information Center, perceived Rosenthal's columns and his references to "negative historical images of Germany" as indicative of "resentment and distrust" against "the Germans" in the American Jewish community.[62] Ziefer concluded that

> at least among the readers of the New York Times it is not considered inappropriate to publicly render a judgment in a way a journalist would never dare to speak about blacks or Jews. The climate of opinion that allows Rosenthal to write such nonsense is thus greater cause for concern than the column itself.[63]

The context of Ziefer's statement makes clear that he in fact meant "prominent" members of the New York City Jewish community when speaking of the "readers of the New York Times." Even though phrased in a somewhat coded way, such an analysis corroborated prevailing notions about the negative attitudes of Jews toward Germany and the influence of American Jewish "'anti-German' circles" who allegedly not only held, but also sought to perpetuate negative stereotypes about Germany.[64] Kohl's staff at home appeared to have no inhibitions to express their concerns in this context. Marc Fisher, the Washington Post's correspondent in Germany at the time, recorded in his book After the Wall that the chancellor's security advisor, Horst Teltschik, had said to him: " 'You have people like Safire,' meaning the New York Times columnist William Safire, 'who dangerously feed our radicals every week.' "[65] If Fisher's account of the conversation with Teltschik is correct, it seemed more logical for German officials to blame American Jewish journalists for the radicalization of German rightwing extremists than to make an effort to explain the reasons for the wave of xenophobic violence.

In light of these developments, the arrival of the staunchly conservative Immo Stabreit in early 1992 as the new German ambassador in Washington must appear as an attempt to confront such challenges. Soon nicknamed "the Junker [Prussian aristocrat] from Germany" in Washington,[66] Stabreit was anything but a subtle mediator and acquired a reputation as "a stern figure . . . known to rail often against the American obsession with the Nazi period."[67] Born in 1933 in Berlin, Stabreit had studied at Princeton University during the 1950s before returning to the Federal Republic to attend law school and join the Foreign Service. In the 1970s, he was stationed at the Boston consulate general and also participated in the Advanced Studies Program at Harvard University. He was among Kohl's confidants and served as Teltschik's deputy in the Chancellery from 1983 to 1987, the year he was appointed ambassador in

South Africa.[68] In 1992, Kohl installed Stabreit against the will of Foreign Minister Genscher as the new ambassador in Washington, according to an article in *Der Spiegel* in early 1992.[69]

Later that year, Stabreit expressed his outrage over right-wing extremism in Germany in a candid letter to Peter Hartmann, Teltschik's successor in the Chancellery.[70] Yet he also complained to Hartmann about how difficult it was for him to explain the inability of the German government to stop the wave of violence: "You will also have to understand that we are slowly getting in a difficult position to sell a policy that exhausts itself in 'examining', 'investigating', 'considering' etc."[71] To Stabreit a number of American Jewish journalists posed a particular problem for the Federal Republic, and he chastised Rosenthal and others, who had "not changed their judgment about Germany since Auschwitz and who are now triumphantly proclaiming, 'I always said it!' "[72] Still, the ambassador considered the American press all in all balanced in late 1992. But he was concerned about the general lack of understanding among Americans about the political conditions in Germany and feared that the climate would change significantly if the wave of violence could not be stopped. If the federal government did not "succeed in creating the impression to have reversed the trend"—by which Stabreit meant right-wing extremism and violence—the Federal Republic would lose the support of its "friends" in the United States. This would even reflect upon the highest political levels. While President Bush had already expressed his concerns about right-wing extremism to Stabreit, the ambassador feared even more tensions with the incoming Clinton administration, which, as he ominously explained, included "many members of minorities."[73]

Of course, it was part of Stabreit's assignment as ambassador to be concerned with the Federal Republic's image in the United States. Yet it is questionable whether he, who had on his previous post in South Africa attempted to reduce public criticism of the Apartheid regime, was suitable to "correct" what he perceived to be a wrong image of Germany.[74] For instance, the aforementioned letter to Peter Hartmann also contained an analysis of postunification neo-Nazism by Stabreit, which illuminated his political convictions. According to the ambassador, the chancellor's hands to confront right-wing extremism in an effective way were tied. Kohl lacked the necessary parliamentary majorities and instruments of power to fight right-wing extremism. Stabreit wrote,

> With regard to combatting right-wing extremism, we are today confronted with the consequences of the reduction of governmental authority since the mid-1960s and the toleration of left-wing terror for decades (Runway West, Hafenstrasse, Brockdorf [sic], Wackersdorf, Kreuzberg, WWF-meeting in Berlin etc. etc.). Today we suffer from the distrust in the executive branch of our democratic state, boosted

by Mr. Baum and Mr. Hirsch [leading representatives of the FDP's left-liberal wing] in an absurd manner; the overly "liberal" laws based on this distrust; and the demoralization of the police ("Hamburg police encirclement"). This was all too predictable. Let's not even talk about the question of asylum seekers [*Asylantenfrage*]. Is it a coincidence that, of all places, allegedly so "reactionary" Bavaria has seen relatively few attacks on foreigners?[75]

In short, Stabreit was not denouncing terrorism but instead viewed liberal legislation and the toleration of the peace and environmentalist movements of the 1980s—which had, for example, opposed the construction of an additional "runway west" at Frankfurt airport or the construction of a nuclear power plant at Brokdorf—as major prerequisites of the wave of neo-Nazi violence in Germany. As such, he fundamentally called the liberalization of West German society since the 1960s into question. This, however, was a position he could hardly make public in the United States to explain the origins of postunification neo-Nazi violence.

Stabreit's assessment illustrated a reductive approach to the challenge the rise of neo-Nazism imposed upon the Federal Republic. Such a stance also precluded Stabreit from comprehending the true extent of the shock the murder of innocent men, women, and children caused in the United States, which, after all, had helped to rebuild West German democracy after World War II. Stabreit also did not take into consideration the fact that to many Americans, Germany still represented a country they had either fled from or whose dictatorship they had opposed and fought against. Such insights probably escaped the eyes of those fixated on finding evidence of anti-German sentiments in the American media. Also in the Federal Republic, as the *Süddeutsche Zeitung* reported, the American coverage of the events in Germany propelled stereotypes about opinion pages "dominated by Jews" in major American newspapers as well as the "ignorance of Americans" more generally.[76]

In accordance with his critical position vis-à-vis American Jewish journalists, Stabreit expressed a rather uncompromising stance toward American Jewish organizations. He prided himself for "being the last person" to give in to the pressure from a Jewish organization and insisted that "we should finally put an end to all of these payments," by which he meant compensation payments for victims of National Socialism.[77] But he also clearly pointed to the damage the wave of right-wing violence caused for the Federal Republic abroad:

But I am happy about every Jew who immigrates to Germany and finds his new home there, and it is simply unacceptable that we are going to let a few radical thugs destroy everything we have built in terms of good will and willingness to cooperate with us over the years.

Considering the position of the chancellor and some of his staff vis-à-vis the USHMM and American Holocaust memorial culture more generally, it was probably no coincidence that Kohl had deemed Stabreit, an unapologetic patriot ready to stand his ground, suitable to represent the Federal Republic in Washington at this time. This decision, however, backfired. American observers criticized Stabreit's reluctance to openly address the Nazi past or the wave of neo-Nazi violence and considered him a failure as ambassador.[78]

In this context, the AJC tried to intervene with the Chancellery. Taking advantage of the close connections formed during the 1980s, AJC president Alfred H. Moses contacted Kohl in late 1992. He expressed his concerns about the wave of neo-Nazi violence and even offered to help confront the issue of extremism in the Federal Republic by sharing information about AJC programs designed to "promote pluralism and tolerance."[79] More importantly, however, he pointed to what many observers in the United States perceived as a specific flaw of the Kohl government's reaction to the rise of neo-Nazism, namely a lack of action by the chancellor himself. Moses concluded:

> We would urge you further to assert forcefully and unequivocally through your own public words and by your physical presences at the scene of recent crimes that there is no place in Germany for the purveyors of neo-Nazi hatred nor for their supporters and sympathizers.[80]

Organizations who had previously taken a more critical stance toward the Federal Republic now also had harsh words about Kohl. Marvin Hier, for instance, stated in a television interview that he had warned the chancellor about the danger of neo-Nazism, a warning the latter had not, according to Hier, taken seriously.[81] Organizations of Holocaust survivors also expressed their worries to German diplomats in the United States concerning the rise of neo-Nazism in unified Germany. They bluntly asked: "Is the new Germany beginning to resemble the old one?"[82]

If nothing else, the wave of right-wing and neo-Nazi violence in the early 1990s illustrated to German officials how closely observers in the United States watched over the development of postunification Germany. That attacks on foreigners, Jews, and synagogues provoked analogies or comparisons to the Third Reich was anything but surprising, as Kohl acknowledged in 1993.[83] Yet the chancellor showed in this context much more empathy for the leadership of European Jewish organizations than for their American counterparts:

They are, in stark contrast to many a visitor from the United States, personally affected in a very different way.... If you talk to them about this topic, it is always a very personal topic, it is not a theoretical topic, because their own personal background and the experiences of their own family immediately comes to their mind. That is why it is important vis-à-vis foreign countries, but also domestically, that this is a disgrace for us. We have to get away from this attitude that it is a trivial offense if some one walks around and glorifies National Socialism. This is not a trivial offense.[84]

Some German officials, however, clearly reverted the causal chain of events. Instead of addressing the roots of neo-Nazism, they fixated on the impact on the Federal Republic's reputation abroad and perceived critical coverage in the press as an expression of an anti-German worldview. Even more, they saw this coverage as an indicator that prominent American Jewish journalists, for example in the *New York Times*, could not dissociate the Federal Republic from the Holocaust. Yet they also became increasingly aware that there was very little they could actually do to influence this coverage—other than "reversing the trend," as Stabreit had said, in the Federal Republic. This connection between events *in* Germany and Holocaust-related references *to* Germany in the American media was a crucial lesson to German officials, corroborated over the course of the 1990s.

Assessing the Holocaust Industry

The opening of major Holocaust museums in the United States in the early 1990s overlapped with German concerns about the negative impact of the coverage on neo-Nazi attacks. Of course, the fears of the federal government connected to the USHMM dated back to the early 1980s. But the plans for other Holocaust museums, memorials, and related projects provided even more cause for concern in the early 1990s. This was particularly problematic from the German perspective, as these developments came at a time when xenophobic incidents and electoral successes of right-wing parties in Germany seemed to confirm to American Jewish critics the potential consequences of German unification. Moreover, German observers feared the emergence of a "Holocaust industry," which instrumentalized the Holocaust for political and commercial purposes. These included fundraising programs of museums and other organizations, but also the production of books and movies.[85] According to a statement by members of the Atlantik-Brücke in 1993, the designated American ambassador to Germany, Richard Burt, had coined the term "Holocaust industry" in describing the high-volume output of publications and movies about the Holocaust.[86]

In this context, Marvin Hier again catalyzed German fears. In spring 1991, Michael Mertes informed Kohl about Hier's latest endeavor, the construction of the Museum of Tolerance—Beit Hashoah ("House of the Holocaust") in Los Angeles. Mertes wrote to Kohl that this museum would become a "kind of 'Holocaust-Disneyland.'"[87] That he was in a position to make such an assessment was a result of the network established with the AJC in the 1980s. Mertes had attended an annual meeting of the AJC in New York, where "a Jewish interlocutor" had explained Hier's goals to him. Mertes summarized for Kohl:

> The more he [Hier] could suggest to the public that the Germans were on their way to a new Holocaust, the more funds he could raise.... My interlocutor uttered the concern that Rabbi Hier's aggressive anti-German campaigns would—with increasing temporal distance from the Holocaust—not diminish but intensify, with detrimental consequences for the image of Germany among Jews *and* non-Jews in the US.[88]

The relationship between the Kohl government and Hier was truly ambivalent. Hier publicly attacked the Federal Republic for failing to embrace the legacies of the Holocaust, for instance in the context of German unification or, even more strikingly, in the run-up to the First Gulf War of 1990-91. In this context, Hier not only pointed to the use of German equipment in Iraq's chemical weapons program, but also accused German companies of having participated in the construction of gas chambers, modeled on those used in Nazi extermination camps, for the liquidation of Iranian POWs.[89] The Chancellery considered such—factually wrong—accusations by Hier, a "radical" by the estimation of German diplomats, as "perfidious."[90] But the federal government could not dismiss Hier's efforts when he reached out to the Chancellery, maybe because of Kohl's admiration for the namesake of the SWC, Simon Wiesenthal. For example, when Hier asked for Kohl's help in establishing a Holocaust archive at the SWC, the Chancellery supported this project.[91] Hier had also publicly spoken out on behalf of Kohl when the *Los Angeles Times* published a cartoon that portrayed Kohl as Hitler.[92] However, there were limits to the federal government's willingness to cooperate. When the SWC sought to establish a "dialogue with Chancellor Kohl" and campaigned for "a major financial contribution" from the German government for the construction of the Museum of Tolerance, the reaction in Bonn was lukewarm.[93] In light of the accusations and preceding tensions with the SWC, it is hardly surprising that the German government did not consider such a contribution. As Hier's campaigns against anti-Semitism and for the security of Israel were at times based on crassly exaggerated or even factually wrong analogies between policies of the Nazi regime and the Federal Republic, his accusations were bound to create the impression in Bonn that he instrumentalized the Holocaust to damage the Federal Republic's reputation. Maybe unwillingly, Hier provided a plausible reason for German governmental officials to fear the impact of the institutions he oversaw, the SWC and the Museum of Tolerance in Los Angeles, on the image of the Federal Republic in the United States.

Diagnosis and Therapy

The German Foreign Office also pondered these issues. In July 1992, it held an internal general meeting (*Hausbesprechung*) to come up with a comprehensive strategy to engage with American Holocaust memorial culture. In a broad analysis of this development, the Foreign Office drew some conclusions about its impact on German–American relations as well as on possible responses.[94] The numbers alone provided cause for concern. All in all, Foreign Office staff assumed that American Jewish organizations would open thirteen Holocaust museums in 1993.[95] These museums aimed at keeping the "memory of the shared history of persecution alive" and thus at guaranteeing solidarity among Jews in the United States. The Foreign Office also pointed to an evolving dimension of American engagement with the Holocaust, which was perceived as even more threatening to the image of the Federal Republic than the commemorative projects. The analysis stated that

> certain Jewish organizations are consciously instrumentalizing the fostering of the memory of the Holocaust for fund-raising purposes. We have to anticipate that the impending series of openings of Holocaust memorials will again awake anti-German sentiment in Jewish circles and beyond. Holocaust studies, which already exist or are in preparation at many schools and universities, will probably receive new impulses.[96]

The Atlantik-Brücke, instrumental for the implementation of the Kohl government's policies concerning American Holocaust memorial culture, shared these fears. It went even further in its efforts to confront the issue of American Holocaust memory and set up a Permanent Commission for German-American Jewish Questions (Ständiger Ausschuss für Deutsch-Amerikanisch/Jüdische Fragen), which convened in early 1993 for the first time.[97] Under the veil of secrecy (*vertraulich*),[98] this commission intended to openly discuss the challenges American Holocaust memorial culture imposed on the Federal Republic's reputation in the United States as well as to suggest possible reactions. In addition to Walther Leisler Kiep and Beate Lindemann of the Atlantik-Brücke, the commission comprised several current and former high-ranking members of federal and state governments, the Foreign Office, the Federal Press Office, and the Konrad Adenauer Foundation, as well as a number of people who had dealt with this issue during the 1980s, such as the historian Michael Stürmer, the director of the House of History Hermann Schäfer, the diplomat Wolf Calebow, and the Armonk Institute's William Trosten. This group, combining experience, expertise, and political power, divided its proceedings into two steps: "diagnosis" and "therapy." Already the language chosen to describe the agenda illustrates that the commission understood Holocaust memory in the United States not only as a challenge to the Federal Republic, but also as an almost pathological phenomenon for which Germans had to find a remedy.

The diagnosis was based on above all two assumptions, which some of its participants had already established in the 1980s or even before. They held that the growing presence of the Holocaust in the United States damaged the Federal Republic's image and that American Jews held a disproportionate influence on the "political class" in the United States.[99] The connection between the impact of American Jewish organizations on American politics and the negative consequences for Germany were often implied and at times explicitly stated. Given the level of expertise and the intensity of the discussion, the commission's analysis was differentiated and complex. The commission made a distinction between a "Holocaust movement" (*Holocaust-Bewegung*) and a "Holocaust industry."[100] It considered the former an "identity movement" (*Identitätsbewegung*) of American Jews, which the Federal Republic neither should nor could influence. The latter, however, instrumentalized the Holocaust for political and commercial reasons and posed a political challenge. Members of the commission agreed that this facet of American Holocaust memorial culture required action. Not only did it currently have a negative influence on the Federal Republic's image, but it also showed that the "inhibition threshold [*Schamschwelle*] for anti-German attitudes" in the United States was sinking, a truly alarming scenario for the future development of German–American relations.[101]

However, the participants of the commission disagreed about the means and the potential effects of a therapy for these challenges. In particular, members of the commission wrestled with the question of whether the German government should become more active in the United States or try to change Holocaust memorial culture in Germany. While some suggested an intensification of German cultural diplomacy in the United States, to spread more information about present-day Germany, others remained skeptical as to the potential effect of such initiatives. Some doubted that efforts by the Atlantik-Brücke and the Armonk Institute to change the discourse about the Holocaust in the United States by addressing teachers and educators actually led to tangible results. There was also no consensus over the Federal Republic's efforts to shape the content of existing or future Holocaust museums. For instance, one participant in the discussion suggested that plans to invest millions of Deutschmark in the Holocaust Memorial Center in Detroit, as pursued by Werner Weidenfeld, pointed to a fundamentally flawed policy: the Federal Republic should not invest money in Holocaust museums, but rather in projects dealing with post-war Germany.[102]

Even less consensus emerged over the question of public commemoration of the Holocaust in the Federal Republic itself. At least one member of the commission suggested the establishment of a Holocaust museum in Germany—possibly even modeled after the USHMM—not only to demonstrate a sincere engagement with the recent wave of neo-Nazism. More importantly, it could become a "symbol for the willingness to confront what was bad and terrible in the German past."[103] According to this perspective, the Federal Republic had "repressed" and "tabooed" the Nazi past and it was not the establishment of the USHMM that was "scandalous" (*anstößig*), but the lack of such a museum in the Federal Republic.[104] Other discussants rejected this suggestion and stated that it ran counter to projects designed to reduce the presence of the Holocaust in the United States—it was merely a sign of "escapism."[105] Nevertheless, this debate illustrated that those concerned about the impact of American Holocaust memorial culture on the image of Germany began to see more clearly the connection between the public commemoration of the Holocaust in the Federal Republic—or the lack thereof—and its reputation abroad. A process thus gained momentum that not only analyzed and objected to American Holocaust memorial culture, but also made German observers more sensitive toward the problems and contradictions in German Holocaust memorial culture itself.

Deutschland = Holocaustland?

German unification, neo-Nazi violence, and the impending opening of Holocaust museums made German officials act. Postunification Germany continued and launched a series of new initiatives to reduce concerns about the new German nation-state and to promote a positive image of Germany more generally. Geared toward a variety of audiences, such endeavors also targeted manifestations of Holocaust memorial culture as well as the American Jewish community, whom the Foreign Office explicitly identified as a "distinctive problem" for German public diplomacy in the United States.[106]

A number of examples underscore this trend in the early 1990s. For instance, the Federal Republic opened a new Goethe Institute in Washington (December 1990) and proposed exhibitions and conferences at this institute as well as at the city's German Historical Institute. These programs intended to address topics somehow related to the Holocaust, but had to avoid the impression that they were conceived of as "counter-events" to the opening of the USHMM at all cost. The Foreign Office proclaimed that German self-representation in the United States in 1993 should not be entirely "dominated by the Holocaust-problem" (*Holocaust-Problematik*).[107] The proposed projects included, for example, exhibitions about the postwar reconstruction of the Jewish community in Frankfurt and on "The Value of the Human Being: Medicine in Germany, 1918–1945."[108] The Federal Republic also financially contributed to a large festival dedicated to German culture at the John F. Kennedy Center for the Performing Arts in Washington in 1992. Titled "A Tribute to Germany," the German embassy hoped to address a wide range of audiences, specifically including American Jews.[109] Originally an American initiative and an expression of American support for unified Germany, the Chancellery perceived the festival as a great opportunity for a "*comprehensive presentation* of unified Germany,"[110] especially in light of the impending opening of the USHMM in Washington.[111]

Furthermore, Werner Weidenfeld, the coordinator for German-American Cooperation, completed his master plan for German public relations work in the United States.[112] He had been working on this concept since the late 1980s, but unification had delayed its completion. In 1992, building on already implemented projects, such as the Centers of Excellence, he recommended a complete overhaul of German public relations work in the United States. Above all, he suggested a modernization and a centralized coordination of efforts to create a "more realistic image of Germany" in the United States.[113] His proposals included the creation of a task force for public relations in the United States, the modernization of the German Information Center, and the use of modern technology. Weidenfeld was again thinking big: he hoped to create a "multimedia show" about Germany to be shown in airports and shopping malls as well as to completely revise the Germany Pavilion in Walt Disney's EPCOT Center in Florida.[114] While the memory of the Holocaust—which had according to Weidenfeld "deeply penetrated America's collective perception" of Germany—provided, among others, a primary motivation for such projects, contemporary events, such as the press coverage about the rise of right-wing extremism in the Federal Republic, increased their urgency.[115] It was the overall goal of all these efforts to portray the Federal Republic as a "liberal, democratic, cosmopolitan, critical (also self-critical) nation of culture [*Kulturnation*]," conscious of its great cultural achievements, but also of National Socialist injustice and of the "youth" of its democracy. Furthermore, the Federal Republic should be portrayed as a "model" in the fields of educational, social, and environmental policies.[116]

As for the relationship with American Jewish organizations, efforts to further improve the image of the Federal Republic became even more clearly visible. The federal government and its German partner organizations maintained and intensified their close connections with the AJC and the Armonk Institute. In addition, it worked toward improving relations with other American

Jewish organizations, such as the American Jewish Congress, the WJC, B'nai B'rith International, and the ADL. The Bitburg controversy and the tensions about German unification still overshadowed relations with these organizations; the rise of neo-Nazism in Germany as well as a meeting between Kohl and the Austrian president Kurt Waldheim, internationally outlawed because of his unclear involvement in Nazi atrocities, further strained them.[117] Nevertheless, these organizations were willing to deepen their ties with the Federal Republic. The American Jewish Congress, for example, a liberal and rather small organization, hoped to establish a "new, positive relationship" with Germany and a dialogue with the Chancellery.[118] B'nai B'rith went even further, hoping to establish an exchange program with the Konrad Adenauer Foundation, modeled after the exchange between the latter and the AJC.[119] And the European District of B'nai B'rith even signaled to the Chancellery a willingness to discuss measures to avoid a reduction of the image of the Federal Republic to the Nazi period.[120] Applauding the work of the AJC, B'nai B'rith—the largest American Jewish organization—suggested that it could significantly increase the number of people reached by future cooperation programs.[121] The Chancellery welcomed this new openness. For example, after discussing this suggestion with Michael Mertes, Peter Hartmann outlined the potential benefits of closer cooperation with the ADL to Kohl by pointing to its "significant" impact in the US media (*sehr einflußreich*) as well as the fact that an ADL member had recently published "several *balanced articles*" in the *New York Times* about the Federal Republic.[122] Thus, Kohl's advisors confirmed existing notions about the influence of American Jews on American public opinion, but also suggested intensifying these relationships to take advantage of their influence.

The cooperation with the AJC and the Atlantik-Brücke most clearly played out in the field of Holocaust education. In fact, German politicians and diplomats had expressed concerns about Holocaust courses in American high schools since their inception in the late 1970s.[123] Efforts to revise the teaching of European and German history during the 1980s—to include more information about the transformation of (West) Germany since 1945—had not, however, been successful. In the late 1980s, the AJC had, with funding from the German government, initiated the project Phoenix from the Ashes, which aimed to raise awareness of postwar German history among American high school students.[124] In the 1990s, it was the alliance between the Armonk Institute and the Atlantik-Brücke that made a concerted effort to change the teaching of postwar German history in the United States. Both organizations criticized the establishment of Holocaust Commissions or similar institutions in many US states, which were responsible for the production of teaching materials about the Holocaust. Their focus, as Trosten pointed out to Teltschik in 1991, was limited to the time period between Kristallnacht and the liberation of concentration camps, but they did not include any information about postwar German history, including West German economic and political support for Israel: "The image of Germany communicated in this way is restricted to the time period from 1933 [*sic*] to 1945 and keeps notions based on this time alive up to the present."[125] At this point in time, Teltschik had left politics and chaired the Bertelsmann Foundation. Trosten hoped that the foundation could fund a poll to measure the actual impact of American Holocaust memorial culture on young Americans.

The Atlantik-Brücke and the Armonk Institute thus initiated a program that offered seminars to American teachers and educators in the United States and (for a smaller number) in Germany, in order to acquaint them with the history of the Federal Republic. German policy-makers, such as Teltschik and Weidenfeld, who counted defining the image of the Federal Republic in the United States among their responsibilities, as well as the chancellor himself, fully supported these efforts.[126] The attitude of officials within the Chancellery toward the engagement with the Holocaust continued to be based on the parameters established in the 1980s: they perceived Holocaust education, just as Holocaust museums, not as "directly anti-German" (*keine anti-deutsche Stoßrichtung*), but assumed that they nevertheless bore the risk of negatively shaping the Federal Republic's image with "Jewish and non-Jewish students" alike, especially in light of neo-Nazi violence in Germany.[127]

Given the number of institutions involved, the implementation of these programs was no easy task. After all, two private organizations, the Atlantik-Brücke and the Armonk Institute, had to coordinate their efforts with a variety of German governmental institutions, the Chancellery, the Foreign Office, and the Federal Press Office, but also with an even larger number of institutions in the respective US states. Nevertheless, by the mid-1990s, annual seminars for about 250 to 300 American teachers in New York, Ohio, Illinois, and Virginia took place, and three groups of sixteen American teachers each went on two-week excursions to the Federal Republic. Funded in part by the Armonk Institute and the Atlantik-Brücke, the German Federal Press Office initially provided the majority of financial support.[128] Considering the financial burden these programs imposed on the Armonk Institute and the Atlantik-Brücke as well as the fact that the German Federal Press Office would at some point withdraw its funding, the Atlantik-Brücke started a rather candid fundraising campaign in Germany to secure the program's future. In a brochure titled "Deutschland = Holocaustland?" it emphasized the success of seminars and excursions for teachers and the financial challenges it faced. The brochure painted a gloomy picture of the "long-term dangers" of American Holocaust memorial culture for the image of Germany in the United States: "Generations of students" were only exposed to the "dark image" of Germany, TV programs and movies about the Holocaust were commercially very successful, and numerous monuments portrayed "Nazi atrocities." The brochure ended with the sobering conclusion that "the termination of these programs is not in the interest of Germany."[129]

While the Atlantik-Brücke and the Armonk Institute administered the seminars and exchange programs, scholars with good connections to the Kohl government provided their intellectual content. For example, the historian Hans-Peter Schwarz, a member of the Atlantik-Brücke and leading biographer of Adenauer (and later also of Kohl), wrote a brochure about the Federal Republic to be used in American high schools.[130] The House of History of the Federal Republic (only a foundation at that time), produced a film about postwar Germany to be distributed by the Armonk Institute in the United States.[131] Titled "Responsibility in Facing History" (*Verantwortung vor der Geschichte*), it intended to "motivate American Holocaust-teachers and their students to also engage with the postwar history of Germany."[132] Here the network established between the Chancellery, the Atlantik-Brücke, and the Armonk Institute clearly paid off: as part of a private initiative, American educators traveled to seminars in the United States or in Germany to gain a positive, affirmative interpretation of the Federal Republic and its history.

Judging by the impressions of participants of the excursions to Germany, the program had the desired effect. The experiences of Gaye Chappel, for example, a supervisor of social studies and humanities for public schools in the Chesapeake region, indicate as much. Chappel participated in an Atlantik-Brücke/Armonk Institute seminar in Germany in 1994. In contrast to earlier cohorts, which were composed of teachers, Chappel's cohort included administrators in charge of the design of future curricula at American high schools. In the seminar, she designed a "model curriculum for educators that looks at Germany in terms of its achievements and contributions since 1945." Summarizing her experiences, Chappel stated: "The more knowledge you have about a subject or a people or a nation, the more apt you are to make knowledgeable decisions about them." Beyond such a universal and undoubtedly true conclusion, Chappel also summed up the message she had received from the program organizers: "Germany should not be held so negatively around the world."[133]

Against Hitler

It was certainly a question of perspective whether or not the Federal Republic was really "held so negatively" in the United States. In 1994, in any case, the German government finally managed to implement a goal it had pursued for many years: acquainting Americans with the history of German resistance against the Nazi regime, above all the assassination attempt on Hitler on July 20, 1944. The chancellor himself saw this event—even though historians have argued the contrary—as a sacrifice for "human dignity and freedom, justice and truth."[134] In July, the traveling exhibition "Against Hitler: German Resistance to National Socialism, 1933–1945," "produced and paid for by the Bonn government," as the *Washington Post* reported, opened in the Library of Congress's Madison Gallery. Its reception in Washington was, however, lukewarm at best.[135]

American historians, journalists, and museum experts greeted "Against Hitler" with considerable suspicion, mostly because of the involvement of politicians in the run up to its opening, its political message, and its historically problematic depiction of anti-Nazi resistance. According to the *Washington Post*, the German embassy, including Ambassador Stabreit, had pressured the Librarian of Congress, James Billington, to provide space for the display. It was supposed to coincide with the fiftieth anniversary not only of July 20, but also of the D-Day celebrations of the former Allies, which took place without Kohl. Thus, an exhibition about German resistance in one of the most prominent spaces in Washington seemed like an ideal venue to present German attempts at self-liberation, as it were. According to Stabreit, German resistance against Hitler was "a guiding star, a lesson not for Americans, but for humanity."[136]

Yet the exhibition's content triggered strong reactions. As a matter of fact, "Against Hitler" did not contain a single reference to the role of the United States in the postwar establishment of democracy in West Germany. In a review of the exhibit, left-wing historian and journalist Jon Wiener called it "highly misleading," as it "overstates the political importance of the resistance, distorts the goals of the anti-Hitler Germans and inflates their role in establishing democracy after the war."[137] Based on a concept developed by German experts of the German Resistance Memorial Center in Potsdam,[138] the exhibition was tailored to conform with Stabreit's—and maybe what embassy staff expected to be some American visitors'—expectations. In contrast to the original concept, it also made no reference to communist anti-Nazi resistance. According to Marc Fisher, Stabreit had explained: "What these people did after 1945 was a betrayal. . . I'm not uncomfortable with communist resisters. I am uncomfortable with Pieck and Ulbricht,'" communist leaders of the GDR.[139] That critical engagement with the German past might indeed be "uncomfortable" did not seem to resonate well with the ambassador. At least for an American audience, he clearly favored a sanitized version of this history.

Some observers were not at all surprised by this concept. For example, the USHMM's senior historian, Sybil Milton, chastised the exhibition, as it took German resistance completely out of its historical context. Milton criticized that it neglected to mention that German resistance "did not stop one deportation train" and that the designers of the exhibit were "taking the exception and making it the rule."[140] She also reported her impressions of the exhibition back to the USHMM. In particular, Milton stressed that "Against Hitler" "at best was a boring replay of the debates of the late 1960s and, at worst, a tendentious reinterpretation of West German national character linked to the failed 1944 coup d'etat [sic]."[141] Other critics confirmed that the Kohl government was "abusing the history of the resistance to reshape the foreign views of wartime Germany."[142] If German officials had hoped to avoid the impression to create counterevents to the opening of the USHMM at all cost, as the Foreign Office had stated in 1992, "Against Hitler" certainly was a failure.[143]

Public Debates about American Holocaust Memorial Culture in the Federal Republic

With the impending opening of the USHMM and other Holocaust museums, the German press also began to debate and comment on American Holocaust memorial culture and its most prominent products. Discussing the opening of the Museum of Tolerance in Los Angeles in February and of the USHMM in Washington in April 1993, the German media featured a series of articles, explaining American remembrance of the Holocaust to their readers. Henryk M. Broder, one of Germany's most acerbic pundits on Holocaust memory, pondered at length in Der Spiegel the "bizarre phenomenon" of the "Shoah-Business" as exemplified by the Museum of Tolerance.[144] He particularly saw the commercial use of the Holocaust and the seemingly tactless appropriation of its symbols as very problematic and inappropriate. While the interactive multimedia museum in Los Angeles offered its visitors the experience of the replica of a gas chamber, it also included a gift shop and aimed to generate donations, offering "a sale of indulgences with the guilty conscience of the survivors and the fears of the next generations."[145] A commentator in the Frankfurter Allgemeine Zeitung sarcastically remarked that the museum unwillingly had decided the Historians' Controversy by equating the Holocaust with other genocides.[146]

Not surprisingly, the opening of the USHMM generated even more coverage. Explaining the museum's history, concept, and exhibition design to their readers, Germany's leading newspapers published a series of mostly positive articles.[147] Germans could even read about some of the concerns the Kohl government had expressed during the planning phase of this institution. Referencing the coverage in the Washington Post, the liberal newspaper Süddeutsche Zeitung explained the efforts of German emissaries to change the design of the exhibition. The article concluded with the striking assessment that it was not the memory of the Holocaust, but German insecurities and fears connected to this memory, that alienated Americans.[148] Given the sensitivity of the subject, it was probably not a coincidence that German newspapers abstained from direct criticism of the museum in Washington. Yet there were two notable exceptions, namely disapproval by prominent German Jewish authors, such as Michael Wolffsohn, Henryk M. Broder, and Raphael Seligman, and criticism delivered indirectly, by quoting American commentators.[149] In this format, the *Frankfurter Allgemeine Zeitung* dared to ask why Americans had to build a "memorial to the European Holocaust before they commemorate slavery or the extinction of the Indians."[150] Even though it is possible that readers shared such concerns, this was a debate German newspapers were reluctant to enter into. This accusation—a deflection of attention from crimes and atrocities in American history by building a national museum dedicated to the Holocaust—had been mostly absent in the negotiations of German emissaires with the United States Holocaust Memorial Council.[151] German officials had wanted to include references to other genocides as well as "human rights violations more generally."[152]

The results of American engagement with the history of the Holocaust continued to preoccupy the German public during the following years. More precisely, a movie and a book by an American director and an American scholar, respectively, contributed to a change in discourse about the Holocaust in the Federal Republic: Steven Spielberg's *Schindler's List* (1993/1994) and Daniel J. Goldhagen's *Hitler's Willing Executioners* (1996). The fact that both were Jewish played less of a role in the case of the former, but a more significant role in the case of the latter. The film and the book, as well as the debates they generated, were drastically different in format, but had a similar effect: they confronted their audiences in graphic ways with the violence the Nazi regime unleashed against Jews in Eastern Europe. Observers in the United States and elsewhere paid close attention to the Germans' responses.

The reaction to *Schindler's List* was overall positive in Germany, where it opened in early 1994.[153] While the film, given the widespread knowledge of the history of the Holocaust, did not have an impact comparable to the NBC miniseries of the late 1970s, it nevertheless confronted its viewers with "realistic" images of the annihilation of European Jews, epitomized by the film's depiction of the liquidation of the Krakow Ghetto.[154] Spielberg had intentionally given the movie the aura of a documentary, filming it in black and white and at original locations whenever possible.[155] He specifically tells the story of Oskar Schindler, who saved the lives of over one thousand Jewish inmates by giving them employment in an enamelware factory he had bought in the vicinity of the Plaszow concentration camp. In contrast to *Holocaust, Schindler's List* left more room for a nuanced portrayal of its hero, a human being with flaws and weaknesses. The majority of commentators, including historians, no longer doubted that film was an inappropriate medium to depict mass murder, even though they disagreed on questions of authenticity and the extent to which violence could and should be portrayed in a movie.[156] Prominent witnesses and survivors, such as the chairman of the Central Council of Jews in Germany, Ignatz Bubis, attested that the images produced by Spielberg corresponded to reality.[157]

Even though the film confronted its viewers with an unprecedented graphic depiction of violence, its hero was the somewhat morally ambivalent "good German" Oskar Schindler.[158] Maybe for that reason, the movie did not cause significant concerns in the Chancellery or among German diplomats. Before it premiered in Germany, some American critics, such as the German-born film-maker Billy Wilder, had expressed worries about how the "country of the skin-heads" would react to the film, yet there were no significant protests against it.[159] Leaders of Bavaria's conservative party, the CSU, which had opposed the airing of *Holocaust* on German television fifteen years earlier, even recom-mended that all Germans see this film.[160] It premiered in Germany under the patronage of Federal President Richard von Weizsäcker.[161] Germany's head of state, widely considered a moral authority on the engagement with the Nazi past since his speech on May 8, 1985, thus granted the movie official approval. Kohl, however, did not attend the premiere, even though he had been invited and was even in Frankfurt, the city where the premiere took place, that day.[162] All told, *Schindler's List* was a tremendous commercial success in the Federal Re-public and was widely acknowledged as a legitimate and authentic representa-tion of the Holocaust.[163] It became a central point of reference for the German engagement with the history of the annihilation of European Jews and the most important source of information for tens of thousands of German high school students.[164]

Only a few years after *Schindler's List*, Daniel J. Goldhagen's highly contro-versial book about the role of ordinary Germans in the mass murder of Euro-pean Jewry provided a further example of the interconnection between Ameri-can and German discourse about the Holocaust. In contrast to Spielberg's movie, *Hitler's Willing Executioners: Ordinary Germans and the Holocaust* caused a brief—but intense—flare of fear among German diplomats and within the Chancellery. This debate, however, also showed that the parameters of Holo-caust angst were changing, underscoring that the Kohl government paid in-creasing attention to German reactions to American exports, as well as to the impact of Germany's confrontation with the Holocaust on its image in the United States more generally. Goldhagen, a political scientist and an assistant professor at Harvard at the time, published this book, his revised dissertation, with a popular press, Alfred A. Knopf in New York. He intended to "create a sen-sation,"[165] but also to fundamentally revise an established scholarly framework of interpretation of the motivations that made "ordinary Germans" participate in the Holocaust. Above all, Goldhagen attacked the path-breaking work of historian Christopher Browning, who had demonstrated that a combination of ideological and situational factors had made *Ordinary Men*—not just members of the SS or other Nazi elites—participate in mass killings of Jews in Eastern Europe.[166] In contrast, Goldhagen provided a graphic account of German violence against Jews and argued that these men were representative of *all* Germans. According to his central claim, the latter exhibited the

> long-incubating, pervasive, virulent, racist, eliminationist antisemitism of German culture, which was mobilized by a criminal regime beholden to an eliminationist, genocidal ideology, and which was given shape and energized by a leader, Hitler, who was adored by the vast majority of the German people, a leader who was known to be committed wholeheartedly to the unfolding, brutal eliminationist program.[167]

Goldhagen's broad generalizations, calling to mind the discourse about collective guilt after the end of the war, proved untenable within the historical profession. Most historians, in the United States as well as in Germany, severely criticized or outright rejected the book for its interpretive and methodological flaws. Historian Jürgen Matthäus, for instance, has called it a book "laden with preconceived, largely outdated notions."[168] While *Hitler's Willing Executioners* did not cause a second Historians' Controversy, it resulted in—at least in an indirect way—some shifts in the historiography of the Holocaust, leading to a more detailed analysis of Nazi anti-Semitism and research on the perpetrators of the Holocaust.[169]

German diplomats, however, closely scrutinized the discussion of Goldhagen's book in the United States. Before the book appeared in Germany, they were quite nervous about its potential impact on the Federal Republic's image. The consul general in Los Angeles, Hans-Alard von Rohr, for example, sent a detailed assessment to the Foreign Office, which sent it on to the Chancellery.[170] According to Rohr's analysis, *Hitler's Willing Executioners* had the potential to further damage the Federal Republic's image in the American Jewish community. The book, explaining the Holocaust as an inevitable consequence of the "soul" of the German people (*Volksseele*), was, according to this assessment, tremendously popular in the "Jewish circles of Los Angeles" and received favorable reviews in the media. The columnist A. M. Rosenthal, for example, had praised the book in the *New York Times*.[171] In an almost professorial tone, Rohr clearly rejected Goldhagen's findings and stated: "His bold thesis should have been refuted early on in his dissertation defense, but should not have been propagated by mass circulation and media circus." He further suggested that this issue be discussed with the AJC, but also that opportunities in the United States, at symposia or in the press, to "counter" Goldhagen's assumptions in an "academically competent" way be arranged. From this perspective, Gold-hagen appeared as an agent provocateur who exploited, and at the same time facilitated, anti-German sentiment among American Jews—not as a scholar. Referring to Goldhagen as a "junior historian" (*Nachwuchshistoriker*) and to *Hitler's Willing Executioners* as a deficient "dissertation," diplomats like Rohr aimed to delegitimize his book and portray it as an anti-German diatribe.

In light of such reports, Hubertus von Morr, in charge of public relations in the Chancellery, prepared an analysis to brief Kohl, illustrating the sensitivity with which German officials monitored American debates about the Holocaust.[172] Morr, a critic of American Holocaust memory in the Chancellery, considered two questions of political importance: how Goldhagen's book would influence Americans' attitude toward Germany and how the Chancellery should react.[173] He suggested, for the time being, not to publicly comment on *Hitler's Willing Executioners*, but only to react if foreign critics raised this issue vis-à-vis the Chancellery. In this case, German government officials should especially avoid pointing to one of the major objections brought forward against Goldhagen's claims, namely that anti-Semitism was not a uniquely German phenomenon. While Morr shared this assessment, he assumed that such a line of argumentation could only be interpreted as apologetic. Instead, the government should point to Goldhagen's findings and corresponding statements in the press, namely that Germany had fundamentally changed since 1945. The Chancellery thus prepared itself to confront Goldhagen with the results of his own research.

The following month the diplomat Rolf Schütte received an opportunity to gather more information about the debate and to gauge its impact on the Federal Republic's image. The German Information Center in New York sent him on a lecture tour through the United States in May 1996 to contribute to a better understanding between Germany and the American Jewish community. In his report to Foreign Minister Kinkel, which also ended up in the Chancellery's Goldhagen Files, Schütte reminded his readers of what his colleagues had been transmitting to the Federal Republic for decades, namely that Jews were "in American politics and society very influential."[174] On this tour, he delivered eighteen presentations to American Jewish audiences about German-Israeli relations and noted that they still had a rather distorted understanding of contemporary Germany. He warned that the "Holocaust cult," epitomized by the recently completed museums, movies, and Goldhagen's book, led to an "almost knee-jerk association Germany = National Socialist period = Holocaust." But he also pointed to the limits of German efforts to change these patterns of thought: the interest in the Holocaust resulted from an American Jewish "search for identity" or even an "identity crisis." The "Holocaust cult" was an expression of this, not connected in any way to the Federal Republic. Hence, Schütte concluded, it was virtually impossible for German officials to shape this discourse. He recommended that cooperation with the AJC and other American Jewish individuals, who were open to a dialogue with the Federal Republic, be continued and intensified: they "can be our best lawyers and 'bridge-heads.'"[175] Despite these challenges, Schütte concluded that the majority of the audiences showed understanding for the German fears that Goldhagen's book could damage the image of contemporary Germany and of the Germans.[176]

While the German press had reported about *Hitler's Willing Executioners*, published excerpts, and printed reviews of the book by historians already by the spring, general readers had to wait until a translation was published several months later.[177] In the fall of 1996, *Hitlers willige Vollstrecker*, the slightly edited German version of the book, sparked a controversy in Germany about the role of "ordinary Germans and the Holocaust" comparable to the impact of *Holocaust* or *Schindler's List*. Goldhagen went on a promotional tour and participated in several public discussions with leading German scholars and journalists, which were broadcast on the Federal Republic's major television networks. While German historians, in reviews and in public discussions with Goldhagen, pointed to its flaws as a scholarly work, general audiences, especially young Germans, greeted Goldhagen with great enthusiasm, almost like a "pop star" or a "messiah."[178] Meeting an audience prepared by *Schindler's List* to confront the horrors of Nazi violence against Jews, but also attesting that Germans born after the war were *not* responsible for the Holocaust, Goldhagen "absolved younger Germans from the legacy of a grim past" according to Jürgen Matthäus.[179] In this sense, as Norbert Frei has observed, *Hitler's Willing Executioners* was more an "event" than a book: "another self-confrontation of German society with the Holocaust."[180]

Having monitored the debate and Goldhagen's book tour, the Chancellery decided to drop this issue in the fall of 1996.[181] It is safe to assume that Kohl's advisors did not change their opinion about Goldhagen's argument that "eliminationist antisemitism" had been inherent in German culture until 1945. This radically contradicted Kohl's earlier statements about the Third Reich. However, the message the generations of Germans born after World War II seemed to take away from the book was not so distant from what the Kohl government had tried to convey in a number of ways in the Federal Republic as well as in the United States since the 1980s: that the Federal Republic was indeed a "new" Germany. For instance, in an interview with one of his fiercest critics, the founder and editor in chief of *Der Spiegel*, Rudolf Augstein, Goldhagen stated:

> Let me say one more thing: Yesterday, I sat outside in the pedestrian zone in Hamburg and had a snack. I looked around: young Germans, boyfriends and girlfriends. People shopping and taking a walk. I thought: What do they have to do with the past, what do they have in common with it? Nothing. If I had sat in Boston, I could have

watched very similar people. These young people should not be obligated to feel tormented by the past.[182]

Strongly resonating with a statement of Ronald Reagan prior to Bitburg, according to which Germans born after the war had an "unnecessary" "guilt feeling that's been imposed upon them,"[183] Goldhagen acknowledged, maybe unwillingly so, also a core principle of Kohl's politics of history. In the end, he even seemed to legitimize the notion about the "grace of late birth," for which Kohl had been criticized severely twelve years earlier.[184]

The Best Germany That Ever Existed

Anyone in Germany who may have still believed at the beginning of the decade that American Holocaust memory was a fleeting phenomenon or could be directly managed by German officials must have realized in the mid-1990s that neither was the case. Regardless which stratum one considered more decisive for the further development of American Holocaust memory—American Jewish identity or the so-called Holocaust industry—and regardless of which German strategy one favored in the United States, it had become obvious that the effect of German efforts would be indirect at best. Of course, the direct intervention vis-à-vis the USHMM had failed. Yet even if other long-term projects, such as the programs pursued by the Atlantik-Brücke in the field of Holocaust education, actually worked, it would take years or even longer for them to show any substantial results.[185] The reactions to *Schindler's List* and *Hitler's Willing Executioners* in Germany had at the very least served to make the products of American engagement with the Holocaust appear less threatening in Germany. However, during the 1990s, German political actors also realized that incidents in Germany had a greater impact on the American image of Germany against the backdrop of the Holocaust than German efforts to correct an allegedly "distorted" image in the United States.

In 1997, the AJC strongly reinforced such lessons by publicly attacking the Kohl government for failing to address a neglected legacy of the Holocaust, namely financial compensation for Eastern European Holocaust survivors. Already in 1990, the end of the Cold War had brought several unresolved questions about compensation and restitution for victims of Nazi persecution back onto the political agenda.[186] The GDR had refused to address this issue almost until the very end of the regime and only the fall of the Iron Curtain put Holocaust survivors in Eastern Europe in a position to demand compensation payments or to receive the support of Western agencies in this context.[187] In late 1992, the Claims Conference negotiated an agreement with the Kohl government about the establishment of a hardship fund (Article-2 Fund) to provide pensions for a number of Eastern European Holocaust survivors who had left their home countries.[188] De facto, this meant that only those who had moved to Israel or the United States would receive pensions from this fund. Most Jewish victims of Nazi persecution who still resided in Eastern Europe, however, were not eligible for any form of compensation from the Federal Republic. The Kohl government refused to increase the number of those entitled to compensation out of fear that other so far uncompensated victim groups, above all non-Jewish Eastern European forced laborers, would follow suit.[189]

Since 1993, the Claims Conference pursued the issue of Eastern European victims of Nazi persecution with the German government, an initiative that the AJC picked up and expanded in 1994.[190] In the Federal Republic, the opposition parties in the Bundestag, the Social Democrats and the Green Party, also appealed to the Kohl government to provide compensation, which it declined.[191] After several years of futile exchange, which also involved American diplomats and officials like Stuart Eizenstat, the Kohl government still refused to establish a fund to compensate Eastern European victims.[192] Kohl feared a wave of new demands for financial compensation from the Federal Republic if he gave in to the Claims Conference. Furthermore, he also expected this would damage his party's standing in the Federal Republic as a majority of Germans indeed opposed these demands.[193]

The AJC then shifted gears. On the one hand, it called on the Clinton White House to confront Kohl with this issue. On the other hand, it signaled to the Chancellery that it "would go public with our campaign in two months' time if no progress were forthcoming."[194] The position of the federal government was particularly precarious as Eastern European Waffen-SS veterans could claim a "war victim's pension" from Germany if they had been wounded in combat.[195] Pointing to the almost $60 billion the Federal Republic had paid to Holocaust survivors, but also intent on not creating a precedent for further claims, the Kohl government did not react. Consequently, on May 7, 1997, the AJC placed an advertisement in the *New York Times*, contrasting a photo of an old man, identified as a "survivor of a Nazi Ghetto in Eastern Europe" with that of a man giving the Hitler salute, a "veteran of the Latvian Legionnaires and the Waffen-SS," under the headline: "Guess Which One Receives a War Victims Pension from the German Government."[196] In July, Bill Clinton raised the issue during a state visit to Germany with Kohl. After having resisted for several years, the Kohl government now accepted new negotiations with the Claims Conference. During the following month, a letter signed by eighty-two US senators, who asked Kohl for "meaningful compensation" for the "forgotten group of Holocaust survivors," further underscored the necessity to act.[197]

After the Kohl government agreed to provide compensation payments to victims of Nazi persecution in Central and Eastern Europe as well as the former Soviet Union, the AJC, essential to this agreement, stressed that the

Guess Which One Receives a War Victims Pension from the German Government.

Survivor of a Nazi Ghetto in Eastern Europe

Veteran of the Latvian Legionnaires and the Waffen-SS

If you guessed the survivor, you're wrong, sad to say. While Holocaust survivors in other parts of the world are eligible to receive German pensions, Holocaust survivors in Eastern Europe and the former Soviet Union have never received a pension of any kind from Bonn. Inexplicably, the German government has simply drawn the line at providing such direct assistance to this group of survivors.

Not so, however, for many of the survivors' former tormentors. Believe it or not, the German government provides generous monthly pensions to Nazi war veterans, whose injuries or even mild, chronic ailments qualify them for "war victims pensions."

In the U.S. alone, there are 3,377 pensions sent each month to veterans of the armies of the Third Reich or their dependents!

After the fall of communism, many Waffen-SS veterans in the Baltic states and elsewhere in Eastern Europe discovered they, too, were eligible and are now receiving such pensions from Germany, while their victims are not.

Today, an estimated 15,000-20,000 Jewish survivors of ghettos and concentration camps live in Eastern Europe and the former Soviet Union. They are old, many are in poor health and financially destitute. Surely, they deserve some help and comfort in the last years of their lives.

Join our call to the German government to correct this grievous wrong. Bring justice to the real victims of the Holocaust. Contact us to see how you can help.

 The American Jewish Committee

Robert S. Rifkind   David A. Harris
President   *Executive Director*

165 East 56th Street, New York, New York 10022
(212) 751-4000, ext. 271
Visit our web site at www.ajc.org

Figure 5.1 AJC ad in the *New York Times*, May 7, 1997. American Jewish Committee.

media campaign had been a last resort after several years of German "refusal to settle the issue."[198] That the AJC had established an office in Germany in 1997, the first American Jewish organization to do so, certainly facilitated its negotiations with German authorities.[199] Despite the tensions about compensation payments and the AJC's public campaign, high-ranking members of the

German government, including Klaus Kinkel and Federal President Roman Herzog, participated in the official opening ceremony of this office in February 1998.[200] Kohl also publicly applauded the contribution of the AJC to German–American relations during the celebrations of the fiftieth anniversary of the Berlin Airlift in 1998.[201] Clearly, the Kohl government was intent on smoothing the waters with the AJC. It probably also drew some further conclusions from this confrontation. While overall friendly and constructive relations had been established over the past two decades, the AJC knew where the Kohl government's weak spot was—and was not afraid to hit it. Andrew Baker of the AJC, instrumental in the negotiations with the federal government, expressed it more diplomatically:

> It is hard to imagine that left to themselves either German leaders or those Americans working in the general arena of German-American relations would have acted at all without prodding from the American Jewish community.[202]

To the Kohl government, this must have been an alarming change in strategy. That even the federal government's closest partner among American Jewish organizations resorted to tactics that had caused great concern for the Chancellery in the 1980s and early 1990s, pointed to what was at stake here: a relationship, which the federal government had been so invested in building for two decades. Moreover, the heightened interest Nazi crimes received in the context of these debates in the United States ran counter to the policies the Kohl government had pursued in promoting a "new" Germany since the 1980s. During the first decade after the end of the Cold War, the issue of compensation payments, looted Holocaust assets, and Nazi slave labor had even become a global affair in which American nongovernmental organizations and institutions acted as the main protagonists and received the full support of the Clinton administration. Against this backdrop, the Americanization of the Holocaust probably reached its apex. Not only did the Clinton administration facilitate efforts to deal with the "unfinished business" of the twentieth century, but in doing so it also accelerated a process that rendered the Holocaust a negative foil for American policies as well as a main theme of the post-Cold War human rights regime in the entire Western world.[203]

One can only speculate about whether the AJC's campaign revived fears about a Jewish lobby or Jewish influence over the American media in the German Chancellery.[204] As a matter of fact, placing an advertisement in the *New York Times* was anything but a sign of power, but a last resort after all efforts to convince the Kohl government behind closed doors to accept responsibility for the forgotten victims had failed. Regardless of how the chancellor's staff perceived the campaign, the lesson the Kohl government drew from this face-off was clear. While it had rejected compensation payments for financial reasons, the negative effects of this refusal on the image of the Federal Republic in the United States led to a change in policy. Out of the sheer necessity to avoid bad press, in a quite literal sense, the Kohl government had altered its policy concerning compensation.

These lessons became perhaps more apparent in the way Helmut Kohl publicly argued for the construction of a Monument to the Murdered Jews of Europe in Berlin in late 1998. In fact, the journalist Lea Rosh and others had called for the establishment of such a monument since 1988, and it had received the backing of the German government in 1992.[205] From this point onward, a private initiative (the so-called Förderkreis zur Errichtung eines Denkmals für die ermordeten Juden Europas e.V.), the Federal Ministry of the Interior, and the Berlin Senate jointly pursued the project, albeit without a clear concept. The monument, only completed in 2005, thus has a long and complex history, which included fierce controversies over the necessity and meaning of such a monument, the question of whether it should be dedicated only to Jewish or also to other victims of Nazi persecution and extermination policies, its location and relationship to other memorial sites in Berlin, and, of course, its design.[206] Kohl, who at critical moments personally intervened in the planning phase of the monument, publicly expressed his support in 1993, while at the same time rejecting a monument or museum modeled after the USHMM.[207]

Kohl's backing for the monument in Berlin was at least in part also a strategy intended to avoid opposition by the leadership of Germany's Jewish community against a project very near to Kohl's heart, namely a Central Memorial of the Federal Republic of Germany for the Victims of War and Tyranny (Zentrale Gedenkstätte der Bundesrepublik Deutschland für die Opfer von Krieg und Gewaltherrschaft). Stalled after the Bitburg controversy, Kohl was able to realize this project after unification at the Neue Wache, an early nineteenth-century guardhouse in Berlin, which had been used as a memorial in the Third Reich and the GDR. The establishment of the Central Memorial was controversial for a number of reasons, above all because its inscription dedicated the site to the abstract group of "victims of war and tyranny."[208] The chairman of the Central Council of Jews in Germany, Ignatz Bubis, only accepted an invitation to the opening ceremony after the federal government had agreed to attach a plaque to the Neue Wache, providing a specific enumeration of those killed by the Nazi regime.[209] However, Bubis later revealed, his decision not to publicly oppose the Central Memorial, which after all did not recognize Jews as the main victims of National Socialism, resulted from Kohl's promise to support the establishment of a Holocaust monument in Berlin, solely dedicated to the murdered Jews of Europe.[210]

This was not an easy promise to keep, and the prolonged and controversial debate about the Holocaust monument also affected the Bundestag election campaigns during the second half of 1998.[211] Michael Naumann, the shadow state minister for cultural affairs of the SPD's candidate for chancellor Gerhard Schröder, publicly opposed the plans for the monument, and Schröder himself was also less than enthusiastic about this project. While Kohl postponed the final decision until after the Bundestag elections on September 27, he publicly reaffirmed his support for the monument. In the long interview with the conservative *Frankfurter Allgemeine Zeitung* quoted at the beginning of this chapter, the chancellor contemplated his government's accomplishments in preparing the "intellectual-cultural conditions for a good future."[212] To the chancellor, aware that he was likely to lose the elections against his popular opponent Schröder, this specifically applied to the enshrining of the German past. Justifying and praising his achievements in this field—his museum projects as well as the Central Memorial in Berlin—he also strongly backed the plans for a Holocaust monument. Much to the surprise of the *Frankfurter Allgemeine Zeitung* journalists, Kohl even suggested that "maybe we should have—with much closer temporal proximity to the events—been thinking about a

Figure 5.2 Opening of Central Memorial of the Federal Republic of Germany for the Victims of War and Dictatorship at the Neue Wache on November 14, 1993 (Memorial Day). Pictured from right to left are Roman Herzog, Henning Voscherau, Richard von Weizsäcker, Rita Süssmuth, and Helmut Kohl. Bundesregierung/Christian Stutterheim.

monument already 30 years ago." In the light of the politics of history Kohl had pursued during the 1980s, his statement now reflected a fundamental change in position toward the memory of the Nazi past. Whether he indeed drastically changed his opinion on these matters or merely tried to respond to what he perceived as the opinion of a majority of Germans is hard to say. In 1998, in any event, he positioned himself as the candidate—in contrast to the skeptical Schröder—who supported a Holocaust monument in Berlin.

Kohl also tried to convince the opponents of the monument of its necessity by pointing to what was at stake in terms of the Federal Republic's foreign relations. With a clear reference to the Federal Republic's reputation abroad, he stated: "The whole world would curse [verfluchen] us if we now said: Because this is so difficult, let's just stop it."[213] A few weeks earlier, he had been even more straightforward in his efforts to gather support for the monument. In a television interview, Kohl suggested that it had to be built because the "American East Coast" expected it.[214] Thus while the chancellor left no doubt that he openly embraced the legacies of the Holocaust, he justified this position by pointing to the assumed effects on Germany's reputation abroad.[215] Although the monument should certainly not be reduced to a result of foreign policy considerations only, Kohl's hardly veiled reference to American Jewish organizations make clear that such considerations indeed played a significant role.

American Jewish organizations welcomed the creation of a Holocaust monument in Berlin, and the AJC facilitated the dialogue between the monument's architect, Peter Eisenman, and German authorities after 1999.[216] It is safe to say that suddenly halting the plans for the project could have caused considerable irritation, not only within American Jewish organizations, but also within a variety of political, religious, and other interest groups in Germany and abroad. But there are no indicators that American Jewish organizations actually applied any kind of pressure on the Kohl government or even threatened to "curse" the Germans if the monument was not built. In the light of the actual implications of Kohl's suggestion—building the Holocaust monument to "please American Jews," as a journalist stated—it is surprising that his statement did not trigger a public controversy.[217] It is possible that the majority of the viewers of the interview, broadcasted on RTL, a lowbrow channel with a wide impact, did not understand Kohl's coded language when he spoke about the "East Coast." However, it is also quite possible that they understood him perfectly and agreed with him. After all, prominent journalists like Rudolf Augstein also suggested that the Kohl government pursued the "mark of shame" in Berlin out of fear and as a "courtesy to the New York press and sharks in their lawyers costumes."[218] Whether the monument really was a concession to what German politicians perceived to be "moral and legal pressure," as Augstein implied, must remain subject to speculation.[219] It must be stressed that Kohl was, after all, only one player in the controversy over the monument, and that in

1998 he alone could have neither realized nor prevented this project, which was completed only under Gerhard Schröder. On June 25, 1999, in its last session in Bonn, the Bundestag rendered the final decision to build the Monument to the Murdered Jews of Europe.[220] In the end it was up to the individual members of the Bundestag to cast their votes according to their individual convictions.

By that time, Kohl had lost the elections and had become an ordinary member of the Bundestag. During his last month as chancellor, however, he had provided a most striking illustration of how his policies concerning the significance of Holocaust memory for the Federal Republic's foreign affairs had changed. Of course, he still feared that the Federal Republic's image abroad would remain connected to the Holocaust. Instead of trying to change the discourse on the Holocaust abroad, however, the chancellor focused on pursuing such policies at home. He publicly advocated a German Holocaust memorial culture that rendered the Federal Republic immune to, as it were, the kind of criticism from abroad that the chancellor and his staff had feared for so many years. According to this logic, changing Holocaust memorialization *in* Germany—and irrevocably putting the Jewish victims of Nazism at the center—would also serve to improve the Federal Republic's reputation in the United States more generally, specifically with American Jewish organizations. In short, if the Federal Republic were able to point to a massive Holocaust

Figure 5.3 Construction of the Monument to the Murdered Jews of Europe in Berlin (July 2004). Bundesregierung/Ralf Maro.

monument in the new capital Berlin, who could still claim that the Germans were tabooing their past and who could still make credible analogies to the policies of the Third Reich? Kohl must have realized that the Nazi past did not necessarily have to weaken Germany's international reputation. Instead, an open, unapologetic engagement with this past actually bore the potential to strengthen it.[221] As if to confirm such expectations, journalist Josef Joffe remarked in 1999 that the monument would become a symbol for "the best Germany that ever existed," a Germany that wanted to be, and succeeded in being, "fundamentally different" from the monstrous Third Reich.[222] In contrast to, indeed despite, his government's former politics of history, Kohl had in the end helped to bring about an utter transformation, one that made the Holocaust the "core" of Germany's "self-concept as a nation."[223]

Epilogue

Holocaust Angst and the Universalization
of the Holocaust

In 2013, the United States Holocaust Memorial Museum celebrated its twentieth anniversary with a series of high-profile events, ceremonies, and conferences in Washington and four other major American cities.[1] The 20th Anniversary National Tribute, which took place under the slogan "Never Again. What You Do Matters" in Washington on April 29, marked the culmination of these celebrations. It included speeches by the Museum's founding figures, most importantly Elie Wiesel, and former president Bill Clinton, who had both overseen the Museum's opening in 1993. The ceremony also featured a number of roundtable discussions, including one on the topic of "Holocaust Memory in Europe." This discussion did not involve scholars from European universities, Holocaust memorials, or museums, but a very select group of the museum's "closest partners," as the moderator and USHMM director, Sara Bloomfield, put it. These partners included François Zimeray, French Ambassador-at-large for Human Rights and Ambassador for Holocaust issues; Polish Culture and National Heritage Minister Bogdan Zdrowjewski; and Thomas de Maizière, German Minister of Defense under the CDU-led government of Angela Merkel.[2]

In the course of the discussion, de Maizière, also a member of the CDU, positioned his government and the Federal Republic more generally in the discussion about Holocaust memory in contemporary Europe as well as vis-à-vis the USHMM. As Minister of Defense, he addressed the involvement of the Wehrmacht in the Holocaust as well as the positive traditions of the postwar (West) German Bundeswehr, including the memory of the military resistance against Hitler and the training of "soldiers as citizens." He explained in detail the Federal Republic's accomplishments, as it were, in the field of Holocaust memory and education, including a large number of memorial projects and educational programs, Germany's strong alliance with the state of Israel, and support for Jews in Germany. He congratulated the Museum on its permanent exhibition on Holocaust history and its more than thirty-four million visitors, who he hoped "left this museum with hope." De Maizière even suggested that Germany could "learn a lot" from the Museum on how to deal with this history: appealing to reason only—as in the case of Germany, he said—was not sufficient, and the museum perfectly demonstrated the necessity to "reach the hearts of the young generation" in order to transmit the message "never again."[3]

De Maizière's words marked a striking contrast to the fears that had characterized the confrontation with American Holocaust memorial culture undertaken by the government of his fellow Christian Conservative, Helmut Kohl, twenty years earlier. De Maizière, born in 1954, represented a very different Germany than Kohl's Republic. Not only had the country's engagement with the Nazi past fundamentally changed since the 1980s, but Germany also played a more confident role in Europe and the world, which had experienced a most significant transformation since the end of the Cold War. As part of these processes, the most prominent institution of American Holocaust memory, the USHMM, had lost its threatening character. Moreover, a top-level representative of the German government now even considered an emotional approach to commemorating the Holocaust—a central point of criticism of the Kohl government—highly desirable.

The ceremony unmistakably illustrated the extent to which "never again" represented the central "lesson" of the Holocaust. De Maizière's copanelists forcefully demonstrated that this was the case beyond the United States and Germany. Zimeray, for example, passionately explained that in France, the memory of the Holocaust had become "a part of our DNA and our identity" and the transmission of its lessons was the nation's highest "responsibility."[4] Of course, the anniversary celebration of the USHMM would have been the wrong occasion to question the political relevance of the Holocaust's legacies, but the ceremony showed how much the engagement with the Holocaust in the West had evolved since the opening of the USHMM in 1993. Top-level representatives of the Federal Republic, Poland, and France joined prominent Americans in affirming the centrality of Holocaust memory for European and North American societies. Indeed, they attested both to its significance for memorial cultures and historical consciousness and to its use, as Aleida Assmann has observed, as a "hegemonic instrument to export Western values and to expand the range of Western influence."[5]

In fact, the ceremony in Washington itself demonstrated the "universalization" of the Holocaust, which has occurred in Europe, North America, and many other places over previous decades. The mass murder of European Jews by the Nazi regime and its allies has been characterized as a transnational event, affecting almost all territories occupied by German forces during World War II and even beyond, but its commemoration has also become a transnational phenomenon.[6] The Holocaust has evolved to become a symbol for mass crime and genocide, a metaphor for barbarism and human rights violations, and the fate of the Jews has developed into a universally recognized point of reference for other victim groups.[7] Today, the mass murder of Europe's Jews forms a centerpiece for the West as a community of memory, where it plays a crucial role in political culture, the media, and educational systems, at least for the mainstream or majority societies.[8]

The origins of this transnational phenomenon lie in developments of the 1960s and 1970s. Events such as the Eichmann Trial and the broadcast of the NBC miniseries *Holocaust* in the late 1970s helped to transform a multitude of anti-Jewish measures and murderous policies pursued by Nazi Germany and its allies into a distinct event, the Holocaust—the "rupture of civilization."[9] However, the universalization of the Holocaust only began to approach its apogee in the 1990s, when Holocaust remembrance, especially in the West but also on a global level, experienced dramatic growth. The past two decades have seen the formation of interconnected international and transnational Holocaust memorial cultures, which have resulted in the founding of memorials, museums, educational programs, and scholarly and academic institutions dedicated to the study of this event.[10] It is certainly no coincidence that major cities such as Berlin, Paris, and Jerusalem have opened new or renovated Holocaust memorials or museums within the past decade or so.[11]

Within Europe, the end of the Cold War and the continuing process of European integration have turned the Holocaust into a negative "founding myth" of the European political community.[12] In 2005, for example, Tony Judt observed that "Holocaust recognition is our contemporary European entry ticket."[13] Not only the acknowledgment of responsibility for crimes committed during the Holocaust, a difficult process for many collaborators of the Nazi regime, but also the need to derive and promote lessons from this event have become key elements in what it means to belong to Europe. Such an endeavor is perhaps best exemplified by the founding of the intergovernmental Task Force for International Cooperation on Holocaust Education, Remembrance, and Research. Initiated in Stockholm in 1998, it resulted two years later in the first international summit of the new millennium, with six hundred delegates from more than forty countries, including twenty-three heads of states.[14] This Task Force, which recently changed its name to the International Holocaust Remembrance Alliance, aims to highlight the lessons to be learned from the Holocaust and provides regulations for both commemoration ceremonies and high school education.[15] A further example of efforts to promote the memory of the Holocaust on a pan-European or even global level was the designation of January 27 as Holocaust Remembrance Day. January 27 is the day Auschwitz was liberated by the Red Army in 1945, and it is commemorated today in most EU member states. Since 2005, the United Nations also officially remembers the victims of National Socialism on this day annually.

Despite such developments, there are also indicators that run counter to a "homogenization" of Holocaust memory and point instead to the strengthening and accentuation of national differences and distinctions.[16] For example, the actual commemoration ceremonies of January 27 vary widely, depending on the respective national context.[17] The Federal Republic established January 27 as a national day of commemoration for the victims of National Socialism shortly after the ceremonies around May 8, 1995. Since 1996, the Federal Republic has recognized this day with an official ceremony in the Bundestag, during which the federal president or the president of the Bundestag and prominent survivors of Nazi persecution address the parliament and prominent guests. Great Britain has held a national commemoration ceremony on this day since 2001, during which the "universal" lessons of the Holocaust for fighting racism and preventing future genocides are stressed. Compared to Germany and Great Britain, this day has only marginal importance in other European countries. France and Austria, for instance, officially recognize January 27 as a Holocaust commemoration day. In France, however, July 16, the day of the Vel' d'Hiv Roundup in 1942, has far greater significance for the commemoration of the victims of National Socialism. Austria, on the other hand, focuses on May 5, the day of the liberation of the Mauthausen concentration camp in 1945.

These transformations in European memorial cultures have left room for national particularities but have also changed the position of the Federal Republic. For non-German Europeans, accompanying the universalization of the Holocaust, and the expansion of its commemoration in many European countries, was a critical examination of their own collaboration with the Nazi regime and involvement in the extermination of Europe's Jews.[18] This has led, as Aleida Assmann and Sebastian Conrad have pointed out, to "a European discourse of guilt with respect to the Holocaust, which, in the 1990s, undermined many a self-serving national myth in countries such as Austria, Poland, France, the Netherlands or Switzerland."[19] The fact that the Holocaust has become a focal point of European memory beyond Germany has also served to "spread guilt evenly" across the European continent.[20]

Holocaust memorial cultures have emerged in the non-European world as well, in places far removed from the historical sites of Nazi extermination policies. They extend far beyond Jewish communities and organizations for whom the memory of the Holocaust has obviously had a special significance. The Association of Holocaust Organizations lists several hundred full and affiliate members worldwide.[21] For example, New Zealand not only boasts a well-developed infrastructure of Holocaust museums, memorials, and educational programs, but here the fate of the Jews during the Third Reich also marks the focal point of debates about the country's own violent history. Over the past decade or so, New Zealand has witnessed a number of public controversies over statements by representatives of the indigenous Maori community, who have compared

British colonialism to the Holocaust.[22] Regardless of whether statements about a "Maori Holocaust" have been made to break taboos, to draw attention to neglected events in New Zealand's history, or to illustrate the aftereffects of a history of victimization, they further attest to the "universalized," symbolic significance of the Holocaust around the globe.[23] In New Zealand, it is not uncommon for the indigenous minority to reference the Holocaust when talking about its own victimization.[24]

While Holocaust memory has shaped political debates and historical consciousness in many countries, the commemoration of the crimes committed by Nazi Germany and its allies in the United States deserves particular attention. The Holocaust has become part of American life, while the products of American Holocaust memorial culture have shaped debates, the imagery, and the understanding of this event well beyond the North American continent.[25] Tremendously successful films, such as *Holocaust* and *Schindler's List*, or books, such as *Hitler's Willing Executioners*, represent the mere tip of an enormous iceberg. In contemporary America, the mass murder of Europe's Jews symbolizes—unlike any other historical event, including the dark chapters of American history—absolute evil and the antithesis to the values of America's civil religion. As Tony Judt has remarked in conversation with Timothy Snyder, the Holocaust has become the ultimate benchmark for assessing human behavior, "a single catastrophic moment, a historical and ethical reference against which the rest of human experience is implicitly compared and found wanting" as well as the "moral measure of every political action we undertake."[26] The tendency to appropriate this event for comparative purposes can take extreme and extremely ahistorical forms, such as comparing abortion or even the breeding and slaughtering of animals for human consumption to the Holocaust.[27]

At the twentieth anniversary of the USHMM in 2013, Bill Clinton gave a pitch-perfect illustration of this development, when he reminded his fellow citizens as well as the foreigners present, that "the Holocaust Memorial will be our conscience and will be here as our conscience from now—forever."[28] In his eloquent address, Clinton further lamented "the fever and the sickness that the Nazis gave to the Germans," which ultimately could be reduced to "the idea that our differences are more important than our common humanity." According to the former president, this "human disease" was not only responsible for anti-Semitism and the mass murder of Europe's Jews, but was also to blame for the discrimination of women in Pakistan or the 2013 terrorist attack on the Boston marathon. Through this completely ahistorical reduction and distortion of the origins of German anti-Semitism and the Holocaust, and by using the suffering of Jews during the Third Reich as a prism through which to reach moral judgments, Clinton suggested that promoting the "truth" of the Holocaust to "all of human kind" would make the world a better place.

Unintentionally, and in passing, Clinton's ponderings also exculpated the perpetrators of the Holocaust—at least to some extent. Who, after all, could be blamed for catching a virus? Perhaps Clinton's moralizing—though forward-looking—words confirmed to German onlookers that the discourse about the Holocaust in America had grown mostly detached from the event's actual historical context and that such presentist, ethical considerations would hardly reflect negatively on the image of the Federal Republic in the United States. In fact, Thomas de Maizière pointed out that the ceremony in Washington had taken place completely without "anti-German sentiment" (*nicht ein einziger anti-deutscher Zungenschlag*).[29] For roughly two decades, however, from the late 1970s until well into the 1990s, a number of powerful and influential (West) German politicians, government officials, and diplomats watched America's multifaceted confrontation with the extermination of Europe's Jews with what this book calls Holocaust angst. At the center of this study are a few German actors with a Nazi past (along with a few individuals born after the war), but mostly its protagonists are part of a generation of decision-makers who were born during the Third Reich, but were too young to have been actively involved in Nazi crimes. In dealing with the legacies of the Holocaust on an international stage, they faced a predicament not of their own choosing, but one they could not escape. In a sense, they were the test subjects of managing the afterlife of genocide in modern times.

This book specifically exposes the perceptions and reactions of the German leadership around Helmut Kohl, chancellor from 1982 to 1998, to the inscription of Holocaust memory into American historical consciousness and popular culture, a development often referred to as the "Americanization of the Holocaust."[30] This network of politicians, government officials, and diplomats, as well as their associates in private organizations and foundations, lobbyists, and scholars, mostly in the conservative spectrum, perceived themselves as the "victims" of the afterlife of the Holocaust in America. Not all of them were involved in this dimension of German–American relations for the entire duration of Kohl's tenure as chancellor. However, the cooperation between Kohl and several key advisors in this context, such as Walther Leisler Kiep and Werner Weidenfeld, predated his election and continued well into the 1990s. Others, like Peter Hartmann, who succeeded Horst Teltschik in the Chancellery, ascribed to the views and positions of their predecessors. As such, there was a significant amount of continuity among the leadership around Kohl. They were concerned that public manifestations of engagement with the Holocaust could severely damage the Federal Republic's reputation in the United States and even cause Americans to call into question the Federal Republic's status as an ally. From their perspective, American Holocaust memorial culture was a stumbling block for (West) German–American relations from the late 1970s up to the 1990s. Their fears propelled a number of responses and reactions, examined in the preceding pages.

Even though West Germans had been concerned with the international consequences of the Nazi past and the horrendous crimes committed by Germans during World War II since the founding of the Federal Republic, the origins of Holocaust angst lie in the late 1970s. At this historical juncture, West German diplomats abroad and officials at home began to see American Holocaust memorial culture as a concrete political and diplomatic challenge to the Federal Republic. These years also saw a new escalation in Cold War tensions, for example in the context of the controversial NATO Double-Track Decision, as well as antagonism in West German–American political and societal relations. The exponential growth of the public commemoration as well as political, academic, and social engagement in the United States with the history of the Holocaust thus appeared as a political problem for West Germany, which depended on the alliance with the United States. Indeed, the late 1970s marked a clear turning point for American society's public confrontation with this history, and American Holocaust consciousness experienced a transformation during this period. The creation of Holocaust museums and memorials, the institutionalization of educational and academic programs, and the NBC miniseries *Holocaust* of 1978 established a permanent infrastructure of Holocaust memory in America. The miniseries in particular forced German diplomats to weigh possible responses to a growing American interest in the history of the destruction of European Jews. These developments helped to place the issue of American Holocaust memorial culture permanently on West Germany's diplomatic and political agenda and shaped how German officials dealt with this phenomenon in subsequent years.

By the early 1980s, West German diplomats had come to view American Holocaust memorial culture as a distinct problem. Yet Holocaust angst reached a new level with the arrival of Helmut Kohl in the Chancellery in late 1982. Unlike any German chancellor before or after him, he actively tried to shape the Federal Republic's confrontation with its history. Kohl worked toward normalizing this relationship, enabling a positive identification with the achievements and accomplishments of German history. The unprecedented boom in American Holocaust memorial culture since the late 1970s, however, challenged such policies, especially with regard to the image of Germany abroad. The Kohl government perceived manifestations of American engagement with the Holocaust as representing Germany in the United States. As a result, the products of American Holocaust memorial culture became screens for the projection of German fears. Under Kohl, American Holocaust memory became an issue the chancellor and his closest advisors personally dealt with, and they perceived relations with American Jewish organizations as a particular challenge in this context.

Shaping America's image of the Federal Republic was a comprehensible and legitimate concern of German diplomats and politicians, especially at a time when this alliance, the pillar of West German security and prosperity during the Cold War, experienced serious challenges. Such concerns, however, coexisted and overlapped with exaggerated fears. At times, assumptions about the influence of American Jews over the political process and the mass media in the United States, as well as notions about collective Jewish character traits, explicit references to a Jewish lobby, and coded language to identify Jews as antagonists for German policies, characterized Holocaust angst. A specific form of West German secondary anti-Semitism supplemented such fears, which suggested that Jews refused to forgive the Germans for the Holocaust and that they exploited Holocaust memory for political and commercial reasons at the expense of postwar Germany.[31] Some German actors, however, showed sincere dedication in their efforts for reconciliation and the establishment of long-term ties between Germany and the American Jewish community.

Indeed, the relationship between the West German government, including nongovernmental organizations and foundations, and American Jewish organizations experienced a fundamental transformation during the 1980s. While in the late 1970s few official contacts existed and a certain degree of antagonism as well as stereotypes on both sides strained this relationship, a decade later the Kohl government had managed to establish a stable and productive partnership with several American Jewish organizations. Trying to build closer ties with such organizations stemmed from the wish to normalize relations with the American Jewish community, but also from fear of the perceived influence of American Jewish organizations over politics and the media in the United States. Debate over the legitimacy of Kohl and Reagan's visit to a German military cemetery in Bitburg in 1985, where not only German soldiers, but also Waffen-SS members are buried, marked the decisive, yet unforeseeable, turning point in this relationship.

Bitburg was the low point of West German–American Jewish relations during the 1980s. Though they mainly focused their energies on opposing Reagan's plans to travel to Bitburg, American Jewish organizations (and many others) also considered the visit an attempt by the German government to finally blur the lines between Nazi perpetrators and their victims integrating fallen German soldiers, and especially Waffen-SS men, into the latter category. They vehemently opposed such policies, as did many others in the United States and in Germany. Among German officials, the opposition of American Jewish organizations confirmed preconceived notions about the power of a Jewish lobby and its allegedly anti-German position. Germans did not undertake in-depth analysis of the criticisms surrounding Bitburg, which came from Holocaust survivors as well as representatives from a broad range of other religious, political, and veteran groups. However, due to the intensity of this confrontation, both German officials and representatives from several American Jewish organizations realized that continuing an antagonistic stance toward each other would hurt the longer-term political interests of both sides.

Interactions and conversations between representatives of the Federal Republic and American Jewish organizations were also a necessary precondition for the implementation of German policies in the United States. As the German government set out to shape its image and the discourse about a history it shared with Americans, it could not pursue such a project with traditional diplomatic tools. It required a network of nongovernmental partners, friends, and allies. In this context, the Konrad Adenauer Foundation constructed and maintained a network with representatives of American Jewish organizations. Together with the Atlantik-Brücke, an elitist and officially nonpartisan association, it functioned as a broker for the interests of the Chancellery in the United States. These two organizations built a long-term partnership with the AJC and, even more importantly, the Armonk Institute, which exclusively focused on German–American Jewish relations, and became the Kohl government's most important ally in this context in the United States. German officials were fully aware of the necessity and importance of such "bridgeheads," if they wished to foster a long-term, positive impact on the image of Germany in the United States, for which American Jewish organizations were considered the gatekeepers.[32] Of course, such close cooperation was not a one-way street. This relationship offered to American Jewish organizations, such as the AJC, an opportunity to contribute to the shaping of West German foreign policy, as well as its domestic engagement with the Nazi past. Concerns about the negative impact of American Holocaust memorial culture on German–American relations therefore also resulted in an intensification and eventual improvement of the West German–American Jewish dialogue.[33]

A fundamental claim for a right of codetermination of how the history of the Holocaust should be told abroad supplemented Holocaust angst. The opposition of the Kohl government to the establishment of the USHMM in Washington represents the most striking example of this constellation. Kohl and his advisors perceived the USHMM to be a state-sanctioned reduction of German history to the Holocaust and, as the German ambassador Peter Hermes stated it in the early 1980s, an "anti-German museum."[34] The debates about the USHMM marked, in a way, the climax of Holocaust angst, and this museum became its central fixation. For more than a decade, German emissaries tried to integrate postwar German history, and the history of German resistance to Nazism into the exhibition concept, in order to show that not all Germans had been Nazis during the Third Reich and that the Federal Republic was distinctly different from Nazi Germany. While diplomats were involved to some extent in these negotiations, it was primarily unofficial messengers who tried to accomplish the goals of the official emissaries of the German state. As representatives of the German government considered the Holocaust to be above all

German history, they claimed for themselves, as it were, a right to be consulted about the museum's content based on their nationality. To them, it was beyond comprehension that Germans would not be allowed to participate in the creation of a museum dedicated to Germany's most heinous crime.

All efforts to change the content of this museum, located on the National Mall, failed. Those in charge of building the museum considered German requests for a modification of the Holocaust narrative either illegitimate or irrelevant to the history of the Holocaust. A complex tension and almost a contradiction existed between the expression of sincere feelings of guilt for the crimes committed against the Jews of Europe on behalf of German emissaries and fears of what they believed to be the power and influence of American Jews. The key German official in the negotiations with the USHMM, the Bundestag member Peter Petersen (CDU), personified the transformation of (West) Germany from Nazi perpetrator to America's Cold War ally. He demanded recognition and respect for this indeed remarkable metamorphosis. Holocaust survivors, on the other hand, having been instrumental in the creation of the USHMM, hesitated to show such respect. Based on their personal experience of persecution and suffering at the hands of the Nazi regime, they held a critical attitude toward Germany and toward Germans. To assume, however, that the USHMM was designed as an "anti-German" institution demonstrates how German emissaries misread developments in the United States.

Negotiations with the USHMM were not the only avenue the Kohl government pursued to make a lasting impact on the image of Germany in the United States. Among a number of possible fields of investigation, the crucial role of scholars stands out. Kohl, who considered it a central goal of his government to furnish Germans with an affirmative narrative about their country's history, closely collaborated with scholars who shared such views. They provided the intellectual framework for his government's politics of history. The founding of the German Historical Institute in Washington and Centers of Excellence for German Studies at American elite universities, such as Harvard, Georgetown, and Berkeley, illustrate the determination of the Kohl government to intensify and shape the dialogue with American academic elites. In accordance with Kohl's history-related projects in the Federal Republic, and the attempts to negotiate the design of the USHMM's permanent exhibition, his government wanted to lay the foundations for defining the discourse about Germany and German history for the foreseeable future.

Both the German Historical Institute and the Centers of Excellence were the products of a partnership between politicians and professors. German scholars were supposed to bestow academic legitimacy on an affirmative interpretation of German history. To conservatives, history and historical scholarship served exactly this purpose: to affirm the Federal Republic as a nation-state, strengthen its inner coherence, and improve its reputation abroad. In order to achieve this goal, the Federal Republic had to establish effective and legit-imate bases within the American academic community. As both cases strik-ingly show, however, this constellation imposed significant limitations on the actual impact these institutions could have on American scholarship about Germany. In the end, scholars and universities succeeded in protecting their domain from direct interference by a foreign government. The goal to inscribe the success story of the Federal Republic into the historical consciousness of Americans and reduce the presence of the Nazi past and the Holocaust could thus only be attempted indirectly—if at all. Yet despite their short-term fail-ure, these initiatives led to the founding of institutions that continue to shape German–American relations today.

After German unification, Holocaust angst experienced an additional evolu-tion. In the postunification years, a series of new developments further stoked German fears. These included the skeptical view held by some American Jewish organizations at the prospect of a unified Germany, as well as critical American press coverage of a series of attacks on foreigners and asylum seekers by right-wing extremists and neo-Nazi groups in Germany. The end of the Cold War also breathed new life into an old issue, namely compensation payments for Eastern European victims of the Holocaust. Furthermore, by the early 1990s, German officials had grown increasingly worried about what they dubbed a burgeoning Holocaust industry in the United States—the instrumentalization of the Holo-caust for commercial reasons.

Simultaneously, the Federal Republic witnessed an unprecedented concen-tration of debates about the Nazi past and the Holocaust during the 1990s.[35] During the first decade after German unification and the end of the Cold War, the mass murder committed in the Holocaust became an issue of national identity for the citizens of the Federal Republic.[36] American products, such as *Schindler's List* and *Hitler's Willing Executioners*, but also German initiatives, such as a traveling exhibition about the participation of Wehrmacht soldiers in the mass murder in Eastern Europe and the Soviet Union, created by the In-stitute for Social Research in Hamburg, made Nazi crimes and Nazi perpetra-tors front-page news. New demands for compensation for the victims of Nazi persecution and forced labor, receiving the support of the US government and American courts, underscored the moral as well as the political urgency of these debates.[37] In the context of these developments, the absence of a central me-morial in the Federal Republic for the Jewish victims of the Holocaust became strikingly apparent. Indeed, such plans had existed since the late 1980s, but only now did they receive both broad public backing and strong opposition. For the Kohl government's politics of history, this constellation posed signifi-cant challenges, but it also provided new opportunities. In the domestic con-text, backing the Holocaust monument eased opposition from German Jewish groups against the establishment of a monument dedicated to all victims of war and tyranny, which Kohl had pursued since the 1980s. In 1993, the Central Memorial of the Federal Republic was inaugurated at the Neue Wache in Berlin.

These transformations in the Federal Republic's public and political engagement with the Nazi past also translated into a new attitude toward American Holocaust memorial culture. The leadership around Kohl and its transatlantic network still feared that the image of Germany abroad might be overshadowed by the Holocaust. Over the course of the 1980s and 1990s, this circle of German political decision-makers, diplomats, lobbyists, and scholars acknowledged that American Holocaust memory was not an anti-German plot by American Jews and realized that they could not significantly impede its development, nor change its content.[38] As part of this learning process, the Kohl government not only accepted the significance of this memory, but also came to understand that making the memorialization of the Holocaust a national political priority would not weaken the Federal Republic's international reputation, but in fact strengthen it.[39] Kohl's support for the Monument to the Murdered Jews of Europe in Berlin must also be understood in this context. The chancellor thus responded to, but also contributed to, a development that rendered Holocaust memory the "core," as he said toward the end of his tenure as chancellor in 1998, of the Federal Republic's "self-concept as a nation."[40]

German confrontation with American Holocaust memory consequently contributed to a more open engagement with this memory on the part of the German government in unified Germany and eventually rendered it a "positive resource" for German self-representation abroad, epitomized by the Berlin memorial.[41] As such, the confrontation with American Holocaust memorial culture since the late 1970s had a deep impact on the Federal Republic's coping with the Nazi past at home as well as abroad. By the end of the 1990s, the Federal Republic had fervently committed itself to accepting responsibility for the crimes perpetrated by the Nazi regime, but also renounced any claim to codetermine how its victims abroad remember their suffering.[42] However, the failure to control the growing presence of Holocaust memory abroad—in the United States and elsewhere—has also given the Federal Republic the opportunity to actively fashion itself as the model state for dealing with the afterlife of genocide.[43] In post-Cold War Europe, Germany now acts as a "memory partner" or even "memory tutor," as historian Wulf Kansteiner has remarked.[44] In the eyes of its political leadership, the Federal Republic has—that much is certain—set an example for the mastering of an "unmasterable past."[45] This process includes not only the acceptance of a highly criminal past, but also the active self-identification with that past in reference to others.

In March 2011, in Washington, DC, the German ambassador Klaus Scharioth met with a group of historians to present *Das Amt und die Vergangenheit*.[46] This book, an account of the German Foreign Office's involvement in the Holocaust and the role of former Nazi diplomats in the postwar West German Foreign Office, had been completed just a few months earlier by an independent international commission of historians.[47] With statements by two of its authors, Norbert Frei and Peter Hayes, and commentators like Christopher Browning, the presentation of this incriminating and controversial study addressed a general audience in the representative conference room of the German Historical Institute. Internal debates about the continuity in personnel had propelled the Foreign Office to commission this report, which indeed painted a rather critical image of the Foreign Office's participation in the Holocaust and of former Nazis within the postwar West German institution.[48]

The complicity of German diplomats in Nazi crimes was not really news to historians, and an American audience with no stake in saving the reputation of former West German diplomats, whose careers began in the Third Reich, could not be easily shocked by such revelations. Yet it is telling that a German ambassador to the United States participated in the publicizing of such a critical examination of German history, which accentuated continuities between Nazi Germany and the "new" Germany, at the German Historical Institute—the very institution the Kohl government had destined for the promotion of an affirmative interpretation of German history. The event highlights the fundamental change in policies and official attitudes toward the Nazi past since the 1980s. To the (West) German protagonists of this book—Petersen, Calebow, Kiep, Weidenfeld, Stabreit, and Kohl—it would have been nothing short of unthinkable that a German ambassador actively advertised the history of Nazi crimes and even the deficiencies of West German democracy abroad, rendering them a crucial component of German self-promotion. Indeed, we have come a long way since the days of Holocaust angst.

Notes

Introduction

1. BArch B 136/42205, Kohl to Hier, February 28, 1990. This book is the revised version of my dissertation: Eder, "Holocaust Angst."
2. Novick, *Holocaust in American Life.*
3. The literature on German–American postwar relations is extensive. The most recent comprehensive account is Steininger, *Deutschland und die USA*; for a detailed overview see the two-volume handbook by Junker, ed., *United States and Germany.* For general overviews of West German foreign policy see Hacke, *Außenpolitik*; Haftendorn, *Außenpolitik*; Schöllgen, *Hitler.* For German foreign policy after unification see, e.g., Hampton and Peifer, "Reordering," and Markovits and Reich, *Predicament.* Recent monographs on German–American relations include Berghahn, *America*; Goedde, *GIs and Germans*; Granieri, *Ambivalent Alliance*; Ninkovich, *Germany*; Poiger, *Jazz*: Reuther, *Normalisierung*; Rupieper, *Wurzeln.*
4. Offical engagement with the Nazi past in the GDR above all focused on the legacies and heroism of (especially communist) resistance against Nazi "fascism." As such, the GDR considered itself as the legitimate heir of the resistance, while simultaneously perceiving the Federal Republic as a continuation of fascism. This approach resulted in a distinctly different form of memory of the Nazi past in comparison to West Germany, which did not lead to comparable concerns about the "image" of the GDR abroad among the East German leadership. For a general genealogy of "divided memory" see Herf, *Divided Memory.* Important studies on the GDR regime's attitude toward Jews, including the American Jewish community, and the issue of compensation payments are Meining, *Judenpolitik*, esp. 368–502; Timm, *Jewish Claims.*
5. Quoted in Leonard Silk, "Economic Scene: What Victory Of Kohl Means," *New York Times*, March 9, 1983. See Kohl's statement in Deutscher Bundestag, Plenarprotokoll 10/4, May 4, 1983, 56. See also Buchstab and Kleinmann, "Einleitung," xliii–lii; Dettling and Geske, "Helmut Kohl," 224–226; Herbert, *Geschichte*, 979f.; Hoeres, "'Wende,'" 104–119; Schwarz, *Kohl*, 326–341; Wirsching, *Abschied*, 49–55.
6. Kirsch, "Kern," 43.
7. Wolfrum, *Geschichtspolitik*, 354f. See also, Kirsch, "Wir," 92f.
8. Kohl, "Earth," 100. See also Kansteiner, *Pursuit*, 252f.
9. This explicitly excludes private forms of engagement with the Holocaust or commemoration as well as the (individual) memory of survivors of the Holocaust. For backround on public forms of memory see, for example, Bösch and Goschler, eds., *Public History*; Cornelißen, "Erinnerungskulturen"; Bielefeld University, "Communicative Space."
10. Wolfrum, *Geschichtspolitik*, 354f
11. Rogers, "Chancellors," 241f.; Meyer, *SPD*, 386f. See with regard to Israel: Leber, "Chancellor Helmut Schmidt."

12. For thoughts about the connections between political and cultural history see Mergel, "Überlegungen"; Bösch and Domeier, "Cultural History."
13. For the role of emotions in history, see, e.g., Frevert, "Gefühle," and for international relations in particular Bormann, Freiberger, and Michel, *Angst*, and Kreis, *Diplomatie mit Gefühl.*
14. Cf. Barkan, *Guilt.*
15. Berger, "Power"; Conze et al., *Amt*, 570–620; Etheridge, "'Antideutsche Welle'"; Etheridge, *Enemies to Allies*; Trommler, *Kulturmacht*, 572–583 and 646–660. See also Frei, "'Renazification?'" and Frei, *Vergangenheitspolitik*, esp. 307–396 and 399f.
16. For the competing "memory narratives" about West Germany after the Second World War cf. Etheridge, "*Desert Fox.*" See also Schildt, "Umgang mit der NS-Vergangenheit," 44; Wiesen, "Germany's PR Man"; Wiesen, *West German Industry.*
17. Trommler, *Kulturmacht*, 581.
18. Conze et al., *Amt*, 612–614; Weinke, "Waning Confidence," 209–214.
19. Trommler, *Kulturmacht*, 694f. See also Leber, "Protest"; Pendas, *Auschwitz Trial*, 254.
20. Kansteiner, "Losing," 120f.
21. Kölsch, "Politik und Gedächtnis," 142–146.
22. Hildegard Hamm-Brücher, "Wirtschaftsriese als Kulturgartenzwerg," *Die Zeit*, September 23, 1977. See also Trommler, *Kulturmacht*, 689–691.
23. Kreis, "Bündnis"; Smyser, *Beziehungen*, 63–70. See also Feldman, "Societal Relations."
24. Cf. Wirsching, *Abschied*. See also Taberner and Cooke, "Introduction," 4–7.
25. Wolfrum, *Geschichtspolitik*, 25–32.
26. Kohl, "Lagebericht," October 13/14, 1985, 350f.
27. Kansteiner, "Losing," 125f.
28. For the 1950s see Shafir, *Ambiguous Relations*, 159–178; Etheridge, "*Desert Fox*," 223f. See also Steinweis, "Legacy."
29. Gramberger, *Wider den häßlichen Deutschen.*
30. Berger, "Learning," 99. Deidre Berger was the former correspondent for National Public Radio in Germany and joined the Berlin office of the American Jewish Committee (AJC) in 1999.
31. Schwarz, *Kohl*, 376.
32. I borrow the term "usable past" from Moeller, *War Stories.*
33. Moses, *Intellectuals*, 247.
34. Ibid., 248.
35. Schmid, "'Vergangenheitsbewältigung.'" See also Meyer, *SPD.*
36. Wirsching, *Abschied*, 474f.
37. Cf. Jarausch, *Umkehr*; Winkler, *Westen*; Wolfrum, *Demokratie.*
38. Cf. Moller, *Entkonkretisierung.*
39. Kohl, "Earth," 100.
40. Cf. Gramberger, *Wider den häßlichen Deutschen.*
41. Cf. Ibid., 84–86.
42. Haftendorn, *Außenpolitik*, 432–445; Kießling, "Täter," 223f.; Berger, "Power," 84–89. See also Beattie, "Past in the Politics," 31f.; Brockman, "'Normalization'"; Kansteiner, *Pursuit*, 280–315; Taberner and Cooke, "Introduction"; Wicke, *Quest for Normality.*
43. Cf. Feldman, *Foreign Policy.*
44. Cf. Aguilar, *Diplomacy*; for an overview consult Cull, "Public Diplomacy"; Snow and Taylor, *Routledge Handbook*. See also Bösch and Hoeres, "Bann."
45. Paulmann, "Repräsentationen," 1–13. See also Paulmann, "Deutschland"; Trommler, *Kulturmacht*, 593–602.
46. Historian Johannes Paulmann has labeled this "reflexive self-perception" (*reflexive Selbstwahrnehmung*). See Paulmann, "Repräsentationen," 2.
47. Cf. Paulmann, "Repräsentationen," 31.
48. Trommler, *Kulturmacht*, 569–712. See also Aguilar, *Diplomacy*; Köpke, "Third Pillar"; Michels, *Akademie*; Littmann, *Partners.*
49. As a *pars pro toto* for a very large body of scholarship see Doering-Manteuffel, *Wie westlich sind die Deutschen?*

50. Tuch, "American Cultural Policy"; Kreis, *Orte.*
51. Weidenfeld, "Geschichte und Politik," 24. See also Tuch, *Burns*; Smyser, *Beziehungen*, 63–70; Kreis, "Bündnis."
52. Cf. Kreis, "Bündnis," 609–613.
53. Köpke, "Third Pillar" and Kreis, "Bündnis."
54. Eckel and Moisel, "Einleitung," 18f. A notable examaple is Etheridge, "*Desert Fox*" and Etheridge, *Enemies to Allies*, 266–278.
55. It is impossible to provide a complete list of these works. Important and recent contributions include Assmann and Frevert, *Geschichtsvergessenheit*; Dubiel, *Niemand*; Fischer and Lorenz, eds., *Lexikon*; Gassert and Steinweis, eds., *Coping*; Herf, *Divided Memory*; Kansteiner, *Pursuit*; Marcuse, *Legacies*; Moses, *Intellectuals*; Moeller, *War Stories*; Reichel, *Vergangenheitsbewältigung*; Reichel, Schmid, and Steinbach, eds., *Nationalsozialismus*; Sharples, *Postwar Germany*; Weinke, *Gesellschaft*; Weinke, *Verfolgung.*
56. See for the early years of the Federal Republic: Frei, *Vergangenheitspolitik*; Brochhagen, *Nürnberg*. Examples for recent trends in memory studies are Schmid, *Erinnern*; Hikel, *Sophies Schwester*; Welzer, Moller, and Tschuggnall, *Opa*. For the political discourse see Frei, *1945.*
57. Cf. Hockerts, "Wiedergutmachung," 26. See also Biess and Moeller, eds. *Aftermath*; Brunner, Goschler, and Frei, eds., *Globalisierung*; Feldman, *Foreign Policy*; Frei, ed., *Transnationale Vergangenheitspolitik*; Frei, Brunner, and Goschler, eds., *Praxis*; Feldman, "Principle"; Lagrou, *Legacy*; Schrafstetter, "Diplomacy"; Stahl, *Nazi-Jagd*. The role of the Foreign Office in the Holocaust and its coping with the past is examined by Conze et al., *Amt*. Responses to this study include Browning, "Foreign Office"; Evans, "Foreign Office"; Hürter, "Amt"; for a summary of the debate see Sabrow and Mentel, eds., *Amt.*
58. Finkelstein, *Holocaust Industry*; Novick, *Holocaust in American Life*. For an early journalistic overview see Miller, *One*, 220–275.
59. See for example Neusner, *Stranger*, 61–81. For critical engagement with Novick's findings see, for example, Judt, "The Morbid Truth," *The New Republic*, July 19–26, 1999, 36–40; Diner, *We Remember*, 8–17.
60. Novick, *Holocaust in American Life*, 207 and 12. Cf. Flanzbaum, ed., *Americanization.*
61. Zimmermann, "Holocaust-Erinnerung," 211f. See also Langer, "Americanization"; Rosenfeld, "Americanization."
62. For an overview of the scholarship see Stier, "Holocaust"; Steinweis, "American Culture." See also Cohen, *Case*; Cole, *Selling*; Greenspan, *Listening*; Flanzbaum, *Americanization*; Niroumand, "*Americanization*."
63. Linenthal, *Preserving Memory*, 255f. See also Saidel, *Remember.*
64. Linenthal, *Preserving Memory*, 251f. The same applies to Shandler, *America.*
65. While Pieper gives an overview over German attitudes toward the USHMM, Haß completely ignores this dimension. Pieper, *Musealisierung*, 163–171; Haß, *Gedenken*, 243–358. The same applies to Young, *Texture;* Young, *Edge.*
66. Shafir, *Ambiguous Relations*. Shafir only devotes marginal attention to the GDR. See also Peck, *German-Jewish Legacy* and Schenderlein, "*Germany on Their Minds.*"
67. Examples of the vast literature are "AHR Conversation: On Transnational History"; Budde, Conrad, and Janz, eds. *Transnationale Geschichte*; Clavin, "Transnationalism"; Gassert, "Transnationale Geschichte"; Iriye, *Global and Transnational History*; Iriye, ed., *Interdependence*; Patel, "'Transnations'"; Patel, "Perspektiven"; Stelzel, "Transnationalism"; Thelen, "Nation and Beyond."
68. Here again, the literature is so vast that it is impossible to give a comprehensive overview. For a focus mostly on Germany, see above all the recent magisterial study Trommler, *Kulturmacht*; see also Kathe, *Kulturpolitik*; Mallinckrodt, *Selbstdarstellung*; Michels, *Akademie*; Renvert, *Machtmakler*. For a focus on the United States, Western Europe, and beyond see, e.g.,: Bender, ed., *Rethinking*; De Grazia, *Irresistible Empire*; Gienow-Hecht, *Transmission*; Gienow-Hecht, ed., *Decentering America*; Gienow-Hecht and Donfried, eds., *Cultural Diplomacy*; Gienow-Hecht and Schumacher, eds., *Culture*;

Hart, *Ideas*; Osgood and Etheridge, eds., *Public Diplomacy*; Kreis, *Orte*; Ostrowski, *Public Diplomacy*; Patel and Weisbrode, eds., *European Integration*.

69. E.g., Assmann, "Holocaust"; Eckel and Moisel, eds., "Universalisierung"; Goldberg and Hazan, eds., *Marking Evil*; Kroh, *Erinnerung*; Levy and Sznaider, *Holocaust and Memory*; MacDonald, *Identity*; Rupnow, "Transformationen"; Schmid, "Europäisierung." See also Rothberg, *Memory* and Allwork, *Holocaust Remembrance*. See also Steininger, ed., *Umgang*.

70. Judt, *Postwar*, 803f.; Kübler, *Erinnerungspolitik*; Heerten, "A wie Auschwitz"; Steinweis, "Analogy."

71. See for example Shain, *Roots* and Miles, "Third World Views."

72. See the volume on Holocaust memory in global perspective, which I am coediting with Philipp Gassert and Alan E. Steinweis (Göttingen: Wallstein, 2016).

73. Zimmermann, "Holocaust-Erinnerung," 212; Caplan, "Reflections," 151f. For a German perspective see Brinkmann, "Amerika"; Schweitzer, *Amerika*.

74. Tony Judt, "The Morbid Truth," *The New Republic*, July 19–26, 1999, 39. See, e.g., Surmann, *Shoah-Erinnerung*.

75. Cf. Etheridge, "*Dessert Fox*," 213.

76. Müller, "Introduction," 1f.

77. Morina, *Legacies*, 2–5.

78. For theoretical background see, for example, Landwehr, "Diskurs," 109; Müller, "Introduction," 25–31; Etheridge, "*Dessert Fox*," 213. See also: Wolfrum, *Geschichtspolitik*, 25–34.

79. The extent of this collaboration is underestimated, e.g., in the most recent account of the Historians' Controversy, see Dworok, "*Historikerstreit*," 430–433.

80. Cf. Bormann, Freiberger, and Michel, eds., *Angst*.

81. Quoted in Weingardt, "Israelpolitik," 23.

82. Shafir, *Ambiguous Relations*, 344. See also Diner, *We Remember*, 216–265; Cherfas et al., "Atrocities"; Mittleman, "American Jewish Perceptions."

83. Cherfas et al., "Atrocities," 76.

84. Benz, *Antisemitismus*, 19f. See also Bergmann, "Sekundärer Antisemitismus"; Claussen, *Judenhaß*, 41f.; Mertens, "Antizionismus," 90–93; Salzborn, *Antisemitismus*, 43–63.

85. Benz, *Antisemitismus*, 137–145. See also Eder and Mentel, "Finkelstein-Debatte."

86. All quotations will be explained in more detail and referenced in the respective chapter. On anti-Semitism in the Federal Republic see Bergmann, *Antisemitismus*, 58–61.

87. See Suri, "Non-governmental Organizations"; Conze, Lappenküper, and Müller, eds., *Geschichte*; Loth and Osterhammel, eds., *Internationale Geschichte*; Osterhammel, "Transnationale Gesellschaftsgeschichte."

88. Bösch and Domeier, "Cultural History," 580. See also Bielefeld University, "Communicative Space."

89. Kershaw, "Begriffe."

90. Conze, "Nation und Staat."

91. Buchstab and Kleinmann, "Einleitung," xvf.; Conze, *Sicherheit*, 584–591; Wirsching, *Abschied*, 171–199; Rödder, *Bundesrepublik*, 78f. For recent essayistic, scholarly, and biographic assessments of Helmut Kohl see Bahners, *Mantel*; Buchstab, Kleinmann, and Küsters, eds. *Kohl*; Clemens and Paterson, eds., "Chancellorship"; Dreher, *Kohl*; Köhler, *Kohl*; Langguth, *Kohl*; Noack and Bickerich, *Kohl*; Schwarz, *Kohl*; Wicke, *Quest for Normality*.

92. The exception was Juliane Weber, the chief of Kohl's office.

93. Eduard Ackermann quoted in Wirsching, *Abschied*, 179.

94. With the exception of German-Israli relations: Rogers, "Chancellors," 237.

95. For a detailed study of Genscher's foreign policy during the time period examined in this book see Bressensdorf, *Frieden*.

96. See Hockerts, "Zeitgeschichte."

97. These include Kohl, *Erinnerungen: 1982–1990*; Reagan, *American Life*; Shultz, *Turmoil and Triumph*; Calebow, *Normalisierung*.

98. For a complete list of interviews see page 257.

99. Ambassador Peter Hermes as quoted in BArch N 1396/3, Petersen to Kohl, February 5, 1985.

Chapter 1

1. PA AA, Zwischenarchiv, Bd. 110.298, Staden to AA, July 9, 1977. See also PA AA, AV Neues Amt, Bd. 16.850, GIC, Draft "Holocaust," June 28, 1977.
2. PA AA, Zwischenarchiv, Bd. 110.298, Staden to AA, July 9, 1977.
3. See, e.g., Schrafstetter, "Diplomacy"; Wiesen, "Germany's PR Man," 294–308. See also: Etheridge, *"Desert Fox."* For West German–American Jewish relations prior to the 1970s see Shafir, *Ambiguous Relations*, 21–280 and Shafir, "Twisted Road." For West German reactions to *Night and Fog* in this context see Knaap, *"Nacht und Nebel,"* 66–82 and Kramer, "Nacht und Nebel."
4. Conze et al., *Amt*, 600–620; Aguilar, *Diplomacy*, 246–248; Shafir, *Ambiguous Relations*, 200–237; Tempel, *Legenden*, 81–88; Weinke, "Waning Confidence."
5. PA AA, Zwischenarchiv, Bd. 110.298, Staden to AA, July 9, 1977. Cf. Paulmann, "Repräsentationen," 1–4.
6. PA AA, AV Neues Amt, Bd. 16.850, Ungerer to Embassy Washington, May 3, 1977.
7. Fallace, *Education*, 34–37.
8. Ibid., 27f. and 34–40. See also Temple University Libraries, Special Collections, Franklin Littell Papers, Littell, "Public Support for Teaching the Holocaust," September 14, 1977.
9. Hoepfner, *Organizations*, 100–111.
10. Nick, *Guide*, 5f.
11. This has been examined in great detail by Diner, *We Remember*. See also Diner, *Jews*, 330–334; Sarna, *Judaism*, 334–338.
12. For a comprehensive account see Diner, *We Remember*. See also Surmann, *Shoah-Erinnerung*, 27–34; Novick, *Holocaust in American Life*, 148–151; Finkelstein, *Holocaust Industry*, 11–38; for a contemporary view: Neusner, *Stranger*, 82–91.
13. Wieviorka, *Era of the Witness*, 96–144. See also Greenspan, *Listening*, 45–47.
14. Mintz, *Culture*, 3.
15. Popkin, "Memories," 51. See also the portrait of Wiesel in Steinweis, "Reflections," 167f.
16. Sicher, "Future," 63.
17. Greenspan, *Listening*, 46f.
18. Novick, *Holocaust in American Life*, 83f. and 189f.
19. Even though Hasia Diner convincingly demonstrates the central role the Holocaust played for Jewish communal life already in the early postwar period, she does not show that this preoccupation with the Holocaust had a significant impact on non-Jewish Americans: Diner, *We Remember*. Cf. Detlef Junker, "Die Amerikanisierung des Holocaust," *FAZ*, September 9, 2000.
20. Neusner, *Stranger*, 84. See also Fallace, *Education*, 94.
21. Neusner, *Stranger*, 84f. See also Novick, *Holocaust in American Life*, 11.
22. Ismar Schorsch quoted in Shafir, *Ambiguous Relations*, 287.
23. Surmann, *Shoah-Erinnerung*, 27–29 and Dollinger, *Quest for Inclusion*, 164–190.
24. Peck, "Confrontations," 403.
25. Linenthal, *Preserving Memory*, 4f.
26. Linenthal, *Preserving Memory*, 11–15; Greenspan, "Survivors," 45–47.
27. Novick, *Holocaust in American Life*, 234. Cf., e.g., Zwerin, *Holocaust*, and the almost grotesque: Alternatives in Religious Education, *Gestapo*. An excellent overview provides: Friedrich Ebert Stiftung, *Unterrichtsthema*.
28. Novick, *Holocaust in American Life*, 11–15.
29. Quoted in Cole, *Selling*, 154.
30. Cf. Detlef Junker, "Die Amerikanisierung des Holocaust," *FAZ*, September 9, 2000; and Junker, "'History Wars,'" 53f.
31. PA AA, AV Neues Amt, Bd. 16.850, Ungerer to Embassy Washington, May 3, 1977.
32. Ibid.
33. Ibid.
34. Cf. Etheridge, *"Desert Fox,"* 223.

35. *Munzinger Online/Personen—Internationales Biographisches Archiv*, s.v. "Werner Ungerer," www.munzinger.de/document/00000017660; "Personalien: Werner Ungerer 60," *FAZ*, April 22, 1987.

36. Personal information and quotes are taken from a letter Ungerer sent to a German Jewish émigré in the aftermath of the airing of the NBC miniseries *Holocaust* in the United States: PA AA, AV Neues Amt, Bd. 23.207, Ungerer to Wicclair, July 5, 1978.

37. Moses, "Die 45er," 235; Moses, *Intellectuals*, 55–73; Rigoll, *Staatsschutz*, 13f.

38. All quotes in this paragraph in PA AA, AV Neues Amt, Bd. 23.207, Ungerer to Wicclair, July 5, 1978.

39. PA AA, AV Neues Amt, Bd. 16.970, Kalkbrenner, "Kulturpolitscher Jahresbericht 1976."

40. PA AA, Zwischenarchiv, Bd. 110.298, Staden to AA, July 9, 1977.

41. Staden, *Ende*, 42–69, quotes on 42f. See also: Staden, *Eiszeit*, 133–148; *Munzinger Online/Personen—Internationales Biographisches Archiv*, s.v. "Berndt von Staden," www.munzinger.de/document/00000013494; "Hoffnungen und Gefahren fuer die deutsch-amerikanische Verwandtschaft," *FAZ*, October 26, 1983; Reinhard Veser, "Berndt von Stadens baltische Jugenderinnerungen," *FAZ*, August 9, 1999.

42. Staden, *Nacht*, 67–94. Wendelgard von Staden's memoirs were also translated into English: Staden, *Darkness*

43. Staden, *Eiszeit*, 133–148. See also Steininger, *Deutschland und die USA*, 607–609; Wiegrefe, *Zerwürfnis*, 359f.

44. *Munzinger Online/Personen—Internationales Biographisches Archiv*, s.v. "Berndt von Staden," www.munzinger.de/document/00000013494.

45. Schmidt's speech to the SPD party council on September 12, 1978, as quoted in Hepperle, *SPD*, 271. See also Leber, "Chancellor Helmut Schmidt."

46. Quoted in "Deutsche und Juden: Kniefall wiederholen?," *Der Spiegel* 20 (1981), 22, 25–28, quote on 28.

47. Rogers, "Chancellors," 241f. See also: Shafir, *Ambiguous Relations*, 274.

48. PA AA, AV Neues Amt, Bd. 16.850, GIC, Draft "Holocaust," June 28, 1977.

49. PA AA, Zwischenarchiv, Bd. 110.298, Staden to AA, July 9, 1977.

50. Ibid.

51. Etheridge, *"Desert Fox,"* 230.

52. PA AA, Zwischenarchiv, Bd. 110.298, Staden to AA, July 9, 1977.

53. Doneson, *American Film*, 145. See also Shandler, *America*, 158–163 and Thiele, *Kontroversen*, 298–338. For a contemporary view see "'Holocaust:' Die Vergangenheit kommt zurück," *Der Spiegel* 5 (1979), 17–28.

54. PA AA, Zwischenarchiv, Bd. 110.298, Staden to AA, July 9, 1977.

55. PA AA, Zwischenarchiv, Bd. 110.298, AA, "Holocaust," July 14, 1977. For an overview see Conze et al., *Amt*, 570–620. See also: Shafir, *Ambiguous Relations*, 281–297.

56. PA AA, AV Neues Amt, Bd. 16.850, AA to Embassy Washington, September 9, 1977.

57. Officially, the process of compensation was supposed to have been completed in 1965. See Goschler, *Schuld*, 293.

58. PA AA, AV Neues Amt, Bd. 16.850, AA to Embassy Washington, September 9, 1977. See also Goschler, *Schuld*, 323–344; Shafir, *Ambiguous Relations*, 278.

59. PA AA, AV Neues Amt, Bd. 16.850, AA to Embassy Washington, September 9, 1977.

60. Ibid.

61. PA AA, AV Neues Amt, Bd. 16.850, Ungerer to Embassy Washington, May 3, 1977.

62. Ibid.

63. Cf. Schuldiner, *Contesting Histories*, 103–117, and for the past decade: Lange, *"Herman the German,"* 104–112.

64. PA AA, AV Neues Amt, Bd. 16.850, Riestenberg to Schlosse (President of NBC Network), July 7, 1977.

65. Draft Paper of the German-American Committee as quoted in PA AA, AV Neues Amt, Bd. 23.207, Ungerer, "Schulbuch über den Holocaust," May 9, 1977.

66. PA AA, AV Neues Amt, Bd. 23.207, Ungerer to Embassy Washington, October 4, 1977.

67. Ibid.
68. PA AA, AV Neues Amt, Bd. 23.207, Ungerer, "Aufnahme des Holocaust in den Lehrplan der Schulen von Philadelphia," September 26, 1977.
69. PA AA, AV Neues Amt, Bd. 23.207, Barbye to D.A.N.K. members, October 9, 1977.
70. PA AA, AV Neues Amt, Bd. 23.207, Peters, "German American Committee of Greater New York," November 10, 1977.
71. PA AA, AV Neues Amt, Bd. 16.970, Haide Russel, "Kulturpolitscher Jahresbericht 1977," 9f. That such fears existed from the beginning of the "Holocaust debate" shows PA AA, AV Neues Amt, Bd. 23.207, Ungerer, "Deutschamerikaner—Holocaust Diskussion," November 29, 1977. See also Shafir, *Ambiguous Relations*, 196f.
72. PA AA, AV Neues Amt, Bd. 23.207, Ungerer to Embassy Washington, July 28, 1978.
73. PA AA, AV Neues Amt, Bd. 23.207, Ungerer, "Schulbuch über den Holocaust," May 9, 1977.
74. Pape is quoted in Fallace, *Education*, 36. On Ungerer's conversation with Pape see PA AA, AV Neues Amt, Bd. 23.207, Ungerer, "Deutschamerikaner—Holocaust Diskussion," November 29, 1977.
75. PA AA, AV Neues Amt, Bd. 23.207, Ungerer, "Deutsch-amerikanisches Komitee von Gross-New York," March 1, 1978. Cf. Fallace, *Education*, 36–38.
76. The ADL had sent an invitation to von Staden already in May: PA AA, AV Neues Amt, Bd. 23.207, Kameny to Staden, May 26, 1977.
77. "Conference Rationale," attached to PA AA, AV Neues Amt, Bd. 23.207, Kameny to Staden, May 26, 1977.
78. PA AA, AV Neues Amt, Bd. 16.850, Staden to AA and BPA, October 14, 1977.
79. PA AA, AV Neues Amt, Bd. 16.850, AA to Bachmann (incl. a dossier on compensation payments), August 5, 1977.
80. PA AA, AV Neues Amt, Bd. 16.850, Embassy Washington to AA, October 26, 1977 (incl. Report by Bachmann, October 18, 1977).
81. PA AA, AV Neues Amt, Bd. 16.850, Staden to AA and BPA, October 14, 1977.
82. Hilberg, *Politics*.
83. PA AA, AV Neues Amt, Bd. 16.850, Report by Bachmann, October 18, 1977.
84. PA AA, AV Neues Amt, Bd. 16.850, Staden to AA, October 26, 1977.
85. See the recommendations of a study group of German and American Experts: *Recent History of the Federal Republic of Germany and the United States*. In the 1990s, the Atlantik-Brücke cooperated with the AJC and the Armonk Institute on programs related to Holocaust education in high schools, see chapter 5 of this book.
86. The ADL even planned to expand this initiative nation-wide: PA AA, AV Neues Amt, Bd. 16.850, Ungerer to Embassy Washington, November 29, 1977.
87. PA AA, AV Neues Amt, Bd. 16.850, Staden to Bonn AA, December 19, 1977.
88. PA AA, AV Neues Amt, Bd. 16.850, AA, "Holocaust als Schulunterrichtsthema," October 17, 1977.
89. PA AA, AV Neues Amt, Bd. 16.850, Ungerer to Embassy Washington, November 29, 1977.
90. Ibid.
91. PA AA, AV Neues Amt, Bd. 16.850, Staden to Bonn AA, December 19, 1977.
92. See for example the relevant passages in Linenthal, *Preserving Memory*, 11–15; Novick, *Holocaust in American Life*, 209–214; Greenspan, "Survivors," 45–47; Herf, "'Holocaust' Reception," 37f.; Shafir, "Conscience," 129f.; Shandler, *America*, 155–178.
93. Cf. Sanua, *Let Us Prove Strong*, 251–259.
94. Feigin, "Office of Special Investigations," 1–20.
95. That this was a controversial decision in the American Jewish community shows, Linenthal, *Preserving Memory*, 12–15.
96. Ibid., 17–28. See also Miller, *One*, 255–257; Judith Miller, "Holocaust Museum: A Troubled Start," *New York Times Magazine*, April 22, 1990, 35.
97. Young, *Texture*, 336.
98. See for example the recent examination of this issue by Breitman and Lichtman, *F.D.R. and the Jews*, 295–314.
99. Young, *Texture*, 290–349.

100. For a history of the Museum of Jewish Heritage see: Saidel, *Remember.*
101. Belzberg Architects, *Museum.*
102. No official history of the founding of this museum exist, but relevant information can be accessed on the museum's website: www.holocaustcenter.org.
103. Linenthal, *Preserving Memory*, 11–15; Greenspan, "Survivors," 45–47.
104. PA AA, Zwischenarchiv, Bd. 110.298, Staden to AA, July 9, 1977; PA AA, AV Neues Amt, Bd. 23.207, Staden to AA, March 5, 1978. In March 1978, a representative of the German Information Center had previewed parts of *Holocaust* and the embassy's assessment is based on her impressions as well as on publicly available information about the miniseries.
105. PA AA, AV Neues Amt, Bd. 16.850, Staden to AA, December 19, 1977.
106. PA AA, Zwischenarchiv, Bd. 110.298, Staden to AA, July 9, 1977.
107. Shandler, *America*, 175. See also: ACDP, Michael Mertes Papers, 01–747, Armonk-Institute/William S. Trosten (1986–1990), Wolf Calebow, "Erfahrungsbericht, Washington, D.C.," October 18, 1988, 2.
108. Wilke, "Fernsehserie."
109. Shandler, *America*, 156f.
110. Doneson, *American Film*, 156.
111. Novick, *Holocaust in American Life*, 209.
112. Elie Wiesel, "Trivializing the Holocaust: Semi-Fact and Semi-Fiction," *New York Times*, April 16, 1978. See also: Institute of Human Relations, *Americans*; Novick, *Holocaust in American Life*, 209–214; Shandler, *America*, 163–165.
113. Shandler, *America*, 163.
114. Doneson, *American Film*, 190. See also Shandler, *America*, 175.
115. PA AA, AV Neues Amt, Bd. 23.207, Ungerer to Embassy Washington, July 31, 1978.
116. PA AA, AV Neues Amt, Bd. 16.850, Embassy Washington to Bonn AA, September 27, 1977.
117. PA AA, AV Neues Amt, Bd. 16.850, GK Detroit to Embassy Washington, August 12, 1977 (incl. attachments).
118. PA AA, AV Neues Amt, Bd. 23.207, GK NY, "NBC-Sendung Holocaust," April 17, 1978; PA AA, AV Neues Amt, Bd. 23.207, Ungerer to AA, April 18, 1978.
119. PA AA, AV Neues Amt, Bd. 23.207, GK NY, "NBC-Sendung 'Holocaust,'" April 18, 1978.
120. PA AA, AV Neues Amt, Bd. 23.207, Staden to AA, April 20, 1978. See also Shafir, *Ambiguous Relations*, 291.
121. PA AA, AV Neues Amt, Bd. 23.207, AA to all German representations abroad, May 29, 1978. For the long-term perspective see: PA AA, AV Neues Amt, Bd. 16.850, GIC to AA, January 22, 1979.
122. PA AA, AV Neues Amt, Bd. 23.207, Staden to AA, April 20, 1978; PA AA, AV Neues Amt, Bd. 16.850, Embassy Washington to AA, May 8, 1978.
123. PA AA, AV Neues Amt, Bd. 23.207, Embassy Washington to AA, May 8, 1978.
124. PA AA, AV Neues Amt, Bd. 16.850, Embassy Washington to AA, May 5, 1978.
125. Ibid.
126. Moeller, *War Stories.* Cf. Hikel, *Sophies Schwester*, 115–155.
127. For this interpretation of the history of the Third Reich see Frei, *Vergangenheitspolitik*, 397–406.
128. PA AA, AV Neues Amt, Bd. 16.850, Staden to AA, BPA, etc., [January] 1979.
129. PA AA, AV Neues Amt, Bd. 23.207, Embassy Washington to Inter Nationes, March 28, 1979.
130. PA AA, AV Neues Amt, Bd. 23.207, AA to all German representations abroad, January 26, 1979.
131. For its impact on the historical profession see Bösch, "Film," 4f.
132. Contemporary observers spoke of the Federal Republic as a "shocked" (*betroffene*) nation. See Märthesheimer and Frenzel, eds., *Kreuzfeuer*; Wilke, "Fernsehserie." See also Sharples, *Postwar Germany*, 127–140.
133. Classen, "Fernsehserie."
134. Wilke, "Fernsehserie," 7f. See also Bösch, "Film."

135. Herf, "'Holocaust' Reception," 32–36.
136. "Fernsehen: Gaskammern à la Hollywood," *Der Spiegel* 20 (1978), 228–231.
137. Herf, "'Holocaust' Reception," 51; Meyer, *SPD*, 392–399.
138. Herf, "'Holocaust' Reception," 36; "Endlösung im Abseits," *Der Spiegel* 3 (1979), 133.
139. IfZ, ED 379, Bd. 90, Hildegard Hamm-Brücher, "Aufgaben und Ziele der auswärtigen Kulturpolitik als dritte Dimension der deutsche Außenpolitik," July 5, 1979, 19; emphasis in the original. See also Kölsch, "Politik und Gedächtnis," 141.
140. Reichel, *Vergangenheitsbewältigung*, 182–198. See also: Dubiel, *Niemand*, 160–174.
141. For the precise legal argument see: Dubiel, *Niemand*, 160–174.
142. PA AA, AV Neues Amt, Bd. 16.850, Embassy Washington, "Holocaust an amerikanischen Schulen und Universitäten," February 2, 1979.
143. PA AA, AV Neues Amt, Bd. 16.850, Staden to AA, January 29, 1979.
144. Ibid.
145. Reichel, *Vergangenheitsbewältigung*, 195f. See also Leber, "Protest."
146. PA AA, Zwischenarchiv, Bd. 115.945, Ungerer to Well (AA), November 10, 1977.
147. Ibid.
148. Shafir, *Ambiguous Relations*, 279.
149. PA AA, Zwischenarchiv, Bd. 115.945, AA, "Einladung von 5 prominenten Vertretern jüdischer Organisationen aus den USA," August 16, 1978.
150. Tempel, *Legenden*, 96–101 and 106; Shafir, *Ambiguous Relations*, 261–280.
151. These were the impressions of the former AJC president, Howard I. Friedman, on the occasion of delivering the Alois Mertes Memorial Lecture on October 29, 1991, as quoted in Shafir, *Ambiguous Relations*, 352f.
152. Ibid., 87–178.
153. Diner, *We Remember*, 216. See also Tempel, *Legenden*, 15–22.
154. PA AA, Zwischenarchiv, Bd. 115.945, AA, "Einladung prominenter Vertreter jüdischer Organisationen aus den USA," May 16, 1978.
155. PA AA, Zwischenarchiv, Bd. 115.945, "Vorschlag des GK New York," January 17, 1978.
156. PA AA, Zwischenarchiv, Bd. 115.945, AA, "Einladung prominenter Vertreter jüdischer Organisationen," October 18, 1978.
157. PA AA, AV Neues Amt, Bd. 16.853, GK Los Angeles to AA, March 22, 1979.
158. Shafir, *Ambiguous Relations*, 274–280.
159. See Sanua, *Let Us Prove Strong*; Peck, *Tradition*; Hoepfner, *Organizations*, 86–100.
160. PA AA, Zwischenarchiv, Bd. 115.945, GK NY to AA, March 9, 1979.
161. Shafir, *Ambiguous Relations*, 293–297; Neuss, "Brückenbauen," 42f.
162. Shafir, *Ambiguous Relations*, 275.
163. Conversation between Chancellor Schmidt and a Delegation of the AJC, March 29, 1979, AAPD 1979 I, doc. 95: 428–431.
164. Ibid.: 430.
165. Deutschkron, *Israel*, 404–424; Lavy, *Germany and Israel*, 198–201; Leber, "Chancellor Helmut Schmidt"; Leber, "Leopard"; Meyer, *SPD*, 386.
166. Leber, "Chancellor Helmut Schmidt." As this is an online publication, page numbers are not available.
167. Ibid.
168. Tempel, *Legenden*, 23–33.
169. Ibid., 96–101.
170. DuBow, "'The Adenauer,'" 64.
171. NYPL, Oral Histories, Box 111 No. 6, transcript of interview by Alice Shapiro with William Trosten, May 6, 1980, 30.
172. Ibid.
173. Calebow, *Normalisierung*, 21–24.
174. Neuss, "Brückenbauen," 42f. See also "William Trosten gestorben," *FAZ*, March 26, 2001; "Paid Notice: Deaths Trosten, William," *New York Times*, March 11, 2001.
175. Cf. BArch B 136/29850, Memorandum for Helmut Schmidt, September 9, 1981.

176. BArch B 136/29850, AA, "Analyse zu einem Treffen von Helmut Schmidt mit Vertretern des AJC für AA und Bundeskanzleramt," March 19, 1979.

177. PA AA, Zwischenarchiv, Bd. 115.939, Staden to AA, March 16, 1979. The AJC invited Schmidt to speak at the 1979 Annual Meeting of the AJC in NYC as the first German "leader" ever invited for this occasion (see: PA AA, Zwischenarchiv, Bd. 115.939, AJC to Schmidt, March 9, 1979). Schmidt could not accept the invitation due to time constraints.

178. PA AA, Zwischenarchiv, Bd. 115.939, Staden to AA, March 16, 1979.

179. Shafir, *Ambiguous Relations*, 279f.

180. ACDP, Michael Mertes Papers, 01–747, Armonk-Institute/William S. Trosten (1986–1990), Wolf Calebow, "Erfahrungsbericht, Washington, D.C.," October 18, 1988, 7f. Cf. the published and expanded version of this report: Calebow, *Normalisierung*, 21–24.

181. BArch B 136/29850, Untitled AJC Proposal, n.d.

182. Kreis, "Bündnis"; Scott-Smith, "Transatlantic Community."

183. Thesing, "Kooperation," 23–28.

184. Ibid., 25.

185. AJC Archives, William Trosten Files, Box 5, AJC, "Exchange Program for Future Leaders in the Federal Republic of Germany and of the American Jewish Community," Dezember 1982. The initators of this program on both sides did not know about the cooperation in the 1950s. See ACDP, Michael Mertes Papers, 01–747, Armonk-Institute/William S. Trosten (1986–1990), Wolf Calebow, "Erfahrungsbericht, Washington, D.C.," October 18, 1988, 7.

186. Quoted in Carole Coyn, "Plurality of American Jewry a Surprise," *Long Island Jewish World*, April 10–16, 1981; parentheses in original. For a video recording of a television interview with Trosten, Pordzik and others see American Jewish Committee, *Jewish Dimension: German Jewish Exchange*, WPIX-TV, 23:04, August 10, 1983, accessed July 23, 2015, www.ajcarchives.org/main.php?DocumentId=15860.

187. All quotes in Marc Fisher, "Friend or Foe?," *Washington Post*, November 27, 1995.

188. All quotes in ibid. See also: Marc Fisher, "Pordzik Suit Unresolved," *Washington Post*, February 16, 1996; "Klage gegen deutschen Stiftungschef abgewiesen," *SZ*, March 30, 1996; Robert von Rimscha, "US-Präsidentschaftswahlkampf," *Der Tagesspiegel*, August 2, 2000, accessed July 23, 2015, www.tagesspiegel.de/politik/us-praesidentschaftswahlkampf-warum-der-parteitag-der-republikaner-ein-fest-fuer-die-deutsche-post-ist/157228.html.

189. For the Atlantik-Brücke's earlier involvement in West German–American Jewish affairs, see Shafir, *Ambiguous Relations*, 186 and 205.

190. Michael Sontheimer, "Walther Leisler Kieps Memoiren: Ein Mann für heikle Missionen," *Spiegel Online*, January 10, 2006, accessed July 23, 2015, www.spiegel.de/politik/deutschland/0,1518,394269,00.html. Kiep maintained that the Atlantik-Brücke did not engage in negotiations with the USHMM (Interview, Walther Leisler Kiep). Cf. chapter 3 and 5 of this book.

191. AJC Archives, William Trosten Files, Box 5, Weiss to Pordzik, July 27, 1983. See also the selected and edited reports in the section "Erfahrungsberichte von amerikanischen Teilnehmern" in Berger and Paulus, eds., *"Experience,"* 34–68.

192. AJC Archives, William Trosten Files, Box 2, Deborah E. Lipstadt, "Germany, 1982. Hiding from History?," n.d., 11.

193. Ibid., 13; italics and German in the original.

194. Lübbe, "Nationalsozialismus," 579.

195. AJC Archives, William Trosten Files, Box 2, Weiss to Trosten, November 12, 1982; Wolfgang Vogel, "Bericht über die USA-Reise von 14.4. bis 2.5.1982," June 1, 1982. For example, for such attitudes during the 1970s, see Shafir, *Ambiguous Relations*, 288.

196. AJC Archives, William Trosten Files, Box 2, Trosten to Mesnekoff, August 5 1982.

197. Neuss, "Brückenbauen," 49. See for example: AJC Archives, William Trosten Files, Box 2, Philip R. Scheier, "AJC Visitors at Holocaust Memorial," *The Jewish Transcript*, May 12, 1983; Frederick Case, "'Thou Shalt Not Forget," *The Seattle Times*, n.d.

198. AJC Archives, William Trosten Files, Box 2, Geoffrey Fisher, "Guilt Lingers On For Young Germans," *San Francisco Jewish Bulletin*, July 23, 1982.
199. AJC Archives, William Trosten Files, Box 2, Trosten to Moses, April 20, 1983.
200. AJC Archives, William Trosten Files, Box 2, Wolffsohn to Heck, May 10, 1982.
201. Neuss, "Brückenbauen," 45. See also Eisel and Koecke, eds., *Deutschland*.
202. Neuss points to Michael Mertes: Neuss, "Brückenbauen," 57.
203. Ibid., 57.
204. Quoted in BArch B 136/29850, Petersen, Report, July 28, 1981.
205. ACDP, Michael Mertes Papers, 01-747, Armonk-Institute/William S. Trosten (1986–1990), Wolf Calebow, "Erfahrungsbericht, Washington, D.C.," October 18, 1988, p 3.
206. BArch B 136/17558, BPA, "Politische Öffentlichkeitsarbeit in den Vereinigten Staaten," February 9, 1982.
207. Ibid. See also Bressensdorf, *Frieden*.
208. For debates about the NATO Double-Track Decision see Gassert, Geiger, and Wentker, eds., *Kalter Krieg*.
209. "Kein Partygänger," *Der Spiegel* 25 (1984), 33; Walter Henkels, "Secretarius fidelis et prudens," *FAZ*, June 11, 1976.
210. "Hermes, Peter," Website of the Konrad Adenauer Foundation, accessed July 23, 2015, www.kas.de/wf/de/71.11540/.
211. Hermes, *Zeitgeschichte*, 275–287, quote on 275.
212. Ibid., 285f.
213. BArch B 136/17552, AA, "Überlegungen zur Verbesserung unserer Selbstdarstellung in den USA," February 11, 1982. See also BArch B 136/17551, Hermes to AA, July 4, 1981.
214. Wiegrefe, *Zerwürfnis*; Steininger, *Deutschand und die USA*, 563–641. See also Feldman, "Societal Relations."
215. BArch B 136/17552, Hermes to AA, May 4, 1982; BArch B 136/17557, Embassy Washington to AA, April 30, 1981; ACDP, Michael Mertes Papers, 01-747, Armonk-Institute/William S. Trosten (1986–1990), Wolf Calebow, "Erfahrungsbericht, Washington, D.C.," October 18, 1988, 5. For the assessment of contemporaries see Szabo, ed., *Successor Generation* and Tuch, *Arthur Burns*. See also Kreis, "Bündnis"; Scott-Smith, "Transatlantic Community."
216. Smyser, *Beziehungen*, 63–70.
217. Kreis, "Bündnis," 611–613.
218. BArch B 136/17552, Seitz to Genscher, February 25, 1982; emphasis in original.
219. Ibid.; emphasis in original.
220. BArch B 136/17552, BKA, "Sprechzettel," meeting with group of German American parliamentarians on February 11, 1982, n.d.
221. BArch B 136/17557, Hamm-Brücher to the chairmen of all parties in the Bundestag, August 12, 1981.
222. BArch B 136/17557, BKAmt, Gablentz to Schmidt, August 31, 1981; BKAmt, Gablentz to Schmidt, September 25, 1981; AA, Ad hoc measures for 1982/1983, n.d.
223. BArch B 136/17552, AA, "Überlegungen zur Verbesserung unserer Selbstdarstellung in den USA," February 11, 1982.
224. Ibid.
225. Smyser, *Beziehungen*, 20.
226. Ibid., 64f.

Chapter 2

1. Cf. for this chapter my article Eder, "'Holocaustsyndrom.'"
2. See Clemens, "Image"; Wirsching, "Beziehungen."
3. For an overview: Seuthe, "Geistig- moralische Wende."
4. Reichel, "Judenmord," 376.
5. Frei, *1945*, 26f. and 34–37.

6. Kießling, "Täter," 209. Cf. Paulmann, "Repräsentationen," 21f.; Brockman, "'Normalization'"; Kansteiner, *Pursuit*, 280–315 and Wicke, *Quest for Normality.*

7. Feldman, "Jewish Role," 180–182.

8. AJC Archives, William Trosten Files, Box 5, Wolffsohn to Bruno Heck, May 10, 1982.

9. Clemens, "Image," 185.

10. Kansteiner, *Pursuit*, 315. See also Wirsching, *Abschied*, 470–481 and 563–572.

11. Quote in Kohl, "Lagebericht," June 18, 1987, 543; similar statement in Deutscher Bundestag, Plenarprotokoll 9/121, October 13, 1982, 7220. See also Buchstab and Kleinmann, "Einleitung," xxvi–xxix; Herbert, *Geschichte*, 1022–1027; Wirsching, "Beziehungen."

12. Clemens, "Image," 182f.

13. Ninkovich, *Germany*, 153–158.

14. Wirsching, *Abschied*, 473. See also Wicke, *Quest for Normality*, 170–198.

15. Kohl, *Erinnerungen: 1982–1990*, 626.

16. Wirsching, *Abschied*, 470–481.

17. Herbert, *Geschichte*, 1010–1014, quote on 1014.

18. Schmid, "'Vergangenheitsbewältigung.'" See also Meyer, *SPD*, 426f.

19. For this paragraph see: Herbert, *Geschichte*, 1014f.; Hoeres, "'Tendenzwende,'" 104–119; Maier, *Past*, 9–16; Kirsch, "*Wir*," 79–86; Seuthe, "*Geistig-moralische Wende*," 309–320; Wolfrum, *Geschichtspolitik*, 354f.; Schwarz, *Kohl*, 374–380.

20. Wicke, *Quest for Normality*, 63–88.

21. Müchler and Hofman, *Kohl*, 32f.

22. Kohl, *Erinnerungen: 1982–1990*, 218–234, quote on 230.

23. Cf. Mommsen, "Polarisierung," 78f.; Kirsch, "*Wir*," 95.

24. Kohl, "Mahnung und Verpflichtung."

25. Quote in ibid. Cf. Gleason, *Totalitarianism*, 157–166.

26. Kohl, "Earth," 97.

27. Cf. Moller, *Entkonkretisierung*, 31–39.

28. Trommler, *Kulturmacht*, 695. See also see Frei, *Vergangenheitspolitik.*

29. Seuthe, "*Geistig-moralische Wende*," 62 and 311; Wirsching, *Abschied*, 475.

30. Kirsch, "*Wir*," 84f.

31. Quoted in Kohl, *Erinnerungen: 1982–1990*, 220.

32. Deutscher Bundestag, Plenarprotokoll 9/121, October 13, 1982, 7227 and Deutscher Bundestag, Plenarprotokoll 10/4, May 4, 1983, 73f. Cf. Kohl, "Lagebericht," March 23, 1983, 71–73. See also Dettling and Geske, "Helmut Kohl," 224–226.

33. Meyer, *SPD*, 439–461, 471–479. Cf. Dworok, "*Historikerstreit*," 429–433.

34. Kattago, *Memory*, 52.

35. Deutscher Bundestag, Plenarprotokoll 10/4, May 4, 1983, 19651. See also Meyer, *SPD*, 473f.

36. Deutscher Bundestag, Plenarprotokoll 10/4, May 4, 1983, 19656f.; emphasis in original.

37. Cf. Mommsen, "Geschichtsbilder."

38. Hildegard Hamm-Brücher, "Mehr Behutsamkeit!," *Deutsches Allgemeines Sonntagsblatt*, February 22, 1987.

39. Meyer, *SPD*, 471–479.

40. Seuthe, "*Geistig-moralische Wende*," 37; Moller, *Entkonkretisierung*, 13–21 and 40–71.

41. Moller, *Entkonkretisierung*, 12 and 137–140.

42. Deutschkron, *Israel*, 425–439; Dreher, *Kohl*, 339–342; Lavy, *Germany and Israel*, 201f.; Meyer, *SPD*, 444-448.

43. Quoted in Kohl, *Erinnerungen: 1982–1990*, 226f.

44. Bergmann, *Antisemitismus*, 385–391; Dubiel, *Niemand*, 200–206. The expression "Gnade der späten Geburt" goes back to Günter Gaus, see "Verschwiegene Enteignung," *Der Spiegel* 38 (1986), 47. For the debate in the Bundestag see Deutscher Bundestag, Plenarprotokoll 10/53, February 9, 1984, 3725–3729.

45. Rosumek, *Kanzler*, 174. Cf. Wolffsohn, *Guilt*, 35.

46. Deutscher Bundestag, Plenarprotokoll 10/53, February 9, 1984, 3730. See also Meyer, *SPD*, 444–447.
47. Deutscher Bundestag, Plenarprotokoll 10/53, February 9, 1984, 3741.
48. Ibid.
49. Kohl, *Erinnerungen: 1982–1990*, 228f. See also Deutschkron, *Israel*, 432; Rosumek, *Kanzler*, 174f.; Wolffsohn, *Guilt*, 35. For negative press coverage see, e.g., Jürgen Leinemann, "'Einen schönen Salat hat man euch serviert,'" *Der Spiegel* (5) 1984, 27f.
50. For example: Hoeres, "'Tendenzwende,'" 104–119; Seuthe, *"Geistig-moralische Wende,"* 309f.; Wirsching, *Abschied*, 473f.
51. Kirsch, *"Wir,"* 81f.; Kirsch, "Kern," 43.
52. Kirsch, *"Wir,"* 92 and also Taberner and Cooke, "Introduction."
53. Seuthe, *"Geistig-moralische Wende,"* 311 and Wirsching, *Abschied*, 473f.
54. "'Auf Kohl's Rat hören wir nicht wieder,'" *Der Spiegel* (18) 1985, 19.
55. Kohl, "Lagebericht," May 13, 1985, 304.
56. Clemens, "Image," 185.
57. Kohl, "Lagebericht," May 3, 1993, 450. Cf. Mann, *Rebellion*, 227f.
58. Kohl, "Lagebericht," June 11, 1990, 141.
59. Kohl made this statement when critizing the World Jewish Congress's opposition to Steffen Heitmann's (CDU) candidacy for the office of federal president. See Kohl, "Lagebericht," October 1/2, 1993, 504.
60. Quoted in BArch, B 136/29854, Perlmutter to Bialkin, November 16, 1982. See also Kohl, *Erinnerungen: 1982–1990*, 64; Shafir, *Ambiguous Relations*, 294.f.
61. Cf. Dubiel, *Niemand*, 200–206. For an opposing view by a former official in the Chancellery under Kohl: Mertes, "Legacy," 75f.
62. BArch B 136/29854, Bialkin to Kohl, November 17, 1982.
63. A deal with a long history indeed: see, e.g., "Keine Kompetenz zum Mitregieren," *FAZ*, October 22, 2014.
64. For East German arms deals with Syria, the PLO, and other opponents of Israel in the Middle East, see Herf, "'At War.'"
65. Wolffsohn, *Guilt*, 30–34; Leber, "Chancellor Helmut Schmidt"; Leber, "Leopard."
66. "Deutsche und Juden: Kniefall wiederholen?," *Der Spiegel* 20 (1981), 22–28, quote on 28. Cf. Schmid, "'Vergangenheitsbewältigung,'" 181f.
67. BArch B 136/29854, Teltschik to Bialkin and Foxman, January 9, 1984.
68. The AJC had intervened with the German embassy against this deal already in 1981. See AJC Archives, William Trosten Files, Box 2, Bookbinder to Hermes, Janaury 22, 1981; Marc Tannenbaum, "Germany's Arms Sales to Saudi Arabia is Morally Unbearable," January 22, 1984.
69. American Gathering of Jewish Holocaust Survivors, "How Many Jews Will German Weapons Kill This Time?," advertisement, *New York Times*, January 20, 1984.
70. Elie Wiesel, "People Without Memories," *Jewish Chronicle*, February 24, 1984. Cf. AJC Archives, William Trosten Files, Box 4, Mertes to Wiesel, August 27, 1984.
71. BArch B 136/30019, Hermes to AA and ChBK, February 10,1984.
72. Message transmitted as part of BArch B 136/30019, Hermes to AA and ChBK, February 10, 1984; lower case spelling in the original.
73. Interview, Michael Berenbaum.
74. BArch B 136/30019, Embassy Washington, "Minutes, Meeting with representatives of the American Gathering of Jewish Holocaust Survivors," February 13, 1984.
75. For the postwar debate on German "collective guilt" and Heuss's suggestion to speak of "collective shame" see Frei, *1945*, 145–155.
76. BArch B 136/30019, Embassy Washington, "Minutes, Meeting with representatives of the American Gathering of Jewish Holocaust Survivors," February 13, 1984.
77. BArch B 136/30019, Hermes to AA and ChBK, February 10, 1984.
78. Steven R. Weisman, "Reagan and Kohl Discuss Soviet Parley," *New York Times*, March 6, 1984. Cf. BArch B 136/30019, BKAmt, "Teilnehmerliste für das Gespräch mit Vertretern jüdischer Organisationen," n.d.

79. BArch B 136/30019, BKAmt, "Gesprächsvorschlag zu möglichen Rüstungslieferungen an Saudi-Arabien," n.d.

80. Ibid. The following quotes are also taken from this document.

81. Deutscher Bundestag, Plenarprotokoll 10/53, February 9, 1984, 3729.

82. BArch B 136/30019, BKAmt, "Gesprächsvorschlag zu möglichen Rüstungslieferungen an Saudi-Arabien," n.d. Cf. Benz, *Antisemitismus*, 146–154 and Salzborn, *Antisemitismus*, 56–63.

83. For background information on this meeting see Steven R. Weisman, "Reagan and Kohl Discuss Soviet Parley," *New York Times*, March 6, 1984.

84. BArch B 136/33866, Hermes to AA, April 9, 1984.

85. AJC Archives, William Trosten Files, Box 4, Tanenbaum to Mertes, September 11, 1984.

86. BArch B 136/30522, Well to AA, ChBK, etc., November 3, 1984.

87. Ibid.

88. Ibid.

89. "Bitburg" has resulted in a large amount of scholarship; for an overview for the specific angle pursued here see Shafir, *Ambiguous Relations*, 299–315. See also: AJC Archives, International Relations Department, File B, Theodore Ellenoff, "AJC Presidential Address," November 22, 1987.

90. Mentel, "Bitburg-Affäre," 53. Cf. Kießling, "Täter," 224; Seuthe, *"Geistig-moralische Wende,"* 313.

91. Maier, *Past*, 9–16, quote on 10. According to Maier, "Bitburg History" encompassed a denial of German collective responsibility for the legacies of the Holocaust and rejected the notion of the singularity of the Holocaust.

92. Cf. Schwarz, *Kohl*, 378.

93. For the opposition in Germany, especially by the German left, see: Meyer, *SPD*, 462-470; Seuthe, *"Geistig-moralische Wende,"* 60–66; Kirsch, *"Wir,"* 82f. and 86–95. For the debate in the Bundestag: Deutscher Bundestag, Plenarprotokoll 10/137, May 14, 1985.

94. Meyer, *SPD*, 463f.

95. Cf. Shafir, "Conscience," 131.

96. Seuthe, *"Geistig-moralische Wende,"* 313.

97. "Auf Kohl's Rat hören wir nicht wieder," *Der Spiegel* 18 (1985), 19. Cf. Kießling, "Täter," 209. Kohl denies this in Kohl, "Lagebericht," April 22, 1985, 288f.

98. Kohl, "Lagebericht," April 22, 1985, 288.

99. Dreher, *Kohl*, 362–366; Seuthe, *"Geistig-moralische Wende,"* 51f.; Steininger, *Deutschland und die USA*, 701–710.

100. Morris, "Bitburg Revisited," 94–97. See also "'Jetzt stehen die Deutschen stramm,'" *Der Spiegel* 19 (1985), 22–32.

101. Kohl, "Lagebericht," April 22, 1985, 287–295.

102. Reagan explicitly wanted to model Bitburg after this ceremony. See the documents in preparation of a press conference by Reagan in Ronald Reagan Library, James Rentschler Files, Box 90417, Bitburg (3), "Q and A," n.d. See also Steininger, *Deutschland und die USA*, 701f.

103. Kirsch, *"Wir,"* 82. The Waffen-SS, the armed wing of the General SS, had committed war crimes during World War II, also against American soldiers. Cf. Maier, *Past*, 10f.

104. Wirsching, *Abschied*, 478–480.

105. Lipstadt, "Bitburg," 22f.

106. Quoted in Hartman, "Chronology," xiii.

107. Quoted in Lipstadt, "Bitburg," 26.

108. Quoted in Rosenfeld, "Revisionism," 94. Cf. Surmann, *Shoah-Erinnerung*, 32–34.

109. Etheridge, *"Desert Fox."* 233.

110. Quoted in "Auf Kohl's Rat hören wir nicht wieder," *Der Spiegel* 18 (1985), 19.

111. Quoted in Lipstadt, "Bitburg," 29.

112. Kohl, "Earth," 96–100. See also Morina, *Legacies*, 226f.; Kirsch, *"Wir,"* 75–77; Reichel, *Politik*, 286; Siebeck, "'Einzug ins verheißene Land.'"

113. See the account of the ghostwriter of Kohl's memoirs: Schwan and Jens, *Vermächtnis*, 80. See also Dreher, *Kohl*, 366. The press coverage summarizes Kirsch, *"Wir,"* 86–91.

114. Weizsäcker, in fact, used the same words in his speech on May 8. See Weizsäcker, "Truth," 201. Jureit and Schneider, *Gefühlte Opfer*, 9f., interprete Weizsäcker's use of this quote as a "tempting offer" for West German society in the 1980s.
115. All quotes in this paragraph in Kohl, "Lagebericht," April 22, 1985, 288–294.
116. Kirsch, *"Wir,"* 92.
117. Ronald Reagan Library, James Rentschler Files, Box 90417, Bitburg (1), USIA, Memorandum of Conversation, April 24, 1985.
118. Ibid. The reference to the Rhineland may have been made because of upcoming state elections, but the source does not speak to this issue.
119. Bernhard Weinraub, "Reagan Joins Kohl in Brief Memorial at Bitburg Graves," *New York Times*, May 6, 1985.
120. The main source for this phone conversation is Shultz, *Turmoil and Triumph*, 550. This phone conversation has been, however, the subject of much speculation, see Wirsching, *Abschied*, 479f. For the considerations in the White House see Ronald Reagan Library, James Rentschler Files, Box 90417, Bitburg (1), Wick to McFaralane, April 24, 1985.
121. Ronald Reagan Library, James Rentschler Files, Box 90417, Bitburg (1), "Suggested Language for Part of a Presidential Statement," n.d.; emphasis in the original. Reagan stated in his autobiography that he "never regretted not cancelling the trip to Bitburg." See Reagan, *American Life*, 384.
122. Ronald Reagan Library, Marshall Breger Files, OA 10856, Box 1, Breger to Donald Regan, April 30, 1985.
123. For this interpretation of history see Frei, *Vergangenheitspolitik*, 397–406, esp. 405. Bergmann, *Antisemitismus*, 397, suggest that the Federal Republic was supposed to be "turned" into a member of the Western Allies.
124. Dregger, "Congressional Letter," 95. Cf. Reichel, *Politik*, 283. That Dregger had been a member of the Nazi Party shows Rigoll, *Staatsschutz*, 420.
125. Kohl, "Lagebericht," April 22, 1985, 293f.
126. Tom Morganthau et al., "Judgment At Bitburg," *Newsweek*, April 29, 1985.
127. David Gelman et al., "Forgive—But Don't Forget," *Newsweek*, April 29, 1985.
128. Linenthal, *Preserving Memory*, 130.
129. USHMM IA, Accession No. 1997–013, Records Wiesel, Bitburg 2/9, USHMC Emergency Meeting, April 15, 1985, 5.
130. Ibid., 19.
131. Ibid., 38.
132. Rabinbach, "Explosion," 226.
133. "Reagan at Bitburg," YouTube video, 18:49–19:15, televised as an NBC News Special on May 5, 1985, posted by "craig80909," October 9, 2013, accessed July 23, 2015, www.youtube.com/watch?v=7pAebjd_-aU.
134. B 145/21051, Embassy Washington to AA, February 13, 1993.
135. AJC Archives, Bitburg File, Friedman to AJC Leaders, May 9, 1985. Cf. Tannenbaum, "American Jewish Committee," 330–334; Sanua, *Let Us Prove Strong*, 304–308; Shafir, *Ambiguous Relations*, 302f.
136. Sanua, *Let Us Prove Strong*, 306f.
137. Shafir, *Ambiguous Relations*, 302f.
138. Calebow, *Normalisierung*, 32–36.
139. Sanua, *Let Us Prove Strong*, 306f.
140. Calebow, *Normalisierung*, 34f.
141. Sanua, *Let Us Prove Strong*, 307f. See also Reagan, "Never again. . . ."
142. Bole, "Bitburg," 66f. and Etheridge, *Enemies to Allies*, 266f.
143. Mentel, "Bitburg-Affäre," 52.
144. Ronald Reagan Library, James Rentschler Files, Box 90417, Bitburg (1), Rentschler to McFarlane, April 18, 1985. Cf. Schwarz, *Kohl*, 377f.
145. Lipstadt, "Bitburg," 27–32.
146. Participants of the debate did not make a clear distinction between the SS and the Waffen-SS. While the latter was technically not in charge of Nazi extermination camps,

the label "SS" symbolized, as it were, the Holocaust. Cf. Ronald Reagan Library, James Rentschler Files, Box 90417, Bitburg (3), "Q and A," n.d.

147. Bergmann, *Antisemitismus*, 414.
148. All communications between the embassy and the Foreign Office in this context was forwarded to the ChBK.
149. Cf. Clemens, "Image," 187.
150. BArch B 136/30207, Wallau to AA, April 29, 1985.
151. Elizabeth Kastor, "Bitburg Visit Assailed," *Washington Post*, April 22, 1985.
152. BArch B 136/33866, Well to AA, March 7, 1985.
153. BArch B 136/30207, Wallau to AA, ChBK etc., April 13, 1985.
154. BArch B136/30207, Wallau to AA, ChBK etc., April 21, 1985.
155. BArch B136/30207, Well to AA, ChBK etc., April 23, 1985, telex no. 2029.
156. BArch B136/30207, Well to AA, ChBK etc., April 23, 1985, telex no. 2028.
157. BArch B136/30207, Well to AA, ChBK etc., April 23, 1985, telex no. 2029; lower case spelling in the original.
158. Such an assessment came very close to the notions of a latent secondary anti-Semitism. Cf. Benz, *Antisemitismus*, 19f.
159. BArch B136/30207, Well to AA, ChBK etc., April 23, 1985, telex no. 2037; BArch B 136/30206, Well to AA, ChBK etc., May 8, 1985.
160. BArch B136/30207, Well to AA, ChBK etc., April 25, 1985; lower case spelling in the original.
161. Ibid.
162. BArch B136/30207, Wallau to AA, ChBK etc., April 29, 1985.
163. Bergmann, *Antisemitismus*, 411–415; Bergmann, "Sekundärer Antisemitismus."
164. Fritz Ullrich Fack, "Ein Scherbenhaufen," *FAZ*, April 29, 1985.
165. R. H., "Tägliches Störfeuer," *FAZ*, April 15, 1985.
166. German diplomats monitored the reactions to this article in the American press: BArch B 136/30207, GK NY to AA, April 26, 1985. Cf. Mentel, "Bitburg-Affäre," 53; Funke, "Bitburg und 'die Macht der Juden,'" 41–52; and Funke, "Bitburg, Jews, and Germans."
167. Quoted in Shultz, *Turmoil and Triumph*, 554. Teltschik allegedly made a similarly critical remark about the Jewish journalist William Safire to the *Washington Post's* correspondent in Germany, Marc Fisher. See Fisher, *Wall*, 319.
168. B 136/30206, Wallau to AA, ChBK, etc., May 3, 1985, telex no. 2247.
169. Ibid.
170. Ibid.
171. Ibid.
172. BArch B 136/30206, Well to AA, ChBK etc., May 8, 1985.
173. Ibid. For a similar result in the Federal Republic see Kirsch, "Wir," 95.
174. Cf. AJC Archives, Bitburg File, Friedman to AJC Leaders, May 9, 1985.
175. Shafir, *Ambiguous Relations*, 310–315.
176. BArch B 136/30523, GK NY to AA etc., May 10, 1985. Mertes had already given a talk to the AJC on May 2: Mertes, "Western Europe."
177. BArch B 136/30523, GK NY to AA etc., May 10, 1985.
178. BArch B 136/30529, Well to AA, ChBK etc., May 21, 1985.
179. BArch B 136/29854, Well to AA, ChBK etc., May 21, 1985.
180. Cf. Dubiel, *Niemand*, 206–215 and Siebeck, "'Einzug ins verheißene Land.'" For a critical approach see Jureit and Schneider, *Gefühlte Opfer*, 9f.
181. Quoted in Shafir, *Ambiguous Relations*, 296; cf. Feldman, "Jewish Role," 182.
182. BArch B 136/29854, Well to AA, ChBK etc., May 21, 1985.
183. Shafir, *Ambiguous Relations*, 310f.
184. Lucy S. Dawidowicz, "Germany's Answer to Bitburg," *Wall Street Journal*, December 6, 1985.
185. BArch B 136/30405, Speech by Kohl to the members of the Atlantik-Brücke, June 25, 1985.
186. Ibid.

187. Hermann, "Hitler," 17.

188. The monument was installed only after German unification at the Neue Wache in Berlin. See Wirsching, *Abschied*, 480f.

189. Feldman, "Jewish Role," 182.

190. BArch B 136/30523, AA, "Sprechzettel," October 16, 1985.

191. See BArch B 136/30532, Embassy Washington to AA, January 5, 1988; BArch B 136/30032, AA, "Sachstand deutsch-amerikanische Beziehungen," February 4, 1988.

192. Morris B. Abram, "Don't Be Misled By the Bitburg Trip," *New York Times*, May 19, 1985. See also Ronald Reagan Library, Marshall Breger Files, OA 10856, Box 1, Friedman to Reagan, May 7, 1985; and AJC Archives, Bitburg File, AJC National Advisory Panel, "Post-Bitburg Analysis," May 22, 1985.

193. Shafir, *Ambiguous Relations*, 310f. and Calebow, *Normalisierung*, 54f.

194. The AJC had been in a conversation with the FES prior to Bitburg, but the controversy led to the decision to establish a joint educational program. See AJC Archives, William Trosten Files, Box 2, AJC, "Education," May 11, 1987.

195. Quoted in Shafir, *Ambiguous Relations*, 310f. See also "Amerikas Juden sehen Deutschland positiv," *Die Welt*, March 21, 1986.

196. William Trosten Files, Box 2, Summary of a meeting of the "AJC/German Joint Task Force on Images in Education," November 12, 1986, AJC Archives.

197. USHMM IA, Accession No. 1997-014, Records Weinberg, Box 86, Minutes of the USHMM/IRC Meeting, February 8, 1988, 2.

198. USHMM IA, Accession No. 1997-014, Records Weinberg, Box 86, Proceedings of the USHMM/IRC Meeting, April 25, 1990, 45.

199. ACDP, Michael Mertes Papers, 01-747, Armonk-Institute/William S. Trosten (1986–1990), Trosten to Kohl, March 20, 1989. In part, this can be attributed to the fact that a well-respected partner, Alois Mertes (Foreign Office), had died in June 1985.

200. Tempel, *Legenden*, 114; Interview, Wolf Calebow.

201. ACDP, Michael Mertes Papers, 01-747, Armonk-Institute/William S. Trosten (1986–1990), Wolf Calebow, "Erfahrungsbericht, Washington, D.C.," October 18, 1988, 15f. Cf. Calebow, *Normalisierung*, 41–44.

202. Wolf Calebow, Letter to the Editor: "Ungeklärtes im deutsch-jüdischen Verhältnis," *FAZ*, May 22, 2001.

203. Ibid.; cf. Wolf Calebow, Letter to the Editor: "Ein deutsch-jüdischer Dialog der achtziger Jahre," *FAZ*, April 13, 1995.

204. Wolf Calebow, Letter to the Editor: "Was das amerikanische Deutschlandbild bestimmt," *FAZ*, December 19, 2000.

205. Wolf Calebow, Letter to the Editor: "Element von Unaufrichtigkeit," *FAZ*, November 11, 2006.

206. Wolf Calebow, Letter to the Editor: "Der Einfluß der Neokonservativen," *FAZ*, November 17, 2004. Cf. Wolf Calebow, Letter to the Editor: "Groß-Israel als langfristiges Ziel," *FAZ*, March 31, 2004.

207. ACDP, Michael Mertes Papers, 01-747, Armonk-Institute/William S. Trosten (1986–1990), Wolf Calebow, "Erfahrungsbericht, Washington, D.C.," October 18, 1988, 15f.

208. Ibid., 3.

209. Ibid., 27.

210. Ibid., 28.

211. Ibid., 25.

212. Calebow reports about tensions between the AJC and other American Jewish organizations about the extent to which to engage with the Federal Republic. See Calebow, *Normalisierung*, 42.

213. ACDP, Michael Mertes Papers, 01-747, Armonk-Institute/William S. Trosten (1986–1990), Wolf Calebow, "Erfahrungsbericht, Washington, D.C.," October 18, 1988, 20.

214. The Foreign Office considered this project very important and had provided funding for an initial period. See BArch B 136/34162, AA, "Gespräch des Herrn Bundeskanzlers mit

Herrn Walther Leisler Kiep von der Atlantikbrücke e.V. und mit Herrn William Trosten vom American Jewish Committee (AJC)," December 7, 1988.

215. No documentation on this program is available in the AJC Archives.

216. BArch B 136/42209, AA, "Armonk-Institut New York," December 2, 1993.

217. BArch B 136/34162, Atlantik-Brücke e.V. and AJC, "Presseerklärung," November 23, 1987.

218. AJC Archives, International Relations Department, File A, AJC-Atlantik-Brücke Conference Report, Executive Summary, February 24, 1988, 2.

219. Ibid.

220. In addition to Bitburg, they mentioned the controversy about an allegedly anti-Semitic play by Rainer Werner Fassbinder and the Historians' Controversy. For futher information see, for example Bergmann, *Antisemitismus*, 424–440 and Maier, *Past*.

221. AJC Archives, International Relations Department, File B, Alvin H. Rosenfeld, "Germany and American Jews," November 21–23, 1987, 15. See also AJC Archives, International Relations Department, File B, Theodore Ellenoff, "AJC Presidential Address," November 22, 1987, 5.

222. AJC Archives, International Relations Department, File A, AJC-Atlantik-Brücke Conference Report, Executive Summary, February 24, 1988, 1.

223. Ibid.

224. Ibid.

225. Ibid., 3.

226. BArch B 136/30032, AA, Sachstand deutsch-amerikanische Beziehungen," February 4, 1988.

227. BArch B 136/34162, AA, "Gespräch des Herrn Bundeskanzlers mit Herrn Walther Leisler Kiep von der Atlantikbrücke e.V. und mit Herrn William Trosten vom American Jewish Committee (AJC)," December 7, 1988.

228. ACDP, Michael Mertes Papers, 01-747, Armonk-Institute/William S. Trosten (1986–1990), Mertes to Klein, February 27, 1990.

229. ACDP, Michael Mertes Papers, 01-747, Armonk-Institute/William S. Trosten (1986–1990), "Deutsch-amerikanisches Verhältnis, hier: Fortsetzung der Verständigungspolitik zwischen amerikanischen Juden und Deutschen," 1988. For a precedent see Wiesen, "Germany's PR Man."

230. ACDP, Michael Mertes Papers, 01-747, Armonk-Institute/William S. Trosten (1986–1990), Trosten to Kohl, October 26, 1989. See also the concept for the Armonk Institute: ACDP, Michael Mertes Papers, 01-747, Armonk-Institute/William S. Trosten (1986–1990), "The Private Initiative," November 20, 1989. The Foreign Office stressed that a cooperation with the Armonk Institute should not lead to tensions with the AJC: ACDP, Michael Mertes Papers, 01-747, Armonk-Institute/William S. Trosten (1986–1990), Moltke to ChBK, November 8, 1989. See also BArch 136/42209, Embassy Washington to AA September 7, 1989. About the Armonk Institute see: Calebow, *Normalisierung*, 76f.; Shafir, *Ambiguous Relations*, 280; New York Companies, The Armonk Institute, accessed July 23, 2015, www.nycompaniesindex.com/the-armonk-institute-te7o/.

231. See the Armonk Institute website, "About us," archived at https://web.archive.org/web/19990128125324/http://www.armonkinstitute.org/aboutus.htm (accessed July 23, 2015).

232. Ibid.

233. Ibid.

234. Armonk Institute, "The Vernon A. Walters Award," archived at https://web.archive.org/web/19990203032029/http://www.armonkinstitute.org/vernon.htm (accessed July 23, 2015). See also Schuler, *Die Mohns*, 255–258.

235. Quoted in Schanetzky, "Distanzierung," 135.

236. Ibid., 134–136; Thomas Schuler, "Neues von der Front," *Die Zeit*, January 20, 2000; Schuler, *Die Mohns*, 255–266. The commissions report is published as Friedländer et al., *Bertelsmann*.

237. Michael Stürmer, "Bill Trosten—ein jüdischer Amerikaner für Deutschland," *Die Welt*, March 31, 2001, accessed July 23, 2015, www.welt.de/print-welt/article442866/Bill-Trosten-ein-juedischer-Amerikaner-fuer-Deutschland.html.

238. BArch B 136/34310, William S. Trosten, "Die jüdische Gemeinschaft der Vereinigten Staaten von Amerika—ein unterschätzter Aspekt der deutsch-amerikanischen Beziehungen," June 13, 1989, 8.

239. ACDP, Michael Mertes Papers, 01-747, Armonk-Institute/William S. Trosten (1986–1990), The Armonk-Institute, "Fact Sheet," n.d.

Chapter 3

1. Kohl records his concerns in his memoirs, but does not speak of efforts to negotiate the design of the exhibition with museum representatives: Kohl, *Erinnerungen: 1982–1990*, 134f. Cf. for this chapter my article Eder, "Holocaust-Erinnerung."

2. Pieper, *Musealisierung*, 163.

3. Linenthal, *Preserving Memory*, 38–51 and Niven, *Past*, 2f. See also Jureit and Schneider, *Gefühlte Opfer*, 95–103.

4. For the importance of national "honor" to Kohl see Kirsch, "Kern," 43f.

5. In his memories, Kohl points out that he was above all concerned about the impact of the museum on American high school students who would visit the USHMM: Kohl, *Erinnerungen: 1982–1990*, 134f.

6. Quoted in Fisher, *Wall*, 287.

7. Young, *Texture*, 336.

8. Linenthal, *Preserving Memory*, 35–51. Cf. Wiesel to Carter, September 27, 1979, in *Report to the President: President's Commission on the Holocaust* (Reprinted by the United States Holocaust Memorial Museum, Washington, DC, 1999), i–vi. Cf. Levy and Sznaider, *Erinnerung*, 179–182.

9. Linenthal, *Preserving Memory*, 35–51; Rosenfeld, *End*, 58f.

10. Wiesel to Carter, September 27, 1979, in *Report to the President*, iii; emphasis in the original.

11. Wiesel to Carter, September 27, 1979, in *Report to the President*, iii.

12. Linenthal, "Boundaries," 429 (see also 425). Cf. Novick, *Holocaust in American Life*, 201 and 219.

13. Novick, *Holocaust in American Life*, 11.

14. For an overview over these debates see Linenthal, *Preserving Memory*, 17–57.

15. Linenthal, *Preserving Memory*, 37f.; Steinweis, "Analogy," 283.

16. Miller, *One*, 258.

17. See Harvey M. Meyerhoff, "Yes, the Holocaust Museum Belongs on the Mall," *Washington Post*, July 18, 1987.

18. Wiesel, *Report to the President*, 10.

19. Weinberg and Elieli, *Museum*, 26. For more information about the design of the building see, for example, Berenbaum, *World*; Weinberg and Elieli, *Museum*; Young, *Texture*, 335–347.

20. Weinberg and Elieli, *Museum*, 26.

21. For illustrations see, e.g., Weinberg and Elieli, *Museum*.

22. Weinberg and Elieli, *Museum*, 49–72. See also Berenbaum, *World*, 1–222; Leo Wieland, "Ein Ort der Mahnung und der Danksagung," *FAZ*, April 2, 1993.

23. Weinberg and Elieli, *Museum*, 162. See also Miller, *One*, 252.

24. Hilberg, *Politics*, 42f.

25. Cf. Linenthal, *Preserving Memory*, 20–38.

26. A general examination of this issue is Cherfas et al., "Atrocities," especially 76f.

27. Diner, *We Remember*, 216–265; Cherfas, "Atrocities," 76f.; Etheridge, "*Desert Fox*," 223f.; Shafir, *Ambiguous Relations*, 159–178.

28. See the information provided by the USHMM online on Meed, accessed July 23, 2015, www.ushmm.org/information/press/in-memoriam/benjamin-meed-1918-2006, and also the obituary "Benjamin Meed, 88; Holocaust Survivor Helped Create Museums," *Los Angeles Times*, October 27, 2006, accessed July 23, 2015, http://articles.latimes.com/2006/oct/27/local/me-meed27.

29. See chapter 2.

30. Interview, Michael Berenbaum.

31. PA AA, AV Neues Amt, Bd. 16.850, Embassy Washington, "Holocaust," March 12, 1979.

32. PA AA, AV Neues Amt, Bd. 23.207, AA to Embassy Washington, January 24, 1979.

33. PA AA, AV Neues Amt, Bd. 23.207, Staden to AA etc., "Mahnmal zur Erinnerung an die Opfer des Holocaust" [date illegible]. According to Foreign Office records available through the Chancellery's files, the USHMC only decided in 1981 that it would definitely not want a financial contribution from the Federal Republic: BArch 136/17551, Embassy Washington to AA, December 18, 1981.

34. PA AA, AV Neues Amt, Bd. 23.207, Staden to AA etc., "Mahnmal zur Erinnerung an die Opfer des Holocaust" [date illegible].

35. BArch 136/17551, Embassy Washington to AA, December 18, 1981.

36. Ibid. In order to avoid expenses, the Foreign Office met Hermes suggestion with some reservation and agreed to finance a trip to Germany only if the embassy considered such an invitation unavoidable: BArch B 136/17551, AA to Embassy Washington, April 23, 1982.

37. BArch N 1396/4, Petersen to Rühe, September 11, 1985.

38. BArch N 1396/3, Petersen to Kohl, February 5, 1985. See also: Miller, *One*, 260. Miller states the conversation tooks place in 1980, but it actually took place in summer of 1982. Kohl notes in his memoirs that he only learned about the USHMM in April 1983, which is not plausible considering Petersen's remark. See Kohl, *Erinnerungen: 1982–1990*, 134f.

39. Quoted in Miller, *One*, 260.

40. See chapter 1.

41. USHMM IA, Accession No. 1997-013, Records Wiesel, Box 8, Hermes to Wiesel, March 18, 1983.

42. Cf. Hermes, *Zeitgeschichte*, 286.

43. AJC Archives, William Trosten Files, Box 2, Bookbinder to Hermes, Janaury 22, 1981. See also Novick, *Holocaust in American Life*, 157 and 319 note 35.

44. Petersen mentions his "friends" Eliot Levitas and James Scheuer in BArch N 1396/2, Petersen to Talisman [Vice Chairman USHMC], October 11, 1984.

45. BArch N 1396/3, Petersen to Kohl, February 5, 1985.

46. BArch B 136/33866, Hermes to AA, March 5, 1983.

47. Hermes referred to Phil McCombs, "Holocaust Museum for Mall," *Washington Post*, March 3, 1983.

48. BArch B 136/33866, Hermes to AA, ChBK, etc., March 5, 1983.

49. BArch B 136/33866, Embassy Washington to AA, ChBK, etc., March 18, 1983; and USHMM IA, Accession No. 1997-013, Records Wiesel, Box 8, Hermes to Wiesel, March 18, 1983.

50. USHMM IA, Accession No. 1997-013, Records Wiesel, Box 8, Wiesel to Hermes, June 16, 1983. As a later remark of Petersen shows, the meeting between Hermes and Wiesel did not take place: Miller, *One*, 260.

51. Kohl, "Lagebericht," April 25, 1983, 83.

52. Cf. Buchstab and Kleinmann, "Einleitung," xii.

53. Kohl, "Lagebericht," April 25, 1983, 83f.

54. BArch N 1396/4, Petersen to Rühe, September 11, 1985.

55. BArch N 1396/3, Petersen to Kohl, February 5, 1985.

56. BArch N 1396/2, Petersen to Talisman, Ocotober 11, 1984; English in the original.

57. E.g.: BArch N 1396/33, Petersen to Wörner, September 12, 1984.

58. Cf. Kirsch, "Kern," 47; Wirsching, *Abschied*, 178–183.

59. BArch N 1396/47, Petersen, "Leserbrief," June 4, 1986. See also Miller, *One*, 260f.

60. Cf. Steinhoff, *Voices*, 8f.

61. Miller, *One*, 260.

62. UVM Library, Record Group 074.005, Raul Hilberg Papers, Carton 15, Hilbergs handwritten notes on the meeting of the Joint United-States-West German Committee on June 24, 1985.

63. BArch N 1396/47, Portait in "Loyal 6/86," 17. He had held a number of party functions in the Baden-Wurttemberg CDU and was also a member of the "Deutsche Gesellschaft für Auswärtige Politik" and the "Nordatlantischen Versammlung." See Vierhaus and Herbst, "Petersen, Peter," 637f.; USHMM IA, Accession No. 1997-014, Records Weinberg, Box 154, Folder 4, USHMC, Joint United-States-West German Committee, June 24, 1985, 34.

64. Petersen, *Sind wir noch zu retten?*

65. USHMM IA, Accession No. 2000.051, USHMC, Minutes of the Council Meetings, Fiscal Year Council Meeting, December 4, 1986, 12–16.

66. BArch N 1396/4, Petersen to Rühe, September 11, 1985.

67. BArch B 136/29850, Petersen to *Kreisrundschau*, June 16, 1981.

68. Ibid.

69. See also Leber, "Chancellor Helmut Schmidt." As this is an online publication, page numbers are not available.

70. BArch B 136/29850, Franke to Schmidt, July 6, 1981.

71. BArch N 1396/4, Petersen to Rühe, September 25, 1985. See also BArch B 136/29850, Petersen to Huonker, August 11, 1981.

72. BArch N 1396/4, Petersen to Rühe, September 25, 1985.

73. BArch B 136/29850, Petersen, Report on American Jewish Community, July 28, 1981.

74. Ibid.

75. BArch N 1396/4, Petersen to Rühe, September 25, 1985.

76. Miller, *One*, 260f. Miller states that the two met in winter 1983 for the first time, which is not correct as Petersen stated in October 1984 that he had not yet met Wiesel. See BArch N 1396/2, Petersen to Talisman, Ocotober 11, 1984.

77. Miller, *One*, 260f.

78. Ibid.; Interview, Raul Hilberg.

79. Elie Wiesel, e-mail message to author, July 26, 2006.

80. Richard Zoglin and Mitch Gelman, "Peace: Elie Wiesel," *Time Magazine*, October 27, 1986, accessed July 23, 2015, www.time.com/time/magazine/article/0,9171,962649-2,00.html.

81. BArch B 136/33866, Neuer, "Vermerk," November 27, 1984.

82. Calebow, *Normalisierung*, 50; James M. Markham, "Elie Wiesel gets Nobel for Peace as 'Messenger,'" *New York Times*, October 15, 1986. See also: Miller, *One*, 35; Interview, Michael Berenbaum; USHMM IA, Accession No. 2000.035, Oral History Branch, Transcript of Interview with William J. Lowenberg, conducted by Joan Ringelheim, March 14, 2000, tape 2, side B, 23.

83. USHMM IA, Accession No. 1997-014, Records Weinberg, Box 154, USHMC, Memorandum, March 13, 1986.

84. BArch N 1396/5, Petersen to Jenninger, November 11, 1986, and BArch N 1396/11, Petersen to Geißler, August 28, 1989; BArch N 1396/47, "Pressemitteilung Büro Petersen," October 15, 1986.

85. BArch N 1396/1, Petersen to Hauser and Wilz, December 12, 1984.

86. BArch N 1396/3, Petersen to Dregger, April 22, 1985. See also BArch N 1396/4, Petersen to Rühe, September 25, 1985.

87. BArch N 1396/3, Petersen to Dregger, April 22, 1985.

88. Ibid.

89. Dregger, "Congressional Letter," 95.

90. Rigoll, *Staatsschutz*, 420f.

91. "NAPOLA-Hundertschaftsfüherer führt Holocaust-Komitee," *Deutsche National-Zeitung*, April 25, 1986.

92. BArch N 1396/3, Petersen to Dregger, Februay 5, 1985. He also mentioned his involvement in the campaign and the press coverage in the American media about the efforts to Wiesel directly: USHMM IA, Accession No. 1997-014, Records Weinberg, Box 154, Petersen to Wiesel, March 28, 1985.

93. Quoted in Stefan Kanfer, "Books: Author, Teacher, Witness Holocaust Survivor," *Time Magazin*, March 18, 1985, accessed July 23, 2015, www.time.com/time/magazine/article/0,9171,963362,00.html#ixzz1SkqVN5OA. See also UVM Library, Record Group 074.005, Raul Hilberg Papers, Carton 16, "Bundestag Deputies Nominate Wiesel for Nobel Peace Prize," *The Week in Germany*, January 31, 1986.

94. BArch N 1396/11, Petersen to Friedrich Bohl, February 3, 1989.

95. Ibid.

96. USHMM IA, Accession No. 2000.035, Oral History Branch, Transcript of Interview with William J. Lowenberg, conducted by Joan Ringelheim, March 14, 2000, tape 2, side B, 23. Similarly: Interview, Michael Berenbaum.

97. BArch N 1396/4, Petersen to Rühe, September 25, 1985. See also Petersen's letter about Wiesel, BArch N 1396/3, Petersen to Dregger, February 5, 1985.

98. See USHMM IA, Accession No. 2001.165, Reports to the USHMC, Chamberlin, Draft Report on Document Collections Related to the Holocaust in Selected European Archives, Museums and other Institutions, January 1985.

99. This seminar took place from November 17–20, 1985 in West Berlin. See USHMM IA, Accession No. 2005.154, Research Subject Files Milton, Chamberlin to Milton, November 4, 1985. For Milton's presentation see Milton, "Memorial Museum." For the reactions of the participants to Milton's presentation see USHMM IA, Accession No. 2005.154, Research Subject Files Milton, Rolf Krieg, "Protokoll Plenum, 19.11.1985, Referat von Dr. S. Milton: Das Konzept des United States Holocaust Memorial Council," 2f.

100. This was a fairly common objection as several scholars have shown. See for example: Krondorfer, "Kulturgut," 103. See also Junker, "'History Wars,'" 53–56.

101. USHMM IA, Accession No. 2001.165, Reports to the USHMC, Chamberlin to Wiesel, December 12, 1985.

102. Quoted in ibid.

103. Ibid., 4–5. Milton cites a Kohl speech from Gedenkstätte Deutscher Widerstand, *Der 20. Juli 1944*, 215.

104. USHMM IA, Accession No. 1997-017, Historian's Office, Box 4, Sybil Milton, "Survey of Holocaust Exhibits," October 14, 1986, 11.

105. USHMM IA, Accession No. 2001.165, Reports to the USHMC, Chamberlin to Wiesel, December 12, 1985. Milton also alludes to a critical article in *Der Spiegel* about Kohl's museum project in Berlin: Karl-Heinz Krüger, "Wir planen hier nicht Kleinkleckersdorf," *Der Spiegel* 48 (1985), 64–71.

106. USHMM IA, Accession No. 2001.165, Reports to the USHMC, Chamberlin to Wiesel, December 12, 1985.

107. Hence the title of Linenthal's book, *Preserving Memory*.

108. Shafir, *Ambiguous Relations*, 301–308; Linenthal, *Preserving Memory*, 130; Miller, *One*, 228. Cf. USHMM IA, Accession No. 1997-013, Records Wiesel, Bitburg 2/9, Wiesel to Reagan, April 15, 1985.

109. USHMM IA, Accession No. 1997-013, Records Wiesel, Bitburg 7/9, "Chronology"; and USHMM IA, Accession No. 1997-013, Records Wiesel, Bitburg 2/9, USHMC Emergency Meeting, April 15, 1985, 13.

110. AJC Archives, International Relations Department, File B, Theodore Ellenoff, "AJC Presidential Address," November 22, 1987, 5f.; Shafir, *Ambiguous Relations*, 301–308.

111. USHMM IA, Accession No. 1997-013, Records Wiesel, Bitburg 2/9, USHMC Emergency Meeting, April 15, 1985, 38; the Council member is not identified by name in the minutes.

112. For Kohl's speech at Bergen-Belsen on April 21, 1985, for example, see: Morina, *Legacies*, 226.

113. For an important text on the significance of personal experience for the shaping of scholarly arguments see Herbert, "Historikerstreit," 107.
114. Linenthal, *Preserving Memory*, 251f.; Miller, *One*, 261; Pieper, *Musealisierung*, 164f.
115. BArch B 136/33866, Well to AA, Mertes, etc., March 7, 1985.
116. BArch N 1396/3, Petersen to Kohl, February 15, 1985.
117. Ibid.
118. USHMM IA, Accession No. 1997-014, Records Weinberg, Box 154, Folder 3, Wiesel to the American members of the United States-German Committee on Learning and Remembrance, May 17, 1985. See also Hilberg, *Politics*, 80 and 129.
119. Calebow, *Normalisierung*, 50.
120. USHMM IA, Accession No. 1997-014, Records Weinberg, Box 154, Folder 3, Wiesel to the American members of the United States-German Committee on Learning and Remembrance, May 17, 1985. The American delegation further included Joseph Asher, Franklin Littell, Bayard Rustin, Sigmund Strochlitz, and in 1986 Norbert Wollheim. In addition to Petersen, the German delegation included Wolfgang Bergsdorf, Eugen Biser, Klaus Hildebrand, Klaus Schütz, and Erika Wolf.
121. "Sehstoff auf Lager," *Der Spiegel* 37 (1981), 68f.; Katrin Richter, "Trauer um Klaus Schütz," *Jüdische Allgemeine*, December 5, 2012, accessed July 23, 2015, www.juedische-allgemeine.de/article/view/id/14632.
122. Jürgen Habermas, "Eine Art Schadensabwicklung," *Die Zeit*, July 11, 1986. According to historian Gerrit Dworok, Elie Wiesel had "probably" referred to Nolte, Hildebrand, Hillgruber, and Stürmer as the "Gang of Four" (*Viererbande*), but he does not provide evidence to support this claim. See Dworok, *"Historikerstreit,"* 64. See also Grosse Kracht, *Zunft*, 91–114. For a critical comment on Hildebrand's role on the advisory boards of German research institutes see Wehler, "Wissenschaftspolitik," 1092f. See also Hildebrand, "Das Zeitalter der Tyrannen," in *Historikerstreit*, 84–92.
123. BArch N 1396/3, Petersen to Rühe, Februay 28, 1985.
124. BArch N 1396/3, Petersen to Dregger, February 5, 1985.
125. Herf, *Divided Memory*, 348–350.
126. BArch N 1396/3, Petersen to Jenninger, June 18, 1985.
127. USHMM IA, Accession No. 1997-014, Records Weinberg, Box 154, folder 4, USHMC, Joint United-States-West German Committee, Meeting of June 24, 1985.
128. "Holocaust Panel Formed," *Washington Post*, June 25, 1985 and "Wiesel Announces New Panel," *New York Times*, June 25, 1985.
129. USHMM IA, Accession No. 1997-014, Records Weinberg, Box 154, folder 4, USHMC, Joint United-States-West German Committee, Meeting of June 24, 1985, 1–3 and 80. See also Hilberg, "Symbol," 24.
130. USHMM IA, Accession No. 1997-014, Records Weinberg, Box 154, folder 4, USHMC, Joint United-States-West German Committee, Meeting of June 24, 1985, 6–10.
131. Ibid., 9.
132. Kirsch, *"Wir,"* 95; Pohl, "Holocaust-Forschung," 13f.
133. USHMM IA, Accession No. 1997-014, Records Weinberg, Box 154, folder 4, USHMC, Joint United-States-West German Committee, Meeting of June 24, 1985, 51–53. For Kohl's position on the German Historical Museum see Kohl, *Erinnerungen: 1982–1990*, 624–634.
134. USHMM IA, Accession No. 1997-014, Records Weinberg, Box 154, folder 4, USHMC, Joint United-States-West German Committee, Meeting of June 24, 1985, 52.
135. Ibid., 11. Wiesel later referred to Petersen as the "emissary" of "the German people and Chancellor Kohl." See USHMM IA, Accession No. 1997-014, Records Weinberg, Box 154, folder 5, Wiesel to Petersen, July 1, 1985.
136. Kohl, *Erinnerungen: 1982–1990*, 134f.
137. USHMM IA, Accession No. 1997-014, Records Weinberg, Box 154, folder 4, USHMC, Joint United-States-West German Committee, Meeting of June 24, 1985, 44. See also Petersen's remarks as quoted in "Holocaust Panel Formed," *Washington Post*, June 25, 1985.

138. USHMM IA, Accession No. 1997-014, Records Weinberg, Box 154, folder 4, USHMC, Joint United-States-West German Committee, Meeting of June 24, 1985, 73–76.

139. Hilberg particularly mentioned Uwe Adam, Hans-Heinrich Wilhelm, and Götz Aly.

140. Hilberg, *Politics*, 80; Interview, Raul Hilberg; similar opinion in interview, Henry Friedlander. See also Matthäus, "Holocaust-Forschung," 32–37.

141. See USHMM IA, Accession No. 1997-014, Records Weinberg, Box 154, folder 4, USHMC, Joint United-States-West German Committee, Meeting of June 24, 1985, 61f.

142. B 136/33866, Embassy Washington to AA, June 26, 1985.

143. Ibid.

144. No official minutes are available for this meeting; see USHMM IA, Accession No. 1997-014, Records Weinberg, Craig to Wollheim, November 10, 1986. Wiesel summarized the results of this meeting in: USHMM IA, Accession No. 1997-013, Records Wiesel, Box 13, Wiesel to Shultz, January 30, 1986.

145. Hinners, "Haus" and Kühling, "Schullandheim."

146. USHMM IA, Accession No. 2000.051, USHMC, Minutes of the Council Meetings, Fiscal Year Council Meeting, December 4, 1986, 15f.

147. See the announcement in USHMM IA, Accession No. 1997-014, Records Weinberg, Box 154, Folder 5, "German-American Committee on Learning and Remembrance Holds Second Meeting in Germany," Washington, DC, January 22, 1986. See also "Elie Wiesel Back in Germany after 41 Years," *New York Times*, January 23, 1986; USHMM IA, Accession No. 1997-014, Records Weinberg, Box 154, Folder 4, Elie Wiesel, "Memory and Reconciliation."

148. Petersen had announced in June 1985 that Kohl planned to attend the next meeting of the committee. See "Holocaust Panel Formed," *Washington Post*, June 25, 1985. See also USHMM IA, Accession No. 1997-013, Records Wiesel, Box 13, Wiesel to Schultz, January 7, 1986; UVM Library, Record Group 074.005, Raul Hilberg Papers, Carton 16, Hilberg, handwritten notes on "Bonn Meeting," n.d.; Calebow, *Normalisierung*, 50.

149. Petersen as quoted in: UVM Library, Record Group 074.005, Raul Hilberg Papers, Carton 16, Hilberg, handwritten notes on "Bonn Meeting," n.d.

150. Ibid.

151. Quoted in ibid.

152. UVM Library, Record Group 074.005, Raul Hilberg Papers, Carton 16, *The Week in Germany*, "Wiesel, Holocaust Memorial Committee in Berlin," January 24, 1986.

153. Calebow, *Normalisierung*, 50f. Cf. USHMM IA, Accession No. 2000.051, USHMC, Minutes of the Council Meetings, Agenda of the Fiscal Year Council Meeting, December 4. 1986.

154. BArch N 1396/5, Petersen to Jenninger, November 11, 1986.

155. Calebow, *Normalisierung*, 50f. See also USHMM IA, Accession No. 2000.051, USHMC, Minutes of the Council Meetings, Fiscal Year Council Meeting, December 4, 1986, 93–95.

156. USHMM IA, Accession No. 1997-013, Records Wiesel, Box 11, Wiesel to Reagan, December 1, 1986.

157. Linenthal, *Preserving Memory*, 136; Interview, Michael Berenbaum. In addition, Wiesel was discontent with competition between American Jewish organizations for seats on the Council: Judith Miller, "Holocaust Museum: A Troubled Start," *New York Times Magazine*, April 22, 1990, 48. Meyerhoff became Wiesel's successor, and chaired the Council until 1993. William J. Lowenberg replaced Mark E. Talisman as vice chairman.

158. USHMM IA, Accession No. 2000.051, USHMC, Minutes of the Council Meetings, Fiscal Year Council Meeting, December 4, 1986, 12–16. Calebow argued that both Petersen and Schütz were probably too shy to raise the issue of the museum design in front of the Council: Calebow, *Normalisierung*, 51.

159. Judith Miller, "Holocaust Museum: A Troubled Start," *New York Times Magazine*, April 22, 1990, 42.

160. Quoted in Miller, *One*, 262.

161. BArch B 136/34310, Kiep to Kohl, August 17, 1989.

162. Interview, Raul Hilberg. On Wiesel's resignation see Linenthal, *Preserving Memory*, 133. Wiesel's letter of resignation is available in USHMM IA, Accession No. 1997-013, Records Wiesel, Box 11, Wiesel to Reagan, December 1, 1986.

163. Judith Miller, "Holocaust Museum: A Troubled Start," *New York Times Magazine*, April 22, 1990, 42 and 47; Miller, *One*, 261f.; Pieper, *Musealisierung*, 164; Leo Wieland, "Ein Ort der Mahnung und Danksagung," *FAZ*, April 2, 1993.

164. Miller maintains that the negotioations ended at this point in time, which is incorrect: Miller, *One*, 216f.

165. Pieper briefly references these talks between Petersen and the IRC, while Linenthal mentions Petersen's position, but not the position of Lerman and the IRC: Pieper, *Musealisierung*, 164f.; Linenthal, *Preserving Memory*, 251f.

166. USHMM IA, Accession No. 1997-014, Records Weinberg, Box 86, "Summary of discussion with Peter Petersen," June 30, 1987; see also USHMM IA, Accession No. 1997-014, Records Weinberg, Box 154, Folder 4, Weinstein to Robert Beecroft (West German Desk Officer, Department of State), July 7, 1987.

167. Lerman agreed to such a meeting in principle, but it never took place as Petersen had to cancel for personal reasons: USHMM IA, Accession No. 1997-014, Records Weinberg, Box 86, Minutes from the Meeting of the IRC, February 8, 1988, 2.

168. USHMM IA, Accession No. 1997-014, Records Weinberg, Box 86, Meeting of the IRC, July 8, 1987, 3f.

169. Ibid. Cf. Pieper, *Musealisierung*, 165.

170. The IRC discussed the meeting between Lermann, Meed, and Petersen on February 8: USHMM IA, Accession No. 1997-014, Records Weinberg, Box 86, Meeting of the IRC, February 8, 1988. See also Pieper, *Musealisierung*, 165; Linenthal, *Preserving Memory*, 252.

171. Minutes from the Meeting of the IRC, Monday, February 8, 1988, Records Weinberg, Box 86, USHMM IA, Accession No. 1997-014, 2.

172. Ibid., 3.

173. Ibid., 2.

174. Ibid., 3.

175. No minutes are available from this meeting, yet Lerman provides some information about the IRC's decision to contact Petersen as well as Petersen's reply to Lerman. See USHMM IA, Accession No. 1997-014, Records Weinberg, Box 86, Lerman to IRC, June 28, 1988.

176. USHMM IA, Accession No. 1997-014, Records Weinberg, Box 86, Petersen to Lerman, June 6, 1988; English in the original.

177. USHMM IA, Accession No. 1997-014, Records Weinberg, Box 86, Meeting of the IRC, September 14, 1988; Lerman to Members and Guests of the IRC, August 15, 1988; and Lerman/Craig to Petersen, September 16, 1988.

178. USHMM IA, Accession No. 1998-004, Chamberlin Files, Box 5, Minutes from the Meeting of the IRC, July 11, 1989, 3–5.

179. BArch N 1396/9, Petersen to Jenninger, September 19, 1988. See also BArch N 1396/9, Petersen to Jenninger, September 1, 1988.

180. Petersen summarizes this conversation in BArch N 1396/4, Petersen to Rühe, September 11, 1985.

181. See "Kompliment vom Zivi," *Der Spiegel* 13 (1994), 28.

182. BArch N 1396/4, Petersen to Rühe, September 11, 1985.

183. In 1989, the parliamentary secretary of the CDU/CSU parliamentary group Friedrich Bohl replaced Petersen on the Bundestag's Foreign Affairs Committee with Philipp Jenninger, who needed a new position after his resignation as Bundestag president in the aftermath of scandal about his speech commemorating Kristallnacht in November 1988. See BArch N 1396/11, Petersen to Bohl, February 3, 1989.

184. BArch N 1396/11, Petersen to Kohl, May 23, 1989. Wiesel had provided Petersen with this information.

185. Ibid.

186. USHMM IA, Accession No. 1998-011, Records Berenbaum, Box 24, Milton to Berenbaum et al., September 20, 1988.

187. At the time of writing, Roik was in charge of "Group K 4, history and memory" in the Chancellery under Angela Merkel's Commissioner for Culture and Media, Monika Grütters.

188. Quoted in USHMM IA, Accession No. 1998-011, Records Berenbaum, Box 24, Milton to Berenbaum et al., September 20, 1988.

189. Ibid.

190. See USHMM IA, Accession No. 1998-004, Chamberlin Files, Box 5, Minutes from the Meeting of the IRC, July 11, 1989, 3–5.

191. Ibid., 5.

192. USHMM IA, Accession No. 1997-014, Records Weinberg, Box 86, Minutes of the IRC Meeting, April 25, 1990, 26; and Agenda of the IRC Meeting, April 25, 1990.

193. Rosensaft to Lerman, n.d., quoted in: USHMM IA, Accession No. 1997–014, Records Weinberg, Box 86, Proceedings of the IRC Meeting, April 25, 1990, 30f.; USHMM IA, Accession No. 1997-014, Records Weinberg, Box 87, Wollheim to Lerman, April 17, 1990.

194. USHMM IA, Accession No. 1997-014, Records Weinberg, Box 86, Proceedings of the IRC Meeting, April 25, 1990; Minutes of the IRC Meeting, April 25, 1990.

195. USHMM IA, Accession No. 1997-014, Records Weinberg, Box 86, Minutes of the IRC Meeting, April 25, 1990, 39.

196. Ibid., 40–50.

197. USHMM IA, Accession No. 1998-011, Records Berenbaum, Box 21, "Agreement on Co-operation between the United States Holocaust Memorial Council and the National Memorials and Museums of the German Democratic Republic," 1–3.

198. Meining, *Judenpolitik*, 493–500; Goschler, *Schuld*, 482; Calebow, *Normalisierung*, 99–101.

199. USHMM IA, Accession No. 1997-014, Records Weinberg, Box 86, Minutes of the IRC Meeting, April 25, 1990, 40.

200. Ibid., 47.

201. "Exhibit Evokes Mixed Reactions From Germans," *St. Louis Post-Dispatch*, April 23, 1993. See also USHMM IA, Accession No. 1997-014, Records Weinberg, Box 86, Minutes of the IRC Meeting, April 25, 1990, 41f.

202. USHMM IA, Accession No. 2000.035, Oral History Branch, Transcript of Interview with William J. Lowenberg, conducted by Joan Ringelheim, March 14, 2000, tape 2, side B, 21.

203. For the following quote see: USHMM IA, Accession No. 1997-014, Records Weinberg, Box 86, Minutes of the IRC Meeting, April 25, 1990, 42. Cf. also Calebow, *Normalisierung*, 114.

204. ACDP, Michael Mertes Papers, 01-747, Armonk-Institute/William S. Trosten (1986–1990), Trosten to Kohl, January 28, 1990. Quote taken from the attached "Fact Sheet." See also Calebow, *Normalisierung*, 113f.; USHMM IA, Accession No. 1997-014, Records Weinberg, Box 86, Proceedings of the IRC Meeting, April 25, 1990, 49.

205. ACDP, Michael Mertes Papers, 01-747, Armonk-Institute/William S. Trosten (1986–1990), Trosten to Kohl, January 28, 1990. Quote taken from the attached "Fact Sheet."

206. USHMM IA, Accession No. 1997-014, Records Weinberg, Box 86, Proceedings of the IRC Meeting, April 25, 1990, 44f.

207. See for instance Leo Wieland, "Weizsäcker willkommen," *FAZ*, March 23, 1993; "Weizsäcker nach Besuch im Washingtoner Holocaust-Museum," *SZ*, May 25, 1993.

208. Judith Weinraub, "The Man Who Never Forgot," *Washington Post*, January 3, 2000, accessed July 23, 2015, www.washingtonpost.com/wp-srv/WPcap/2000-01/03/038r-010300-idx.html.

209. USHMM IA, Accession No. 1997-014, Records Weinberg, Box 86, Proceedings of the IRC Meeting, April 25, 1990, 45.

210. Ibid., 48.

211. Ibid., 44–49. See also Pieper, *Musealisierung*, 170.
212. See chapter 5.
213. Calebow, *Normalisierung*, 115.
214. ACDP, Michael Mertes Papers, 01-747, Armonk-Institute/William S. Trosten (1986–1990), Mertes to Trosten, January 31, 1990 and Mertes to Kohl, February 8, 1990.
215. BArch B 136/33866, AA internal memorandum, "Deutsche Öffentlichkeitsarbeit in den USA," February 19, 1990.
216. ACDP, Michael Mertes Papers, 01-747, Armonk-Institute/William S. Trosten (1986–1990), Kohl to Schäfer, March 1, 1990.
217. BArch B 136/33866, Exhibition Concept, "Umgang mit der nationalsozialistischen Vergangenheit in der Bundesrepublik Deutschland und deutsche Identität heute (Arbeitstitel)," May 1990.
218. Calebow, *Normalisierung*, 114–118.
219. ACDP, Michael Mertes Papers, 01-747, Armonk-Institute/William S. Trosten (1986–1990), Wolf Calebow, "Erfahrungsbericht, Washington, D.C.," October 18, 1988.
220. Calebow, *Normalisierung*, 9–14.
221. Ibid., 112–123. See USHMM IA, Accession No. 1998-011, Records Berenbaum, Box 36, Bloomfield to Weinberg and Berenbaum, January 29, 1990.
222. Calebow, *Normalisierung*, 118–120.
223. ACDP, Michael Mertes Papers, 01-747, Armonk-Institute/William S. Trosten (1991–1992), Trosten to Kohl, April 22, 1991.
224. USHMM IA, Accession No. 1998-011, Records Berenbaum, Calebow to Berenbaum, January 9, 1992. In his memoirs, Jürgen Ruhfus devotes one and a half pages to "German-Jewish relations in the United States," but does not speak of the issue of the USHMM: Ruhfus, *Aufwärts*, 373f.
225. USHMM IA, Accession No. 1998-011, Records Berenbaum, Calebow to Hoffmann (cc: Berenbaum), January 9, 1992.
226. See, e.g., Kershaw, *Nazi Dictatorship*, 188f.
227. Weinberg and Elieli, *Museum*, 163.
228. Interview, Raul Hilberg.
229. ACDP, Michael Mertes Papers, 01-747, Armonk-Institute/William S. Trosten (1991–1992), Embassy Washington to AA, December 20, 1991.
230. Calebow, *Normalisierung*, 120–123.
231. BArch B 136/42199, BKAmt, "Holocaust-Memorial," February 24, 1992; emphasis in original.
232. BArch B 136/42199, Morr, "Holocaust-Museum in Washington," February 10, 1992; BArch B 136/42199, AA, "Künftiges Holocaust-Museum in Washington, " February 11, 1992.
233. Originally, integrating the Brandt image was Berenbaum's idea (Interview, Michael Berenbaum). See also Linenthal, *Preserving Memory*, 252.
234. Interview, Michael Berenbaum; Linenthal, *Preserving Memory*, 252.
235. Weinberg and Elieli, *Museum*, 165.
236. BArch 136/42199, GIC to AA, March 10, 1992.
237. Calebow, *Normalisierung*, 122f.
238. Ibid., 122.
239. ACDP, Michael Mertes Papers, 01-747, Armonk-Institute/William S. Trosten (1992–1995), Morr to Kohl, October 6, 1993 [the chronology indicates that this is a typo and the document is actually from 1992].
240. Ibid; emphasis in the original.
241. Ibid; emphasis in the original.
242. Günther Gillessen, "Bedenkliche Art der Erinnerung," *FAZ*, August 4, 1992.
243. See BArch B 136/33866, Embassy Washington to AA, August 2, 1985.
244. BArch B 136/42199, AA, "Erweiterung des Holocaust Memorial Centers," June 25, 1993.
245. Ibid.
246. BArch B 136/33866, Embassy Washington to AA, August 2, 1985; BArch B 136/33866, Holocaust Memorial Center to AA and ChBK, June 21, 1991.

247. BArch B 136/33866, GK Detroit to AA, June 24, 1991.

248. Ibid.

249. BArch B 136/34308, Weidenfeld to Kohl, October 8, 1992.

250. Ibid.

251. BArch B 136/42199, AA, "Erweiterung des Holocaust Memorial Centers," June 25, 1993. See also: BArch B 136/42199, Weidenfeld to Rosenzveig, May 14, 1993.

252. Marc Fisher, "Germany's Holocaust Fears," *Washington Post*, March 30, 1993. See also Leon Wieseltier, "After Memory," *The New Republic*, May 3, 1993, 16–26, who has remarked: "There is something comic about the Germans asking the Jews to help them with the image of what the Germans did to the Jews."

253. B 136/42199, Langguth to Hartmann, March 31, 1993. See also B 136/42199, Hartmann to Kohl, March 31, 1993.

254. BArch B 136/42199, Pordzik to *Washington Post*, March 30, 1993.

255. BArch B 136/42199, *Washington Post* (Michael Getler) to Pordzik, March 31, 1993.

256. B 136/42199, Hartmann to Kohl, March 31, 1993.

257. Dieter Vogel, "The Holocaust Museum: Two Replies," *Washington Post*, April 3, 1993. This article also contains a letter by Wolfgang Pordzik. Cf. Kurt Kister, "Plötzlich ist da diese Wand aus Geruch," *SZ*, April 22, 1993.

258. Pieper, *Musealisierung*, 168.

259. See Fisher, *Wall*, 286f.

260. Calebow, *Normalisierung*, 113.

261. Stephan Walter to Wallmann, June 8, 1989 and Walter to Gauland, July 20, 1989. Both letters were made available to historian Katrin Pieper by the Kreisverband CDU, Frankfurt am Main. I would like to thank her for sharing them with me. See also Pieper, *Musealisierung*, 169, n. 469.

262. Lerman spoke of $25 million (interview, Miles Lerman), while Berenbaum spoke of $10 million (interview, Michael Berenbaum). William Lowenberg suggests a sum between $25 million and $50 million (USHMM IA, Accession No. 2000.035, Oral History Branch, Transcript of Interview with William J. Lowenberg, conducted by Joan Ringelheim, March 14, 2000, tape 2, side B, 21f).

263. BArch B 136/42205, GK Los Angeles to AA, January 4, 1991.

264. No records exist on this interaction between Lerman and Petersen. Cf. p. 114.

265. BArch B 136/42199, Embassy Washington to AA and ChBK, March 30, 1993.

266. Ibid.

267. BArch B 136/42199, Hartmann to Kohl, March 31, 1993; emphasis in original.

268. BArch B 136/42199, AA, "Erweiterung des Holocaust Memorial Centers," June 25, 1993.

269. Schwarz, *Kohl*, 870-896; "Empörung über angebliche jüdische Vermächtnisse," *Der Tagesspiegel*, January 18, 2000.

270. ACDP, Michael Mertes Papers, 01-747, Armonk-Institute/William S. Trosten (1992–1995), Kaul, Report on a "USA-Vortragsreise 'deutsch-israelische Beziehungen' vor meist US-jüdischen Kreisen (17.04.–01.05.93)," June 22, 1993.

271. USHMM IA, Accession No. 1997-004, Eskenazi Files, Box 7, Meyerhoff to Kohl, October 28, 1992.

272. "Kohl besucht Holocaust-Museum," *FAZ*, March 3, 1993. See also BArch B 136/42199, BKAmt, "Besuch des Herrn Bundeskanzlers im Holocaust Memorial Museus in Washington," November 28, 1996; "Erklärung des Bundeskanzlers zur Eröffnung des Holocaust Memorial Museums," *Bulletin*, April 24, 1993, 292.

273. Marc Fisher, "Germany's Holocaust Fears," *Washington Post*, March 30, 1993.

274. Botschaft Washington to AA, February 12, 1993, B 145/21051. Krondorfer, "Kulturgut," 91, states that Kohl did not attend the opening ceremony because of the issue of a German financial contribution to the USHMM.

275. Kohl, "Lagebericht," May 3, 1993, 450. See also Steininger, *Deutschland und die USA*, 747f.

276. See for example Henryk M. Broder, "Das Shoah-Business," *Der Spiegel* 16 (1993), 248–256; Michael Wolffsohn, "Eine Amputation des Judentums?," *FAZ*, April 15,

1993; Josef Joffe, "Erinnerung als Götzendienst?," *SZ*, April 22, 1993; Günther Gillessen, "Mit Gedenkstätten ist es nicht getan," *FAZ*, July 18, 1994. See also AJC, "Current Concerns in Germany and in German-American Jewish Relations: Summary of a Conference Held by the American Jewish Committee, and the Atlantik-Brücke, in New York City, January 17–19, 1993." For the reactions of the Foreign Office see: BArch B 136/42199, AA to Bundespräsidialamt, ChBK etc., March 25, 1993.

277. BArch B 136/42199, Embassy Washington to AA, April 20, 1993.
278. Ibid.
279. BArch B 136/42199, Bierett to Kohl, May 3, 1993.
280. BArch B 136/42199, Pohlmann, "Das Holocaust Memorial Museum in Washington D.C.," April 29, 1993.
281. Interview, Michael Mertes, July 20, 2006.
282. As expressed in ACDP, Michael Mertes Papers, 01-747, Armonk-Institute/William S. Trosten (1992–1995), Kaul, Report on a "USA-Vortragsreise 'deutsch-israelische Beziehungen' vor meist US-jüdischen Kreisen (17.04.–01.05.93)," June 22, 1993.
283. Quoted in Marc Fisher, "Germany's Holocaust Fears," *Washington Post*, March 30, 1993.
284. Cf. Pieper, *Musealisierung*, 168.

Chapter 4

1. For an overview see Littmann, *Partners*, 73–250.
2. See chapter 1 and Kreis, "Bündnis."
3. See also Dworok, "*Historikerstreit*," 429–433.
4. Ibid., 376–379.
5. "Die SPD gründet Historische Kommission," *FAZ*, February 9, 1982. See also Dworok, "*Historikerstreit*," 437–443.
6. See Hans Mommsen, "Geschichtsbilder." See also Meyer, *SPD*, 424–431.
7. Cf. Dworok, "*Historikerstreit*," 430–433.
8. Basic considerations in this context are provided by Wolfrum, *Geschichtspolitik*, 13–38 and 303–345; Rudloff, "Einleitung"; with emphasis on the natural sciences: Weingart, *Stunde der Wahrheit?*, 127–170. In contrast to the period of the Third Reich and the GDR, the relationship between the West German historical profession and government institutions has so far not been a major focus of historical research. See Blaschke and Raphael, "Kampf um Positionen," 108f.
9. Doering-Manteuffel and Raphael, *Boom*, 10. See also Dworok, "*Historikerstreit*," 107–184.
10. Cf. Podewils, ed., *Tendenzwende?*. See also Dworok, "*Historikerstreit*," 376–379; Hoeres, "'Tendenzwende;'" and Wehrs, *Protest*, 430–452.
11. Wirsching, "'Konstruktion,'" 129; Bösch, "Krise als Chance"; Zolleis, *CDU*, 183–213; Schildt, *Konservatismus*, 245–250.
12. See Dettling, "Ursachen," 363; Dettling, "Folgen," 457–468.
13. See Szatkowski, *Carstens*, 358–360.
14. ACDP, CDU-Bundespartei, 07-001, 1909, Teltschik to members of "Unterkommission III: Selbstverständnis der BRD," April 16, 1973.
15. ACDP, CDU-Bundespartei, 07-001, 1909, Weidenfeld, "Die Frage nach der deutschen Nation: Überlegungen zum Selbstverständnis der Bundesrepublik Deutschland."
16. Moses, *Intellectuals*, 5–10.
17. Ibid., 9f.
18. Berger, *Normality*, 88–93.
19. Wolfrum, *Geschichtspolitik*, 303–310.
20. See, also for the next paragraph: Winkler, *Westen*, 440; Herbert, *Geschichte*, 1010–1022; Conze, *Sicherheit*, 654–664; Wirsching, *Abschied*, 466–491; Wolfrum, *Geschichtspolitik*, 316–345.

21. For anti-Israel and anti-Semitic position and actions of the extreme left see Kraushaar, *"Kampf."*
22. See chapter 1.
23. Knoch, "Rückkehr," 121–125 and Rürup, *Schatten*, 130–134.
24. E.g., Mommsen, "Realisierung." See also Kershaw, "Moral High Ground," 28.
25. Mommsen, "Polarisierung." See also Wolfrum, *Geschichtspolitik*, 339–342.
26. Wirsching, *Abschied*, 476.
27. A good recent summary is provided by Große Kracht, *Zunft*, 91–114. See also Maier, *Past*; for the most recent detailed analysis see Dworok, *"Historikerstreit."*
28. Herbert, "Historikerstreit," 97 and 105. See also Berger, *Normality*, 77–108; and Stelzel, "Rethinking," 294–300.
29. Stürmer, "History in a Land without History," 16. For more information on Stümer see Maier, *Past*, 44f.; Steinbach, "Kontroversen," 165.
30. Berghahn, "Große Politik," 33–35. See also Wehrs, *Protest*, 68-147.
31. Berger, *Normality*, 79. See also Moeller, *War Stories*, 13.
32. E.g. Weidenfeld, ed., *Identität der Deutschen*. See also Dworok, *"Historikerstreit,"* 432f.
33. Weidenfeld, "Suche nach Identität," 91.
34. Weidenfeld, "Identität der Deutschen," 42f.
35. Ibid.
36. "Die Souffleure der Kanzler," *Die Zeit*, July 8, 1983. See also Werner Weidenfeld, "Am Pulsschlag der verletzten Nation," *Die Zeit*, April 10, 1987; Werner Weidenfeld, "Deutschland, Deutschland—und kein Ende . . . ," *Die Zeit*, July 17, 1987.
37. Wolfrum, *Geschichtspolitik*, 303–310.
38. For example, Weidenfeld contributed to Kohl's first state of the nation address: Kohl, *Erinnerungen: 1982–1990*, 49. See also Dettling and Geske, "Helmut Kohl," 220–222.
39. For this and the following see: "Die Souffleure der Kanzler," *Die Zeit*, July 8, 1983.
40. Conze, *Sicherheit*, 584–591; Wirsching, *Abschied*, 171–199; Rödder, *Bundesrepublik*, 78f.
41. Langguth, *Kohl*, 88.
42. Wirsching, *Abschied*, 488. See also Leggewie, *Geist*, 205. See also the January/February 1987 issue of *Die Politische Meinung* (no. 230).
43. Steinbach, "Kontroversen," 165. See also Dworok, *"Historikerstreit,"* 432.
44. See Langguth, *Kohl*, 88 and Maier, *Past*, 43f.
45. Stürmer, "History in a Land without History," 16f.
46. See for example a summary of this approach: Stürmer, "Nation und Demokratie."
47. Evans, *Hitler's Shadow*, 104f. See also Berger, *Normality*, 114–116 and Maier, *Past*, 43–47. Cf. Calleo, *German Problem*. Cf. also Dworok, *"Historikerstreit,"* 308f.
48. E.g., ACDP, CDU-Bundespartei, 07-001, 1909, Weidenfeld, "Die Frage nach der deutschen Nation: Überlegungen zum Selbstverständnis der Bundesrepublik Deutschland." This was in accordance with the conservative strategy, above all advocated by Wolfgang Bergsdorf, to coin terms: Steinbach, "Kontroversen," 159.
49. Weidenfeld, "Identität der Deutschen," 18–23. See also Berger, *Normality*, 87.
50. Deutscher Bundestag, Plenarprotokoll 9/121, October 13, 1982, 7227. See also Kohl, *Erinnerungen: 1982–1990*, 49.
51. Quoted in Szatkowski, *Carstens*, 359.
52. Stelzel, "Rethinking," 224f.
53. Stürmer, "Deutsche Identität."
54. Ibid., 209. See also Berger, *Normality*, 79.
55. Kohl, "Weichenstellung."
56. BArch B 136/24443, BMFT, "Bericht zur Errichtung eines Deutschen Historischen Instituts in den USA," October 30, 1985. For a precedent see Conze et al., *Amt*, 615–620 and Stelzel, "Fischer," 68–73.
57. The history of the GHI Paris, for example, is documented in: Pfeil, ed., *Gründungsväter*; Pfeil, *Vorgeschichte*; Babel and Große, eds., *Institut Paris*.
58. Pfeil, *Vorgeschichte*, 96–164, quote on 162.
59. Ibid., 162.

60. Pfeil, "Gründung," 1. For the founding of the GHI London see: German Historical Institute London, *Institute*, 9–16.

61. PA AA, AV Neues Amt, Bd. 16.970, Embassy Washington, "Deutsches Institut in den USA: Sachstand," March 11, 1980; BArch B 136/24443, Anglo-Amerikanische Abteilung des Historischen Seminars der Universität Köln, "Ein Deutsches Historisches Institut in den USA," n.d.

62. PA AA, AV Neues Amt, Bd. 16.970, Embassy Washington, "Deutsches Institut in den USA: Sachstand," March 11, 1980; Cf. BArch B 136/24443, Anglo-Amerikanische Abteilung der Uni Köln: "Ein Deutsches Historisches Institut in den USA," n.d. For a detailed analysis of this generation of German-born emigrant historians see Stelzel, "Rethinking," 113–129.

63. Junker, "Introduction," 29f.

64. Quoted in PA AA, Zwischenarchiv, Bd. 117.562, Pfeiffer (Alexander von Humboldt Stiftung) to AA, February 2, 1977. See also: PA AA, Zwischenarchiv, Bd. 117.562, Littmann (Fulbright-Kommission) to AA, March 7, 1977.

65. PA AA, Zwischenarchiv, Bd. 117.562, AA, "Wissenschaftsaustausch mit den USA," March 8, 1977.

66. Ibid.

67. PA AA, Zwischenarchiv, Bd. 117.562, BMFT to AA, October 11, 1978.

68. PA AA, Zwischenarchiv, Bd. 117.562, AA to BMFT, May 16, 1977.

69. PA AA, AV Neues Amt, Bd. 16.970, Embassy Washington, "Deutsches Institut in den USA: Sachstand," March 11, 1980.

70. PA AA, Zwischenarchiv, Bd. 117.562, GK Boston to AA, December 5, 1978.

71. PA AA, Zwischenarchiv, Bd. 117.562, Embassy Washington to AA, December 29, 1978.

72. PA AA, AV Neues Amt, Bd. 16.970, Embassy Washington, "Deutsches Institut in den USA: Sachstand," March 11, 1980.

73. PA AA, Zwischenarchiv, Bd. 124.739, AA, "Gründung eines deutschen Instituts in den USA," August 25, 1980.

74. BArch B 136/17557, Livingtson to Lahnstein, August 4, 1981,

75. BArch B 136/17557, "Institute for Contemporary German Studies: Preliminary Proposal," n.d.

76. BArch B 136/17558, AA to Schmidt, May 4, 1982.

77. BArch B 136/17558, "Vermerk," June 25, 1982. For an evaluation of the AICGS's first year of activities see BArch B 136/42221, Embassy Washington to AA, ChBK, etc., March 15, 1985.

78. "Bonn plant neue Institute im Ausland," *SZ*, February 18, 1984.

79. BArch B 136/24443, Lutz to Kohl, November 7, 1988.

80. BArch B 136/33866, Teltschik to Kohl, April 5, 1984.

81. BArch B 136/30523, Farmer to Kiep, March 4, 1984; emphasis added by Chancellery. This letter included an attachment titled "Plans for a German Historical Institute in the United States," from which the quote is taken.

82. BArch B 136/24443, Wissenschaftsrat, "Stellungnahme zur Errichtung eines Deutschen Historischen Instituts in den USA," November 16, 1984. See also Stucke, "Wissenschaftsrat."

83. In fact, the GHI's first major project dealt in 1988 precisely with this group of historians. See Epstein, "Account," and the volume based on this conference: Lehmann and Sheehan, eds., *Interrupted Past*. See also Daum, "Second Generation" and Daum, Lehmann, and Sheehan, eds., *Second Generation*.

84. BArch B 136/24443, Wissenschaftsrat, "Stellungnahme zur Errichtung eines Deutschen Historischen Instituts in den USA," November 16, 1984, 8f.

85. BArch B 136/24443, BMFT, "Errichtung von zwei neuen Auslandsinstituten," May 2, 1985.

86. Willy Brandt quoted in Siegel, "Marshall Fund," 2.

87. BArch B 136/24443, Haunschild to Kiep, August 8, 1985.

88. BArch B 136/24443, Kiep to Haunschild, August 12, 1985.

89. "Dankspende an Amerika," *Die Zeit*, December 6, 1985; BArch B 136/24443, BKAmt, "Kabinettsitzung am Mittwoch, dem 6. November 1985," October 30, 1985.

90. BArch B 136/24443, BMFT, "Errichtung eines Deutschen Historischen Instituts in den USA," March 6, 1985.

91. BArch B 136/24443, Witte to Rembser, n.d.

92. BArch B 136/24443, Riesenhuber to Schäuble, October 4, 1985.

93. BArch B 196/97446, BMFT, "Ein Deutsches Historisches Institut in den USA," n.d.

94. BArch B 136/24443, BMFT, "Errichtung eines Deutschen Historischen Instituts in den USA," March 6, 1985; BArch B 136/24443, BMFT, "Errichtung von zwei neuen Auslandsinstituten," May 2, 1985; BArch B 136/24443, BKAmt, "Kabinettsitzung am Mittwoch, dem 6. November 1985," October 30, 1985.

95. Wehler, "Wissenschaftspolitik," 1091.

96. BArch B 136/24443, BMFT, "DHI USA," April 8, 1986.

97. BArch B 136/24443, Lutz to Schäuble, April 16, 1986.

98. See Eckard Jesse, "Ideologien und Totalitarismus," *Die Zeit*, March 13, 1988.

99. BArch B 136/33866, Teltschik to Kohl, April 5, 1984. Teltschik had asked Bracher for a list of historians whom the Chancellery could send to negotiations with the United States Holocaust Memorial Council, and Bracher had recommended, among others, Karl Dietrich Erdmann, Martin Broszat, Rudolf Vierhaus, Gerhard A. Ritter, Thomas Nipperdey, Eberhard Bethge, Eberhard Jäckel, Andreas Hillgruber, Michael Stürmer, and himself. No further sources were available on this exchange.

100. BArch B 136/24443, Lutz to Kohl, May 6, 1986.

101. "Thomas Nipperdey (1927–1992), Historiker," Portal Rheinische Geschichte; Baumeister, "Nipperdey." See also Breuilly, "Telling It As It Was?"; Evans, *Rereading*, 23–43 and Dworok, *"Historikerstreit,"* 306–309. For his history of Germany see Nipperdey, *Deutsche Geschichte* (3 vols.).

102. BArch B 136/24443, Stürmer to Lutz, June 18, 1986.

103. BArch B 136/24443, Lutz to Kohl, May 6, 1986.

104. Lehmann, "Österreich-Ungarn"; Lehmann, *Pietismus*.

105. Lehmann, *Absolutismus*.

106. "The Staff of the Institute as of mid-September." *Bulletin of the German Historical Institute* 1 (1987): 17.

107. BArch B 136/24443, Lutz to Kohl, May 6, 1986.

108. Ibid.

109. All quotes in this paragraph in BArch B 136/24443, Stürmer to Lutz, June 18, 1986.

110. Wolfrum, *Geschichtspolitik*, 307f.

111. Berghoff and Wetzell, "Institute," 9.

112. BArch B 136/24443, Lutz to Bergsdorf, February 12, 1987.

113. Ibid.

114. Archiv des Liberalismus, N49-0059, Hildegard Hamm-Brücher's Office, Untitled memorandum of conversation with Arnulf Baring, July 2, 1987.

115. BArch B 136/24443, Ruhfus to AA, December 1, 1987.

116. Dietze and Wetzell, "Early Years," 40f.

117. Berghoff and Wetzell, "Institute," 8.

118. BArch B 196/97462, Embassy Washington to AA, February 11, 1988.

119. "Thousands of Sites, Millions of Fates: New Insights into the Universe of Nazi Camps," report on the event held on May 13, 2010, accessed July 23, 2015, www.ghi-dc.org/index.php?option=com_content&view=article&id=1045&Itemid=935.

120. See, for example, Lazar, "Foreign Service."

121. BArch B 196/97462, Embassy Washington to AA, February 11, 1988.

122. BArch B 196/97463, BMFT, "Zusammenarbeit mit den USA," March 10, 1988.

123. Ibid.

124. BArch B 196/97457, DHI Stiftungsrat, "Ergebnisprotokoll," August 22, 1988 and Lehmann to the Members of the GHI's Academic Advisory Board, Rembser, Maier, etc., October 14, 1988.

125. Wolfrum, *Geschichtspolitik*, 342f.
126. BArch B 196/97457, Lehmann to the Members of the GHI's Academic Advisory Board, Rembser, Maier, etc., October 14, 1988.
127. See the report on the conference by Ledford, "1949–1989."
128. Maier, *Past*, 9–16.
129. BArch B 196/97457, Maier, "Conference Proposal: '1949–1989: The Federal Republic as History,'" July 27, 1988.
130. BArch B 196/97457, Lehmann to the Members of the GHI's Academic Advisory Board, Rembser, Maier, etc., October 14, 1988.
131. Ibid.
132. Charles S. Maier, "Immoral Equivalence: Revising the Nazi past for the Kohl Era," *The New Republic*, December 1, 1986, 36–41, 41.
133. BArch B 196/97457, Angermann to Members of the GHI's Academic Advisory Board, the Board of Trustees, and the Directors of the GHI London and Washington, October 3, 1988.
134. Ibid.
135. BArch B 196/97457, Maier, "Revised Conference Proposal, 'The Federal Republic as History: 1949–1989,'" October 25, 1988.
136. BArch B 196/97457, DHI Wissenschaftlicher Beirat, "'Ergebnisprotokoll der 5. Sitzung des Wissenschaftlichen Beirats des Deutschen Historischen Instituts—USA,' November 25, 1988," January 31, 1989; emphasis in the original.
137. BArch B 196/97457, Angermann to Rembser, December 5, 1988.
138. BArch B 196/97457, Rembser to Angermann, December 30, 1988.
139. Cf. Wehler, "Wissenschaftspolitik," 1093-1096. See also Stelzel, "Rethinking," 298f.
140. Cf. Wehler, "Wissenschaftspolitik," 1092f.
141. BArch B 136/24443, Lutz to Kohl, November 7, 1988.
142. BArch B 136/24443, Kohl to Heck, November 8, 1988.
143. ACDP, Michael Mertes Papers, 01-747, Armonk-Institute/William S. Trosten (1991–1992), Embassy Washington to AA, December 20, 1991.
144. Deutscher Bundestag, Plenarprotokoll 11/4, March 18, 1987, 68.
145. Ibid.
146. Ibid., 64f.
147. See, e.g., Deutscher Bundestag, Plenarprotokoll 10/53, 9.2.1984, 7227f. Cf. Wolfrum, *Geschichtspolitik*, 307f.
148. BArch B 136/30532, BKAmt, "Stichworte zum Gespräch mit Charles Wick zum Thema: Öffentlichkeitsarbeit und Deutschlandbild in den USA," April 23, 1987; and BArch B 136/30532, BKAmt, "Politische Öffentlichkeitsarbeit und Deutschlandbild in den USA," n.d.
149. BArch B 136/30532, Untitled 25-page position paper on West German public relations in the United States, n.d. [1987]; emphasis in original.
150. See, e.g., BArch B 136/30532, BKAmt, "Deutsches Fernsehangebot für Nordamerika," October 31, 1985.
151. E.g., BArch B 136/30535, Weidenfeld to Genscher, March 10, 1989.
152. For the competition over the design of foreign policy between the Chancellery and the Foreign Office under Genscher see Bierling, *Außenpolitik*, 46–48.
153. Leggewie, *Geist*, 32.
154. See bibliography.
155. Weidenfeld, ed., *Geschichtsbewußtsein*.
156. Weidenfeld, "Geschichte und Politik," 16.
157. Ibid., 18f.
158. Ibid., 22–28.
159. Cf. Kreis, "Bündnis," 631.
160. "Rede von Professor Dr. Werner Weidenfeld anläßlich seiner Amtseinführung als Koordinator für die deutsch-amerikanische Zusammenarbeit," in *Brücken über den Atlantik*, 36.
161. Ibid., 38.

162. "Jahresbericht des Koordinators, Professor Dr. Werner Weidenfeld, über seine Tätigkeit vom 1.10.1987 bis 31.12.1988," in *Brücken über den Atlantik*, 13.
163. "Wortlaut der gemeinsamen Resolution des 100. Kongresses der Vereinigten Staaten von Amerika," in *Brücken über den Atlantik*, 39. See also BArch B 136/30033, Embassy Washington, "Deutsch-amerikanischer Freundschaftsgarten," February 19, 1988.
164. BArch B 138/56199, Embassy Washington to AA, May 19, 1988; BArch B 136/30530, Embassy Washington to AA, June 30, 1988.
165. Littmann, *Partners*, 225.
166. BArch B 136/42221, AA, "Sachstand: Bundeskanzlerinitiative vom Juli 1988 Initiative zur Förderung des deutsch-amerikanischen Wissenschaftsaustauschs, hier: Centers of Excellence," September 29, 1990.
167. BArch B 136/34308, AA, "Tätigkeitsbericht des Koordinators für die deutsch-amerikanische Zusammenarbeit," January 20, 1992.
168. BArch B 138/56199, BMBW, "Gespräch zwischen Herrn St und Herrn Prof. Weidenfeld, dem neuen Koordinator für die deutsch-amerikanischen Beziehungen, vom 27.11.1987," November 30, 1987.
169. BArch B 136/30534, AA, "Einladung des BKs an Präsidenten führender US-Hochschulen, 6.–8. Juli 1988," June 27, 1988.
170. BArch B 138/56199, Weidenfeld to Böning, March 16, 1988.
171. See BArch B 136/30534, AA, "Einladung des BKs an Präsidenten führender US-Hochschulen, 6.–8. Juli 1988," June 27, 1988.
172. BArch B 138/56199, BMBW, "Besuch von Präsidenten amerikanischer Spitzenuniversitäten vom 6.–9. Juli 1988 auf Einladung des Bundeskanzlers," July 4, 1988.
173. This applied for example to the project of a German American Academy for the Humanities: BArch B 138/56199, BMBW, "Gespräch zwischen Herrn St und Herrn Prof. Weidenfeld, dem neuen Koordinator für die deutsch-amerikanischen Beziehungen, vom 27.11.1987," November 30, 1987.
174. For example BArch B 138/65324, BMBW, "Bundeskanzlerinitiative vom Juli 1988 zur Intensivierung der deutsch-amerikanischen Wissenschaftsbeziehungen," December 13, 1989.
175. BArch B 136/30534, AA, "Vermerk: Einladung des Bundeskanzlers an Präsidenten amerikanischer Spitzenuniversitäten, 6.–9. Juli 1988," May 27, 1988; BArch B 138/56199, BMBW, "Besuch von Präsidenten amerikanischer Spitzenuniversitäten vom 6.–9. Juli 1988 auf Einladung des Bundeskanzlers," July 4, 1988.
176. BArch B 138/56199, BMBW, "Besuch US-amerikanischer Universitätspräsidenten in der undesrepublik Deutschland," July 11, 1988.
177. In fact, all in all seventeen universities applied for funding to establish a Center of Excellence.
178. BArch B 136/34311, BKAmt, "Gespräch des Herrn Bundeskanzlers mit u.a. den Präsidenten amerikanischer Privatstiftungen, 27.9.1989," October 4, 1989. See also BArch B 138/65324, Embassy Washington to AA, November 18, 1989; BArch B 138/65324, AA, "Deutsch-amerikanische Akademie der Geistes- und Sozialwissenschaften," July 25, 1989. Cf. Littmann, *Partners*, 243f.
179. BArch B 136/30534, AA, "Vermerk: Einladung des Bundeskanzlers an Präsidenten amerikanischer Spitzenuniversitäten, 6.–9. Juli 1988," May 27, 1988.
180. Cf. Littmann, *Partners*, 225–228.
181. BArch B 136/30536, AA, "Anlage: Gesprächsführungsvorschlag," September 18, 1989.
182. For the following paragraph: BArch B 136/34311, BKAmt, "Gespräch des Herrn Bundeskanzlers mit u.a. den Präsidenten amerikanischer Privatstiftungen, 27.9.1989," October 4, 1989; BArch B 136/34311, Embassy Washington, "Besuch von Präsidenten amerikanischer Stiftungen in Bonn am 27. und 28.09.1989," October 2, 1989.
183. BArch B 136/30536, AA, "Anlage: Gesprächsführungsvorschlag," September 18, 1989.
184. BArch B 136/34311, BKAmt, "Gespräch des Herrn Bundeskanzlers mit u.a. Präsidenten amerikanischer privater Stiftungen am 27.9.1989," October 2, 1989.

185. BArch B 136/34311, AA, "Einladung des Herrn Bundeskanzlers an hochrangige Vertreter amerikanischer Stiftungen und wissenschaftliche Institutionen, hier: Bewertung des Besuchs," October 5, 1989.

186. Kohl, "Lagebericht," October 31, 1988, 658.

187. BArch B 136/30034, "Reise des Bundeskanzlers in die USA," October 28, 1988; emphasis in the original.

188. BArch B 136/30033, AA, "Vorlage: Zur Unterrichtung und mit dem Vorschlag der Weiterleitung an den Chef des Bundeskanzleramtes im Hinblick auf den Bundeskanzlerbesuch in New York und Washington (12.–15.11.)," October 20, 1988.

189. BArch B 136/32873, GK NY to AA, September 29, 1988. Attached to this message was the calendar "Kritalnacht 1938–1988: Remembrance Week November 4–10, 1988" for New York City, Long Island and Westchester. See also Saidel, *Remember*, 174.

190. Dubiel, *Niemand*, 215–218; Herf, "Jenninger"; Schmid, *Erinnern*, 429–448.

191. Quoted in BArch B 136/30034, GK NY to AA, November 10, 1988.

192. Quoted in BArch B 136/30034, Embassy Washington to AA, November 11, 1988.

193. Kohl, *Erinnerungen: 1982–1990*, 793f. See also Kohl, "Lagebericht," November 21, 1988, 669.

194. BArch B 136/30530, "Pressemitteilung zum Jahresbericht 1988 des Koordinators für die deutsch-amerikanische zwischengesellschaftliche, kultur- und informationspolitische Zusammenarbeit," n.d.

195. BArch B 136/34310, BKAmt, "Deutsche Öffentlichkeitsarbeit in den USA," September 12, 1990. In early 1991, Weidenfeld provided a short proposal of ten suggestions of how to improve German–American relations: BArch B 136/34308, Weidenfeld, "10 Leitsätze zur Zukunft der deutsch-amerikanischen Beziehungen," February 20, 1991.

196. BArch B 136/34311, Weidenfeld to Kohl, April 30, 1992.

197. BArch B 136/34310, Horstmann, "Draft Proposal for a Comprehensive Public Relations and Information Plan to be carried out by the German government and German companies (including banks) in the United States of America," February 21, 1989.

198. BArch B 136/34310, "Kernpunkte eines intern ad referendum verabschiedeten Entwurfs des New Yorker Arbeitskreises zu einem 'Gesamtkonzept für die Informations- und Öffentlichkeitsarbeit in den USA,'" n.d.; emphasis in original.

199. BArch B 136/34310, "Ergebnisprotokoll der Tagung 'Politische Öffentlichkeitsarbeit in den USA,'" February 28, 1989, esp. 20. See also BArch B 136/34310, "Ergebnis-Protokoll der Sitzung des Arbeitskreises USA am 9. März 1989 zum Thema 'Öffentlichkeitsarbeit in den USA,'" n.d.

200. See chapter 3.

201. BArch B 136/34311, Weidenfeld, "Konzept für die deutsche Öffentlichkeitsarbeit in den Vereinigten Staaten von Amerika," n.d. [April 30, 1992].

202. BArch B 136/34318, "Initiativen des Herrn Bundeskanzlers in der deutsch-amerikanischen Wissenschaftskooperation (Bundeskanzlerstipendien, Centers of Excellence etc.)," October 16, 1989. One of Kohl's sons, Walter, was an undergraduate student there at the time. See Kohl, *Leben*, 245–250.

203. BArch B 136/34318, AA, "Finanzierung Bundeskanzlerstipendien und Centers of Excellence," n.d. [before June 23, 1989]; BArch B 138/65324, BMBW, "Bundeskanzlerinitiative vom Juli 1988 zur Intensivierung der deutsch-amerikanischen Wissenschaftsbeziehungen, hier: Sachstand," December 13, 1989.

204. BArch B 138/65324, BMBW, "Bundeskanzler-Initiative vom Juli 1988 zur Intensivierung des deutsch-amerikanischen Wissenschaftsaustausches, hier: Stand der einzelnen Projekte," October 27, 1989.

205. BArch B 136/42401, Teltschik to Kohl, August 17, 1989.

206. BArch B 136/42401, Weidenfeld to Kohl, April 23, 1990.

207. BArch B 145/17812, "Vertrag zwischen dem Deutschen Akademischen Austauschdienst und den Regents der University of California," November 1, 1990.

208. BArch B 136/42401, AA, "Zentren für Deutschland- und Europastudien an amerikanischen Universitäten, hier: Bericht über die Evaluierung," April 22, 1996.

Chapter 5

1. For the history of the monument see: Kirsch, *Nationaler Mythos*; Leggewie and Meyer, *"Ein Ort"*; Stavginski, *Holocaust-Denkmal*.
2. "Ich stelle mich in eine Ecke, wo man gar nicht bemerkt wird," Interview with Helmut Kohl, *FAZ*, September 17, 1998. Cf. Kirsch, "Kern," 43f.
3. Kohl, "Earth."
4. Kirsch, "Kern," 43. See also Beattie, "Past in the Politics," 32.
5. The term "Holocaustland" is used in a fundraising brochure of the Atlantik-Brücke: BArch B 145/21051, "Deutschland—Holocaustland?," n.d. [1995 or later].
6. See, e.g., Rödder, *Deutschland*; Zelikow and Rice, *Germany Unified*.
7. Kohl allegedly referred to Merkel as "mein Mädchen" ("my girl"). See for example Severin Weiland, "Kohls unterschätztes Mädchen," *Spiegel Online*, May 30, 2005, accessed July 23, 2015, www.spiegel.de/politik/deutschland/0,1518,357997,00.html.
8. For the following see Niven, *Past*, 1–9; König, *Zukunft*, 17 and 143–163; Beattie, "Past." See also Müller, *Another Country*.
9. See Herf, *Divided Memory*, 162–200.
10. This was, for example, the position taken by Alfred Dregger during the Bitburg controversy. See chapter 2.
11. Beattie, "Past," 32; Herbert, *Geschichte*, 1205f.
12. König, *Zukunft*, 51–72.
13. Müller, *Another Country*, 98–102. See also Hampton and Peifer, "Reordering" and Markovits and Reich, *Predicament*.
14. König, *Zukunft*, 17.
15. For an overview see Niven, *Past*.
16. Kansteiner, *Pursuit*, 283. See also Kirsch, *Nationaler Mythos*, 152f.
17. Niven, *Past*, 143–174; Rürup, *Schatten*, 186–200; Thamer, "Tabubruch."
18. In the early 2000s, however, the Federal Republic saw a number of debates on this issue, for instance about the suffering of Germans during Allied bombing raids. This debate was, among others, sparked by a controversial book: Friedrich, *Brand*.
19. Martin Walser, "Erfahrungen beim Verfassen einer Sonntagsrede aus Anlaß der Verleihung des Friedenspreises des Deutschen Buchhandels," *FAZ*, October 12, 1998.
20. See, e.g., also the essays in Wickert, ed., *Angst vor Deutschland*.
21. In spring 1990, 56 percent of Jewish American and 77 percent of all Americans supported German unification. See Hanhardt, "Vereinigung," 409.
22. Cf. Neuss, "Brückenbauen," 39.
23. Shafir, *Ambiguous Relations*, 342f.
24. USHMM IA, Accession No. 1998-011, Records Berenbaum, Box 36, International Council of B'nai B'rith, "German Unification. A Fact Sheet," April 12, 1990; and the comprehensive account by Shafir, *Ambiguous Relations*, 341–357. For the concerns of the West German Left, see Moses, *Intellectuals*, 229–235.
25. USHMM IA, Accession No. 1998-011, Records Berenbaum, Box 36, International Council of B'nai B'rith, "German Unification. A Fact Sheet," April 12, 1990.
26. Timm, *Jewish Claims*, 180–189; Meining, *Judenpolitik*, 503–514.
27. E.g., Charles Krauthammer, "The German Revival. The Berlin Wall Came Down Too Soon," *The New Republic*, March 26, 1990.
28. Quoted in BArch B 136/42205, Hier to Kohl, February 9, 1990. A further example is USHMM IA, Accession No. 1998-011, Records Berenbaum, Box 36, Meed to Kohl, September 6, 1990. Cf. Neuss, "Brückenbauen," 39; ACDP, Michael Mertes Papers, 01–747, Armonk-Institute/William S. Trosten (1986–1990), William S. Trosten, "Die jüdische Gemeinschaft von Amerika und die Vereinigung Deutschlands," May 30, 1990.
29. "Interview mit Elie Wiesel, Deutschland ist noch nicht bereit," *Der Spiegel* 1 (1990), 105–110.
30. BArch B 136/42205, Hier to Kohl, February 9, 1990.

31. Hier had also sent his letter to the *New York Times*, which had published an excerpt in Robert Pear, "Bush and Kohl on TV," *New York Times*, February 25, 1990.
32. BArch B 136/42205, Hier to Kohl, February 9, 1990.
33. See, e.g., Herf, "'At War.'"
34. For an overwiew of the teaching of the Nazi past see Sharples, *Postwar Germany*, 149–164.
35. Kohl always used a thick black pen, despite the fact that a chancellor (or any head of a governmental office) ususally uses green ink: ACDP, Michael Mertes Papers, 01-747, Armonk-Institute/William S. Trosten (1986–1990), Hier to Kohl, February 9, 1990. Kohl made this note on the German translation of Hier's letter.
36. BArch B 136/42205, Kohl to Hier, February 28, 1990.
37. Cf. Kohl, *Erinnerungen: 1982–1990*, 788–792.
38. Kohl to Wiesenthal, February 28, 1990, BArch B 136/42205. Cf. Sheldon Teitelbaum and Tom Waldman, "The Unorthodox Rabbi," *Los Angeles Times Magazine*, July 15, 1990.
39. BArch B 136/42205, Hier to Kohl, March 1, 1990.
40. BArch B 136/42205, Ruhfus to AA, March 9, 1990.
41. BArch B 136/42205, Ruhfus to Bonn AA, March 13, 1990.
42. Ibid.
43. ACDP, Michael Mertes Papers, 01-747, Armonk-Institute/William S. Trosten (1986–1990), Trosten to Mertes, January 13, 1990; parentheses in original. See also ACDP, Michael Mertes Papers, 01-747, Armonk-Institute/William S. Trosten (1986–1990), William S. Trosten, "Die jüdische Gemeinschaft von Amerika und die Vereinigung Deutschlands," May 30, 1990.
44. ACDP, Michael Mertes Papers, 01-747, Armonk-Institute/William S. Trosten (1986–1990), "Vorlage von Michael Mertes zur Unterrichtung an Helmut Kohl," February 8, 1990.
45. See BArch B 136/42209, Theodore Ellenoff to the *New York Times*, February 21, 1990.
46. AJC Archives, William Trosten Files, Box 226, AJC, "Statement on German Unification," May 17, 1990.
47. See for example Niven, *Past*, 19–24; and Shafir, *Ambiguous Relations*, 319–337.
48. See Trommler, "Culture," 266–268.
49. See, for example, the essays in Hoffmann and Maaß, eds., *Freund oder Fratze?*
50. BArch B 136/42209, Neuer to Kohl, February 19, 1991.
51. For an overview see Kurthen, "Antisemitism and Xenophobia"; Kurthen and Minkenberg, "Transition"; Ohlemacher, "Public Opinion."
52. BArch B 136/42401, Embassy Washington to AA, November 24, 1992.
53. Herf, *Divided Memory*, 366.
54. "Ernstes Zeichen an der Wand," *Der Spiegel* 36 (1992), 18–29.
55. Robert Leicht, "Hoyerswerda in den Köpfen," *Die Zeit*, September 27, 1991.
56. See Ohlemacher, "Public Opinion," 222–236.
57. Kansteiner, *Pursuit*, 269f.
58. E.g., "Ernstes Zeichen an der Wand," *Der Spiegel* 36 (1992), 18–29; "Heilloses Chaos," *Der Spiegel* (48) 1993, 34–36.
59. BArch B 136/34311, Stabreit to Hartmann, November 30, 1992. Stabreit refered to a phone conversation with Hartmann about the attacks and Kohl's reactions.
60. Cf. Kurt Kister, "Der häßliche Deutsche—wie gehabt!," *SZ*, December 16, 1992.
61. A. M. Rosenthal, "Our German Business," *New York Times*, September 22, 1992. See also A.M. Rosenthal, "Das Land, das Angst macht," *Die Zeit*, October 2, 1992.
62. BArch B 136/34311, Ziefer to AA, September 29, 1992.
63. Ibid.
64. Clemens, "Image," 185.
65. Quoted in Fisher, *Wall*, 319.
66. "Junker aus Germany," *Der Spiegel* 17 (1993), 17.
67. Marc Fisher, "The Rewriting on the Wall?," *Washington Post*, July 24, 1994.
68. *Munzinger Online/Personen—Internationales Biographisches Archiv*, s.v. "Immo Stabreit," http://www.munzinger.de/document/00000020335.

69. "Flaschen im Kabinett," *Der Spiegel* 15 (1992), 22f.
70. Cf. Schwarz, *Kohl*, 641f.
71. BArch B 136/34311, Stabreit to Hartmann, November 30, 1992.
72. BArch B 136/42401, Stabreit to AA, November 24, 1992.
73. Ibid.
74. "Ohne Distanz," *Der Spiegel* 30 (1988), 27–29. In contrast to the German foreign minister, Hans-Dietrich Genscher, Stabreit considered the African National Congress a "terrorist organization." *Der Spiegel* suggests that Stabreit's view corresponded with that of the Bavarian prime minister Franz Josef Strauß, who had "cleared the way" for Stabreit to become ambassador in South Africa. See also "Geladene Pistole," *Der Spiegel* 27 (1989), 23f.
75. BArch B 136/34311, Stabreit to Hartmann, November 30, 1992.
76. Quotations from Kurt Kister, "Der häßliche Deutsche—wie gehabt!," *SZ*, December 16, 1992.
77. BArch B 136/34311, Stabreit to Hartmann, November 30, 1992.
78. Clemens, "Image," 184; Marc Fisher, "The Rewriting on the Wall?," *Washington Post*, July 24, 1994.
79. BArch B 136/42206, Moses to Kohl, December 2, 1992.
80. Ibid.
81. Hier's statement is summarized in BArch B 136/42205, GK Los Angeles to AA, September 4, 1992.
82. BArch B 145/21051, Association of Jewish Holocaust Survivors in Philadelphia/Child Holocaust Survivors of Delaware Valley/Sons and Daughters of Holocaust Survivors to Peter Kohler/Generalkonsul, n.d. [1992].
83. Kohl, "Lagebericht," September 12, 1993, 493.
84. Ibid., 493.
85. Flanzbaum, "Introduction," 14f.; Mintz, *Culture*, 32–35.
86. ACDP, Michael Mertes Papers, 01-747, Armonk-Institute/William S. Trosten (1992–1995), "Protokoll der Ersten Sitzung des Ständigen Ausschuss für Deutsch-Amerikanisch/Jüdische Fragen der Atlantik-Brücke e.V.," February 12/13, 1993, 16. Burt thus used this term almost a decade before it was popularized by Finkelstein, *Holocaust Industry*.
87. ACDP, Michael Mertes Papers, 01-747, Armonk-Institute/William S. Trosten (1991–1992), Mertes to Kohl, May 8, 1991.
88. Ibid.; emphasis in the original.
89. BArch B 136/42205, GK Los Angeles to AA, February 8, 1991. See also Novick, *Holocaust in American Life*, 249.
90. Marginal comment on BArch B 136/42205, GK Los Angeles to AA, February 8, 1991.
91. BArch B 136/42205, "Bitte des Simon-Wiesenthal-Zentrums um Unterstützung durch Überlassung deutschen Archivmaterials," January 4, 1990. These negotiations continued well into 1991.
92. The letter by Hier is translated for Kohl in BArch B 136/42205, "Leserbrief von Rabbi Hier an den Chefredakteur der Los Angeles Times zu der Karikatur des Bundeskanzlers, die in dieser Zeitung erschienen ist," March 6, 1990.
93. BArch B 136/42205, Margolis to GK Los Angeles, January 2, 1991.
94. BArch B 145/21051, AA, "Holocaust-Museen in den USA," July 10, 1992.
95. In addition to the USHMM and the Museum of Tolerance, the report listed institutions in Detroit, Houston, and San Francisco.
96. BArch B 145/21051, AA, "Holocaust-Museen in den USA," July 10, 1992.
97. ACDP, Michael Mertes Papers, 01-747, Armonk-Institute/William S. Trosten (1992–1995), "Protokoll der Ersten Sitzung des Ständigen Ausschuss für Deutsch-Amerikanisch/Jüdische Fragen der Atlantik-Brücke e.V.," February 12/13, 1993.
98. Due to this fact, the discussants are—with the exception of the keynote speakers Karl Kaiser, William Trosten, and Dieter Kastrup—not identified in the minutes.
99. ACDP, Michael Mertes Papers, 01-747, Armonk-Institute/William S. Trosten (1992–1995), "Protokoll der Ersten Sitzung des Ständigen Ausschuss für Deutsch-Amerikanisch/Jüdische Fragen der Atlantik-Brücke e.V.," February 12/13, 1993, 6, quotation on 21.

100. Ibid., 16.
101. Ibid., 18.
102. Ibid., 28.
103. Ibid., 14.
104. Ibid., 15–17.
105. Ibid., 28.
106. BArch B 136/42396, AA, "Öffentlichkeitswirkung der Deutschen Auswärtigen Kultur-politik in den USA," January 13, 1993.
107. BArch B 145/21051, AA, "Holocaust-Museen in den USA," July 10, 1992.
108. Ibid. This is the original title of the exhibition according to the Foreign Office.
109. BArch B 136/34308, Embassy Washington to AA, ChBK, etc., November 1, 1991.
110. BArch B 136/34308, Hartmann to Kohl, July 9, 1991; emphasis in original.
111. BArch B 136/34308, Embassy Washington to AA, July 8, 1991. A staff member in the Chancellery had written in large letters "Holocaust Museum" on the memorandum explaining the concept of the festival.
112. BArch B 136/34311, Weidenfeld to Kohl, April 30, 1992, including the attachment "Konzept für die deutsche Öffentlichkeitsarbeit in den Vereinigten Staaten von Amerika"
113. BArch B 136/34311, AA, "1. Sitzung des Arbeitsstabes 'Öffentlichkeitsarbeit USA,'" November 10, 1992.
114. Such plans go back to 1989: Carola Kaps, "Freundschaften wollen gepfelgt sein," *FAZ*, August 11, 1989.
115. BArch B 136/34311, Weidenfeld, "Konzept für die deutsche Öffentlichkeitsarbeit in den Vereinigten Staaten von Amerika," n.d. [April 30, 1992]. See, for example, also the assessment of Gramberger, *Wider den häßlichen Deutschen*, 84–86; BArch B 136/34311, AA, "1. Sitzung des Arbeitsstabes 'Öffentlichkeitsarbeit USA,'" November 10, 1992.
116. BArch B 136/42396, AA, "Öffentlichkeitswirkung der Deutschen Auswärtigen Kultur-politik in den USA," January 13, 1993.
117. E.g.: BArch B 136/42207, Salberg and Foxman to Kohl, February 2, 1993. A year earlier, a meeting between Kohl and Kurt Waldheim had also caused some protest by American Jewish organizations. See for example: BArch B 136/42207, Salberg and Foxman to Kohl, March 30, 1992. Kohl had publicly declared that he did not "need any advice" from Jewish organizations about who he met with or not. See John Tagliabue, "Waldheim is Given Welcome by Kohl," *New York Times*, March 28, 1992.
118. BArch B136/42214, Hartmann to Kohl, April 27, 1993.
119. BArch B 136/42207, Morr, "Gespräch des Weltvizepräsidenten und des Europadirektors von B'nai B'rith, Domberger und Prof. Ehrlich mit StM Pfeifer am 29. Juni 1992," July 2, 1992.
120. BArch B 136/42207, Mertes to Hartmann, June 16, 1992.
121. BArch B 136/42207, Domberger and Ehrlich to Mertes (*Grundlagenpapier*), July 14, 1992.
122. BArch B 136/42207, Hartmann to Kohl, December 9, 1992.
123. For example: Staatsarchiv Wolfenbüttel, 143 N Zg. 2009/069 Nr. 517, Hamm-Brücher to Liedtke, July 13, 1978.
124. See BArch B 136/34162, AA, "Gespräch des Herrn Bundeskanzlers mit Herrn Walther Leisler Kiep von der Atlantikbrücke e.V. und mit Herrn William Trosten vom American Jewish Committee (AJC)," December 7, 1988. No documentation on this program is available in the AJC Archives.
125. ACDP, Michael Mertes Papers, 01-747, Armonk-Institute/William S. Trosten (1991–1992), Trosten to Teltschik, November 13, 1991. Trosten may have overlooked that the Kristallnacht pogrom took place in 1938, not in 1933.
126. BArch B 136/34308, Weidenfeld to Kohl, July 10, 1991; ACDP, Michael Mertes Papers, 01-747, Armonk-Institute/William S. Trosten (1986–1990), Mertes to Klein, February 27, 1990.
127. ACDP, Michael Mertes Papers, 01-747, Armonk-Institute/William S. Trosten (1986–1990), Mertes to Kohl, February 8, 1990. Cf. ACDP, Michael Mertes Papers, 01-747,

Armonk-Institute/William S. Trosten (1992–1995), "Protokoll der Ersten Sitzung des Ständigen Ausschuss für Deutsch-Amerikanisch/Jüdische Fragen der Atlantik-Brücke e.V.," February 12/13, 1993. A member of this commission, not identified in the minutes, made this statement.

128. BArch B 145/21051, Atlantik-Brücke brochure "Deutschland—Holocaustland?," n.d. [1995 or later].

129. Ibid.

130. Calebow, *Normalisierung*, 79. See also Schwarz, *Adenauer: Der Aufstieg*; Schwarz, *Adenauer: Der Staatsmann*; Schwarz, *Kohl*.

131. BArch B 145/21051, Schäfer to Wegener, November 11, 1993.

132. BArch B 145/21051, BPA, internal memorandum, November 18, 1993.

133. All quotations taken from: BArch B 145/21051, Dove Wimbish, "Teachers Putting Germany in Better Light for Students," *The Clipper*, February 3–4, 1994.

134. Kohl, *Erinnerungen: 1990–1994*, 704–706. Kohl dismisses critical voices about the actual motivations of the participants in "July 20." Cf. Kershaw, *Nazi Dictatorship*, 188f.; Herbert, *Geschichte*, 526–529.

135. All information and quotations regarding the exhibition *Against Hitler* are taken, unless otherwise noted, from Marc Fisher, "The Rewriting on the Wall?," *Washington Post*, July 24, 1994. See also Pieper, *Musealisierung*, 169, n. 470.

136. Marc Fisher, "The Rewriting on the Wall?," *Washington Post*, July 24, 1994.

137. Jon Wiener, "Good Germans," *The New Republic*, March 6, 1995, 28.

138. Steinbach, Tuchel, and Walle, eds., *Against Hitler*.

139. Marc Fisher, "The Rewriting on the Wall?," *Washington Post*, July 24, 1994.

140. Quoted in ibid.

141. USHMM IA, Accession No. 2005.154, Research Subject Files Milton, Sybil Milton, "Background Paper," October 12, 1994, 2.

142. Quoted in Marc Fisher, "The Rewriting on the Wall?," *Washington Post*, July 24, 1994.

143. BArch B 145/21051, AA, "Holocaust-Museen in den USA," July 10, 1992.

144. Henryk M. Broder, "Das Shoah-Business," *Der Spiegel* 16 (1993), 248–256. Less critical is Henriette Schroeder, "Das Haus des Holocaust," *SZ*, April 15, 1993. In addition to numerous articles, Border recently published a very critical book on Holocaust memory in Germany: Broder, *Auschwitz*.

145. Henryk M. Broder, "Das Shoah-Business," *Der Spiegel* 16 (1993), 253.

146. Jörg von Uthmann, "Vergangenheit, die nicht vergehen darf," *FAZ*, March 10, 1993.

147. For example: Leo Wieland, "Ein Ort der Mahnung und Danksagung," *FAZ*, April 2, 1993; Leo Wieland, "Die 'Amerikanisierung' des Holocaust," *FAZ*, April 23, 1993; Joseph Giovannini, "Konstruktion des Grauens," *SZ*, May 7, 1993.

148. Kurt Kister, "Plötzlich ist da diese Wand aus Geruch," *SZ*, April 22, 1993.

149. Michael Wolffsohn, "Eine Amputation des Judentums?," *FAZ*, April 15, 1993; Henryk M. Broder, "Das Shoah-Business," *Der Spiegel* 16 (1993), 248–256; Raphael Seligmann, "Ausbruch aus der Märtyrerroll," *SZ*, April 13, 1993. For a critical reply to Wolffsohn and Seligmann see Josef Joffe, "Erinnerung als Götzendienst?," *SZ*, April 22, 1993.

150. Jörg von Uthmann, "Wem gehört der Holocaust?," *FAZ*, May 3, 1993. Uthmann refers to Lance Morrow, "In all its grimness, Washington's controversial Holocaust museum is a necessary, civilizing memorial," *Time Magazine*, April 26, 1993, Vol. 141 Issue 17, 56f.

151. Cf. Krondorfer, "Kulturgut," 103. See also Junker, "'History Wars,'" 53f. and 56. The German Extreme Right made a similar case: "NAPOLA-Hundertschaftsführer führt Holocaust-Komitee: Die wundersame Karriere des MdB Peter Petersen," *Deutsche National-Zeitung*, April 25, 1986.

152. BArch N 1396/3, Petersen to Dregger, February 5, 1985.

153. A detailed analysis of the debate in the German press over *Schindler's List* provides Thiele, *Kontroversen*, 435–459. For example: Wolfgang Benz, "Bilder statt Fußnoten," *Die Zeit*, March 4, 1994. See also Sharples, *Postwar Germany*, 140–145.

154. Weiß, "Sinnliche Erinnerung," 84–86.

155. See Urs Jenny, "Holocaust mit Happy-End?," *Der Spiegel* 21 (1993), 208–213.

156. For the reception of *Schindler's List* in Germany and its interconnection with Holocaust historiography see Bösch, "Film," 16–21.
157. Ibid., 17.
158. See the anthology by Weiss, ed., *"Der gute Deutsche."*
159. Wilder quoted in "Als ob es gestern war: Premiere von 'Schindlers Liste,'" *SZ*, March 3, 1994. See also Thiele, *Kontroversen*, 437.
160. For the CSU's reaction (Hans Zehetmair) see Weiß, "Sinnliche Erinnerung," 87f.
161. Craig R. Whitney, "The German Premiere Of 'Schindler's List' Brings Tears and Praise," *New York Times*, March 2, 1994.
162. Ibid.
163. Weiß, "Sinnliche Erinnerung," 87f.
164. "Es ist unsere Geschichte," *Der Spiegel*, 12 (1994), 97–100.
165. Goldhagen's book proposal as quoted in Frei, "Goldhagen," 141.
166. Both historians used in part the same sources on Reserve Police Battalion 101. See also Browning's reply to Goldhagen: Browning, *Ordinary Men*, 191–223.
167. Goldhagen, *Hitler's Willing Executioners*, 419.
168. Matthäus, "Historiography," 206. For a detailed critique see also Pohl, "Holocaust-Forschung," 14–42.
169. Frei, "Goldhagen," 146f. Frei points out that hardly any of these works explicitly refers to *Hitler's Willing Executioners*.
170. BArch B 136/42205, Rohr to AA, April 2, 1996. Following quotes taken from this telex.
171. A. M. Rosenthal, "Some Ordinary Germans," *New York Times*, April 2, 1996.
172. BArch B 136/42621, Morr to Kohl, April 12, 1996.
173. See for example Fisher, *Wall*, 287.
174. BArch B 136/42205, AA (Schütte) to Kinkel, "Deutschland-Bild amerikanischer Juden: Beobachtungen auf einer Vortragsreise durch die USA," June 4, 1996. See also Schuette [*sic*], *German-Jewish Relations*.
175. BArch B 136/42205, AA (Schütte) to Kinkel, "Deutschland-Bild amerikanischer Juden: Beobachtungen auf einer Vortragsreise durch die USA," June 4, 1996.
176. BArch B 136/42205, AA, Schütte, "Meine Vortragsreise nach USA/Kanada vom 06. bis 22.05.1996 zum Thema 'Deutsch-israelische Beziehungen und deutsche Rolle im Nahost-Friedensprozeß," May 28, 1996.
177. For the debate in Germany see e.g. Eder and Mentel, "Goldhagen-Debatte" and Ullrich, "Provokation."
178. Frei, "Goldhagen," 145–157. See also Grossmann, "'Goldhagen Effect,'" 109–119.
179. Matthäus, "Historiography," 207.
180. Frei, "Goldhagen," 147.
181. BArch B 136/42621, Haibach, "Zur Rezeption von Daniel Goldhagens Buch 'Hitler's willige Vollstrecker,'" September 16, 1996. Haibach prepared a detailed analysis of *Hitler's Willing Executioners*, summarizing Goldhagen's arguments, the replies by his critics, and the favorable reception by nonexpert audiences in Germany. For the Chancellery's decision: BArch B 136/42621, Morr to ChBK, September 19, 1996. Morr had also discussed this with Michael Mertes.
182. Interview with Goldhagen, "Was dachten die Mörder?," *Der Spiegel* 33 (1996), 50–55, quote on 55. See also Rudolf Augstein, "Der Soziologe als Scharfrichter," *Der Spiegel* 16 (1996), 29–32.
183. Quoted in Rosenfeld, *End*, 17.
184. Grossmann, "'Goldhagen Effect,'" 123.
185. ACDP, Michael Mertes Papers, 01–747, Armonk-Institute/William S. Trosten (1991–1992), Trosten to Teltschik, November 13, 1991.
186. Brunner, Goschler, and Frei, eds., *Globalisierung*; Goschler, *Schuld*, 413–421; and Surmann, *Shoah-Erinnerung*, 49–80.
187. For an account on the GDR's handling of this issue see Timm, *Jewish Claims*. For a detailed account on post-1990 *"Wiedergutmachung"* see Goschler, *Schuld*, 413–475 and Hockerts, "Entschädigung," 50–58.

188. This was the so-called Artikel-2 Abkommen. For details see Goschler, "Entschädigung," 127–129 and Goschler, *Schuld*, 442–444.

189. In fact, the Schröder government was confronted with such claimes, which resulted in the establishment of the Foundation Remembrance, Responsibility and Future (Stiftung "Erinnerung, Verantwortung und Zukunft"). See Goschler, *Schuld*, 450–471 and Borggräfe, *Zwangsarbeiterentschädigung*, 286–309.

190. Goschler, *Schuld*, 438–449.

191. Ibid., 446.

192. These included Stuart Eizenstat, Bill Clinton's key official on Holocaust-Era Assets, who would also negotiate with the government of Gerhard Schröder on compensation for slave and forced labor. See Feldman, "Jewish Role," 184f. as well as Eizenstat, *Justice*. For the impact of the debate about Holocaust-Era Assets on American Holocaust memory see Surmann, "Restitution" and Surmann, *Shoah-Erinnerung*.

193. Goschler, *Schuld*, 416f. and 446f. See also Kohl's statement in Kohl, "Lagebericht," February 9, 1998, 968.

194. AJC Archives, Digital Collection, Rifkind and Harris to all AJC members, January 28, 1998, accessed July 23, 2015, www.ajcarchives.org/AJC_DATA/Files/947.pdf. In this letter, the AJC leadership explained the development of the negotiations and the AJC strategy to its members.

195. Alan Cowell, "Germany Defends Pensions for SS Veterans," *New York Times*, May 10, 1997.

196. AJC advertisement, "Guess Which One Receives a War Victims Pension from the German Government," *New York Times*, May 7, 1997.

197. AJC Archives, Digital Collection, Letter from 82 Senators to Kohl, August 1, 1997, accessed July 23, 2015, www.ajcarchives.org/AJC_DATA/Files/940.pdf.

198. AJC Archives, Digital Collection, AJCommitteeNEWS, "ACJCommittee Applauds German Government Announcement to Provide Compensation for Holocaust Survivors in Eastern Europe and Former Soviet Union," January 12, 1998, accessed July 23, 2015, www.ajcarchives.org/AJC_DATA/Files/946.pdf. For details about the settlement see Goschler, *Schuld*, 447–449.

199. Peck, *Tradition*, 19f.

200. AJC Archives, Digital Collection, AJCommitteeNEWS, "American Jewish Committee Opens Historic Berlin Office With Special Dedication Ceremonies," February 9, 1998, accessed July 23, 2015, www.ajcarchives.org/ajc_data/files/929.pdf. See also Feldman, "Jewish Role," 183f.

201. Feldman, "Jewish Role," 183f.

202. Baker, "Jewish Voice," 15.

203. Eizenstat, *Justice;* Kansteiner, *Pursuit*, 296–304; Surmann, *Shoah-Erinnerung*, 259–265. See also Brunner, Goschler, and Frei, "Vernetze Wiedergutmachung."

204. Neuss, "Brückenbauen," 59.

205. The origins of this monument have been amply documented and discussed, for instance, by Kirsch, *Nationaler Mythos;* Leggewie and Meyer, *"Ein Ort"*; Stavginski, *Holocaust-Denkmal;* and Kansteiner, *Pursuit*, 292–296.

206. Especially Sinti and Roma protested the fact that the monument should only be dedicated to Jewish victims of Nazi persecution: Stavginski, *Holocaust-Denkmal*, 58–61. A detailed overview—including images—of the different proposals is provided by Young, *Edge*, 184–223; for images see also Stavginski, *Holocaust-Denkmal*, 314–324.

207. "Kohl plädiert für zentrale Holocaust-Gedenkstätte," *SZ*, September 15, 1993. According to this report, members of the CDU's youth organization (Junge Union) and "others" had called for the German Holocaust monument to be modeled after the USHMM. See also Knoch, "Rückkehr," 133. For Kohl's interventions see Kirsch, *Nationaler Mythos*, 158–160.

208. For a detailed account see Reichel, *Politik*, 231–245.

209. This inscription was based on Federal President Richard von Weizsäcker's speech on the occasion of May 8, 1985.

210. Stavginski, *Holocaust-Denkmal*, 65f. See also Leggewie and Meyer, *"Ein Ort,"* 163; Kirsch, *Nationaler Mythos*, 158–160.

211. Leggewie and Meyer, *"Ein Ort,"* 165–171.

212. "Ich stelle mich in eine Ecke, wo man gar nicht bemerkt wird," interview with Helmut Kohl, *FAZ*, September 17, 1998.

213. Ibid. See also Kirsch, *"Wir,"* 43f., and Niven, *Past*, 218.

214. Quoted in Stefan Reinecke, "Der einzige mögliche Weg," *die tageszeitung*, August 26, 1998.

215. Kirsch, "Kern," 43.

216. Feldman, "Jewish Role," 185.

217. Stefan Reinecke, "Der einzige mögliche Weg," *die tageszeitung*, August 26, 1998. Reinecke stressed that justifying the monument this way would only serve right-wing extremists, who, after all believed in anti-Semitic theories about the "Jewish lobby." And indeed, in an allegedly "objective" analysis, a right-wing author wanted to answer the question "Who and what is the 'East Coast' of Dr. Helmut Kohl?," providing an anti-Semitic dossier about America's largest Jewish organizations. See Denes, *Macht in der Macht*.

218. Rudolf Augstein, "Wir sind alle verletzbar," *Der Spiegel* 49 (1998), 32f. See also Kirsch, *Nationaler Mythos*, 116.

219. Quote is an analysis of Augstein by Niven, *Past*, 218.

220. For a detailed account of the Bundestag's proceedings in this matter see Stavginski, *Holocaust-Denkmal*, 294f.

221. Kirsch, "Kern," 43f.

222. Josef Joffe, "Metaphysik eines Mahnmals," *SZ*, June 26, 1999. See also Kansteiner, *Pursuit*, 295 and Kirsch, *Nationaler Mythos*, 116.

223. "Ich stelle mich in eine Ecke, wo man gar nicht bemerkt wird," Interview with Helmut Kohl, *FAZ*, September 17, 1998. See also Brockman, " 'Normalization,' " 27.

Epilogue

1. 20th Anniversary National Tribute and Tour, United States Holocaust Memorial Museum Online, http://neveragain.ushmm.org/events.

2. United States Holocaust Memorial Museum, *Holocaust Memory in Europe*, C-Span Video, 41:32. April 29, 2013, accessed July 23, 2015, www.c-span.org/video/?312271-2/us-holocaust-museum-panel-future-holocaust-memory-europe.

3. Ibid.

4. Ibid.

5. Assmann, "Holocaust," 113.

6. Schmid, "Europäisierung," 174.

7. Eckel and Moisel, "Einleitung," 17f.; Assmann, "Holocaust," 97f.; Levy and Sznaider, *Holocaust and Memory*.

8. Bauerkämper, *Gedächtnis*, 15f. It is not possible to provide a comprehensive account of recent publications. The most important contributions on this topic include: Eckel and Moisel, "Einleitung"; Assmann, "Holocaust"; Levy and Sznaider, *Holocaust and Memory*; Kroh, *Erinnerung*; Judt, *Postwar*, 803–831; Rupnow, "Transformationen"; Kübler, *Erinnerungspolitik*.

9. Diner, "Vorwort," 9. See also Eckel and Moisel, "Einleitung."

10. Assmann, "Holocaust," 109–112.

11. For a recent overview on Holocaust memorials and museum see: Rotem, *Constructing Memory*.

12. Goldberg, " 'Jewish Narrative,' " 188. See also Kübler, *Erinnerungspolitik*, 11–30; Pakier and Stråth, eds., *European Memory?*; Kühberger and Sedmak, eds., *Europäische Geschichtskultur*.

13. Judt, *Postwar*, 803.

14. Assmann, "Holocaust," 101–105. Cf. Kroh, *Erinnerung*, 111–200; Kübler, *Erinnerungspolitik*, 17f.

15. Allwork, *Holocaust Remembrance*, 147–155.
16. Rupnow, "Transformationen," 70.
17. Schmid, "Europäisierung."
18. Judt, *Postwar*, 803–831.
19. Assmann and Conrad, "Introduction," 5. Cf. Schmid, "Europäisierung," 191.
20. Kübler, *Erinnerungspolitik*, 28.
21. Rosenfeld, *End*, 9f.; Association of Holocaust Organizations Online, accessed July 23, 2015, www.ahoinfo.org/.
22. MacDonald, "Daring to Compare," 104–112.
23. See Eckel and Moisel, "Einleitung," 17f.; Assmann, "Holocaust," 97f.
24. MacDonald, "Daring to Compare," 389–397.
25. Novick, *Holocaust in American Life*.
26. Judt with Snyder, *Thinking*, 273. See also Novick, *Holocaust in American Life*, 11–15.
27. Rosenfeld, *End*, 74f.
28. United States Holocaust Memorial Museum, *U.S. Holocaust Museum 20th Anniversary Tribute*, C-Span Video, 01:05:53. April 29, 2013, accessed July 23, 2015, www.c-span.org/video/?312271-1/us-holocaust-museum-20th-anniversary-tribute. Cf. Surmann, *Shoah-Erinnerung*, 237.
29. Bundesregierung, "USA-Reise de Maizère," May 1, 2013, accessed July 23, 2015, www.bundesregierung.de/ContentArchiv/DE/Archiv17/Artikel/2013/05/2013-05-01-de-maiziere-washington.html.
30. Flanzbaum, "Introduction"; Rosenfeld, "Americanization."
31. Benz, *Antisemitismus*, 19f.
32. Quoted in BArch B 136/42205, AA (Schütte) to Kinkel, "Deutschland-Bild amerikanischer Juden: Beobachtungen auf einer Vortragsreise durch die USA," June 4, 1996.
33. Feldman, "Jewish Role," 180–182.
34. Quoted in BArch N 1396/3, Petersen to Kohl, February 5, 1985.
35. Herbert, *Geschichte*, 1193–1206; Kirsch, *Nationaler Mythos*, 45–80; Rürup, *Schatten*, 127–144.
36. Kirsch, *Nationaler Mythos*, 78.
37. Borggräfe, *Zwangsarbeiterentschädigung*; Brunner, Goschler, and Frei, eds., *Globalisierung*.
38. For the impact on relations with Israel on this learning process in Germany see Wolffsohn, *Guilt*, 30–41.
39. Kirsch, "Kern," 43f.
40. "Ich stelle mich in eine Ecke, wo man gar nicht bemerkt wird," Interview with Helmut Kohl, *FAZ*, September 17, 1998. See also Brockman, "'Normalization,'" 27.
41. Kirsch, "Kern," 43.
42. This is a lesson, by the way, the Turkish government still struggles with as a recognition of the Armenian Genocide stands in its way (in addition to other reasons) to join the EU. See: Judt, *Postwar*, 803.
43. Müller, "Europäische Erinnerungspolitik," 166.
44. Kansteiner, *Pursuit*, 279. See also Assmann, *Unbehagen*, 59f.; Frei, *1945*, 37–40; and Sharples, *Postwar Germany*, 166f.
45. Maier, *Past*.
46. Lazar, "Foreign Service." See also Frei and Hayes, "German Foreign Office," Browning "German Foreign Office Revisited," and a number of other contributions in the same volume of the *Bulletin of the GHI*.
47. Conze et al., *Amt*. The members of the independent commission included Eckart Conze, Norbert Frei, Peter Hayes, Klaus Hildebrand (until 2008), and Moshe Zimmermann. For a full list of contributors to *Das Amt* see ibid., 4. For the debate about the book see Sabrow and Mentel, eds., *Amt*.
48. See the introduction to Conze et al., *Amt*, 10–21.

Bibliography

Archival Sources

ARCHIV DES INSTITUTS FÜR ZEITGESCHICHTE MUNICH-BERLIN, MUNICH (IFZ)

Archives of the Institute for Contemporary History, Munich
  ED 379 (Hildegard Hamm-Brücher Papers).

ARCHIV DES LIBERALISMUS, GUMMERSBACH

Archive of Liberalism, Gummersbach
  N49 (Hildegard Hamm-Brücher Papers).

ARCHIV FÜR CHRISTLICH-DEMOKRATISCHE POLITIK, ST. AUGUSTIN (ACDP)

Archive for Christian Democratic Politics, St. Augustin
  07-001 (CDU Bundespartei).
  01-747 (Michael Mertes Papers).

ARCHIVES OF THE AMERICAN JEWISH COMMITTEE, NEW YORK (AJC ARCHIVES)

NB: The Archives of the AJC offers access to a large number of archival documents via its website, but in most cases, a call number of a document is not available online. These documents can be found on the website www.ajcarchives.org/ajcarchive/DigitalArchive.aspx and hyperlinks have been supplied with the respective collection or document.
  Bitburg File (online).
    http://ajcarchives.org/ajcarchive/FileViewer.aspx?id=16364.
  Digital Collection (online).
    Hyperlinks are provided in endnotes with cited documents.
  International Relations Department.
    File A: Atlantik-Brücke [*sic*]/AJC Conference File, Press releases, reports and memoranda on the conference, 1987, http://ajcarchives.org/ajcarchive/FileViewer.aspx?id=16365.
    File B: Atlantik-Brücke [*sic*]/AJC Conference File, Speeches, proposals, and a paper by Dr. Alvin H. Rosenfeld, 1987, http://ajcarchives.org/ajcarchive/FileViewer.aspx?id=16366.
  William Trosten Files.

BUNDEARCHIV KOBLENZ (BARCH)

German Federal Archives, Koblenz Branch
  B 136 (Bundeskanzleramt/German Chancellery). Access was granted to these files according to IFG or BArchG and files were accessed at the BArch, Koblenz.
  B 138 (Bundesministerium für Bildung und Wissenschaft/Federal Ministry of Education and Science). Access was granted to these files according to IFG or BArchG and files were accessed at the BArch, Koblenz.

B 145 (Presse- und Informationsamt der Bundesregierung/Press and Information Agency of the Federal Government). Access was granted to these files according to IFG or BArchG and files were accessed at the BArch, Koblenz.

B 196 (Bundesministerium für Forschung und Technologie/Federal Ministry of Research and Technology). Access was granted to these files according to IFG and files were accessed in the ministry in Bonn, which is now called Bundesministerium für Bildung und Forschung (Federal Ministry of Education and Research).

N 1396 (Peter Petersen Papers).

INSTITUTIONAL ARCHIVES OF THE UNITED STATES HOLOCAUST MEMORIAL MUSEUM, WASHINGTON, DC (USHMM IA)

Accession No. 1997-004 (Communications Department, Director Sam Eskenazi's Subject Files).

Accession No. 1997-013 (USHMC, Records of the Chairman Elie Wiesel, 1978–1986).

Accession No. 1997-014 (Director's Office, Records of the Museum Director Jeshajahu "Shaike" Weinberg, 1979–1994).

Accession No. 1998-004 (Archives Branch, Subject Files of Archives Director Brewster S. Chamberlin, 1992–1996).

Accession No. 1998-011 (Research Institute, Records of the Director Michael Berenbaum).

Accession No. 2000.035 (Oral History Branch, Audiotape Recordings of the Institutional Oral History Project Featuring the Museum's Founders, 2000).

Accession No. 2000.051 (USHMC, Minutes of the Council Meetings, 1980– 1993).

Accession No. 2001.165 (USHMC, Reports to the USHMC Relating to European Holocaust Archives, Memorials, and Museums, 1980–1989).

Accession No. 2005.154 (Historian's Office, Sybil Milton, Research Subject Files, 1984–1987, A—N, accretion to series 2000.102).

Accession No. 1997- 017 (Historian's Office, Sybil Milton's Correspondence).

NEW YORK PUBLIC LIBRARY, NEW YORK (NYPL)

Dorot Jewish Division, Newspaper Collection.

Oral Histories, Box 111, No. 6 (Oral History William Trosten).

NIEDERSÄCHSICHES LANDESARCHIV-STAATSARCHIV WOLFENBÜTTEL

State Archive of Lower Saxony, Wolfenbüttel Branch

143 N (Georg-Eckert-Institut, Braunschweig).

POLITISCHES ARCHIV DES AUSWÄRTIGEN AMTS, BERLIN (PA AA)

Political Archives of the Foreign Office, Berlin

B 32 204 (USA, GB, Kanada, Nordische Staaten, Österreich, Schweiz).

B 90/600 (Kulturpolitik, Grundsatzangelegenheiten).

B 94-604 (Wissenschaft, Hochschulen, Jugendfragen, Sport).

B 94-621 (Wissenschaft, Hochschulen, Deutsches Archäologisches Institut).

Neues Amt (German Representations Abroad).

RONALD REAGAN PRESIDENTIAL LIBRARY, SIMI VALLEY, CA

James Rentschler Papers.

Marshall Breger Papers.

TEMPLE UNIVERSITY LIBRARIES, SPECIAL COLLECTIONS, PHILADELPHIA, PA

Franklin Littell Papers.

UNIVERSITY OF VERMONT LIBRARIES, SPECIAL COLLECTIONS, BURLINGTON, VT (UVM)

Record Group 074.005 (Raul Hilberg Papers).

Minutes of Plenary Proceedings of the Deutscher Bundestag

Deutscher Bundestag. Plenarprotokoll. Stenographischer Bericht der 121. Sitzung der 9. Wahlperiode (October 13, 1982), 7213–7292.

Deutscher Bundestag. Plenarprotokoll. Stenographischer Bericht der 4. Sitzung der 10. Wahlperiode (May 4, 1983), 55–146.

Deutscher Bundestag. Plenarprotokoll. Stenographischer Bericht der 53. Sitzung der 10. Wahlperiode (February 9, 1984), 3725–3861.

Deutscher Bundestag. Plenarprotokoll. Stenographischer Bericht der 137. Sitzung der 10. Wahlperiode (May 14, 1985), 10159–10238.

Deutscher Bundestag. Plenarprotokoll. Stenographischer Bericht der 253. Sitzung der 10. Wahlperiode (December 4, 1986), 19629–19776.

Deutscher Bundestag. Plenarprotokoll. Stenographischer Bericht der 4. Sitzung der 11. Wahlperiode (March 18, 1987), 51–135.

Newspapers, Magazines, and Periodicals

Commentary, Der Aufbau, Der Tagesspiegel, Der Spiegel, Deutsche National-Zeitung, Deutsches Allgemeines Sonntagsblatt, die tageszeitung, Die Zeit, Frankfurter Allgemeine Zeitung (FAZ), Jewish Chronicle, Jüdische Allgemeine, Long Island Jewish World, Los Angeles Times, Los Angeles Times Magazine, Newsweek, New York Times, New York Times Magazine, San Francisco Jewish Bulletin, Spiegel Online, St. Louis Post-Dispatch, Süddeutsche Zeitung (SZ), The Clipper, The Jewish Transcript, The New Republic, The Seattle Times, The Week in Germany, Time Magazine, Wall Street Journal, Washington Post.

Interviews

Andrew Baker, April 12, 2011 (Washington, DC); Michael Berenbaum, July 19, 2006 (Washington, DC); Wolfgang Bergsdorf, March 1, 2010 (St. Augustin); J.D. Bindenagel, April 12, 2010 (phone interview); Wolf Calebow, March 16, 2010 (Baden-Baden); Dieter Dettke, May 19, 2010 (Washington, DC); Hasia R. Diner, June 16, 2011 (Antwerp); Eugene DuBow, April 22, 2010 (New York City); Raye Farr, June 29, 2006 (Washington, DC); Marc Fisher, May 24, 2010 (Washington, DC); Henry Friedlander, June 30, 2006 (Washington, DC); Lily Gardner Feldman, May 27, 2010 (Washington, DC); Peter Hermes, 2010 (exchange of letters); Raul Hilberg, June 28, 2006 (phone interview); Saul Kagan, April 23, 2010 (New York City); Craig Kennedy, April 16, 2010 (Washington, DC); Walther Leisler Kiep, September 14, 2006 (phone interview); John Kornblum, March 2, 2010 (Berlin); Miles Lerman, July 29, 2006 (phone interview); Vernon Lidtke, May 25, 2010 (Baltimore, MD); Beate Lindemann, February 22, 2010 (Berlin); Michael Mertes, July 20, 2006 (phone interview) and March 4, 2010 (Berlin); Wolfgang Pordzik, April 12, 2010 (Washington, DC); Josef Rembser, March 1, 2010 (Bonn/Wachtberg); Jeffrey Richter, April 14, 2011 (Washington, DC); Heinz Riesenhuber, January 20, 2010 (phone interview); Hanna Schissler, March 3, 2010 (Berlin); Waldemar Schreckenberger, March 24, 2010 (Heidelberg); Paul Shapiro, April 14, 2011 (Washington, DC); Immo Stabreit, March 4, 2010 (Berlin); Michael Stürmer, February 22, 2010 (Berlin); Hans N. "Tom" Tuch, April 28, 2010 (Bethesda, MD); Barthold C. Witte, February 28, 2010 (Bonn/Bad Godesberg).

Video Recordings

American Jewish Committee. *Jewish Dimension: German Jewish Exchange.* WPIX-TV, 23:04. August 10, 1983. www.ajcarchives.org/main.php?DocumentId=15860.

"Reagan at Bitburg." YouTube video, 1:28:33. Televised as an NBC News Special on May 5, 1985. Posted by "craig80909," October 9, 2013. www.youtube.com/watch?v=7pAebjd_-aU.

United States Holocaust Memorial Museum. *Holocaust Memory in Europe*. C-Span Video, 41:32. April 29, 2013. www.c-span.org/video/?312271-2/us-holocaust-museum-panel-future-holocaust-memory-europe.

United States Holocaust Memorial Museum. *U.S. Holocaust Museum 20th Anniversary Tribute*. C-Span Video, 01:05:53. April 29, 2013. www.c-span.org/video/?312271-1/us-holocaust-museum-20th-anniversary-tribute.

Online Resources/Websites

Bundesregierung. www.bundesregierung.de.

Holocaust Memorial Center. www.holocaustcenter.org.

Konrad Adenauer Foundation. "Geschichte der CDU." www.kas.de/wf/de/71.9060/.

Los Angeles Museum of the Holocaust. "History." www.lamoth.org/the-museum/history.

Munzinger Online/Personen—Internationales Biographisches Archiv. www.munzinger.de.

United States Holocaust Memorial Museum. www.ushmm.org.

Books, Articles, and Theses

AAPD 1979 I (Akten zur Auswärtigen Politik der Bundesrepublik Deutschland). Ed. for the Auswärtiges Amt by the Institute für Zeitgeschichte (Horst Möller, Klaus Hildebrand, and Gregor Schöllgen). Munich: Oldenbourg, 2010.

Aguilar, Manuela. *Cultural Diplomacy and Foreign Policy: German-American Relations, 1955–1968*. New York: Peter Lang, 1996.

"AHR Conversation: On Transnational History," with C. A. Bayly, Sven Beckert, Matthew Connelly, Isabel Hofmeyr, Wendy Kozol, and Patricia Seed, *American Historical Review* 111 (December 2006), 1440–1464.

Alternatives in Religious Education, *Gestapo. A Learning Experience about the Holocaust*. Denver, CO: Alternatives in Religious Education, 1976.

Allwork, Larissa. *Holocaust Remembrance between the National and the Transnational: The Stockholm International Forum and the First Decade of the International Task Force*. London et al.: Bloomsbury, 2015.

American Jewish Committee, "Current Concerns in Germany and in German-American Jewish Relations: Summary of a Conference Held by the American Jewish Committee, and the Atlantik-Brücke, in New York City, January 17–19, 1993." New York: AJC, 1993.

Assmann, Aleida. *Das neue Unbehagen an der Erinnerungskultur: Eine Intervention*. Munich: Beck, 2013.

Assmann, Aleida. *Der lange Schatten der Vergangenheit: Erinnerungskultur und Geschichtspolitik*. Munich: Beck, 2006.

Assmann, Aleida. "The Holocaust: A Global Memory? Extensions and Limits of a New Memory Community." In *Memory in a Global Age: Discourses, Practices and Trajectories*, edited by Aleida Assmann and Sebastian Conrad, 97–117. Houndmills: Palgrave Macmillan, 2010.

Assmann, Aleida, and Sebastian Conrad, eds. *Memory in a Global Age: Discourses, Practices and Trajectories*. Houndmills: Palgrave Macmillan, 2010.

Assmann, Aleida, and Sebastian Conrad. "Introduction." In *Memory in a Global Age: Discourses, Practices and Trajectories*, edited by Aleida Assmann and Sebastian Conrad, 1–16. Houndmills: Palgrave Macmillan, 2010.

Assmann, Aleida and Ute Frevert. *Geschichtsvergessenheit—Geschichtsversessenheit: Vom Umgang mit deutschen Vergangenheiten nach 1945*. Stuttgart: Deutsche Verlags-Anstalt, 1999.

Atlantik-Brücke e.V., *Jahresbericht Juni 2010 bis Juni 2011*. Berlin: Atlantik-Brücke e. V., 2011.

Auswärtiges Amt, ed. *Brücken über den Atlantik 1988: Jahresbericht des Koordinators für die deutsch-amerikanische zwischengesellschaftliche, kultur- und informationspolitische Zusammenarbeit; Professor Dr. Werner Weidenfeld.* Bonn: Auswärtiges Amt, n.d.

Babel, Rainer, and Rolf Große, eds. *Das Deutsche Historische Institut Paris: 1958–2008.* Ostfildern: Jan Thorbecke Verlag, 2008.

Baker, Andrew. "The Jewish Voice in German-American Relations." In "The Jewish Voice in Transatlantic Relations," edited by Jeffrey M. Peck. Special issue, *AICGS German-American Issues*, no. 1 (2004): 13–15. www.aicgs.org/site/wp-content/uploads/2011/10/aicgsgermanamerican.pdf.

Bahners, Patrick. *Im Mantel der Geschichte: Helmut Kohl oder Die Unersetzlichkeit.* Berlin: Siedler, 1998.

Baldwin, Peter, ed. *Reworking the Past: Hitler, the Holocaust, and the Historians' Debate.* Boston: Beacon Press, 1990.

Barkan, Elazar. *The Guilt of Nations: Restitution and Negotiating Historical Injustices.* New York and London: W.W. Norton & Company, 2000.

Bartov, Omer. "Chambers of Horror: Holocaust Museums in Israel and the United States." *Israel Studies* 2, no. 2 (Fall 1997): 66–87.

Bauerkämper, Arnd. *Das Umstrittene Gedächtnis: Die Erinnerung an Nationalsozialismus, Faschismus und Krieg in Europa seit 1945.* Paderborn: Ferdinand Schöningh, 2012.

Baumeister, Martin. "Thomas Nipperdey (1927–1992)." In *Münchner Historiker zwischen Politik und Wissenschaft: 150 Jahre Historisches Seminar der Ludwig-Maximilians-Universität München*, edited by Katharina Weigand, 309–328. Munich: Herbert Utz Verlag, 2010.

Beattie, Andrew H. "The Past in the Politics of Divided and Unified Germany." In *Partisan Histories: The Past in Contemporary Global Politics*, edited by Max Paul Friedman and Padraic Kenney, 17–37. New York: Palgrave Macmillan, 2005.

Belzberg Architects. *The Los Angeles Holocaust Museum.* Berkeley: Publishers Group West, 2012.

Bender, Thomas, ed. *Rethinking American History in a Global Age.* Berkeley: University of California Press, 2002.

Benz, Wolfgang. *Was ist Antisemitismus?* Munich: Beck, 2004.

Berenbaum, Michael. *The World Must Know: The History of the Holocaust as Told in the United States Holocaust Memorial Museum.* Boston: Little Brown, 1993.

Berger, Deidre. "Learning to Stop Hating Germans: The Challenge of Journalistic Objectivity." In *A User's Guide to German Cultural Studies*, edited by Scott Denham, Irene Kacandes, and Jonathan Petropoulos, 93–111. Ann Arbor: University of Michigan Press, 1997.

Berger, Deidre, and Jens Paulus, eds. *"A Life-Changing Experience:" 30 Jahre KAS/AJC-Austauschprogramm.* St. Augustin: Konrad Adenauer Foundation, 2010. www.kas.de/wf/doc/kas_19725-544-1-30.pdf?110427115734.

Berger, Stefan. *The Search for Normality: National Identity and Historical Consciousness in Germany Since 1800.* New York and Oxford: Berghahn Books, 1997.

Berger, Thomas. "The Power of Memory and Memories of Power: The Cultural Parameters of German Foreign Policy-Making since 1945." In *Memory and Power in Post-War Europe: Studies in the Presence of the Past*, edited by Jan-Werner Müller, 76–99. Cambridge: Cambridge University Press, 2002.

Berghahn, Volker. *America and the Intellectual Cold Wars in Europe: Shepard Stone between Philanthropy, Academy, and Diplomacy.* Princeton, NJ: Princeton University Press, 2001.

Berghahn, Volker. "Geschichtswissenschaft und Große Politik." *Aus Politik und Zeitgeschichte* 11 (March 1987): 25–37.

Berghoff, Hartmut, and Richard F. Wetzell, "The German Historical Institute in Washington, 1987–2012: A Short History." *Bulletin of the German Historical Institute* 50, supplement 8 (2012): 7–31.

Bergmann, Werner. *Antisemitismus in öffentlichen Konflikten: Kollektives Lernen in der politischen Kultur der Bundesrepublik 1949–1989.* Frankfurt am Main and New York: Campus, 1997.

Bergmann, Werner. "Die Bitburg-Affäre in der deutschen Presse: Rechtskonservative und linksliberale Interpretationen." In Werner Bergmann, Rainer Erb, and Albert Lichtblau, eds. *Schwieriges Erbe: Der Umgang mit Nationalsozialismus und Antisemitismus in Österreich, der DDR und der Bundesrepublik Deutschland*, 408–427. Frankfurt am Main and New York: Campus, 1995.

Bergmann, Werner. "Sekundärer Antisemitismus." In *Handbuch des Antisemitismus: Judenfeindschaft in Geschichte und Gegenwart*, edited by Wolfgang Benz, 3: 300–302. Berlin: Walter de Gruyter, 2010.

Bielefeld University. "Collaborative Research Centre (SFB) 584: The Political as Communicative Space in History." www.uni-bielefeld.de/geschichte/forschung/sfb584/SFB-584-Research-Programme.pdf.

Bierling, Stephan. *Die Außenpolitik der Bundesrepublik Deutschland: Normen, Akteure, Entscheidungen*. Munich: Oldenbourg, 1999.

Biess, Frank, and Robert G. Moeller, eds. *Histories of the Aftermath: The Legacies of the Second World War in Europe*. New York and Oxford: Berghahn Books, 2010.

Blaschke, Olaf, and Lutz Raphael. "Im Kampf um Positionen: Änderungen im Feld der französischen und deutschen Geschichtswissenschaft nach 1945." In *Neue Zugänge zur Geschichte der Geschichtswissenschaft*, edited by Jan Eckel and Thomas Etzemüller, 69–109. Göttingen: Wallstein, 2007.

Bole, William. "Bitburg: The American Scene." In *Bitburg in Moral and Political Perspective*, edited by Geoffrey H. Hartman, 66–79. Bloomington: Indiana University Press, 1986.

Borggräfe, Henning. *Zwangsarbeiterentschädigung: Vom Streit um "vergessene Opfer" zur Selbstaussöhnung der Deutschen*. Göttingen: Wallstein, 2014.

Bormann, Patrick, Thomas Freiberger, and Judith Michel, eds. *Angst in den internationalen Beziehungen*. Bonn: Bonn University Press, 2010.

Bösch, Frank. "Film, NS-Vergangenheit und Geschichtswissenschaft: Von 'Holocaust' zu 'Der Untergang.'" *Vierteljahrshefte für Zeitgeschichte* 55, no. 1 (2007): 1–32.

Bösch, Frank. "Die Krise als Chance: Die Neuformierung der Christdemokraten in den siebziger Jahren." In *Das Ende der Zuversicht? Die siebziger Jahre als Geschichte*, edited by Konrad Jarausch, 288–301. Göttingen: Vandenhoeck & Ruprecht, 2008.

Bösch, Frank, and Norman Domeier. "Cultural History of Politics: Concepts and Debates." *European Review of History/Revue europeenne d'histoire* 15, no. 6 (2008): 577–586.

Bösch, Frank, and Constantin Goschler, eds. *Public History: Öffentliche Darstellung des Nationalsozialismus jenseits der Geschichtswissenschaft*. Frankfurt am Main and New York: Campus, 2009.

Bösch, Frank, and Peter Hoeres, eds. *Außenpolitik im Medienzeitalter: Vom späten 19. Jahrhundert bis zur Gegenwart*. Göttingen: Wallstein, 2013.

Bösch, Frank, and Peter Hoeres. "Im Bann der Öffentlichkeit? Der Wandel der Außenpolitik im Medienzeitalter." In *Außenpolitik im Medienzeitalter: Vom späten 19. Jahrhundert bis zur Gegenwart*, edited by Frank Bösch and Peter Hoeres, 7–35. Göttingen: Wallstein, 2013.

Brebeck, Wulff E., ed. *Zur Arbeit in Gedenkstätten für die Opfer des Nationalsozialismus: Ein internationaler Überblick*. Berlin: Aktion Sühnezeichen Friedensdienste, 1988.

Breitman, Richard, and Allan J. Lichtman. *F.D.R. and the Jews*. Cambridge, MA: The Belknap Press of Harvard University Press, 2013.

Bressensdorf, Agnes Bresselau von. *Frieden durch Kommunikation: Das System Genscher und die Entspannungspolitik im Zweiten Kalten Krieg 1979–1982/83*. Berlin and Boston: Walter de Gruyter, 2015.

Breuilly, J.J. "Telling it as it was? Thomas Nipperdey's History of Nineteenth-Century Germany." *History* 80, no. 258 (1995): 59–70.

Brinkmann, Tobias. "Amerika und der Holocaust: Die Debatte über die 'Amerikanisierung des Holocaust' in den USA und ihre Rezeption in Deutschland." *Neue politische Literatur* 48, no. 2 (2003): 251–270.

Brochhagen, Ulrich. *Nach Nürnberg: Vergangenheitsbewältigung und Westintegration in der Ära Adenauer*. Hamburg: Junius, 1994.

Brockman, Stephen. "'Normalization': Has Helmut Kohl's Vision Been Realized?" In *German Culture, Politics, and Literature into the Twenty-First Century: Beyond Normalization*, edited by Stuart Taberner and Paul Cooke, 17–29. Rochester, NY: Camden House, 2006.

Broder, Henryk M. *Vergesst Auschwitz! Der deutsche Erinnerungswahn und die Endlösung der Israel-Frage*. 2nd ed. Munich: Knaus, 2012.

Browning, Christopher R. "The German Foreign Office Revisited." *Bulletin of the German Historical Institute* 49 (Fall 2011): 71–79.

Browning, Christopher R. *Ordinary Men: Reserve Police Battalion 101 and the Final Solution in Poland*. Reissued ed. New York, HaperCollins Publishers, 1998.

Brunner, José, Constantin Goschler, and Norbert Frei, eds. *Die Globalisierung der Wiedergutmachung: Politik, Moral, Moralpolitik*. Göttingen: Wallstein, 2013.

Brunner, José, Constantin Goschler, and Norbert Frei. "Vernetzte Wiedergutmachung: Die Praxis der Entschädigung von NS-Verbrechen nach dem Kalten Krieg." In *Die Globalisierung der Wiedergutmachung: Politik, Moral, Moralpolitik*, edited by José Brunner, Constantin Goschler, and Norbert Frei, 7–33. Göttingen: Wallstein, 2013.

Buchstab, Günter, and Hans-Otto Kleinmann, eds. *Helmut Kohl: Berichte zur Lage 1982–1989; Der Kanzler und Parteivorsitzende im Bundesvorstand der CDU Deutschlands*. Düsseldorf: Droste, 2014.

Buchstab, Günter, and Hans-Otto Kleinmann. "Einleitung." In *Helmut Kohl: Berichte zur Lage 1982–1989; Der Kanzler und Parteivorsitzende im Bundesvorstand der CDU Deutschlands*, edited by Günter Buchstab, and Hans-Otto Kleinmann, vii–lx. Düsseldorf: Droste, 2014.

Buchstab, Günter, and Hans-Otto Kleinmann, eds. *Helmut Kohl: Berichte zur Lage 1989–1998; Der Kanzler und Parteivorsitzende im Bundesvorstand der CDU Deutschlands*. Düsseldorf: Droste, 2012.

Buchstab, Günter, Hans-Otto Kleinmann, and Hanns Jürgen Küsters, eds. *Die Ära Kohl im Gespräch: Eine Zwischenbilanz*. Cologne: Böhlau, 2010.

Budde, Gunilla, Sebastian Conrad, and Oliver Janz, eds. *Transnationale Geschichte: Themen, Tendenzen und Theorien*. Göttingen: Vandenhoek & Ruprecht, 2006.

Calebow, Wolf. *Auf dem Weg zur Normalisierung: 15 Jahre Dialog mit amerikanischen Juden*. Berlin: Berlin Verlag Arno Spitz GmbH, 1999.

Calleo, David P. *The German Problem Reconsidered: Germany and the World Order, 1870 to the Present*. Cambridge: Cambridge University Press, 1978.

Caplan, Jane. "Reflections on the Reception of Goldhagen in the United States." In *The "Goldhagen Effect:" History, Memory, Nazism; Facing the German Past*, edited by Geoff Eley, 151–162. Ann Arbor: University of Michigan Press, 2000.

Cherfas, Lina, Paul Rozin et al. "The Framing of Atrocities: Documenting and Exploring Wide Variation in Aversion to Germans and German-Related Activities Among Holocaust Survivors." *Peace and Conflict: Journal of Peace Psychology* 12, no. 1 (2006): 65–80.

Classen, Christoph. "Die Fernsehserie 'Holocaust' (1979): Rückblicke auf eine 'betroffene Nation'." In Zeitgeschichte-online (March 2004/October 2005). www.zeitgeschichte-online.de/sites/default/files/documents/classen_einf.pdf.

Claussen, Detlev. *Vom Judenhass zum Antisemitismus: Materialien einer verleugneten Geschichte*. Darmstadt: Luchterhand, 1987.

Clavin, Patricia. "Defining Transnationalism." *Contemporary European History* 14, no. 4 (2005): 421–439.

Clemens, Clay. "Kohl's Image of America." In *Germany and America: Essays in Honor of Gerald R. Kleinfeld*, edited by Wolfgang-Uwe Friedrich, 178–195. New York and Oxford: Berghahn Books, 2001.

Clemens, Clay, and William E. Paterson, eds. "The Kohl Chancellorship." Special Issue of *German Politics* 7, no. 1 (1998).

Cohen, Beth B. *Case Closed: Holocaust Survivors in Postwar America*. New Brunswick, NJ: Rutgers University Press, 2007.

Cole, Tim. *Selling the Holocaust: From Auschwitz to Schindler; How History is Bought, Packaged, and Sold*. New York: Routledge, 1999.

262 *Bibliography*

Confino, Alon. *Germany as a Culture of Remembrance: Promises and Limits of Writing History.* Chapel Hill: University of North Carolina Press, 2006.

Conze, Eckart. "Jenseits von Nation und Staat? Die Renaissance der Politikgeschichte im 21. Jahrhundert." In *Was heißt und zu welchem Ende studiert man Geschichte des 20. Jahrhunderts?*, edited by Norbert Frei, 140–146. Göttingen: Wallstein, 2006.

Conze, Eckart, Ulrich Lappenküper, and Guido Müller, eds. *Geschichte der internationalen Beziehungen. Erneuerung und Erweiterung einer historischen Disziplin.* Cologne: Böhlau, 2004.

Conze, Eckart. *Die Suche nach Sicherheit: Eine Geschichte der Bundesrepublik Deutschland von 1949 bis zur Gegenwart.* Munich: Siedler, 2009.

Conze, Eckart, Norbert Frei, Peter Hayes, and Moshe Zimmermann. *Das Amt und die Vergangenheit: Deutsche Diplomaten im Dritten Reich und in der Bundesrepublik.* Munich: Karl Blessing Verlag, 2010.

Cornelißen, Christoph. "Erinnerungskulturen," in *Docupedia-Zeitgeschichte* (February 2, 2010). http://docupedia.de/zg/Erinnerungskulturen.

Cull, Nicholas J. "Public Diplomacy: Taxonomies and Histories." *The ANNALS of the American Academy of Political and Social Science* 616, no. 1 (2008): 31–54.

Danyel, Jürgen. *Die geteilte Vergangenheit: Zum Umgang mit Nationalsozialismus und Widerstand in beiden deutschen Staaten.* Berlin: Akademie Verlag, 1995.

Daum, Andreas W. "The Second Generation: German Émigré Historians in the Transatlantic World, 1945 to the Present." *Bulletin of the German Historical Institute* 51 (Fall 2012): 116–121.

Daum, Andreas W., Hartmut Lehmann, and James J. Sheehan, eds. *The Second Generation: Émigrés from Nazi Germany as Historians.* New York and Oxford: Berghahn Books, 2015.

De Grazia, Victoria. *Irresistible Empire: America's Advance through Twentieth-Century Europe.* Cambridge, MA: The Belknap Press of Harvard University Press, 2005.

Denes, Ivan. *Macht in der Macht: wer und was ist die "Östküste" des Dr. Helmut Kohl? Jüdische Organisationen in den USA; ein Dossier.* Berlin: Oberbaum, 2000.

Dettling, Benedikt, and Michael Geske. "Helmut Kohl: Krise und Erneuerung." In *"Das Wort hat der Herr Bundeskanzler:" Eine Analyse der großen Regierungserklärungen von Adenauer bis Schröder*, edited by Karl-Rudolf Korte, 217–245. Wiesbaden: Westdeutscher Verlag, 2002.

Dettling, Warnfried. "Politik, Freiheit und Glück: Über Ursachen und Folgen des Wertwandels." *Simmen der Zeit* 6 (June 1979): 363–372.

Dettling, Warnfried. "Politik, Freiheit und Glück: Die Folgen des Wertwandels für die Politik." *Simmen der Zeit* 7 (July 1979): 457–468.

Deutschkron, Inge. *Israel und die Deutschen: Das schwierige Verhältnis.* Rev. ed. Cologne: Verlag Wissenschaft und Politik, 1991.

Dietze, Carola, and Richard F. Wetzell. "The Early Years of the GHI: An Interview with the Institute's Founding Director, Hartmut Lehmann." *Bulletin of the German Historical Institute* 42 (Spring 2008): 39–47.

Diner, Dan. "Vorwort des Herausgebers." In *Zivilisationsbruch: Denken nach Auschwitz*, edited by Dan Diner, 7–13. Frankfurt am Main: Fischer, 1988.

Diner, Dan, ed. *Zivilisationsbruch: Denken nach Auschwitz.* Frankfurt am Main: Fischer, 1988.

Diner, Hasia R. *The Jews of the United States: 1654–2000.* Berkeley: University of California Press, 2004.

Diner, Hasia R. *We Remember with Reverence and Love: American Jews and the Myth of Silence after the Holocaust; 1945–1962.* New York: New York University Press, 2009.

Doering-Manteuffel, Anselm. *Wie westlich sind die Deutschen? Amerikanisierung und Westernisierung im 20. Jahrhundert.* Göttingen: Vandenhoeck und Ruprecht, 1999.

Doering-Manteuffel, Anselm, and Lutz Raphael. *Nach dem Boom: Perspektiven auf die Zeitgeschichte seit 1970.* Göttingen: Vandenhoeck & Ruprecht, 2008.

Dollinger, Marc. *Quest for Inclusion: Jews and Liberalism in Modern America.* Princeton, NJ: Princeton University Press, 2000.

Doneson, Judith E. *The Holocaust in American Film*. 2nd ed. Syracuse, NY: Syracuse University Press, 2002.

Dregger. Alfred. "Congressional Letter Fills Me With Dismay." April 19, 1985. In *Bitburg and Beyond: Encounters in American, German and Jewish History*, edited by Ilya Levkov, 95. New York: Shapolsky Publishers, 1987.

Dreher, Klaus. *Helmut Kohl: Leben mit Macht*. Stuttgart: Deutsche Verlags-Anstalt, 1998.

DuBow, Eugene. "'The Adenauer': Eine persönliche Retrospektive auf dreißig Jahre." In *"A Life-Changing Experience:" 30 Jahre KAS/AJC-Austauschprogramm*, edited by Deidre Berger and Jens Paulus, 63–66. St. Augustin: Konrad Adenauer Foundation. www.kas.de/wf/doc/kas_19725-544-1-30.pdf?110427115734.

Dubiel, Helmut. *Niemand ist frei von der Geschichte: Die nationalsozialistische Herrschaft in den Debatten des Deutschen Bundestages*. Munich: Carl Hanser Verlag, 1999.

Dworok, Gerrit. *"Historikerstreit" und Nationswerdung: Ursprünge und Deutung eines bundesrepublikanischen Konflikts*. Cologne et al.: Böhlau, 2015.

Eckel, Jan, and Thomas Etzemüller, eds. *Neue Zugänge zur Geschichte der Geschichtswissenschaft*. Göttingen: Wallstein, 2007.

Eckel, Jan, and Claudia Moisel. "Einleitung." In "Universalisierung des Holocaust?," edited by Jan Eckel and Claudia Moisel, *Beiträge zur Geschichte des Nationalsozialismus* 24 (2008): 9–25.

Eckel, Jan, and Claudia Moisel, eds. "Universalisierung des Holocaust?" *Beiträge zur Geschichte des Nationalsozialismus* 24 (2008).

Eckert, Astrid M., and Vera Ziegeldorf, eds. *Der Holocaust und die westdeutschen Historiker: Eine Debatte*. Berlin: Clio-online and Humboldt University Berlin, 2004. http://edoc.hu-berlin.de/e_histfor/2/PDF/HistFor_2-2004.pdf.

Eder, Jacob S. "Ein 'Holocaustsyndrom'? Die politischen Beziehungen zwischen der Bundesrepublik und amerikanisch-jüdischen Organisationen in den achtziger Jahren." *Archiv für Sozialgeschichte* 52 (2012): 633–665.

Eder, Jacob S. "Holocaust Angst: The Federal Republic of Germany and Holocaust Memory in the United States, 1977–98." PhD diss., University of Pennsylvania, 2012.

Eder, Jacob S. "Holocaust-Erinnerung als deutsch-amerikanische Konfliktgeschichte: Die bundesdeutschen Reaktionen auf das United States Holocaust Memorial Museum in Washington, D.C." In "Universalisierung des Holocaust?," edited by Jan Eckel and Claudia Moisel, *Beiträge zur Geschichte des Nationalsozialismus* 24 (2008): 109–134.

Eder, Jacob S., Philipp Gassert, and Alan E. Steinweis, eds. *Holocaust Memory in a Globalizing World*. Göttingen: Wallstein, 2016.

Eder, Jacob S., and Christian Mentel. "Finkelstein-Debatte." In *Handbuch des Antisemitismus: Judenfeindschaft in Geschichte und Gegenwart*, edited by Wolfgang Benz, 8: 201–205. Berlin: Walter de Gruyter, 2015.

Eder, Jacob S., and Christian Mentel. "Goldhagen-Debatte." In *Handbuch des Antisemitismus: Judenfeindschaft in Geschichte und Gegenwart*, edited by Wolfgang Benz, 8: 213–217. Berlin: Walter de Gruyter, 2015.

Eisel, Stephan, and Christian Koecke, eds. *Deutschland und die amerikanischen Juden: Versöhnung—Begegnung—Perspektiven*. St. Augustin: Konrad Adenauer Foundation, 1997.

Eizenstat, Stuart E. *Imperfect Justice: Looted Assets, Slave Labor, and the Unfinished Business of World War II*. With a foreword by Elie Wiesel. New York: Public Affairs, 2003.

Eley, Geoff, ed. *The "Goldhagen Effect:" History, Memory, Nazism; Facing the German Past*. Ann Arbor: University of Michigan Press, 2000.

Epstein, Catherine. "Account of the Discussions at the Conference 'German-Speaking Refugee Historians in the United States 1933–1970s' (Washington, DC, December 1–3, 1988)." *Bulletin of the German Historical Institute* 4 (Spring 1989): 5–19.

Etheridge, Brian Craig. "'Die antideutsche Welle:' The Anti-German Wave, Public Diplomacy, and Intercultural Relations in Cold War America." In *Decentering America*, edited by Jessica Gienow-Hecht, 73–106. New York and Oxford: Berghahn Books, 2007.

Etheridge, Brian Craig. *Enemies to Allies: Cold War Germany and American Memory*. Lexington: University of Kentucky Press, 2016.

Etheridge, Brian Craig. *"The Desert Fox*, Memory Diplomacy, and the German Question in Early Cold War America." *Diplomatic History* 32, no. 2, (2008): 207–238.

Etheridge, Brian Craig. "Window and Wall: Berlin, the Third Reich, and the German Question in the United States; 1933–1999." PhD diss., Ohio State University, 2002.

Evans, Richard J. "The German Foreign Office and the Nazi Past." *Neue Politische Literatur* 56, no. 2 (2011): 165–183.

Evans, Richard J. *In Hitler's Shadow: West German Historians and the Attempt to Escape from the Nazi Past*. New York: Pantheon Books, 1989.

Evans, Richard J. *Rereading German History: From Unification to Reunification, 1800–1996*. London and New York: Routledge, 1997.

Falk, Svenja, Dieter Rehfeld, Andrea Römmele, and Martin Thunert, eds. *Handbuch Politikberatung*. Wiesbaden: VS Verlag für Sozialwissenschaften, 2006.

Fallace, Thomas D. *The Emergence of Holocaust Education in American Schools*. New York: Palgrave Macmillan, 2008.

Feigin, Judy. "The Office of Special Investigations: Striving for Accountability in the Aftermath of the Holocaust." Report, 2006. http://documents.nytimes.com/confidential-report-provides-new-evidence-of-notorious-nazi-cases.

Feldman, Lily Gardner. *Germany's Foreign Policy of Reconciliation: From Enmity to Amity*. Lanham, MD: Rowman & Littlefield Publishers, 2012.

Feldman, Lily Gardner. "German-American Societal Relations in Three Dimensions, 1968–1990." In *The United States and Germany in the Era of the Cold War, 1945–1990: A Handbook, Volume 2: 1968–1990*, edited by Detlef Junker, 409–420. Cambridge: Cambridge Universtity Press, 2004.

Feldman, Lily Gardner. "The Jewish Role in German-American Relations." In *The German-American Encounter: Conflict and Cooperation between Two Cultures; 1800–2000*, edited by Frank Trommler and Elliott Shore, 179–187. New York and Oxford: Berghahn Books, 2001.

Feldman, Lily Gardner. "The Principle and Practice of 'Reconciliation' in German Foreign Policy: Relations with France, Israel, Poland and the Czech Republic." *International Affairs* 75, no. 2 (1999): 333–356.

Finkelstein, Norman G. *The Holocaust Industry: Reflections on the Exploitation of Jewish Suffering*. Rev. ed. London: Verso, 2001.

Finney, Patrick, ed. *Palgrave Advances in International History*. New York: Palgrave Macmillan, 2005.

Fisch, Stefan, and Wilfried Rudloff, eds. *Experten und Politik: Wissenschaftliche Politikberatung in geschichtlicher Perspektive*. Berlin: Dunker und Humblot, 2004.

Fischer, Torben, and Matthias N. Lorenz, eds. *Lexikon der "Vergangenheitsbewältigung" in Deutschland: Debatten- und Diskursgeschichte des Nationalsozialismus nach 1945*. 3rd and updated ed. Bielefeld: Transcript, 2015.

Fisher, Marc. *After The Wall: Germany, the Germans and the Burdens of History*. New York: Simon and Schuster, 1995.

Flanzbaum, Hilene, ed. *The Americanization of the Holocaust*. Baltimore, MD: Johns Hopkins University Press, 1999.

Flanzbaum, Hilene. "Introduction: The Americanization of the Holocaust." In *The Americanization of the Holocaust*, edited by Hilene Flanzbaum, 1–17. Baltimore: Johns Hopkins University Press, 1999.

Forever in the Shadow of Hitler? Original Documents of the Historikerstreit, the Controversy Concerning the Singularity of the Holocaust. Translated by James Knowlton and Truett Cates. Atlantic Highlands, NJ: Humanities Press International, 1993.

Freed, James Ingo. "The United States Holocaust Memorial Museum." *Assemblage* 9 (June 1989): 58–79.

Frei, Norbert. *1945 und wir: Das Dritte Reich im Bewußtsein der Deutschen*. Munich: Beck, 2005.

Frei, Norbert. "Goldhagen, die Deutschen und die Historiker: Über die Repräsentation des Holocaust im Zeitalter der Visualisierung." In *Zeitgeschichte als Streitgeschichte: Große Kontroversen nach 1945*, edited by Martin Sabrow, Ralph Jessen, and Klaus Große Kracht, 138–151. Munich: Beck, 2003.

Frei, Norbert. "'Vergangenheitsbewältigung' or 'Renazification'? The American Perspective on Germany's Confrontation with the Nazi past in the Early Years of the Adenauer Era." In *America and the Shaping of German Society*, edited by Michael Ermarth, 47–59. Providence and Oxford: Berg Publishers, 1993.

Frei, Norbert, ed. *Transnationale Vergangenheitspolitik: Der Umgang mit deutschen Kriegsverbrechern in Europa nach dem Zweiten Weltkrieg*. Göttingen: Wallstein, 2006.

Frei, Norbert. *Vergangenheitspolitik: Die Anfänge der Bundesrepublik und die NS-Vergangenheit*. Munich: Beck, 1996.

Frei, Norbert, ed. *Was heißt und zu welchem Ende studiert man Geschichte des 20. Jahrhunderts?* Göttingen: Wallstein, 2006.

Frei, Norbert, Jose Brunner, and Constantin Goschler, eds. *Die Praxis der Wiedergutmachung: Geschichte, Erfahrung und Wirkung in Deutschland und Israel*. Göttingen: Wallstein, 2009.

Frei, Norbert, and Peter Hayes. "The German Foreign Office and the Past." *Bulletin of the German Historical Institute* 49 (Fall 2011): 55–69.

Frei, Norbert, and Sybille Steinbacher, eds. *Schweigen und Bekennen: Die deutsche Nachkriegsgesellschaft und der Holocaust*. Göttingen: Wallstein, 2001.

Frevert, Ute. "Neue Politikgeschichte: Konzepte und Herausforderungen." In *Neue Politikgeschichte: Perspektiven einer historischen Politikforschung*, edited by Ute Frevert and Heinz-Gerhard Haupt, 7–26. Frankfurt am Main and New York: Campus, 2005.

Frevert, Ute. "Was haben Gefühle in der Geschichte zu suchen?" *Geschichte und Gesellschaft* 35, no. 2 (2009): 183–208.

Frevert, Ute, and Heinz-Gerhard Haupt, eds. *Neue Politikgeschichte: Perspektiven einer historischen Politikforschung*. Frankfurt am Main and New York: Campus, 2005.

Friedländer, Saul, Norbert Frei, Trutz Rendtorff, and Reinhard Wittmann. *Bertelsmann im Dritten Reich*. Munich: C. Bertelsmann, 2002.

Friedman, Max Paul, and Padraic Kenney, eds. *Partisan Histories: The Past in Contemporary Global Politics*. New York: Palgrave Macmillan, 2005.

Friedrich Ebert Stiftung. *Der Holocaust als Unterrichtsthema in amerikanischen Schulen: Ergebnisse eines Studienaufenthalts deutscher Lehrer in den USA*. Bonn: Friedrich Ebert Stiftung, 1988.

Friedrich, Jörg. *Der Brand: Deutschland im Bombenkrieg 1940–1945*. Berlin: Propyläen, 2002.

Friedrich, Wolfgang-Uwe, ed. *Die USA und die Deutsche Frage 1945–1990*. Frankfurt am Main and New York: Campus, 1991.

Friedrich, Wolfgang-Uwe, ed. *Germany and America: Essays in Honor of Gerald R. Kleinfeld*. New York and Oxford: Berghahn Books, 2001.

Fröhlich, Claudia. "Rückkehr zur Demokratie: Wandel der politischen Kultur in der Bundesrepublik." In *Der Nationalsozialismus: Die Zweite Geschichte; Überwindung, Deutung, Erinnerung*, edited by Peter Reichel, Harald Schmid, and Peter Steinbach, 105–126. Munich: Beck, 2009.

Fröhlich, Claudia, and Horst-Alfred Heinrich, eds. *Geschichtspolitik: Wer sind ihre Akteure, wer ihre Rezipienten?* Stuttgart: Franz Steiner Verlag, 2004.

Fulbrook, Mary. *German National Identity after the Holocaust*. Cambridge: Polity Press, 1999.

Funke, Hajo. "Bitburg, Jews, and Germans: A Case Study of Anti-Jewish Sentiment in Germany during May, 1985." *New German Critique*, no. 38, *Special Issue on the German-Jewish Controversy* (Spring/Summer 1986): 57–72.

Funke, Hajo. "Bitburg und 'die Macht der Juden:' Zu einem Lehrstück anti-jüdischen Ressentiments in Deutschland/Mai 1985." In *Antisemitismus nach dem Holocaust: Bestandsaufnahme und Erscheinungsformen in deutschsprachigen Ländern*, edited by Alphons Silbermann and Julius H. Schoeps, 41–52. Cologne: Verlag Wissenschaft und Politik, 1986.

Gassert, Philipp. "Transnationale Geschichte." In *Docupedia-Zeitgeschichte* (February 16, 2010). http://docupedia.de/zg/Transnationale_Geschichte.

Gassert, Philipp, Tim Geiger, and Hermann Wentker, eds. *Zweiter Kalter Krieg und Friedensbewegung: Der NATO-Doppelbeschluss in deutsch-deutscher und internationaler Perspektive.* Munich: Oldenbourg Verlag, 2011.

Gassert, Philipp, and Alan E. Steinweis, eds. *Coping with the Nazi Past: West German Debates on Nazism and Generational Conflict; 1955–1975.* New York and Oxford: Berghahn Books, 2006.

Gedenkstätte Deutscher Widerstand, ed. *Der 20. Juli 1944: Reden zu einem Tag der deutschen Geschichte.* Berlin: Gedenkstätte Deutscher Widerstand, 1984.

German Historical Institute London. *German Historical Institute London: 1976–1986.* London: German Historical Institute, 1986.

Gienow-Hecht, Jessica, ed. *Decentering America.* New York and Oxford: Berghahn Books, 2007.

Gienow-Hecht, Jessica. *Transmission Impossible: American Journalism as Cultural Diplomacy in Postwar Germany, 1945–1955.* Baton Rouge: Louisiana State University Press, 1999.

Gienow-Hecht, Jessica, and Mark C. Donfried., eds. *Searching for a Cultural Diplomacy*, New York and Oxford: Berghahn Books, 2010.

Gienow-Hecht, Jessica, and Frank Schumacher, eds. *Culture and International History.* New York and Oxford: Berghahn Books, 2003.

Gleason, Abbott. *Totalitarianism: The Inner History of the Cold War.* New York: Oxford University Press, 1995.

Goedde, Petra. *GIs and Germans: Culture, Gender and Foreign Relations, 1945–1949.* New Haven, CT: Yale University Press, 2003.

Goldberg, Amos. "The 'Jewish Narrative' in the Yad Vashem Global Holocaust Museum." *Journal of Genocide Research* 14, no. 2 (2012): 187–213.

Goldberg, Amos, and Haim Hazan, eds. *Marking Evil: Holocaust Memory in the Global Age.* New York and Oxford: Berghahn Books, 2015.

Goldhagen, Daniel Jonah. *Hitler's Willing Executioners: Ordinary Germans and the Holocaust.* New York: Knopf, 1996.

Goschler, Constantin. "Die Bundesrepublik und die Entschädigung von Ausländern seit 1966." In *Grenzen der Wiedergutmachung: Die Entschädigung für NS-Verfolgte in West- und Osteuropa 1945–2000*, edited by Hans Günther Hockerts, Claudia Moisel, and Tobias Winstel, 94–146. Göttingen: Wallstein, 2006.

Goschler, Constantin. *Schuld und Schulden: Die Politik der Wiedergutmachung für NS-Verfolgte seit 1945.* Göttingen: Wallstein, 2005.

Gramberger, Marc R. *Wider den häßlichen Deutschen: Die verständnisorientierte Öffentlichkeitsarbeit der Bundesrepublik Deutschland in den USA.* Münster: LIT Verlag, 1993.

Granieri, Ronald J. *The Ambivalent Alliance: Konrad Adenauer, the CDU/CSU, and the West, 1949–1966.* New York and Oxford: Berghahn Books, 2002.

Greenspan, Henry. "Imagining Survivors: Testimony and the Rise of Holocaust Consciousness." In *The Americanization of the Holocaust*, edited by Hilene Flanzbaum, 45–67. Baltimore: Johns Hopkins University Press, 1999.

Greenspan, Henry. *On Listening to Holocaust Survivors: Recounting and Life History.* Westport, CT: Praeger, 1998.

Große Kracht, Klaus. *Die zankende Zunft: Historische Kontroversen in Deutschland nach 1945.* Göttingen: Vandenhoeck & Ruprecht, 2005.

Grossmann, Atina. "The 'Goldhagen Effect:' Memory, Repetiton, and Responsibility in the New Germany." In *The "Goldhagen Effect:" History, Memory, Nazism; Facing the German Past*, edited by Geoff Eley, 89–129. Ann Arbor: University of Michigan Press, 2000.

Hacke, Christian. *Die Außenpolitik der Bundesrepublik Deutschland: Von Konrad Adenauer bis Gerhard Schröder.* 2nd ed. Berlin: Ullstein, 2004.

Haftendorn, Helga. *Deutsche Außenpolitik zwischen Selbstbeschränkung und Selbstbehauptung: 1945–2000.* Stuttgart: Deutsche Verlags-Anstalt, 2001.

Hamm-Brücher, Hildegard. *Deutsch-amerikanische Beziehungen: ein neuer Anlauf tut not.* Bonn: Auswärtiges Amt, Referat Öffentlichkeitsarbeit, 1982.

Hampton, Mary N., and Douglas C. Peifer. "Reordering German Identity: Memory Sites and Foreign Policy." *German Studies Review* 30, no. 2 (2007): 371–390.

Hanhardt, Arthur M., Jr. "Die deutsche Vereinigung im Spiegelbild der amerikanischen veröffentlichten Meinung." In *Die USA und die Deutsche Frage 1945–1990*, edited by Wolfgang-Uwe Friedrich, 407–417. Frankfurt am Main and New York: Campus, 1991.

Hart, Justin. *Empire of Ideas: The Origins of Public Diplomacy and the Transformation of U.S. Foreign Policy*. Oxford: Oxford University Press, 2013.

Hartman, Geoffrey H. "Chronology." In *Bitburg in Moral and Political Perspective*, edited by Geoffrey H. Hartman, xiii–xvi. Bloomington: Indiana University Press, 1986.

Hartman, Geoffrey H. "Introduction." In *Bitburg in Moral and Political Perspective*, edited by Geoffrey H. Hartman, 1–12. Bloomington: Indiana University Press, 1986.

Hartman, Geoffrey H. ed. *Bitburg in Moral and Political Perspective*. Bloomington: Indiana University Press, 1986.

Haß, Matthias. *Gestaltetes Gedenken: Yad Vashem, das U.S. Holocaust Memorial Museum und die Stiftung Topographie des Terrors*. Frankfurt am Main and New York: Campus, 2002.

Heerten, Lasse. "A wie Auschwitz, B wie Biafra: Der Bürgerkrieg in Nigeria (1967–1970) und die Universalisierung des Holocaust." *Zeithistorische Forschungen/Studies in Contemporary History* 8, no. 3 (2011). www.zeithistorische-forschungen.de/16126041-Heerten-3-2011.

Heil, Johannes, and Rainer Erb. *Geschichtswissenschaft und Öffentlichkeit: Der Streit um Daniel J. Goldhagen*. Frankfurt am Main: Fischer, 1998.

Hepperle, Sabine. *Die SPD und Israel: Von der Großen Koalition 1966 bis zur Wende 1982*. Frankfurt am Main: Peter Lang, 2000.

Herbert, Ulrich. "Der Historikerstreit: Politische wissenschaftliche, biographische Aspekte." In *Zeitgeschichte als Streitgeschichte: Große Kontroversen nach 1945*, edited by Martin Sabrow, Ralph Jessen, and Klaus Große Kracht, 94–113. Munich: Beck, 2003.

Herbert, Ulrich. *Geschichte Deutschlands im 20. Jahrhundert*. Munich: Beck, 2014.

Herf, Jeffrey. "'At War with Israel': East Germany's Key Role in Soviet Policy in the Middle East." *Journal of Cold War Studies* 16, no. 3 (2014): 129–163.

Herf, Jeffrey. *Divided Memory: The Nazi Past in the Two Germanys*. Cambridge, MA: Harvard University Press, 1997.

Herf, Jeffrey. "The 'Holocaust' Reception in West Germany: Right, Center and Left." *New German Critique*, no 19, Special Issue 1 (1980): 30–52.

Herf, Jeffrey. "Philipp Jenninger and the Dangers of Speaking Clearly." *Partisan Review* 56, no. 2 (1989): 225–236.

Hermann, Ludolf. "Hitler, Bonn und die Wende: Wie die Bundesrepublik ihre Lebenskraft zurückgewinnen kann." *Die politische Meinung* 28, no. 209 (1983): 13–28.

Hermes, Peter. *Meine Zeitgeschichte: 1922–1987*. Paderborn: Ferdinand Schöningh, 2007.

Hikel, Christine. *Sophies Schwester: Inge Scholl und die Weiße Rose*. Munich: Oldenbourg, 2013.

Hilberg, Raul. "Bitburg as Symbol." In *Bitburg in Moral and Political Perspective*, edited by Geoffrey H. Hartman, 15–26. Bloomington: Indiana University Press, 1986.

Hilberg, Raul. *The Politics of Memory: The Journey of a Holocaust Historian*. Chicago: Ivan R. Dee, 1996.

Hinners, Miriam. "Haus der Wannsee-Konferenz." In *Lexikon der "Vergangenheitsbewältigung" in Deutschland: Debatten- und Diskursgeschichte des Nationalsozialismus nach 1945*, edited by Torben Fischer and Matthias N. Lorenz, 294–296. 3rd and updated edition. Bielefeld: Transcript, 2015.

Historikerstreit: Die Dokumentation der Kontroverse um die Einzigartigkeit der nationalsozialistischen Judenvernichtung. Munich: Piper, 1987.

Hockerts, Hans Günter. "Die Entschädigung für NS-Verfolgte in West- und Osteuropa: Eine einführende Skizze." In *Grenzen der Wiedergutmachung: Die Entschädigung für NS-Verfolgte in West- und Osteuropa 1945–2000*, edited by Hans Günther Hockerts, Claudia Moisel, and Tobias Winstel, 7–58. Göttingen: Wallstein, 2006.

Hockerts, Hans Günter, ed. *Koordinaten deutscher Geschichte in der Epoche des Ost-West-Konflikts*. Munich: Oldenbourg Verlag, 2004.

Hockerts, Hans Günter. "Wiedergutmachung: Ein umstrittener Begriff und ein weites Feld." In *Nach der Verfolgung: Wiedergutmachung nationalsozialistischen Unrechts in Deutschland?*, edited by Hans Günter Hockerts and Christiane Kuller, 7–33. Göttingen: Wallstein, 2003.

Hockerts, Hans Günter. "Zeitgeschichte in Deutschland: Begriffe, Methoden, Themenfelder." *Historisches Jahrbuch* 113 (1993): 98–127.

Hockerts, Hans Günter, and Christiane Kuller, eds. *Nach der Verfolgung: Wiedergutmachung nationalsozialistischen Unrechts in Deutschland?* Göttingen: Wallstein, 2003.

Hockerts, Hans Günter, Claudia Moisel, and Tobias Winstel, eds. *Grenzen der Wiedergutmachung: Die Entschädigung für NS-Verfolgte in West- und Osteuropa 1945–2000.* Göttingen: Wallstein, 2006.

Hoepfner, Sebastian. *Jewish Organizations in Transatlantic Perspective: Patterns of Contemporary Jewish Politics in Germany and the United States.* Heidelberg: Universitätsverlag Winter, 2012.

Hoeres, Peter. "Von der 'Tendenzwende' zur 'geistig-moralischen Wende:' Konstruktion und Kritik konservativer Signaturen in den 1970er und 1980er Jahren." *Vierteljahrshefte für Zeitgeschichte* 61, no. 1 (2013): 93–119.

Hoffmann, Hilmar, and Kurt-Jürgen Maaß, eds. *Freund oder Fratze? Das Bild von Deutschland in der Welt und die Aufgaben der Kulturpolitik.* Frankfurt am Main and New York: Campus, 1994.

Hürter, Johannes. "Das Auswärtige Amt, die NS-Diktatur und der Holocaust: Kritische Bemerkungen zu einem Kommissionsbericht." *Vierteljahrshefte für Zeitgeschichte* 59, no. 2 (2011): 167–192.

Institute of Human Relations (American Jewish Committee). *Americans Confront the Holocaust: A Study of Reactions to NBC-TV's Four-Part Drama on the Nazi Era.* New York: American Jewish Committee, Institute of Human Relations, 1978.

Iriye, Akira. *Global and Transnational History: The Past, Present, and Future.* Basingstoke: Palgrave Macmillan, 2013.

Iriye, Akira, ed. *Global Interdependence: The World after 1945.* Cambridge, MA: The Belknap Press of Harvard University Press, 2014.

Jarausch, Konrad H., ed. *Das Ende der Zuversicht? Die siebziger Jahre als Geschichte.* Göttingen: Vandenhoeck & Ruprecht, 2008.

Jarausch, Konrad H. *Die Umkehr: Deutsche Wandlungen 1945–1995.* Munich: Deutsche Verlags-Anstalt, 2004.

Judt, Tony. *Postwar: A History of Europe Since 1945.* New York: Penguin, 2005.

Judt, Tony, with Timothy Snyder. *Thinking the Twentieth Century.* New York: Penguin, 2012.

Junker, Detlef, ed. *The United States and Germany in the Era of the Cold War, 1945–1990: A Handbook; Vol. 1: 1945–1968.* Cambridge: Cambridge University Press, 2004.

Junker, Detlef, ed. *The United States and Germany in the Era of the Cold War, 1945–1990: A Handbook; Vol. 2: 1968–1990.* Cambridge: Cambridge University Press, 2004.

Junker, Detlef. "'History Wars'—Geschichte und nationale Identität der USA." In *Geschichtsdeutungen im internationalen Vergleich*, 49–60. Munich: Bayerische Landeszentrale für Politische Bildungsarbeit, 2003.

Junker, Detlef. "Introduction." In *The German Historical Institute: 1987–1997; A Ten-Year Report*, edited by Detelf Junker, 29–51. Washington, DC: German Historical Institute, 1998.

Jureit, Ulrike, and Christian Schneider. *Gefühlte Opfer: Illusionen der Vergangenheitsbewältigung.* Stuttgart: Klett-Cotta, 2010.

Kansteiner, Wulf. "Losing the War, Winning the Memory Battle: The Legacy of Nazism, World War II, and the Holocaust in the Federal Republic of Germany." In *The Politics of Memory in Postwar Europe*, edited by Richard Ned Lebow, Wulf Kansteiner, and Claudio Fogu, 102–139. Durham, NC: Duke University Press, 2006.

Kansteiner, Wulf. *In Pursuit of German Memory: History, Television, and Politics after Auschwitz.* Athens: Ohio University Press, 2006.

Kathe, Steffen R. *Kulturpolitik um jeden Preis: Die Geschichte des Goethe-Instituts von 1951 bis 1990.* Munich: Meidenbauer, 2005.

Kattago, Siobhan. *Ambiguous Memory: The Nazi Past and German National Identity.* W CT: Praeger, 2001.

Kershaw, Ian. *The Nazi Dictatorship: Problems and Perspectives of Interpretation.* London Press, 2000.

Kershaw, Ian. "Beware the moral high ground." In *Der Holocaust und die westdt Historiker: Eine Debatte*, edited by Astrid M. Eckert und Vera Ziegeldorf, Berlin: H-Soz-u-Kult Forum, 2004. http://edoc.hu-berlin.de/histfor/2/PDF/H 2-2004.pdf.

Kershaw, Ian. "Vier Begriffe für ein Jahrhundert: Was nützt uns eine 'Neue Pc schichte?'" In *Was heißt und zu welchem Ende studiert man Geschichte des 20. J derts?*, edited by Norbert Frei, 148–155. Göttingen: Wallstein, 2006.

Kießling, Friedrich. "Täter repräsentieren: Willy Brandts Kniefall in Warschau." In . *tige Repräsentationen: Deutsche Kulturdiplomatie nach 1945*, edited by Johanne mann, 205–224. Cologne: Böhlau, 2005.

Kirsch, Jan-Holger. "'Hier geht es um den Kern unseres Selbstverständnisses als I Helmut Kohl und die Genese des Holocaust-Gedenkens als bundesdeutscher Si son." *Potsdamer Bulletin für Zeithistorische Studien* 43/44 (2008): 40–48.

Kirsch, Jan-Holger. *Nationaler Mythos oder historische Trauer? Der Streit um ein z "Holocaust-Mahnmal" für die Berliner Republik.* Cologne: Böhlau, 2003.

Kirsch, Jan-Holger. *"Wir haben aus der Geschichte gelernt:" Der 8. Mai als politischer Ge in Deutschland.* Cologne: Böhlau, 1999.

Kleinsteuber, Hans J. "*Deutsche Welle* und *German TV* in den USA: Auswärtige Kultu auf einem schwierigen Markt." In *Die deutsche Präsenz in den USA/The German I in the U.S.A.*, edited by Josef Raab and Jan Wirrer, 451–478. Berlin: LIT Verlag,

Knaap, Ewout van der. *"Nacht und Nebel:" Gedächtnis des Holocaust und intern Wirkungsgeschichte.* Göttingen: Wallstein, 2008.

Knoch, Habbo. "Die Rückkehr der Zeugen: Gedenkstätten als Gedächtnisorte der Bi publik." In *Öffentliche Erinnerung und Medialisierung des Nationalsozialismus: Ei der letzten dreißig Jahre*, edited by Gerhard Paul and Bernhard Schoßig, 116–1 tingen: Wallstein, 2010.

Kohl, Helmut. "Earth Conceal not the Blood Shed on Thee." April 21, 1985. In *Bi Beyond: Encounters in American, German and Jewish History*, edited by Ilya Le' 100. New York: Shapolsky Publishers, 1987.

Kohl, Helmut. "Lagebericht im Bundesvorstand der CDU, 23. März 1983." I *Kohl: Berichte zur Lage 1982–1989; Der Kanzler und Parteivorsitzende im Bund der CDU Deutschlands*, edited by Günter Buchstab and Hans-Otto Kleinmai Düsseldorf: Droste, 2014.

Kohl, Helmut. "Lagebericht im Bundesvorstand der CDU, 25. April 1983." *Kohl: Berichte zur Lage 1982–1989; Der Kanzler und Parteivorsitzende im Bun, der CDU Deutschlands*, edited by Günter Buchstab and Hans-Otto Kleinma Düsseldorf: Droste, 2014.

Kohl, Helmut. "Lagebericht im Bundesvorstand der CDU, 22. April 1985." *Kohl: Berichte zur Lage 1982–1989; Der Kanzler und Parteivorsitzende im Bui der CDU Deutschlands*, edited by Günter Buchstab and Hans-Otto Kleinmai Düsseldorf: Droste, 2014.

Kohl, Helmut. "Lagebericht im Bundesvorstand der CDU, 13. Mai 1985." In *Hel richte zur Lage 1982–1989; Der Kanzler und Parteivorsitzende im Bundesvors Deutschlands*, edited by Günter Buchstab and Hans-Otto Kleinmann, 2ℂ seldorf: Droste, 2014.

Kohl, Helmut. "Lagebericht im Bundesvorstand der CDU, 13./14. Oktober 19ℓ *Kohl: Berichte zur Lage 1982–1989; Der Kanzler und Parteivorsitzende im B der CDU Deutschlands*, edited by Günter Buchstab and Hans-Otto Kleinm Düsseldorf: Droste, 2014.

Kohl, Helmut. "Lagebericht im Bundesvorstand der CDU, 18. Juni 19ℓ *Kohl: Berichte zur Lage 1982–1989; Der Kanzler und Parteivorsitzende im der CDU Deutschlands*, edited by Günter Buchstab and Hans-Otto Kleinmann, 538–563. Düsseldorf: Droste, 2014.

Kohl, Helmut. Lagebericht im Bundesvorstand der CDU, 31. Oktober 1988." In *Helmut Kohl: Berichte zur Lage 1982–1989; Der Kanzler und Parteivorsitzende im Bundesvorstand der CDU Deutschlands*, edited by Günter Buchstab and Hans-Otto Kleinmann, 650–668. Düsseldorf: Droste, 2014.

Kohl, Helmut. "Lagebericht im Bundesvorstand der CDU, 21. November 1988." In *Helmut Kohl: Berichte zur Lage 1982–1989; Der Kanzler und Parteivorsitzende im Bundesvorstand der CDU Deutschlands*, edited by Günter Buchstab and Hans-Otto Kleinmann, 669–683. Düsseldorf: Droste, 2014.

Kohl, Helmut. "Lagebericht im Bundesvorstand der CDU, 11. Juni 1990." In *Helmut Kohl: Berichte zur Lage 1989–1998; Der Kanzler und Parteivorsitzende im Bundesvorstand der CDU Deutschlands*, edited by Günter Buchstab and Hans-Otto Kleinmann, 140–157. Düsseldorf: Droste, 2012.

Kohl, Helmut. "Lagebericht im Bundesvorstand der CDU, 3. Mai 1993." In *Helmut Kohl: Berichte zur Lage 1989–1998; Der Kanzler und Parteivorsitzende im Bundesvorstand der CDU Deutschlands*, edited by Günter Buchstab and Hans-Otto Kleinmann, 448–455. Düsseldorf: Droste, 2012.

Kohl, Helmut. "Lagebericht im Bundesvorstand der CDU, 12. September 1993." In *Helmut Kohl: Berichte zur Lage 1989–1998; Der Kanzler und Parteivorsitzende im Bundesvorstand der CDU Deutschlands*, edited by Günter Buchstab and Hans-Otto Kleinmann, 490–493. Düsseldorf: Droste, 2012.

Kohl, Helmut. "Lagebericht im Bundesvorstand der CDU, 1./2. Oktober 1993." In *Helmut Kohl: Berichte zur Lage 1989–1998; Der Kanzler und Parteivorsitzende im Bundesvorstand der CDU Deutschlands*, edited by Günter Buchstab and Hans-Otto Kleinmann, 494–505. Düsseldorf: Droste, 2012.

Kohl, Helmut. "Lagebericht im Bundesvorstand der CDU, 9. Februar 1998." In *Helmut Kohl: Berichte zur Lage 1989–1998; Der Kanzler und Parteivorsitzende im Bundesvorstand der CDU Deutschlands*, edited by Günter Buchstab and Hans-Otto Kleinmann, 965–976. Düsseldorf: Droste, 2012.

Kohl, Helmut. *Erinnerungen: 1982–1990*. Munich: Droemer, 2005.

Kohl, Helmut. *Erinnerungen: 1990–1994*. Munich: Droemer, 2007.

Kohl, Helmut. "Mahnung und Verpflichtung des 30. Januar 1933." January 30, 1983, Berlin. www.helmut-kohl-kas.de/index.php?menu_sel=17&menu_sel2=&menu_sel3=&menu_sel4=&msg=2269.

Kohl, Helmut. "Weichenstellung für die Zukunft." *Die Politische Meinung* 32, no. 230 (1987): 7–13.

Kohl, Walter. *Leben oder gelebt werden: Schritte auf dem Weg zur Versöhnung*. Munich: Integral Verlag, 2011.

Köhler, Henning. *Helmut Kohl. Ein Leben für die Politik. Die Biografie*. Cologne: Bastei Lübbe, 2014.

Kölsch, Julia. "Politik und Gedächtnis: Die Gegenwart der NS-Vergangenheit als politisches Sinnstiftungspotential." In *Die NS-Diktatur im deutschen Erinnerungsdiskurs*, edited by Wolfgang Bergem, 137–150. Opladen: Leske & Budrich, 2003.

König, Helmut. *Die Zukunft der Vergangenheit: Der Nationalsozialismus im politischen Bewußtsein der Bundesrepublik*. Frankfurt am Main: S. Fischer Verlag, 2003.

Konrad Adenauer Foundation, ed. *Twenty Years of Building Bridges: American Jewish Committee–Konrad Adenauer Foundation*. Ed. by Ursula Carpenter and Sylvia Mitterndorfer. Washington, DC: Konrad Adenauer Foundation, 2000.

Köpke, Wulf. "The Third Pillar of Foreign Policy: West German Cultural Policy in the United States." In *The United States and Germany in the Era of the Cold War, 1945–1990: A Handbook, Volume 2: 1968–1990*, edited by Detlef Junker, 280–286. Cambridge: Cambridge Universtity Press, 2004.

Kramer, Sven. "Nacht und Nebel." In *Lexikon der "Vergangenheitsbewältigung" in Deutschland: Debatten- und Diskursgeschichte des Nationalsozialismus nach 1945*, edited by Torben

Fischer and Matthias N. Lorenz, 123–125. 3rd and updated edition. Bielefeld: Transcript, 2015.

Kraushaar, Wolfgang. *"Wann endlich beginnt bei euch der Kampf gegen die heilige Kuh Israel?" München 1970—über die antisemitischen Wurzeln des deutschen Terrorismus.* Reinbek: Rowohlt Verlag 2013.

Kreis, Reinhild. "Bündnis ohne Nachwuchs? Die 'Nachfolgegeneration' und die deutsch-amerikanischen Beziehungen in den 1980er Jahren." *Archiv für Sozialgeschichte* 52 (2012): 607–631.

Kreis, Reinhild, ed. *Diplomatie mit Gefühl: Vertrauen, Misstrauen und die Außenpolitik der Bundesrepublik Deutschland.* Berlin: De Gruyter Oldenbourg, 2015.

Kreis, Reinhild. *Orte für Amerika: Deutsch-Amerikanische Institute und Amerikahäuser in der Bundesrepublik seit den 1960er Jahren.* Stuttgart: Franz Steiner Verlag, 2012.

Kroh, Jens. *Transnationale Erinnerung: Der Holocaust im Fokus geschichtspolitischer Initiativen.* Frankfurt am Main and New York: Campus, 2008.

Krondorfer, Björn. "Kulturgut 'Holocaust': Gedanken zum neuen U.S. Holocaust Memorial Museum in Washington." *Tribüne* 32, no. 127 (1993): 91–104.

Kübler, Elisabeth. *Europäische Erinnerungspolitik: Der Europarat und die Erinnerung an den Holocaust.* Bielefeld: Transcript, 2012.

Kühberger, Christoph, and Clemens Sedmak, eds. *Europäische Geschichtskultur—Europäische Geschichtspolitik: Vom Erfinden, Entdecken, Erarbeiten der Bedeutung von Erinnerung und Geschichte für das Verständnis und Selbstverständnis Europas.* Innsbruck: StudienVerlag, 2009.

Kühling, Gerd. "Schullandheim oder Forschungsstätte? Die Auseinandersetzung um ein Dokumentationszentrum im Haus der Wannsee-Konferenz (1966/67)." *Zeithistorische Forschungen/Studies in Contemporary History* 5, no. 2 (2008): 211–235.

Kühnhardt, Ludger. *Atlantik-Brücke: Fünfzig Jahre deutsch-amerikanische Partnerschaft; 1952–2002.* Berlin: Propyläen, 2002.

Kurthen, Hermann. "Antisemitism and Xenophobia in United Germany: How the Burden of the Past Affects the Present." In *Antisemitism and Xenophobia in Germany after Unification*, edited by Hermann Kurthen, Werner Bergmann, and Rainer Erb, 39–61. Oxford: Oxford University Press, 1997.

Kurthen, Hermann, Werner Bergmann, and Rainer Erb, eds. *Antisemitism and Xenophobia in Germany after Unification.* Oxford: Oxford University Press, 1997.

Kurthen, Hermann, and Michael Minkenberg. "Germany in Transition: Immigration, Racism, and the Extreme Right." *Nations and Nationalism* 1, no. 2 (1995): 175–196.

Lagrou, Pieter. *The Legacy of Nazi Occupation: Patriotic Memory and National Recovery in Western Europe, 1945–1965.* Cambridge: Cambridge University Press, 2000.

Landwehr, Achim. "Diskurs—Macht—Wissen: Perspektiven einer Kulturgeschichte des Politischen." *Archiv für Kulturgeschichte* 85, no. 1 (2003): 71–117.

Landwehr, Achim. *Historische Diskursanalyse.* Frankfurt am Main and New York: Campus, 2008.

Lang, Berel. "On Peter Novick's 'The Holocaust in American Life'." *Jewish Social Studies*, 7, no. 3 (2001): 149–158.

Lange, Julia. *"Herman the German:" Das Hermann Monument in der deutsch-amerikanischen Erinnerungskultur.* Münster: LIT Verlag, 2013.

Langer, Lawrence L. "The Americanization of the Holocaust on Stage and Screen." In *Admitting the Holocaust: Collected Essays*, edited by Lawrence L. Langer, 157–177. Oxford: Oxford University Press, 1995.

Langguth, Gerd. *Kohl, Schröder, Merkel: Machtmenschen.* Munich: Deutscher Taschenbuch Verlag, 2009.

Lavy, George. *Germany and Israel: Moral Debt and National Interest.* London: Frank Cass, 1996.

Lazar, David. "The German Foreign Service and its Nazi Past," Report on Panel Discussion at the German Historical Institute on March 3, 2011. http://ghi-dc.org/index.php?option=com_content&view=article&id=1139&Itemid=1005.

Leber, Hubert. "Chancellor Helmut Schmidt, His Policy toward Israel, and the German Responsibility for the Jewish People." *AICGS: Transatlantic Perspectives* (December 2015).

www.aicgs.org/publication/chancellor-helmut-schmidt-his-policy-toward-israel-and-the-german-responsibility-for-the-jewish-people/.

Leber, Hubert. "'The Leopard that Forgot the Holocaust'? Israel, West Germany's Arms Export Policy, and the Saudi Tank Deal Debate in 1981/82." Presentation, University of Haifa, January 12–14, 2014 (copy is in the author's possession).

Leber, Hubert. "Zwischen Protest und Diplomatie: Israels Reaktion auf die deutsche Verjährungsdebatte von 1979." Presentation, Institut für Zeitgeschichte Munich-Berlin, Berlin, January 23, 2013 (copy is in the author's possession).

Ledford, Kenneth F. "1949–1989: The Federal Republic as History (Cambridge, Massachusetts, October 27–29, 1989)." *Bulletin of the German Historical Institute* 5 (Fall 1989): 25–33.

Leggewie, Claus. *Der Geist steht rechts: Ausflüge in die Denkfabriken der Wende.* 2nd ed. Berlin: Rotbuch Verlag, 1987.

Leggewie, Claus, and Erik Meyer. *"Ein Ort, an den man gerne geht:" Das Holocaust-Mahnmal und die deutsche Geschichtspolitik nach 1989.* Munich: Carl Hanser Verlag, 2005.

Lehmann, Hartmut. "Österreich-Ungarn und die belgische Frage im ersten Weltkrieg." PhD diss., University of Vienna, 1959.

Lehmann, Hartmut. *Pietismus und weltliche Ordnung in Württemberg vom 17. bis zum 20. Jahrhundert.* Stuttgart: Kohlhammer, 1969.

Lehmann, Hartmut. *Das Zeitalter des Absolutismus: Gottesgnadentum und Kriegsnot.* Stuttgart: Kohlhammer, 1980.

Lehmann, Hartmut, and James J. Sheehan, eds. *An Interrupted Past: German-Speaking Refugee Historians in the United States after 1933.* Washington, DC: German Historical Institute, 1991.

Levkov, Ilya, ed. *Bitburg and Beyond: Encounters in American, German and Jewish History.* New York: Shapolsky Publishers, 1987.

Levy, Daniel, and Natan Sznaider. *The Holocaust and Memory in the Global Age.* Translated by Assenka Oksiloff. Philadelphia: Temple University Press, 2006.

Levy, Daniel, and Natan Sznaider. *Erinnerung im globalen Zeitalter: Der Holocaust.* Frankfurt am Main: Suhrkamp, 2001.

Linenthal, Edward T. "The Boundaries of Memory: The United States Holocaust Memorial Museum." *American Quarterly* 46, no. 3 (September 1994): 406–433.

Linenthal, Edward T. "Committing History in Public." *The Journal of American History* 81, no. 3 (December 1994): 986–991.

Linenthal, Edward T. *Preserving Memory: The Struggle to Create America's Holocaust Museum.* New York: Penguin Books, 2001.

Lipstadt, Deborah E. "The Bitburg Controversy." *American Jewish Year Book* 87 (1987): 1–38.

Littmann, Ulrich. *Partners: Distant and Close; Notes and Footnotes on Academic Mobility Between Germany and the United States of America (1923–1993).* Bonn: Deutscher Akademischer Austauschdienst, 1997.

Loth, Wilfried, and Jürgen Osterhammel, eds. *Internationale Geschichte. Themen, Ergebnisse, Aussichten.* Munich: Oldenbourg, 2000.

Lübbe, Hermann. "Der Nationalsozialismus im deutschen Nachkriegsbewußtsein." *Historische Zeitschrift* 236, no. 3 (1983): 579–599.

MacDonald, David B. "Daring to Compare: The Debate about a Maori 'Holocaust' in New Zealand." *Journal of Genocide Research* 5, no. 3 (2003): 383–403.

MacDonald, David B. *Identity Politics in the Age of Genocide: The Holocaust and Historical Representation.* New York: Routledge, 2008.

Maier, Charles S. *In Search of Stability: Explorations in Historical Political Economy.* Cambridge: Cambridge University Press, 1987.

Maier, Charles S. *The Unmasterable Past: History, Holocaust, and German National Identity.* Rev. ed. Cambridge, MA: Harvard University Press, 1997 (orig. 1988).

Mallinckrodt, Anita M. *Die Selbstdarstellung der beiden deutschen Staaten im Ausland: "Image-Bildung" als Instrument der Außenpolitik.* Cologne: Verlag Wissenschaft und Politik, 1980.

Mann, James. *The Rebellion of Ronald Reagan: A History of the End of the Cold War.* New York: Viking, 2009.

Marcuse, Harold. *Legacies of Dachau: The Uses and Abuses of a Concentration Camp, 1933–2001.* Cambridge: Cambridge University Press, 2001.

Markovits, Andrei S., and Simon Reich. *The German Predicament: Memory and Power in the New Europe.* Ithaca, NY: Cornell University Press, 1997.

Märthesheimer, Peter, and Ivo Frenzel, eds. *Im Kreuzfeuer: Der Fernsehfilm "Holocaust"; Eine Nation ist betroffen.* Frankfurt am Main: Fischer, 1979.

Matthäus, Jürgen. "Historiography and the Perpetrators of the Holocaust." In *The Historiography of the Holocaust,* edited by Dan Stone, 197–215. New York: Palgrave Macmillan, 2004.

Matthäus, Jürgen. "Holocaust-Forschung in Deutschland: Eine Geschichte ohne Zukunft?" In *Der Holocaust in der deutschsprachigen Geschichtswissenschaft: Bilanz und Perspektiven,* edited by Michael Brenner and Maximilian Strnad, 27–41. Göttingen: Wallstein, 2012.

Meining, Stefan. *Kommunistische Judenpolitik: Die DDR, die Juden und Israel.* Münster: LIT Verlag, 2002.

Meng, Michael. *Shattered Spaces: Encountering Jewish Ruins in Postwar Germany and Poland.* Cambridge, MA: Harvard University Press, 2011.

Mentel, Christian. "Bitburg-Affäre (1985)." In *Handbuch des Antisemitismus: Judenfeindschaft in Geschichte und Gegenwart,* edited by Wolfgang Benz, 4: 51–53. Berlin: Walter de Gruyter, 2011.

Mergel, Thomas. "Überlegungen zu einer Kulturgeschichte der Politik." *Geschichte und Gesellschaft* 28, no. 4 (2002): 574–606.

Mertens, Lothar. "Antizionismus: Feindschaft gegen Israel als neue Form des Antisemitismus." In *Antisemitismus in Deutschland: Zur Aktualität eines Vorurteils,* edited by Wolfgang Benz, 89–100. Munich: Deutscher Taschenbuch Verlag, 1995.

Mertes, Alois. "Western Europe Forty Years After World War II." May 2, 1985. In *Bitburg and Beyond: Encounters in American, German and Jewish History,* edited by Ilya Levkov, 119–127. New York: Shapolsky Publishers, 1987.

Mertes, Michael. "Helmut Kohl's Legacy for Germany." *The Washington Quarterly* 25, no. 4 (Autumn 2002): 67–82.

Meyer, Kristina. *Die SPD und die NS-Vergangenheit 1945–1990.* Göttingen: Wallstein, 2015.

Michels, Eckard. *Von der Deutschen Akademie zum Goethe-Institut: Sprach- und auswärtige Kulturpolitik; 1923–1960.* Munich: Oldenbourg, 2005.

Michman, Dan, ed. *Remembering the Holocaust in Germany: 1945–2000; German Strategies and Jewish Responses.* New York: Peter Lang, 2002.

Miles, William F.S. "Third World Views of the Holocaust." *Journal of Genocide Research* 6, no. 3 (2004): 371–393.

Miller, Judith. *One, by One, by One: Facing the Holocaust.* New York: Simon & Schuster, 1990.

Milton, Sybil. "Die Darstellung des Holocaust in den USA im Vergleich zu den beiden deutschen Staaten." In *Die geteilte Vergangenheit: Zum Umgang mit Nationalsozialismus und Widerstand in beiden deutschen Staaten,* edited by Jürgen Danyel, 227–233. Berlin: Akademie Verlag, 1995.

Milton, Sybil. "United States Holocaust Memorial Museum in Washington, D.C." In *Zur Arbeit in Gedenkstätten für die Opfer des Nationalsozialismus: Ein internationaler Überblick,* edited by Wulff E. Brebeck, 113–121. Berlin: Aktion Sühnezeichen Friedensdienste, 1988.

Mintz, Alan. *Popular Culture and the Shaping of Holocaust Memory in America.* Seattle: University of Washington Press, 2001.

Mittleman, Alan. "American Jewish Perceptions of Germany: A Brief Survey." In *Deutschland und die amerikanischen Juden: Versöhnung—Begegnung—Perspektiven,* edited by Stephan Eisel and Christian Koecke, 61–71. St. Augustin: Konrad Adenauer Foundation, 1997.

Moeller, Robert G. "Germans as Victims? Thoughts on a Post-Cold War History of World War II's Legacies." *History & Memory* 17, no. 1/2 (Spring/Summer 2005): 147–194.

Moeller, Robert G. *War Stories: The Search for a Usable Past in the Federal Republic of Germany.* Berkeley: University of California Press, 2001.

Moller, Sabine. *Die Entkonkretisierung der NS-Herrschaft in der Ära Kohl: Die Neue Wache, das Denkmal für die ermordeten Juden Europas, das Haus der Geschichte der Bundesrepublik Deutschland.* Hannover: Offizin, 1998.

Mommsen, Hans. "Die Realisierung des Utopischen: Die 'Endlösung der Judenfrage' im 'Dritten Reich'." *Geschichte und Gesellschaft* 9, no. 3 (1983): 381–420.

Mommsen, Hans. "Stehen wir vor einer neuen Polarisierung des Geschichtsbildes in der Bundesrepublik Deutschland?" In *Geschichte in der demokratischen Gesellschaft: Eine Dokumentation,* edited by Susanne Miller, 71–83. Düsseldorf: Schwann, 1985.

Mommsen, Hans. "Suche nach der 'verlorenen Geschichte'? Bemerkungen zum historischen Selbstverständnis der Bundesrepublik." In *Historikerstreit: Die Dokumentation der Kontroverse um die Einzigartigkeit der nationalsozialistischen Judenvernichtung,* 156–173. Munich: Piper, 1987.

Mommsen, Hans. "Verordnete Geschichtsbilder: Historische Museumspläne der Bundesregierung." *Gewerkschaftliche Monatshefte* 37, no. 1 (1986): 13–24. http://library.fes.de/gmh/main/pdf-files/gmh/1986/1986-01-a-013.pdf.

Morina, Christina. *Legacies of Stalingrad: Remembering the Eastern Front in Germany since 1945.* Cambridge: Cambridge University Press, 2011.

Morris, David B. "Bitburg Revisited: Germany's Search for Normalcy." *German Politics and Society* 13, no. 4 (1995): 92–109.

Moses, A. Dirk. *German Intellectuals and the Nazi Past.* Cambridge: Cambridge University Press, 2007.

Moses, A. Dirk. "Die 45er: Eine Generation zwischen Faschismus und Demokratie." *Neue Sammlung* 40, no. 1 (2000): 233–263.

Müchler, Günter, and Klaus Hofmann. *Helmut Kohl: Chancellor of German Unity.* Bonn: Press and Information Office of the Federal Government, 1992.

Müller, Jan-Werner. *Another Country: German Intellectuals, Unification, and National Identity.* New Haven, CT: Yale University Press, 2000.

Müller, Jan-Werner. "Europäische Erinnerungspolitik Revisited." *Transit: Europäische Revue* 33 (Summer 2007): 166–175.

Müller, Jan-Werner. "Introduction: The Power of Memory, the Memory of Power and the Power over Memory." In *Memory and Power in Post-War Europe: Studies in the Presence of the Past,* edited by Jan-Werner Müller, 1–35. Cambridge: Cambridge University Press, 2002.

Müller, Jan-Werner, ed. *Memory and Power in Post-War Europe: Studies in the Presence of the Past.* Cambridge: Cambridge University Press, 2002.

Münkel, Daniela. "Politische Generationen in der Bundesrepublik." *Zeitschrift für Geschichtswissenschaft* 56, no. 2 (2008): 139–153.

Neumann, Klaus. *Shifting Memories: The Nazi Past in the New Germany.* Ann Arbor: University of Michigan Press, 2000.

Neusner, Jacob. *Stranger at Home: "The Holocaust," Zionism, and American Judaism.* Chicago: University of Chicago Press, 1981.

Neuss, Beate. "Vom Brückenbauen über tiefe Schluchten: Deutsche und amerikanische Juden." In *"A Life-Changing Experience:" 30 Jahre KAS/AJC-Austauschprogramm,* edited by Deidre Berger and Jens Paulus, 35–61. St. Augustin: Konrad Adenauer Foundation, 2010. www.kas.de/wf/doc/kas_19725-544-1-30.pdf?110427115734.

Nick, Ann L. *A Teachers' Guide to the Holocaust.* New York: Anti-Defamation League of B'nai B'rith, 1977.

Ninkovich, Frank A. *Germany and the United States: The Transformation of the German Question since 1945.* Updated edition. New York: Twayne Publishers, 1995.

Nipperdey, Thomas. *Deutsche Geschichte 1800–1866: Bürgerwelt und starker Staat.* Munich: Beck, 1983.

Nipperdey, Thomas. *Deutsche Geschichte 1866–1918; Vol. 1: Arbeitswelt und Bürgergeist.* Munich: Beck, 1990.

Nipperdey, Thomas. *Deutsche Geschichte 1866–1918; Vol. 2: Machtstaat vor der Demokratie.* Munich: Beck, 1990.

Niroumand, Mariam. *"Americanization" of the Holocaust.* Berlin: John F. Kennedy-Institut für Nordamerikastudien/Freie Universität Berlin, 1995.

Niven, Bill. *Facing the Nazi Past: United Germany and the Legacy of the Third Reich.* London: Routledge, 2002.

Niven, Bill. "The Reception of Steven Spielberg's *Schindler's List* in the German Media." In *Images of Germany in the American Media,* edited by Jim Willis, 131–151. Westport, CT: Praeger, 1999.

Noack, Hans-Joachim, and Wolfram Bickerich. *Helmut Kohl. Die Biographie.* Berlin: Rowohlt, 2010.

Novick, Peter. *The Holocaust in American Life.* Boston: Houghton Mifflin, 1999.

Ohlemacher, Thomas. "Public Opinion and Violence Against Foreigners in the Unified Germany." *Zeitschrift für Soziologie* 23, no. 3 (1994): 222–236.

Osgood, Kenneth A., and Brian C. Etheridge, eds. *The United States and Public Diplomacy: New Directions in Cultural and International History.* Leiden: Martinus Nijhoff Publishers, 2010.

Osterhammel, Jürgen. "Transnationale Gesellschaftsgeschichte: Erweiterung oder Alternative?" *Geschichte und Gesellschaft* 27, no. 3 (2001): 464–479.

Ostrowski, Daniel. *Die Public Diplomacy der deutschen Auslandsvertretungen weltweit: Theorie und Praxis der deutschen Auslandsöffentlichkeitsarbeit.* Wiesbaden: VS Verlag für Sozialwissenschaften, 2010.

Pakier, Małgorzata, and Bo Stråth, eds. *A European Memory? Contested Histories and Politics of Memory.* New York and Oxford: Berghahn Books, 2010.

Patel, Kiran Klaus. "Transatlantische Perspektiven transnationaler Geschichte." *Geschichte und Gesellschaft* 29, no. 4 (2003): 625–647.

Patel, Kiran Klaus. "'Transnations' among 'Transnations'? The Debate on Transnational History in the United States and Germany." *Amerikastudien/American Studies* 54, no. 3 (2009): 451–472.

Patel, Kiran Klaus, and Kenneth Weisbrode, eds. *European Integration and the Atlantic Community in the 1980s.* New York: Cambridge University Press, 2013.

Paulmann, Johannes. "Auswärtige Repräsentationen nach 1945: Zur Geschichte der deutschen Selbstdarstellung im Ausland." In *Auswärtige Repräsentationen: Deutsche Kulturdiplomatie nach 1945,* edited by Johannes Paulmann, 1–32. Cologne: Böhlau, 2005.

Paulmann, Johannes, ed. *Auswärtige Repräsentationen: Deutsche Kulturdiplomatie nach 1945.* Cologne: Böhlau, 2005.

Paulmann, Johannes. "Deutschland in der Welt: Auswärtige Repräsentationen und reflexive Selbstwahrnehmung nach dem Zweiten Weltkrieg; eine Skizze." In *Koordinaten deutscher Geschichte in der Epoche des Ost-West-Konflikts,* edited by Hans Günter Hockerts, 63–78. Munich: Oldenbourg Verlag, 2004.

Peck, Abraham J., ed. *The German-Jewish Legacy in America, 1938–1988: From Bildung to the Bill of Rights.* Detroit: Wayne State University Press, 1989.

Peck, Jeffrey M. "Confrontations with the Holocaust in the Era of the Cold War: German and American Perspectives." In *The United States and Germany in the Era of the Cold War, 1945–1990: A Handbook, Volume 2: 1968–1990,* edited by Detlef Junker, 402–407. Cambridge: Cambridge University Press, 2004.

Peck, Jeffrey M. *A Continuous Tradition of Dialogue and Tolerance: AJC in Germany.* New York: American Jewish Committee, 2006. www.ajc.org/atf/cf/%7B42d75369-d582-4380-8395-d25925b85eaf%7D/AJC%20IN%20GERMANY.PDF.

Peck, Jeffrey M., ed. "The Jewish Voice in Transatlantic Relations." Special issue, *AICGS German-American Issues,* no. 1 (2004). www.aicgs.org/site/wp-content/uploads/2011/10/aicgsgermanamerican.pdf.

Pendas, Devin O. *The Frankfurt Auschwitz Trial, 1963–1965: Genocide, History, and the Limits of the Law.* Cambridge: Cambridge University Press, 2006.

Petersen, Peter. *Sind wir noch zu retten? Ein Bundestagsabgeordneter schreibt an seinen 19jährigen Sohn, der sich Sorgen um die Zukunft macht.* Stuttgart-Bonn: Burg Verlag, 1984.

Pfeil, Ulrich, ed. *Das Deutsche Historische Institut Paris und seine Gründungsväter: Ein personengeschichtlicher Ansatz.* Munich: Oldenbourg, 2007.

Pfeil, Ulrich. "Gründung und Aufbau des Instituts: 1958–1968." In *Das Deutsche Historische Institut Paris: 1958–2008*, edited by Rainer Babel and Rolf Große, 1–84. Ostfildern: Jan Thorbecke Verlag, 2008.

Pfeil, Ulrich. *Vorgeschichte und Gründung des Deutschen Historischen Instituts Paris: Darstellung und Dokumentation.* Ostfildern: Jan Thorbecke Verlag, 2007.

Pieper, Katrin. *Die Musealisierung des Holocaust: Das Jüdische Museum Berlin und das U.S. Holocaust Memorial Museum in Washington D.C.; Ein Vergleich.* Cologne: Böhlau, 2006.

Podewils, Clemens, ed. *Tendenzwende? Zur geistigen Situation der Bundesrepublik.* Stuttgart: Klett, 1975.

Pohl, Dieter. "Die Holocaust-Forschung und Goldhagens Thesen." *Vierteljahrshefte für Zeitgeschichte* 45, no. 1 (1997): 1–48.

Poiger, Uta G. *Jazz, Rock, and Rebels: Cold War Politics and American Culture in a Divided Germany.* Berkeley: University of California Press, 2000.

Popkin, Jeremy D. "Holocaust Memories, Historians' Memoirs: First-Person Narrative and the Memory of the Holocaust." *History & Memory* 15, no. 1 (2003): 49–84.

Rabinbach, Anson. "From Explosion to Erosion: Holocaust Memorialization in America since Bitburg." *History & Memory* 9, no. 2 (1997): 226–255.

Rabinbach, Anson. "The Jewish Question in the German Question." *New German Critique*, no. 44 (1988): 159–192.

Reagan, Ronald. *An American Life.* New York: Simon and Schuster, 1990.

Reagan, Ronald. "Never again. . . ." May 5, 1985. In *Bitburg and Beyond: Encounters in American, German and Jewish History*, edited by Ilya Levkov, 131–135. New York: Shapolsky Publishers, 1987.

Recent History of the Federal Republic of Germany and the United States: Recommendations for Treatment in Textbooks. Boulder, CO: Westview Press, 1985.

Reichel, Peter. "Der Judenmord in der deutschen Erinnerungskultur." In *"Transformationen" der Erinnerungskulturen in Europa nach 1989*, edited by Bernd Faulenbach and Franz-Josef Jelich, 367–380. Essen: Klartext, 2006.

Reichel, Peter. *Politik mit der Erinnerung: Gedächtnisorte im Streit um die Nationalsozialistische Vergangenheit.* Munich: Carl Hanser Verlag, 1995.

Reichel, Peter. *Vergangenheitsbewältigung in Deutschland: Die Auseinandersetzung mit der NS-Diktatur von 1945 bis heute.* Munich: Beck, 2001.

Reichel, Peter, Harald Schmid, and Peter Steinbach, eds. *Der Nationalsozialismus: Die Zweite Geschichte; Überwindung, Deutung, Erinnerung.* Munich: Beck, 2009.

Renvert, Nicole. *Machtmakler in schwierigen Zeiten? Die Rolle der deutschen politischen Stiftungen in den transatlantischen Beziehungen.* Trier: WVT, 2014.

Reuther, Thomas. *Die ambivalente Normalisierung: Deutschlanddiskurs und Deutschlandbilder in den USA, 1941–1955.* Stuttgart: Franz Steiner, 2000.

Rigoll, Dominik. *Staatsschutz in Westdeutschland: Von der Entnazifizierung zur Extremistenabwehr.* Göttingen: Wallstein 2013.

Rödder, Andreas. *Die Bundesrepublik Deutschland 1969–1990.* Munich: Oldenbourg, 2004.

Rödder, Andreas. *Deutschland einig Vaterland: Die Geschichte der Wiedervereinigung.* Munich: Beck, 2009.

Rogers, Daniel E. "The Chancellors of the Federal Republic of Germany and the Political Legacy of the Holocaust." In *The Impact of Nazism: New Perspectives on the Third Reich and its Legacies*, edited by Alan E. Steinweis and Daniel E. Rogers, 231–247. Lincoln: University of Nebraska Press, 2003.

Rosenfeld, Alvin H. "The Americanization of the Holocaust." *Commentary*, June 1995, 35–40.

Rosenfeld, Alvin H. "Another Revisionism: Popular Culture and the Changing Image of the Holocaust." In *Bitburg in Moral and Political Perspective*, edited by Geoffrey H. Hartman, 90–102. Bloomington: Indiana University Press, 1986.

Rosenfeld, Alvin H. *The End of the Holocaust.* Bloomington: Indiana University Press, 2011.

Rosenfeld, Gavriel D. "The Politics of Uniqueness: Reflections on the Recent Polemical Turn in Holocaust and Genocide Scholarship." *Holocaust and Genocide Studies* 13, no. 1 (1999): 28–61.

Rosumek, Lars. *Die Kanzler und die Medien: Acht Porträts von Adenauer bis Merkel.* Frankfurt am Main and New York: Campus, 2007.

Rotem, Stephanie Shosh. *Constructing Memory: Architectural Narratives of Holocaust Museums.* Bern et al.: Peter Lang, 2013.

Rothberg, Michael. *Multidirectional Memory: Remembering the Holocaust in the Age of Decolonization.* Redwood City, CA: Stanford University Press, 2009.

Rudloff, Wilfried. "Einleitung: Politikberatung als Gegenstand historischer Betrachtung; Forschungsstand, neue Befunde, übergreifende Fragestellungen." In *Experten und Politik: Wissenschaftliche Politikberatung in geschichtlicher Perspektive,* edited by Stefan Fisch and Wilfried Rudloff, 13–57. Berlin: Dunker und Humblot, 2004.

Ruhfus, Jürgen. *Aufwärts: Erlebnisse und Erinnerungen eines diplomatischen Zeitzeugen, 1955 bis 1992.* Sankt Ottilien: EOS-Verlag, 2006.

Rupieper, Hermann-Josef. *Die Wurzeln der westdeutschen Nachkriegsdemokratie: Der amerikanische Beitrag 1945–1952.* Opladen: Westdeutscher Verlag, 1993.

Rupnow, Dirk. "Transformationen des Holocaust: Anmerkungen nach dem Beginn des 21. Jahrhunderts." *Transit: Europäische Revue* 35 (Summer 2008): 68–88.

Rürup, Reinhard. *Der lange Schatten des Nationalsozialismus: Geschichte, Geschichtspolitik und Erinnerungskultur.* Göttingen: Wallstein, 2014.

Sabrow, Martin, Ralph Jessen, and Klaus Große Kracht, eds. *Zeitgeschichte als Streitgeschichte: Große Kontroversen nach 1945.* Munich: Beck, 2003.

Sabrow, Martin, and Christian Mentel, eds. *Das Auswärtige Amt und seine umstrittene Vergangenheit: Eine deutsche Debatte.* Frankfurt am Main: Fischer, 2014.

Saidel, Rochelle G. *Never Too Late To Remember: The Politics Behind New York City's Holocaust Museum.* New York: Holmes and Meier, 1996.

Salzborn, Samuel. *Antisemitismus: Geschichte, Theorie, Empirie.* Baden-Baden: Nomos, 2014.

Sanua, Marianne R. *Let Us Prove Strong: The American Jewish Committee; 1945–2006.* Waltham, MA: Brandeis University Press, 2007.

Sarna, Jonathan D. *American Judaism: A History.* New Haven, CT: Yale University Press, 2004

Schanetzky, Tim. "Distanzierung, Verunsicherung, Entschädigung: Die deutsche Wirtschaft und die Globalisierung der Wiedergutmachung." In *Die Globalisierung der Wiedergutmachung: Politik, Moral, Moralpolitik,* edited by José Brunner, Constantin Goschler, and Norbert Frei, 104–148. Göttingen: Wallstein, 2013.

Schenderlein, Anne Clara. "'Germany on Their Minds'? German Jewish Refugees in the United States and Relationships to Germany, 1938–1988." PhD diss., University of California, San Diego, 2014.

Schildt, Axel. *Konservatismus in Deutschland: Von den Anfängen im 18. Jahrhundrt bis zur Gegenwart.* Munich: Beck, 1998.

Schildt, Axel. "Der Umgang mit der NS-Vergangenheit in der Öffentlichkeit der Nachkriegszeit." In *Verwandlungspolitik: NS- Eliten in der westdeutschen Nachkriegsgesellschaft,* edited by Wilfried Loth and Bernd-A. Rusinek, 19–55. Frankfurt am Main and New York: Campus, 1998.

Schmid, Harald. *Erinnern an den "Tag der Schuld:" Das Novemberpogrom von 1938 in der deutschen Geschichtspolitik.* Hamburg: Ergebnisse Verlag, 2001.

Schmid, Harald. "Europäisierung des Auschwitzgedenkens? Zum Aufstieg des 27. Januar 1945 als 'Holocaustgedenktag' in Europa." In "Universalisierung des Holocaust?," edited by Jan Eckel and Claudia Moisel, *Beiträge zur Geschichte des Nationalsozialismus* 24 (2008): 174–202.

Schmid, Harald. "Von der 'Vergangenheitsbewältigung' zur 'Erinnerungskultur': Zum öffentlichen Umgang mit dem Nationalsozialismus seit Ende der 1970er Jahre." In *Öffentliche Erinnerung und Medialisierung des Nationalsozialismus: Eine Bilanz der letzten dreißig Jahre,* edited by Gerhard Paul und Bernhard Schoßig, 171–202. Göttingen: Wallstein, 2010.

Schöllgen, Gregor. *Jenseits von Hitler: Die Deutschen in der Weltpolitik von Bismarck bis heute.* Berlin: Propyläen, 2005.

Schrafstetter, Susanna. "The Diplomacy of Wiedergutmachung: Memory, the Cold War, and the Western European Victims of Nazism; 1956–1964." *Holocaust and Genocide Studies* 17, no. 3 (2003): 459–479.

Schuette, Rolf. *German-Jewish Relations, Today and Tomorrow: A German Perspective.* New York: The American Jewish Committee, 2005.

Schuldiner, Michael. *Contesting Histories: German and Jewish Americans and the Legacy of the Holocaust.* Lubbock: Texas Tech University Press, 2011.

Schuler, Thomas. *Die Mohns: Vom Provinzbuchhändler zum Weltkonzern; Die Familie hinter Berteslmann.* Frankfurt am Main and New York: Campus, 2004.

Schwan, Heribert, and Tilman Jens. *Vermächtnis: Die Kohl-Protokolle.* Munich: Heyne, 2014.

Schwarz, Hans-Peter. *Adenauer: Der Aufstieg 1876–1952.* 2nd ed. Munich: Deutsche Verlags-Anstalt, 1986.

Schwarz, Hans-Peter. *Adenauer. Der Staatsmann, 1952–1967.* Munich: Deutsche Verlags-Anstalt, 1991.

Schwarz, Hans-Peter. *Helmut Kohl: Eine politische Biographie.* Munich: Deutsche Verlags-Anstalt, 2012.

Schweitzer, Eva. *Amerika und der Holocaust: Die verschwiegene Geschichte.* Munich: Knaur, 2004.

Scott-Smith, Giles. "Reviving the Transatlantic Community? The Successor Generation Concept in U.S. Foreign Affairs, 1960s–1980s." In *European Integration and the Atlantic Community in the 1980s*, edited by Kiran Klaus Patel and Kenneth Weisbrode, 201–225. New York: Cambridge University Press, 2013.

Seuthe, Rupert."Geistig-moralische Wende"? Der politische Umgang mit der NS-Vergangenheit in der Ära Kohl am Beispiel von Gedenktagen, Museums- und Denkmalprojekten. Frankfurt am Main: Peter Lang, 2001.

Shafir, Shlomo. *Ambiguous Relations: The American Jewish Community and Germany since 1945.* Detroit: Wayne State University Press, 1999.

Shafir, Shlomo. "Constantly Disturbing the German Conscience: The Impact of American Jewry." In *Remembering the Holocaust in Germany: 1945–2000; German Strategies and Jewish Responses*, edited by Dan Michman, 121–141. New York: Peter Lang, 2002.

Shafir, Shlomo. "The Twisted Road toward Rapprochement: American Jewry and Germany until Reunification." In *The United States and Germany in the Era of the Cold War, 1945–1990: A Handbook, Volume 2: 1968–1990*, edited by Detlef Junker, 474–481. Cambridge: Cambridge Universtity Press, 2004.

Shain, Milton. *The Roots of Antisemitism in South Africa.* Charlottesville: University Press of Virginia, 1994.

Shandler, Jeffrey. *While America Watches: Televising the Holocaust.* New York: Oxford University Press, 1999.

Sharples, Caroline. *Postwar Germany and the Holocaust.* London et al.: Bloomsbury, 2016.

Shultz, George P. *Turmoil and Triumph: My Years as Secretary of State.* New York: Scribner, 1993.

Sicher, Efraim. "The Future of the Past: Countermemory and Postmemory in Contemporary American Post-Holocaust Narratives." *History & Memory* 12, no. 2, (Fall/Winter 2000): 56–91.

Siebeck, Cornelia. "'Einzug ins verheißene Land:' Richard von Weizsäckers Rede zum 40. Jahrestag des Kriegsendes am 8. Mai 1985." *Zeithistorische Forschungen/Studies in Contemporary History* 12, no. 1, (2015): 161–169.

Siegel, Nicholas. "The German Marshall Fund of the United States: A Brief History." Washington, DC: GMF, 2012. www.gmfus.org/wp-content/blogs.dir/1/files_mf/1336582663GMF_history_publication_web.pdf.

Smyser, William R. *Deutsch-amerikanische Beziehungen.* Bonn: Europa Union Verlag, 1980.

Snow, Nancy, and Taylor Philip M., eds. *Routledge Handbook of Public Diplomacy.* New York: Routledge, 2009.

Staden, Berndt von. *Ende und Anfang. Erinnerungen 1939–1963.* Vaihingen: IPa Verlag, 2001.

Staden, Berndt von. *Zwischen Eiszeit und Tauwetter. Diplomatie in einer Epoche des Umbruchs; Erinnerungen.* Berlin: wjs Verlag, 2005.

Staden, Wendelgard von. *Darkness over the Valley.* Translated by Mollie Comerford Peters. New Haven, CT and New York: Ticknor & Fields, 1981.

Staden, Wendelgard von. *Nacht über dem Tal. Eine Jugend in Deutschland.* 3rd ed. Munich: Deutscher Taschenbuch Verlag, 2000.

Stahl, Daniel. *Nazi-Jagd: Südamerikas Diktaturen und die Ahndung von NS-Verbrechen.* Göttingen: Wallstein, 2013.

Stavginski, Hans-Georg. *Das Holocaust-Denkmal: Der Streit um das "Denkmal für die ermordeten Juden Europas" in Berlin; 1988–1999.* Paderborn: Schöningh, 2002.

Steinbach, Peter. "Die publizistischen Kontroversen: Eine Vergangenheit, die nicht vergeht." In *Der Nationalsozialismus: Die Zweite Geschichte; Überwindung, Deutung, Erinnerung*, edited by Peter Reichel, Harald Schmid, and Peter Steinbach, 127–174. Munich: Beck, 2009.

Steinbach, Peter, Johannes Tuchel, and Heinrich Walle, eds. *Against Hitler: German Resistance to National Socialism, 1933–1945.* Berlin: Research Institute for Military History, Potsdam, and the German Resistance Memorial Center, 1994.

Steinhoff, Johannes. *Voices from the Third Reich: An Oral History.* Washington, DC: Regnery Gateway, 1989.

Steininger, Rolf, ed. *Der Umgang mit dem Holocaust: Europa, USA, Israel.* Vienna: Böhlau, 1994.

Steininger, Rolf. *Deutschland und die USA: Vom Zweiten Weltkrieg bis zur Gegenwart.* Reinbeck: Lau-Verlag, 2014.

Steinweis, Alan E. "The Auschwitz Analogy: Holocaust Memory and American Debates over Intervention in Bosnia and Kosovo in the 1990s." *Holocaust and Genocide Studies* 19, no. 2 (Fall 2005): 276–289.

Steinweis, Alan E. "The Holocaust and American Culture: An Assessment of Recent Scholarship." *Holocaust and Genocide Studies* 15, no. 2 (2001): 296–310.

Steinweis, Alan E. "The Legacy of the Holocaust in Germany and the United States." In *The United States and Germany in the Era of the Cold War, 1945–1990: A Handbook, Volume 1: 1945–1968*, edited by Detlef Junker, 488–494. Cambridge: Cambridge University Press, 2004.

Steinweis, Alan E. "Reflections on the Holocaust from Nebraska." In *The Americanization of the Holocaust*, edited by Hilene Flanzbaum, 167–180. Baltimore: Johns Hopkins University Press, 1999.

Steinweis, Alan E. "West German *Zeitgeschichte* and the Holocaust: The Importance of an International Context." In *Der Holocaust und die westdeutschen Historiker: Eine Debatte*, edited by Astrid M. Eckert und Vera Ziegeldorf, 47–51. Berlin: H-Soz-u-Kult Forum, 2004. http://edoc.hu-berlin.de/histfor/2/PDF/HistFor_2-2004.pdf.

Steinweis, Alan E., and Daniel E. Rogers, eds. *The Impact of Nazism: New Perspectives on the Third Reich and its Legacies.* Lincoln: University of Nebraska Press, 2003.

Stelzel, Philipp. "Rethinking Modern German History: Critical Social History as a Transatlantic Enterprise; 1945–1989." PhD diss., University of North Carolina at Chapel Hill, 2010.

Stelzel, Philipp. "Fritz Fischer and the American Historical Profession: Tracing the Transatlantic Dimension of the Fischer-Kontroverse." *Storia della Storiografia* 44, no. 1 (2003): 67–84.

Stelzel, Philipp. "Transnationalism and the History of Historiography: A Transatlantic Perspective." *History Compass* 13, no. 2 (2015). 78–87.

Stier, Oren Baruch. "Holocaust, American Style." *Prooftexts* 22, no. 3 (2002): 354–391.

Stone, Dan, ed. *The Historiography of the Holocaust.* New York: Palgrave Macmillan, 2004.

Stucke, Andreas, "Der Wissenschaftsrat." In *Handbuch Politikberatung*, edited by Svenja Falk, Dieter Rehfeld, Andrea Römmele, and Martin Thunert, 248–254. Wiesbaden: VS Verlag für Sozialwissenschaften, 2006.

Stürmer, Michael. *Die Grenzen der Macht: Begegnungen der Deutschen mit der Geschichte.* Berlin: Siedler, 1992.

Stürmer, Michael. *Dissonanzen des Fortschritts: Essays über Geschichte und Politik in Deutschland*. Munich: Piper, 1986.

Stürmer, Michael. "Deutsche Identität: Auf der Suche nach der verlorenen Nationalgeschichte." In *Dissonanzen des Fortschritts: Essays über Geschichte und Politik in Deutschland*, edited by Michael Stürmer, 201–209. Munich: Piper, 1986.

Stürmer, Michael. "History in a Land without History." In *Forever in the Shadow of Hitler? Original Documents of the Historikerstreit, the Controversy Concerning the Singularity of the Holocaust*. Translated by James Knowlton and Truett Cates, 16f. Atlantic Highlands, NJ: Humanities Press International, 1993.

Stürmer, Michael. "Nation und Demokratie: Zur Substanz des deutschen Nationalbewußtseins." *Die Politische Meinung* 32, no. 230 (1987): 15–27.

Suri, Jeremy. "Non-governmental Organizations and Non-state Actors." In *Palgrave Advances in International History*, edited by Patrick Finney, 223–246. New York: Palgrave Macmillan, 2005.

Surmann, Jan. "Restitution Policy and the Transformation of Holocaust Memory: The Impact of the American 'Crusade for Justice' after 1989." *Bulletin of the German Historical Institute* 49 (Fall 2011): 31–49.

Surmann, Jan. *Shoah-Erinnerung: Die US-Geschichtspolitik am Ende des 20. Jahrhunderts*. Stuttgart: Franz Steiner Verlag, 2012.

Szabo, Stephen F., ed. *The Successor Generation: International Perspectives of Postwar Europeans*. London et al.: Butterworths, 1983.

Szatkowski, Tim. *Karl Carstens: Eine Politische Biographie*. Cologne: Böhlau, 2007.

Taberner, Stuart, and Paul Cooke, eds. *German Culture, Politics, and Literature into the Twenty-First Century: Beyond Normalization*. Rochester, NY: Camden House, 2006.

Taberner, Stuart, and Paul Cooke. "Introduction." In *German Culture, Politics, and Literature into the Twenty-First Century: Beyond Normalization*, edited by Stuart Taberner and Paul Cooke, 1–15. Rochester, NY: Camden House, 2006.

Tannenbaum, Marc H. "The American Jewish Committee at the White House." In *Bitburg and Beyond: Encounters in American, German and Jewish History*, edited by Ilya Levkov, 330–334. New York: Shapolsky Publishers, 1987.

Tempel, Sylke. *Legenden von der Allmacht: Die Beziehungen zwischen amerikanisch-jüdischen Organisationen und der Bundesrepublik Deutschland seit 1945*. Frankfurt am Main: Peter Lang, 1995.

Thamer, Hans-Ulrich. "Vom Tabubruch zur Historisierung? Die Auseinandersetzung um die 'Wehrmachtsausstellung'." In *Zeitgeschichte als Streitgeschichte: Große Kontroversen nach 1945*, edited by Martin Sabrow, Ralph Jessen, and Klaus Große Kracht, 171–186. Munich: Beck, 2003.

"The Staff of the Institute as of mid-September." *Bulletin of the German Historical Institute* 1 (Fall 1987): 17–20.

Thelen, David. "The Nation and Beyond: Transnational Perspectives on United States History." *Journal of American History* 86, no. 3 (1999): 965–975.

Thesing, Josef. "30 Jahre Kooperation: KAS und AJC; Einige Gedanken zum Beginn der Zusammenarbeit mit jüdischen Organisationen." In *"A Life-Changing Experience:" 30 Jahre KAS/AJC-Austauschprogramm*, edited by Deidre Berger and Jens Paulus, 17–33. St. Augustin: Konrad Adenauer Foundation, 2010. www.kas.de/wf/doc/kas_19725-544-1-30.pdf?110427115734.

Thiele, Martina. *Publizistische Kontroversen über den Holocaust im Film*. Münster: LIT Verlag, 2001.

"Thomas Nipperdey (1927–1992), Historiker." Portal Rheinische Geschichte. Last modified February 22, 2011. www.rheinische-geschichte.lvr.de/persoenlichkeiten/N/Seiten/ThomasNipperdey.aspx.

"Thousands of Sites, Millions of Fates: New Insights into the Universe of Nazi Camps." Report on Book Presentation, German Historical Institute, Washington, DC, May 13, 2010. www.ghi-dc.org/index.php?option=com_content&view=article&id=1045&Itemid=935.

Timm, Angelika. *Jewish Claims against East Germany: Moral Obligations and Pragmatic Policy.* Budapest: Central European University Press, 1997.

Trommler, Frank. "Culture as an Arena of Transatlantic Conflict." In *The United States and Germany in the Era of the Cold War, 1945–1990: A Handbook, Volume 2: 1968–1990,* edited by Detlef Junker, 257–273. Cambridge: Cambridge Universtity Press, 2004.

Trommler, Frank. *Kulturmacht ohne Kompass: Deutsche auswärtige Kulturbeziehungen im 20. Jahrhundert.* Köln: Böhlau, 2014.

Trommler, Frank, and Elliott Shore, eds. *The German-American Encounter: Conflict and Cooperation between Two Cultures; 1800–2000.* New York and Oxford: Berghahn Books, 2001.

Tuch, Hans N. "American Cultural Policy Toward Germany." In *The United States and Germany in the Era of the Cold War, 1945–1990: A Handbook, Volume 2: 1968–1990,* edited by Detlef Junker, 274–279. Cambridge: Cambridge Universtity Press, 2004.

Tuch, Hans N. *Arthur Burns and the Successor Generation: Selected Writings of and about Arthur Burns.* Lanham, MD: University Press of America, 1988.

Ullrich, Volker. "Eine produktive Provokation: Die Rolle der Medien in der Goldhagen-Kontroverse." In *Zeitgeschichte als Streitgeschichte: Große Kontroversen nach 1945,* edited by Martin Sabrow, Ralph Jessen, and Klaus Große Kracht, 152–170. Munich: Beck, 2003.

Vierhaus, Rudolf, and Ludolf Herbst. "Petersen, Peter." In *Biographisches Handbuch der Mitglieder des Deutschen Bundestages: 1949–2002,* edited by Rudolf Vierhaus and Ludolf Herbst, 2: 637f. Munich: Saur, 2002.

Wehler, Hans-Ulrich. "Neokonservative Wissenschaftspolitik: Eine Anmerkung zum Historikerstreit." *Merkur* 41, no. 12 (1987): 1091–1096.

Wehrs, Nikolai. *Protest der Professoren: Der "Bund Freiheit der Wissenschaft" in den 1970er Jahren.* Göttingen, Wallstein: 2014.

Weidenfeld, Werner, ed. *Die Identität der Deutschen.* Munich: Carl Hanser Verlag, 1983.

Weidenfeld, Werner. "Die Identität der Deutschen: Fragen, Positionen, Perspektiven." In *Die Identität der Deutschen,* edited by Werner Weidenfeld, 13–49. Munich: Carl Hanser Verlag, 1983.

Weidenfeld, Werner. "Geschichte und Politik." In *Geschichtsbewußtsein der Deutschen: Materialien zur Spurensuche einer Nation,* edited by Werner Weidenfeld, 13–32. Cologne: Verlag Wissenschaft und Politik, 1987.

Weidenfeld, Werner. *Geschichtsbewußtsein der Deutschen: Materialien zur Spurensuche einer Nation.* Cologne: Verlag Wissenschaft und Politik, 1987.

Weidenfeld, Werner. "Die Suche nach Identität: Ein deutsches Problem?" In *Nachdenken über Deutschland: Materialien zur politischen Kultur der Deutschen Frage,* edited by Werner Weidenfeld, 89–99. Cologne: Verlag Wissenschaft und Politik, 1985.

Weidenfeld, Werner. *Nachdenken über Deutschland: Materialien zur politischen Kultur der Deutschen Frage.* Cologne: Verlag Wissenschaft und Politik, 1985.

Weidenfeld, Werner. *Politische Kultur und deutsche Frage: Materialien zum Staats- und Nationalbewußtsein in der Bundesrepublik Deutschland.* Cologne: Verlag Wissenschaft und Politik, 1989.

Weidenfeld, Werner. "Die Suche nach Identität: Ein deutsches Problem?" In *Nachdenken über Deutschland: Materialien zur politischen Kultur der Deutschen Frage,* edited by Werner Weidenfeld, 89–99. Cologne: Verlag Wissenschaft und Politik, 1985.

Weidenfeld, Werner and Dirk Rumberg, eds. *Orientierungsverlust: Zur Bindungskrise der modernen Gesellschaft.* Gütersloh: Verlag Bertelsmann Stiftung, 1994.

Weigand, Katharina, ed. *Münchner Historiker zwischen Politik und Wissenschaft: 150 Jahre Historisches Seminar der Ludwig-Maximilians-Universität München.* Munich: Herbert Utz Verlag, 2010.

Weinberg, Jeshajahu, and Rina Elieli. *The Holocaust Museum in Washington.* New York: Rizzoli International Publications, 1995.

Weingardt, Markus A. "Deutsche Israelpolitik: Etappen und Kontinuitäten." *Aus Politik und Zeitgeschichte* 15 (April 2005): 22–31.

Weingart, Peter. *Die Stunde der Wahrheit? Zum Verhältnis der Wissenschaft zu Politik, Wirtschaft und Medien in der Wissensgesellschaft.* Weilerswist: Velbrück Wissenschaft, 2001.

Weinke, Annette. *Eine Gesellschaft ermittelt gegen sich selbst: Die Geschichte der Zentralen Stelle Ludwigsburg 1958–2008*. Darmstadt: Wissenschaftliche Buchgesellschaft, 2008.

Weinke, Annette. *Die Verfolgung von NS-Tätern im geteilten Deutschland: Vergangenheitsbewältigungen 1949–1969 oder: Eine deutsch-deutsche Beziehungsgeschichte im Kalten Krieg*. Paderborn: Schöningh, 2002.

Weinke, Annette. "'Waning Confidence in Germany's Rehabilitation:' Das gespaltene Krisenmanagement der bundesdeutschen Außenpolitik zum Eichmann-Prozess." In *Interessen um Eichmann: Israelische Justiz, deutsche Strafverfolgung und alte Kameradschaften*, edited by Werner Renz, 201–215. Frankfurt am Main and New York: Campus, 2012.

Weiss, Christoph, ed. *"Der gute Deutsche:" Dokumente zur Diskussion um Steven Spielbergs "Schindlers Liste" in Deutschland*. St. Ingbert: Röhrig, 1995.

Weiß, Matthias. "Sinnliche Erinnerung: Die Filme 'Holocaust' und 'Schindlers Liste' in der bundesdeutschen Vergegenwärtigung der NS-Zeit." In *Schweigen und Bekennen: Die deutsche Nachkriegsgesellschaft und der Holocaust*, edited by Norbert Frei and Sybille Steinbacher, 71–102. Göttingen: Wallstein, 2001.

Weizsäcker, Richard von. "We Must Look Truth Straight in the Eye." May 8, 1985. In *Bitburg and Beyond: Encounters in American, German and Jewish History*, edited by Ilya Levkov, 198–207. New York: Shapolsky Publishers, 1987.

Welzer, Harald, Sabine Moller, and Karoline Tschuggnall. *Opa war kein Nazi: Nationalsozialismus und Holocaust im Familiengedächtnis*. Frankfurt am Main: Fischer, 2002.

Wicke, Christian. *Helmut Kohl's Quest for Normality: His Representation of the German Nation and Himself*. New York and Oxford: Berghahn Books, 2015.

Wickert, Ulrich, ed. *Angst vor Deutschland*. Hamburg: Hoffmann und Campe, 1990.

Wiegrefe, Klaus. *Das Zerwürfnis: Helmut Schmidt, Jimmy Carter und die Krise der deutsch-amerikanischen Beziehungen*. Berlin: Propyläen, 2005.

Wiesel, Elie. "Letter to President Carter." September 27, 1979. In *Report to the President: President's Commission on the Holocaust*. Reprinted by the United States Holocaust Memorial Museum, Washington, DC, 1999.

Wiesel, Elie. *Report to the President: President's Commission on the Holocaust; September 27, 1979*. Reprinted by the United States Holocaust Memorial Museum, Washington DC, 1999.

Wiesen, S. Jonathan. "Germany's PR Man: Julius Klein and the Making of Transatlantic Memory." In *Coping with the Nazi Past: West German Debates on Nazism and Generational Conflict; 1955–1975*, edited by Philipp Gassert and Alan E. Steinweis, 294–308. New York and Oxford: Berghahn Books, 2006.

Wiesen, S. Jonathan. *West German Industry and the Challenge of the Nazi Past, 1945–1955*. Chapel Hill: University of North Carolina Press, 2001.

Wieviorka, Annette. *The Era of the Witness*. Translated by Jared Stark. Ithaca, NY: Cornell University Press, 2006.

Wilke, Jürgen. "Die Fernsehserie 'Holocaust' als Medienereignis." *Zeitgeschichte-online* (March 2004). www.zeitgeschichte-online.de/thema/die-fernsehserie-holocaust-als-medienereignis.

Willis, Jim, ed. *Images of Germany in the American Media*. Westport, CT: Praeger, 1999.

Winkler, Heinrich August. *Der lange Weg nach Westen: Deutsche Geschichte vom Dritten Reich bis zur Wiedervereinigung*. Munich, Beck: 2000.

Wirsching, Andreas. *Abschied vom Provisorium: 1982–1990; Geschichte der Bundesrepublik Deutschland*. Munich: Deutsche Verlags-Anstalt, 2006.

Wirsching, Andreas. "Die Beziehungen zu den USA im Kontext der deutschen Außenpolitik 1982–1998." *Historisch-Politische Mitteilungen* 14 (December 2007): 235–244.

Wirsching, Andreas. "Die mediale 'Konstruktion' der Politik und die 'Wende' von 1982/83." *Historisch- Politische Mitteilungen* 9 (December 2002): 127–139.

Wolffsohn, Michael. *Eternal Guilt? Forty Years of German-Jewish-Israeli Relations*. New York: Columbia University Press, 1993.

Wolffsohn, Michael. *Ewige Schuld? 40 Jahre deutsch-jüdisch-israelische Beziehungen*. Munich: Piper, 1988.

Wolfrum, Edgar. *Die geglückte Demokratie: Geschichte der Bundesrepublik Deutschland von ihren Anfängen bis zur Gegenwart.* Stuttgart: Klett-Cotta, 2006.

Wolfrum, Edgar. *Geschichtspolitik in der Bundesrepublik Deutschland: Der Weg zur bundesrepublikanischen Erinnerung 1948–1990.* Darmstadt: Wissenschaftliche Buchgesellschaft, 1999.

Young, James E. *At Memory's Edge: After-Images of the Holocaust in Contemporary Art and Architecture.* New Haven, CT: Yale University Press, 2000.

Young, James E. *The Texture of Memory: Holocaust Memorials and Meanings.* New Haven, CT: Yale University Press, 1993.

Zelikow, Philip, and Condoleezza Rice. *Germany Unified and Europe Transformed: A Study in Statecraft.* Cambridge, MA: Harvard University Press, 1997.

Zimmermann, Moshe. "Die transnationale Holocaust-Erinnerung." In *Transnationale Geschichte: Themen, Tendenzen und Theorien,* edited by Gunilla Budde, Sebastian Conrad, and Oliver Janz, 202–216. Göttingen: Vandenhoek & Ruprecht, 2006.

Zolleis, Udo. *Die CDU: Das politische Leitbild im Wandel der Zeit.* Wiesbaden: VS Verlag für Sozialwissenschaften, 2008.

Zuckermann, Moshe. "The Israeli and German Holocaust Discourses and their Transatlantic Dimension." In *The German-American Encounter: Conflict and Cooperation between Two Cultures; 1800–2000,* edited by Frank Trommler and Elliott Shore, 188–197. New York and Oxford: Berghahn Books, 2001.

Zwerin, Raymond A. *The Holocaust: A Study in Values.* Denver, CO: Alternatives in Religious Education, 1976.

Index